D0734943

Rajasthan, Delhi & Agra

Victoria McCulloch

Credits

Footprint credits

Editor: Nicola Gibbs
Production and layout: Emma Bryers
Maps and cover: Kevin Feeney

Publisher: Patrick Dawson
Managing Editor: Felicity Laughton
Advertising: Elizabeth Taylor
Sales and marketing: Kirsty Holmes

Photography credits
Front cover: Shutterstock/Alvaro Puig
Back cover: Shutterstock/Rafal Cichawa

Printed in Great Britain by Alphaset,
Surbiton, Surrey

Every effort has been made to ensure that
the facts in this guidebook are accurate.
However, travellers should still obtain advice
from consulates, airlines, etc, about travel
and visa requirements before travelling.
The authors and publishers cannot accept
responsibility for any loss, injury or
inconvenience however caused.

The content of Footprint *Focus Rajasthan,
Delhi & Agra* has been taken directly from
Footprint's *India Handbook*, which was
researched and written by David Stott,
Vanessa Betts and Victoria McCulloch.

Publishing information

Footprint *Focus Rajasthan, Delhi & Agra*
1st edition
© Footprint Handbooks Ltd
November 2013

ISBN: 978 1 909268 39 5
CIP DATA: A catalogue record for this book
is available from the British Library

® Footprint Handbooks and the Footprint
mark are a registered trademark of
Footprint Handbooks Ltd

Published by Footprint
6 Riverside Court
Lower Bristol Road
Bath BA2 3DZ, UK
T +44 (0)1225 469141
F +44 (0)1225 469461
footprinttravelguides.com

Distributed in the USA by Globe Pequot
Press, Guilford, Connecticut

Contents

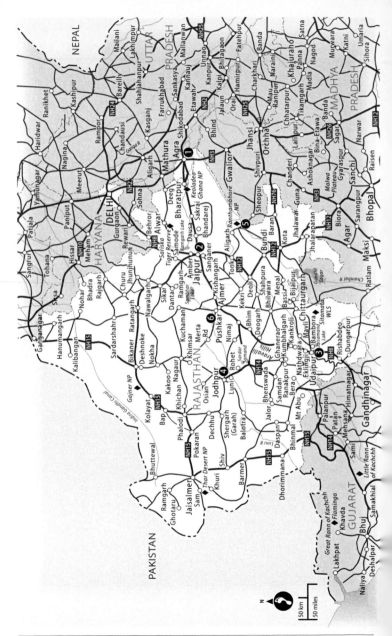

For most visitors to India their priority is the Golden Triangle of Delhi, Agra and Jaipur. In this snapshot alone you will see everything you had imagined India would be – women wrapped in glorious saris, turbaned farmers, imposing fort cities and majestic palaces. Yet venture a little further and you will be richly rewarded, for beyond the Golden Triangle lies Rajasthan, a vast state of sweeping deserts and jungles where tigers still roam.

India's capital, Delhi, is developing at an astonishing rate. Containing both the British-built New Delhi and Shah Jahan's 17th-century capital, modern buildings vie for prominence with the colonial arches of Connaught Place and the Mughal architecture of Qutb Minar. Brash, chaotic and dynamic, the city serves as a perfect introduction to the country and a gateway to some of its most beautiful sights.

From the windows of the ornate wind palace the Hawa Mahal, you can look down onto the bustling streets of Tripolia Bazaar in Jaipur and see camel carts lope passed, going head to head with cycle rickshaws, cars and buses. From an arched window in Agra's Red Fort, you can gaze across the water to the Taj Mahal just as Shah Jahan must have done when he was imprisoned there. In Amber you might look down on lines of elephants transporting people up to the imposing gateway of the fort. In some ways nothing much has changed over the years – it's a window into the history and soul of India.

Even though Delhi, Agra and Rajasthan have the most visitors, their magic continues to charm. The forts are epic, the scenery stunning and the Taj Mahal, no matter how many pictures you might have seen, takes your breath away. And yes India does have its fair share of chaos, noise, heat, dust and people – 1.2 billion of them – it will be overwhelming and enthralling, confusing and intoxicating; but every expectation – be it of beauty, mysticism, poverty, bigotry or bureaucracy – will be outdone by what hits you on the ground.

Planning your trip

Best time to visit Rajasthan, Delhi and Agra

By far the best time to visit North Central India is from October to April. It is intensely hot, especially on the plains, during May and June and then the humidity builds up as the monsoon approaches. The monsoon season lasts for two to three months, from July to September. In 2012, after a hearty monsoon, the desertlands of Rajasthan – especially around Jodhpur and Jaisalmer – were a vibrant green, however this is unusual and Rajasthan sees a lot less rain than the rest of India. The European summer holidays of July and August bring many visitors to Rajasthan despite the temperatures. Hot summers are followed by much cooler and clearer winters; in Delhi, Jaipur and Agra the temperatures can plummet to near freezing in January. Some of the region's great festivals, such as **Diwali** and the **Pushkar Camel Fair**, take place in the autumn and winter.

Getting to Rajasthan, Delhi and Agra

Air

India is accessible by air from virtually every continent. Most international flights arrive in Delhi or Mumbai. Some carriers permit 'open-jaw' travel, arriving in and departing from different cities in India. Some (**Air India**, **Jet Airways** or **British Airways**) have convenient non-stop flights from Europe eg from London to Delhi, takes only nine hours.

On arrival, you can fly to numerous destinations across India with **Jet Airways**, **Indigo** or **Spicejet**. The prices are very competitive if domestic flights are booked in conjunction with **Jet** on the international legs. In 2013 the cheapest return flights to Delhi from London started at around £500, but leapt to £900+ as you approached the high seasons of Christmas, New Year and Easter.

From Europe Despite the increases to Air Passenger Duty, Britain remains the cheapest place in Europe for flights to India. From mainland Europe, major European flag carriers, including **KLM** and **Lufthansa**, fly to Delhi and/or Mumbai from their respective hub airports. In most cases the cheapest flights are with Middle Eastern or Central Asian airlines, transiting via airports in the Gulf. Several airlines from the Middle East (eg **Emirates**, **Gulf Air**, **Kuwait Airways**, **Qatar Airways** and **Oman Air**) offer good discounts to Indian regional capitals from London, but fly via their hub cities, adding to the journey time. Consolidators in the UK can quote some competitive fares, such as: www.skyscanner.net, www.ebookers.com; and **North South Travel** ① *T01245-608291, www.northsouthtravel. co.uk (profits to charity)*.

From North America From the east coast, several airlines, including **Air India**, **Jet Airways**, **Continental** and **Delta**, fly direct from New York to Delhi and Mumbai. **American** flies to both cities from Chicago. Discounted tickets on **British Airways**, **KLM**, **Lufthansa**, **Gulf Air** and **Kuwait Airways** are sold through agents although they will invariably fly via their country's capital cities. From the west coast, **Air India** flies from Los Angeles to Delhi and Mumbai, and **Jet Airways** from San Francisco to Mumbai via Shanghai. Alternatively, fly via Hong Kong, Singapore or Bangkok using one of those countries' national

Don't miss...

1 Early morning at the Taj Mahal, page 67.
2 Hidden temples on the Old City Walking Tour in Jaipur, page 97.
3 Sunset from the Monsoon Palace in Udaipur, page 116.
4 Delicious saffron-laced lassis in Jodhpur, page 152.
5 A jungle trip in Ranthambhore, page 176.
6 Climbing to the Savitri Goddess Temple in Pushkar, page 185.

Numbers relate to the map on page 4.

carriers. **Air Canada** operates between Vancouver and Delhi. **Air Brokers International** ⓘ *www.airbrokers.com*, is competitive and reputable. **STA**, www.statravel.co.uk, has offices in many US cities as well as Toronto. Student fares are also available from **Travel Cuts** ⓘ *www.travelcuts.com*, in Canada.

From Australasia Qantas, Singapore Airlines, Thai Airways, Malaysian Airlines, Cathay Pacific and Air India are the principal airlines connecting the continents, although Qantas is the only one that flies direct, with services from Sydney to Mumbai. **Singapore Airlines**, with subsidiary **Silk Air**, offers the most flexibility. Low-cost carriers including Air Asia (via Kuala Lumpur), **Scoot** and **Tiger Airways** (Singapore) offer a similar choice of arrival airports at substantially lower prices, though long stopovers and possible missed connections make this a slightly more risky venture than flying with the mainstream airlines. **STA** and **Flight Centre** offer discounted tickets from their branches in major cities in Australia and New Zealand. **Abercrombie & Kent** ⓘ *www.abercrombiekent.co.uk*, **Adventure World** ⓘ *www.adventureworld.net.au*, **Peregrine** ⓘ *www.peregrineadventures. com*, and **Travel Corporation of India** ⓘ *www.tcindia.com*, organize tours.

Airport information The formalities on arrival in India have been increasingly streamlined during the last few years and the facilities at the major international airports greatly improved. However, arrival can still be a slow process. Disembarkation cards, with an attached customs declaration, are handed out to passengers during the inward flight. The immigration form should be handed in at the immigration counter on arrival. The customs slip will be returned, but must be handed over to customs on leaving the baggage collection hall. You may well find that there are delays of over an hour at immigration in processing passengers who need help with filling in forms. When departing, note that you'll need to have a printout of your itinerary to get into the airport, and the security guards will only let you into the terminal within three hours of your flight.

  Departure tax Rs 500 is payable for all international departures other than those to neighbouring SAARC countries, when the tax is Rs 250 (not reciprocated by Sri Lanka). This is normally included in your international ticket; check when buying. (To save time 'Security Check' your baggage before checking in on departure.) Some airports have also begun charging a Passenger Service Fee or User Development Fee to each departing passenger. This is normally included in international tickets, but some domestic airlines have been reluctant to incorporate the charge. Keep some spare cash in rupees in case you need to pay the fee on arriving at the terminal.

Transport in Rajasthan, Delhi and Agra

Air

India has a comprehensive network linking the major cities of the different states. Deregulation of the airline industry has had a transformative effect on travel within India, with a host of low-budget private carriers offering sometimes unbelievably cheap fares on an ever-expanding network of routes in a bid to woo the train-travelling middle class. Promotional fares as low as Rs 9 (US$0.20) are not unknown, though such numbers are rendered somewhat meaningless by additional taxes and fuel charges – an extra US$30-50 on most flights. Booking a few days in advance, you can expect to fly between Delhi and Mumbai for around US$100 one way including taxes, while a month's notice and flying with a no-frills airline can reduce the price to US$70-80; regional routes, eg Delhi to Udaipur, are often cheaper than routes between main cities.

Competition from the efficiently run private sector has, in general, improved the quality of services provided by the nationalized airlines. It also seems to herald the end of the two-tier pricing structure, meaning that ticket prices are now usually the same for foreign and Indian travellers. The airport authorities, too, have made efforts to improve handling on the ground.

Although flying is comparatively expensive and has a larger environmental impact, for covering vast distances or awkward links on a route it is an option worth considering, though delays and re-routing can be irritating. For short distances (eg Delhi–Agra), and on some routes where you can sleep during an overnight journey, it makes more sense to travel by train.

The best way to get an idea of the current routes, carriers and fares is to use a third-party booking website such as **www.cheapairticketsindia.com** (toll-free numbers: UK T0800-101 0928, USA T1-888 825 8680), **www.cleartrip.com**, **www.makemytrip.co.in**, or **www.yatra.com**. Booking with these is a different matter: some refuse foreign credit cards outright, while others have to be persuaded to give your card special clearance. Tickets booked on these sites are typically issued as an email ticket or an SMS text message – the simplest option if you have an Indian mobile phone, though it must be converted to a paper ticket at the relevant carrier's airport offices before you will be allowed into the terminal. **Makemytrip.com** and **Travelocity.com** both accept international credit cards.

Rail

Trains can still be the cheapest and most comfortable means of travelling long distances saving you hotel expenses on overnight journeys. Rail travel also gives access to station Retiring Rooms, which can be useful from time to time. Above all, you have an ideal opportunity to meet local travellers and catch a glimpse of life on the ground. See also **www.indianrail.gov.in** and **www.erail.in**.

High-speed trains There are several air-conditioned 'high-speed' services: **Shatabdi** (or 'Century') **Express** for day travel, and **Rajdhani Express** ('Capital City') for overnight journeys. These cover large sections of the network but due to high demand you need to book them well in advance (up to 90 days). Meals and drinks are usually included.

Royal trains You can travel like a maharaja on the **Palace on Wheels** (www.palace onwheels.net), the famous seven-nighter which has been running for many years and gives visitors an opportunity to see some of the 'royal' cities in Rajasthan during the winter months for around US$2500 and affords some special privileges such as private fine dining at Mehrangarh Fort in Jodhpur.

Classes **A/c First Class**, available only on main routes, is very comfortable with two- or four-berth carpeted sleeper compartments with washbasin. As with all air-conditioned Sleeper accommodation, bedding is included, and the windows are tinted to the point of being almost impossible to see through. **A/c Sleeper**, two and three-tier configurations (known as 2AC and 3AC), are clean and comfortable and popular with middle class families; these are the safest carriages for women travelling alone. **A/c Executive Class**, with wide reclining seats, are available on many Shatabdi trains at double the price of the ordinary **a/c Chair Car**, which are equally comfortable. **First Class (non-a/c)** is gradually being phased out, and is now restricted to a handful of routes in the south, but the run-down old carriages still provide a pleasant experience if you like open windows. **Second Class (non-a/c)** two- and three-tier (commonly called **Sleeper**), provides exceptionally cheap and atmospheric travel, with basic padded vinyl seats and open windows that allow the sights and sounds of India (not to mention dust, insects and flecks of spittle expelled by passengers up front) to drift into the carriage. On long journeys Sleepers can be crowded and uncomfortable, and toilet facilities can be unpleasant; it is nearly always better to use the Indian-style squat loos rather than the Western-style ones as they are better maintained. At the bottom rung is **Unreserved Second Class**, with hard wooden benches. You can travel long distances for a trivial amount of money, but unreserved carriages are often ridiculously crowded, and getting off at your station may involve a battle of will and strength against the hordes trying to shove their way on.

Indrail passes These allow travel across the network without having to pay extra reservation fees and Sleeper charges but you have to spend a high proportion of your time on the train to make it worthwhile. However, the advantages of pre-arranged reservations and automatic access to 'Tourist Quotas' can tip the balance in favour of the pass for some travellers.

Tourists (foreigners and Indians resident abroad) may buy these passes from the tourist sections of principal railway booking offices and pay using foreign currency, major credit cards, travellers' cheques or rupees with encashment certificates. Fares range from US$57 to US$1060 for adults or half that for children. Combined rail and air tickets are also to be made available.

Indrail passes can also conveniently be bought abroad from special agents. For people contemplating a single long journey soon after arriving in India, the Half- or One-day Pass with a confirmed reservation is worth the peace of mind; two- or four-day passes are also sold.

The UK agent is **SDEL** ① *103 Wembley Park Dr, Wembley, Middlesex HA9 8HG, UK, T020-8903 3411, www.indiarail.co.uk*. They make all necessary reservations and offer excellent advice. They can also book **Air India** and **Jet Airways** internal flights.

Cost A/c First Class costs about double the rate for two-tier shown below, and non-a/c Second Class about half. Children (aged five to 12) travel at half the adult fare. The young (12-30 years) and senior citizens (65 years and over) are allowed a 30% discount on journeys over 500 km (just show your passport).

Period	US$ A/c 2-tier	Period	US$ A/c 2-tier
½ day	26	21 days	198
1 day	43	30 days	248
7 days	135	60 days	400
15 days	185	90 days	530

Fares for individual journeys are based on distance covered and reflect both the class and the type of train. Higher rates apply on the *Mail* and *Express* trains and the air-conditioned *Shatabdi* and long-distance *Rajdhani* expresses.

Internet services Much information is available online via www.railtourismindia.com, www.indianrail.gov.in, www.erail.in and www.trainenquiry.com, where you can check timetables (which change frequently), numbers, seat availability and even the running status of your train. Internet e-tickets can be bought and printed on www.irctc.in – a great time-saver when the system works properly, though paying with a foreign credit card is fraught with difficulty. If you plan to do a lot of train travel it might be worth the effort to get your credit card recognized by the booking system. This process changes often, so it's good idea is to consult the very active India transport forums at www.indiamike.com. Another good option is to seek a local agent who can sell e-tickets, which can cost as little as Rs 10 (plus Rs 20 reservation fee; some agents charge up to Rs 150 a ticket, however), and can save hours of hassle; simply present the print-out to the ticket collector. However, it is tricky if you then want to cancel an e-ticket which an agent has bought for you on their account.

Tickets and reservations It is now possible to reserve tickets for virtually any train on the network from one of the 1000 computerized reservation centres across India. It is always best to book as far in advance as possible (usually up to 60 days). To reserve a seat on a particular train, note down the train's name, number and departure time and fill in a reservation form while you line up at the ticket window; you can use one form for up to four passengers. At busy stations the wait can take an hour or more. You can save a lot of time and effort by asking a travel agent to get your tickets for a fee of Rs 50-100. If the class you want is full, ask if special 'quotas' are available. **Foreign Tourist Quota** (FTQ) reserves a small number of tickets on popular routes for overseas travellers; you need your passport and either an exchange certificate or ATM receipt to book tickets under FTQ. The other useful special quota is **Tatkal**, which releases a last-minute pool of tickets at 1000 on the day before the train departs. If the quota system can't help you, consider buying a 'wait list' ticket, as seats often become available close to the train's departure time; phone the station on the day of departure to check your ticket's status. If you don't have a reservation for a particular train but carry an Indrail Pass, you may get one by arriving three hours early. Be wary of touts at the station offering tickets, hotels or exchange.

Timetables Regional timetables are available cheaply from station bookstalls; the monthly *Indian Bradshaw* is sold in principal stations. The handy *Trains at a Glance* (Rs 30) lists popular trains likely to be used by most foreign travellers and is available at stalls at Indian railway stations and in the UK from **SDEL** (see page 9).

Road
Road travel is sometimes the only choice for reaching some of the more remote places of interest, particularly national parks or isolated tourist sites. For the uninitiated, travel by road can also be a worrying experience because of the apparent absence of conventional traffic regulations. Vehicles drive on the left – in theory. Routes around the major cities are usually crowded with lorry traffic, especially at night, and the main roads are often poor and slow. There are a few motorway-style expressways, but most main roads are single track. Some district roads are quiet, and although they are not fast they can be a good way of seeing the country and village life if you have the time.

Bus Buses reach virtually every part of India, offering a cheap, if often uncomfortable, means of visiting places off the rail network. Very few villages are now more than 2-3 km from a bus stop. Services are run by the State Corporation from the State Bus Stand (and by private companies, which often have offices nearby). The latter allow advance reservations, including booking printable e-tickets online (check www.redbus.in and www.viaworld.in) and, although ticket prices are a little higher, they have fewer stops and are a bit more comfortable. There are some sleeper buses (a contradiction in terms)– if you must take a sleeper bus, choose a lower berth near the front of the bus. The upper berths are almost always really uncomfortable on bumpy roads.

Bus categories Though comfortable for sightseeing trips, apart from the very best 'sleeper coaches' even **air-conditioned luxury coaches** can be very uncomfortable for really long journeys. Often the air conditioning is very cold so wrap up. Journeys over 10 hours can be extremely tiring so it is better to go by train if there is a choice. **Express buses** run over long distances (frequently overnight); these are often called 'video coaches' and can be an appalling experience unless you appreciate loud film music blasting through the night. Ear plugs and eye masks may ease the pain. They rarely average more than 45 kph. **Local buses** are often very crowded, quite bumpy, slow and usually poorly maintained. However, over short distances, they can be a very cheap, friendly and easy way of getting about. Even where signboards are not in English someone will usually give you directions. Many larger towns have **minibus** services which charge a little more than the buses and pick up and drop passengers on request. Again very crowded, and with restricted headroom, they are the fastest way of getting about many of the larger towns.

Bus travel tips Some towns have different bus stations for different destinations. Booking on major long-distance routes is now computerized. Book in advance where possible and avoid the back of the bus where it can be very bumpy. If your destination is only served by a local bus you may do better to take the Express bus and 'persuade' the driver, with a tip in advance, to stop where you want to get off. You will have to pay the full fare to the first stop beyond your destination but you will get there faster and more comfortably. When an unreserved bus pulls into a bus station, there is usually an unholy scramble for seats, whilst those arriving have to struggle to get off! In many areas there is an unwritten 'rule of reservation' using handkerchiefs or bags thrust through the windows to reserve seats. Some visitors may feel a more justified right to a seat having fought their way through the crowd, but it is generally best to do as local people do and be prepared with a handkerchief or 'sarong'. As soon as it touches the seat, it is yours! Leave it on your seat when getting off to use the toilet at bus stations.

Car A car provides a chance to travel off the beaten track, and gives unrivalled opportunities for seeing something of India's great variety of villages and small towns. Until recently, the most widely used hire car was the Hindustan Ambassador. However, except for the newest model, they are often very unreliable, and although they still have their devotees, many find them uncomfortable for long journeys. Ambassadors are gradually giving way to more efficient (and boring) Tata and Toyota models with mod-cons like air conditioning – and seat belts. A handful of international agencies offer self-drive car hire (**Avis**, **Sixt**), but India's majestically anarchic traffic culture is not for the faint-hearted. It's much more common, and comfortable, to hire not just the car but someone to drive it for you.

Car hire Hiring a car and driver is the most comfortable and efficient way to cover short to medium distances, and although prices have increased sharply in recent years car travel in India is still a bargain by Western standards. A car shared by three or four people can be very good value. Even if you're travelling on a modest budget a day's car hire can help take the sting out of an arduous journey, allowing you to go sightseeing along the way without looking for somewhere to stash your bags. Local drivers often know their way around an area much better than drivers from other states, so where possible it is a good idea to get a local driver who speaks the state language, in addition to being able to communicate with you. The best way to guarantee a driver who speaks good English is to book in advance with a professional travel agency, either in India or in your home country. You can, if you choose, arrange car hire informally by asking around at taxi stands, but don't expect your driver to speak anything more than rudimentary English.

On pre-arranged overnight trips the fee you pay will normally include fuel and interstate taxes – check before you pay – and a wage for the driver. Drivers are responsible for their own expenses, including meals (and the pervasive servant-master culture in India means that most will choose to sit separately from you at meal times). Some tourist hotels provide rooms for drivers, but they often choose to sleep in the car overnight to save money. Urge them to use the drivers' rooms so they are fresh for the road ahead. In some areas drivers also seek to increase their earnings by taking you to hotels and shops where they earn a handsome commission; these are generally hugely overpriced and poor alternatives to the hotels recommended in this book, so don't be afraid to say no and insist on your choice of accommodation. If you feel inclined, a tip at the end of the tour of Rs 100 per day is perfectly acceptable. Be sure to check carefully the mileage at the beginning and end of the trip.

	Tata Indica non-a/c	Tata Indigo non-a/c	Hyundai Accent a/c	Toyota Innova
8 hrs/80 km	Rs 1200	Rs 1600	Rs 2200	Rs 2500
Extra km	Rs 8	Rs 10	Rs 15	Rs 15
Extra hour	Rs 80	Rs 100	Rs 180	Rs 200
Out of town				
Per km	Rs 8	Rs 10	Rs 15	Rs 15
Night halt	Rs 200	Rs 200	Rs 250	Rs 300

Taxi Taxi travel in India is a great bargain, and in most cities you can take a taxi from the airport to the centre for under US$10. Yellow-top taxis in cities and large towns are metered, although tariffs change frequently. These changes are shown on a fare chart which should be read in conjunction with the meter reading. Increased night-time rates apply in most cities, and there might be a small charge for luggage. Insist on the taxi meter being flagged in your presence. If the driver refuses, the official advice is to contact the police. This may not work, but it is worth trying. When a taxi doesn't have a meter, you will need to fix the fare before starting the journey. Ask at your hotel desk for a guide price. As a foreigner, it is rare to get a taxi in the big cities to use the meter – if they are eager to, watch out as sometimes the meter is rigged and they have a fake rate card. Also, watch out for the David Blaine-style note shuffle: you pay with a Rs 500 note, but they have a Rs 100 note in their hand. This happens frequently at the pre-paid booth outside New Delhi train station too, no matter how small the transaction.

At stations and airports it is often possible to share taxis to a central point. It is worth looking for fellow passengers who may be travelling in your direction and sharing a pre-paid taxi. At night, always have a clear idea of where you want to go and insist on being taken there. Taxi drivers may try to convince you that the hotel you have chosen 'closed three years ago' or is 'completely full'. Say that you have a reservation.

Rickshaw **Auto-rickshaws** (autos) are almost universally available in towns across North India and are the cheapest and most convenient way of getting about. It is best to walk a short distance away from a hotel gate before picking up an auto to avoid paying an inflated rate. In addition to using them for short journeys it is often possible to hire them by the hour, or for a half- or full-day's sightseeing. In some areas younger drivers who speak some English and know their local area well may want to show you around. However, rickshaw drivers are often paid a commission by hotels, restaurants and gift shops so advice is not always impartial. Drivers generally refuse to use a meter, often quote a ridiculous price or may sometimes stop short of your destination. If you have real problems it can help to note down the vehicle licence number and threaten to go to the police. Beware of some rickshaw drivers who show the fare chart for taxis.

Cycle-rickshaws and **horse-drawn tongas** are more common in small towns or on the outskirts of a large one. You will need to fix a price by bargaining. The animal attached to a tonga usually looks too undernourished to have the strength to pull the driver, let alone passengers.

Where to stay in Rajasthan, Delhi and Agra

India has an enormous range of accommodation. You can stay safely and very cheaply by Western standards right across the country. In all the major cities there are also high-quality hotels, offering a full range of facilities; in small centres hotels are much more variable. In Rajasthan, old maharajas' palaces and forts have been privately converted into comfortable, unusual hotels. The mainstay of the budget traveller is the ubiquitous Indian 'business hotel': these are usually within walking distance of train and bus stations, anonymous but generally decent value, with en suite rooms of variable cleanliness and a TV showing 110 channels of cricket and Bollywood *MTV*. At the top end, alongside international chains like **ITC Sheraton** and **Radisson Blu**, India boasts several home-grown hotel chains, best of which are the exceptional heritage and palace hotels operated by the **Oberoi** and **Taj** groups. In Delhi, there is a wide range of accommodation from the hostels, and chic B&Bs to super-budget, while in Agra, predictably, rooms are an expensive affair whatever the quality. In the peak season (October to April) hotels get very booked up in popular destinations. It is sometimes possible to book in advance by phone, fax or email, but double check your reservation, and always try to arrive as early as possible in the day.

Hotels
Price categories The category codes used in this book are based on the price of a double room excluding taxes. They are **not** star ratings and individual facilities vary considerably. The most expensive hotels charge in US dollars only. Modest hotels may not have their own restaurant but will often offer 'room service', bringing in food from outside. In temple towns, restaurants may only serve vegetarian food. Expect to pay more in Delhi and Agra. Prices away from large cities tend to be lower for comparable hotels.

Off-season rates Large reductions are made by hotels in all categories out of season. Always ask if any discount is available. You may also request the 10-15% agent's commission to be deducted from your bill if you book direct. Clarify whether the agreed figure includes all taxes.

Price codes

Where to stay
$$$$ over US$150   **$$$** US$66-150
$$ US$30-65   **$** under US$30
For a double room in high season, excluding taxes.

Restaurants
$$$ over US$12   **$$** US$6-12   **$** under US$6
For a two-course meal for one person, excluding drinks and service charge.

Taxes In general most hotel rooms rated at Rs 3000 or above are subject to a tax of 10%. Many states levy an additional luxury tax of 10-25%, and some hotels add a service charge of 10% on top of this. Taxes are not necessarily payable on meals, so it is worth settling your meals bill separately. Most hotels in the **$$** category and above accept payment by credit card. Check your final bill carefully. Visitors have complained of incorrect bills, even in the most expensive hotels. The problem particularly afflicts groups, when last-minute extras appear mysteriously on some guests' bills. Check the evening before departure, and keep all receipts.

Hotel facilities You have to be prepared for difficulties which are uncommon in the West. It is best to inspect the room and check that all equipment (air conditioning, TV, water heater, flush) works before checking in at a modest hotel. Many hotels try to wring too many years' service out of their linen, and it's quite common to find sheets that are stained, frayed or riddled with holes. Don't expect any but the most expensive or tourist-savvy hotels to fit a top sheet to the bed.

In some states **power cuts** are common, or hot water may be restricted to certain times of day. The largest hotels have their own generators but it is best to carry a good torch.

In some regions **water supply** is rationed periodically. Keep a bucket filled to use for flushing the toilet during water cuts. Occasionally, tap water may be discoloured due to rusty tanks. During the cold weather and in hill stations (such as Mount Abu), hot water will be available at certain times of the day, sometimes in buckets, but is usually very restricted in quantity. Electric water heaters may provide enough for a shower but not enough to fill a bath tub. For details on drinking water, see page 16.

Hotels close to temples can be very **noisy**, especially during festivals. Music blares from loudspeakers late at night and from very early in the morning, often making sleep impossible. Mosques call the faithful to prayers at dawn. Some find ear plugs helpful.

Some hotels offer **24-hour checkout**, meaning you can keep the room a full 24 hours from the time you arrive – a great option if you arrive in the afternoon and want to spend the morning sightseeing.

Homestays

At the upmarket end, increasing numbers of travellers are keen to stay in private homes and guesthouses, opting not to book large hotel chains that keep you at arm's length from a culture. Instead, travellers get home-cooked meals in heritage houses and learn about a country through conversation with often fascinating hosts. Delhi has many new and smart family-run B&Bs springing up. Tourist offices have lists of families with more modest homestays. Companies specializing in homestays include **Home & Hospitality** ① *www.homeandhospitality.co.uk*, **MAHout** ① *www.mahoutuk.com*, and **Sundale Vacations** ① *www.sundale.com*.

Food and drink in Rajasthan, Delhi and Agra

Food

You find just as much variety in dishes crossing India as you would on an equivalent journey across Europe. Combinations of spices give each region its distinctive flavour.

The larger hotels, open to non-residents, often offer **buffet** lunches with Indian, Western and sometimes Chinese dishes. These can be good value (Rs 400-500; but Rs 850 in the top grades) and can provide a welcome, comfortable break in the cool. The health risks, however, of food kept warm for long periods in metal containers are considerable, especially if turnover at the buffet is slow. We have received several complaints of stomach trouble following a buffet meal, even in five star hotels.

It is essential to be very careful since food hygiene may be poor, flies abound and refrigeration in the hot weather may be inadequate and intermittent because of power cuts. It is best to eat only freshly prepared food by ordering from the menu (especially meat and fish dishes). Avoid salads and cut fruit, unless the menu advertises that they have been washed in mineral water.

If you are unused to spicy food, go slow. Food is often spicier when you eat with families or at local places. Popular local restaurants are obvious from the number of people eating in them. Try a traditional *thali*, which is a complete meal served on a large stainless steel plate. Several preparations, placed in small bowls, surround the central serving of wholewheat chapati and rice. A vegetarian *thali* would include *dhal* (lentils), two or three curries (which can be quite hot) and crisp poppadums. A variety of pickles are offered – mango and lime are two of the most popular. These can be exceptionally hot, and are designed to be taken in minute quantities alongside the main dishes. Plain *dahi* (yoghurt), or *raita*, usually act as a bland 'cooler'. Simple *dhabas* (rustic roadside eateries) are an alternative experience for sampling authentic local dishes.

Many city restaurants and backpacker eateries offer a choice of so-called **European options** such as toasted sandwiches, stuffed pancakes, apple pies, fruit crumbles and cheesecakes. Italian favourites (pizzas, pastas) can be very different from what you are used to. **Ice creams**, on the other hand, can be exceptionally good; there are excellent Indian ones as well as some international brands.

India has many delicious tropical **fruits**. Some are seasonal (eg mangoes, pineapples and lychees), while others (eg bananas, grapes and oranges) are available throughout the year. It is safe to eat the ones you can wash and peel.

Regional specialities In cities and larger towns, you will see all types of Indian food on the menus, with some restaurants specializing in regional cuisine. North Indian kebabs and the richer flavoursome cuisine of Delhi and the Northwest Frontier are popular. Good Rajasthani dishes to try are *kadhi pakoka* (small veggie dumplings in a yoghurt curry) and *kej sangri* (lightly spiced desert beans). For snacks try the crispy, spicy and delicious *kachori* rather than the usual *samosa*. There are also amazing *kulfis* in Rajasthan, often served in hand-thrown clay pots, or try the delicious saffron *lassis*.

Drink

Drinking water used to be regarded as one of India's biggest hazards. It is still true that water from the tap or a well should never be considered safe to drink since public water supplies are often polluted. Bottled water is now widely available although not all bottled water is mineral water; most are simply purified water from an urban supply. Buy from a shop or stall, check the seal carefully and avoid street hawkers. When disposing of bottles puncture the neck, which prevents misuse but allows recycling.

There is growing concern over the mountains of plastic bottles that are collecting and the waste of resources needed to produce them, so travellers are being encouraged to carry their own bottles and take a portable water filter. It is important to use pure water for cleaning teeth.

Tea and **coffee** are safe and widely available. Both are normally served sweet, and with milk. If you wish, say 'no sugar' (*chini nahin*), 'no milk' (*dudh nahin*) when ordering. Alternatively, ask for a pot of tea and milk and sugar to be brought separately. Freshly brewed coffee is rare in North India; ordinary city restaurants will usually serve the instant variety. Even in aspiring smart cafés, espresso or cappuccino may not turn out quite as you'd expect in the West.

Bottled **soft drinks** such as Coke, Pepsi, Teem, Limca and Thums Up are universally available but always check the seal when you buy from a street stall. There are also several brands of fruit juice sold in cartons, including mango, pineapple and apple – Indian brands are very sweet. Don't add ice cubes as the water source may be contaminated. Take care with fresh fruit juices or *lassis* as ice is often added.

Indians rarely drink **alcohol** with a meal. In the past wines and spirits were generally either imported and extremely expensive, or local and of poor quality. Now, the best Indian whisky, rum and brandy (IMFL or 'Indian Made Foreign Liquor') are widely accepted, as are good Champagnoise and other wines from Maharashtra. If you hanker after a bottle of imported wine, you will only find it in the top restaurants or specialist liquor stores for at least Rs 1000.

For the urban elite, refreshing Indian beers are popular when eating out and are widely available. 'Pubs' have sprung up in the major cities. Elsewhere, seedy, all-male drinking dens in the larger cities are best avoided for women travellers, but can make quite an experience otherwise – you will sometimes be locked into cubicles for clandestine drinking. If that sounds unsavoury then head for the better hotel bars instead; prices aren't that steep. In rural India, local rice, palm, cashew or date juice *toddy* and *arak* are deceptively potent.

Most states have alcohol-free dry days or enforce degrees of prohibition. Some upmarket restaurants may serve beer even if it's not listed, so it's worth asking. In some states there are government approved wine shops where you buy your alcohol through a metal grille.

Festivals in Rajasthan, Delhi and Agra

India has a wealth of festivals with many celebrated nationwide, while others are specific to a particular state or community or even a particular temple. Many fall on different dates each year depending on the Hindu lunar calendar so check with the tourist office, or see the thorough calendar of upcoming major and minor festivals at www.drikpanchang.com.

The Hindu calendar

Hindus follow two distinct eras: The *Vikrama Samvat* which began in 57 BC and the *Salivahan Saka* which dates from AD 78 and has been the official Indian calendar since 1957. The *Saka* new year starts on 22 March and has the same length as the Gregorian calendar. The 29½-day lunar month with its 'dark' and 'bright' halves based on the new and full moons, are named after 12 constellations, and total a 354-day year. The calendar cleverly has an extra month (*adhik maas*) every 2½ to three years, to bring it in line with the solar year of 365 days coinciding with the Gregorian calendar of the West.

Some major national and regional festivals are listed below. A few count as national holidays: **26 January**: Republic Day; **15 August**: Independence Day; **2 October**: Mahatma Gandhi's Birthday; **25 December**: Christmas Day.

Major festivals and fairs

Jan New Year's Day (**1 Jan**) is accepted officially when following the Gregorian calendar but there are regional variations which fall on different dates, often coinciding with spring/harvest time in Mar and Apr. **14 Jan** Makar Sankranti marks the end of winter and is celebrated with kite flying. Very popular in Jaipur.

Feb Vasant Panchami, the spring festival when people wear bright yellow clothes to mark the advent of the season with singing, dancing and feasting. **Naqaur Camel Fair** and **Desert Festival** in Jaisalmer, both in Rajasthan.

Feb-Mar Maha Sivaratri marks the night when Siva danced his celestial dance of destruction (*Tandava*), which is celebrated with feasting and fairs at Siva temples, but preceded by a night of devotional readings and hymn singing.

Mar Holi, the festival of colours, marks the climax of spring. The previous night bonfires are lit symbolizing the end of winter (and conquering of evil). People have fun throwing coloured powder and water at each other and in the evening some gamble with friends. If you don't mind getting covered in colours, you can risk going out but celebrations can sometimes get very rowdy (and unpleasant). Some worship Krishna who defeated the demon Putana.

Apr/May Buddha Jayanti, the 1st full moon night in Apr/May marks the birth of the Buddha.

Jul/Aug Raksha (or Rakhi) Bandhan symbolizes the bond between brother and sister, celebrated at full moon. A sister says special prayers for her brother and ties coloured threads around his wrist to remind him of the special bond. He in turn gives a gift and promises to protect and care for her. Sometimes *rakshas* are exchanged as a mark of friendship. **Narial Purnima** on the same full moon. Hindus make offerings of *narial* (coconuts) to the Vedic god Varuna (Lord of the waters) by throwing them into the sea.

15 Aug is **Independence Day**, a national secular holiday is marked by special events. **Ganesh Chaturthi** was established just over 100 years ago by the Indian nationalist leader Tilak. The elephant-headed God of good omen is shown special reverence. On the last of the 5-day festival after harvest, clay images of Ganesh are taken in procession with dancers and musicians, and are immersed in the sea, river or pond.

Gaining popularity in Rajasthan, Udaipur and Pushkar.

Aug/Sep Janmashtami, the birth of Krishna is celebrated at midnight at Krishna temples.

Sep/Oct Dasara has many local variations. Celebrations for the 9 nights *(navaratri)* are marked with Ramlila, various episodes of the *Ramayana* story are enacted with particular reference to the battle between the forces of good and evil. In some parts of India it celebrates *R*ama's victory over the Demon king Ravana of Lanka with the help of loyal Hanuman (Monkey). Huge effigies of Ravana made of bamboo and paper are burnt on the 10th day *(Vijaya dasami)* of *Dasara* in public open spaces. In West Bengal the focus is on Durga's victory over the demon Mahishasura, and the festival is known as **Durga Puja**

Oct/Nov Gandhi Jayanti (2 Oct), Mahatma Gandhi's birthday, is remembered with prayer meetings and devotional singing.

Diwali/Deepavali (*Sanskrit ideepa* lamp), the festival of lights. Some Hindus celebrate Krishna's victory over the demon Narakasura, some Rama's return after his 14 years' exile in the forest when citizens lit his way with oil lamps. The festival falls on the dark *chaturdasi* (14th) night (the one preceding the new moon), when rows of lamps or candles are lit in remembrance, and *rangolis* are painted on the floor as a sign of welcome. Fireworks have become an integral part of the celebration which are often set off days before Diwali. Equally, Lakshmi, the Goddess of Wealth (as well as Ganesh) is worshipped by merchants and the business community who open the new financial year's account on the day. Most people wear new clothes; some play games of chance.

Guru Nanak Jayanti commemorates the birth of Guru Nanak. **Akhand Path** (unbroken reading of the holy book) takes place and the book itself (*Guru Granth Sahib*) is taken out in procession.

Dec **Christmas Day** (25 Dec) sees Indian Christians celebrate the birth of Christ in much the same way as in the West; many churches hold services/mass at midnight. There is an air of festivity in city markets which are specially decorated and illuminated. Over **New Year's Eve** (31 Dec) hotel prices peak and large supplements are added for meals and entertainment in the upper category hotels. Some churches mark the night with a Midnight Mass.

Muslim holy days

These are fixed according to the lunar calendar. According to the Gregorian calendar, they tend to fall 11 days earlier each year, dependent on the sighting of the new moon.

Ramadan, known in India as "ramzan", is the start of the month of fasting when all Muslims (except young children, the very elderly, the sick, pregnant women and travellers) must abstain from food and drink, from sunrise to sunset.

Id ul Fitr is the 3-day festival that marks the end of Ramzan.

Id-ul-Zuha/Bakr-Id is when Muslims commemorate Ibrahim's sacrifice of his son according to God's commandment; the main time of pilgrimage to Mecca (the Hajj). It is marked by the sacrifice of a goat, feasting and alms giving.

Muharram is when the killing of the Prophet's grandson, Hussain, is commemorated by Shi'a Muslims. Decorated *tazias* (replicas of the martyr's tomb) are carried in procession by devout wailing followers who beat their chests to express their grief. Lucknow is famous for its grand *tazias*. Shi'as fast for the 10 days.

Essentials A-Z

Accident and emergency

Contact the relevant emergency service (police T100, fire T101, ambulance T102) and your embassy (see under Directory in major cities). Make sure you obtain police/medical reports required for insurance claims.

Drugs

Be aware that the government takes the misuse of drugs very seriously. Anyone charged with the illegal possession of drugs risks facing a fine of Rs 100,000 and a minimum 10 years' imprisonment. Several foreigners have been imprisoned for drugs-related offences in the last decade.

Electricity

India's supply is 220-240 volts AC. Some top hotels have transformers. There may be pronounced variations in the voltage, and power cuts are common. Power back-up by generator or inverter is becoming more widespread, even in humble hotels, though it may not cover a/c. Socket sizes vary so take a universal adaptor; low-quality versions are available locally. Many hotels, even in the higher categories, don't have electric razor sockets. Invest in a stabilizer for a laptop.

Embassies and consulates

For information on visas and immigration, see page 24. For a comprehensive list of embassies (but not all consulates), see http://india.gov.in/overseas/indian_missions.php or http://embassy.goabroad.com. Many embassies around the world are now outsourcing the visa process which might affect how long the process takes.

Health

Local populations in India are exposed to a range of health risks not encountered in the Western world. Many of the diseases are major problems for the local poor and destitute and, although the risk to travellers is more remote, they cannot be ignored. Obviously 5-star travel is going to carry less risk than backpacking on a budget.

Health care in the region is varied. There are many excellent private and government clinics/hospitals. As with all medical care, first impressions count. It's worth contacting your embassy or consulate on arrival and asking where the recommended (ie those used by diplomats) clinics are. You can also ask about locally recommended medical dos and don'ts. If you do get ill, and you have the opportunity, you should also ask your medical insurer whether they are satisfied that the medical centre/hospital you have been referred to is of a suitable standard.

Before you go

Ideally, you should see your GP or travel clinic at least 6 weeks before your departure for general advice on travel risks, malaria and vaccinations. Make sure you have travel insurance, get a dental check (especially if you are going to be away for more than a month), know your own blood group and if you suffer a long-term condition such as diabetes or epilepsy make sure someone knows or that you have a Medic Alert bracelet/necklace with this information on it. Remember that it is risky to buy medicinal tablets abroad because the doses may differ and India has a huge trade in false drugs.

Vaccinations

If you need vaccinations, see your doctor well in advance of your travel. Most courses must be completed by a minimum of 4 weeks. Travel clinics may provide rapid courses of vaccination, but are likely to be more expensive. The following vaccinations are recommended: typhoid, polio, tetanus, infectious hepatitis and diptheria. For details of malaria prevention, contact your GP or local travel clinic.

The following vaccinations may also be considered: rabies, possibly BCG (since TB is still common in the region) and in some cases meningitis and diphtheria (if you're staying in the country for a long time). Yellow fever is not required in India but you may be asked to show a certificate if you have travelled from Africa or South America. Japanese encephalitis may be required for rural travel at certain times of the year (mainly rainy seasons). An effective oral cholera vaccine (Dukoral) is now available as 2 doses providing 3 months' protection.

Websites

Blood Care Foundation (UK), www.bloodcare.org.uk A Kent-based charity 'dedicated to the provision of screened blood and resuscitation fluids in countries where these are not readily available'. They will dispatch certified non-infected blood of the right type to your hospital/clinic. The blood is flown in from various centres around the world.

British Travel Health Association (UK), www.btha.org This is the official website of an organization of travel health professionals.

Fit for Travel, www.fitfortravel.scot.nhs.uk This site from Scotland provides a quick A-Z of vaccine and travel health advice requirements for each country.

Foreign and Commonwealth Office (FCO) (UK), www.fco.gov.uk This is a key travel advice site, with useful information on the country, people, climate and lists the UK embassies/consulates. The site also promotes the concept of 'know before you go' and encourages travel insurance and appropriate travel health advice. It has links to Department of Health travel advice site.

The Health Protection Agency, www.hpa. org.uk Up-to-date malaria advice guidelines for travel around the world. It gives specific advice about the right drugs for each location. It also has useful information for those who are pregnant, suffering from epilepsy or planning to travel with children.

Medic Alert (UK), www.medicalalert.com This is the website of the foundation that produces bracelets and necklaces for those with existing medical problems. Once you have ordered your bracelet/necklace you write your key medical details on paper inside it, so that if you collapse, a medic can identify you as having epilepsy or a nut allergy, etc.

Travel Screening Services (UK), www. travelscreening.co.uk A private clinic dedicated to integrated travel health. The clinic gives vaccine, travel health advice, email and SMS text vaccine reminders and screens returned travellers for tropical diseases.

World Health Organisation, www.who.int The WHO site has links to the *WHO Blue Book* on travel advice. This lists the diseases in different regions of the world. It describes vaccination schedules and makes clear which countries have yellow fever vaccination certificate requirements and malarial risk.

Language

Hindi, spoken as a mother tongue by over 400 million people, is India's official language. The use of English is also enshrined in the Constitution for a wide range of official purposes, notably communication between Hindi and non-Hindi speaking states. The most widely spoken Indo-Aryan languages are: Bengali (8.3%), Marathi (8%), Urdu (5.7%), Gujarati (5.4%), Oriya (3.7%) and Punjabi (3.2%). Among the Dravidian languages Telugu (8.2%), Tamil (7%), Kannada (4.2%) and Malayalam (3.5%) are the most widely used.

English now plays an important role across India. It is widely spoken in towns and cities and even in quite remote villages it is usually not difficult to find someone who speaks at least a little English. Outside of major tourist sites, other European languages are almost completely unknown. The accent in which English is spoken is often affected strongly by the mother tongue of the speaker and there have been changes in common grammar which sometimes make it sound unusual.

Many of these changes have become standard Indian English usage, as valid as any other varieties of English used around the world. It is possible to study a number of Indian languages at language centres.

Money → *UK £1 = Rs 98.8, €1 = Rs 83.6, US$1 = Rs 61.5 (Nov 2013)*

Indian currency is the Indian Rupee (Re/Rs). It is **not** possible to purchase these before you arrive. If you want cash on arrival it is best to get it at the airport bank, although see if an ATM is available as airport rates are not very generous. Rupee notes are printed in denominations of Rs 1000, 500, 100, 50, 20, 10. The rupee is divided into 100 paise. Coins are minted in denominations of Rs 10, 5, Rs 2, Rs 1 and (the increasingly uncommon) 50 paise. **Note** Carry money in a money belt worn under clothing but keep a small amount in an easily accessible place.

ATMs

By far the most convenient method of accessing money, ATMs can be found all over India, usually attended by security guards, with most banks offering some services to holders of overseas cards. Banks whose ATMs will issue cash against Cirrus and Maestro cards, as well as Visa and MasterCard, include **Bank of Baroda, Citibank, HDFC, HSBC, ICICI, IDBI, Punjab National Bank, State Bank of India (SBI), Standard Chartered** and UTI. A withdrawal fee is usually charged by the issuing bank on top of the conversion charges applied by your own bank. Fraud prevention measures quite often result in travellers having their cards blocked by the bank when unexpected overseas transactions occur; advise your bank of your travel plans before leaving.

Credit cards

Major credit cards are increasingly acceptable in the main centres, though in smaller cities and towns it is still rare to be able to pay by credit card. Payment by credit card can sometimes be more expensive than payment by cash, whilst some credit card companies charge a premium on cash withdrawals. **Visa** and **MasterCard** have an ever-growing number of ATMs in major cities and several banks offer withdrawal facilities for Cirrus and Maestro cardholders. It is however easy to obtain a cash advance against a credit card. Railway reservation centres in major cities take payment for train tickets by Visa card which can be very quick as the queue is short, although they cannot be used for Tourist Quota tickets.

Currency cards

If you don't want to carry lots of cash, pre-paid currency cards allow you to preload money from your bank account, fixed at the day's exchange rate. They look like a credit or debit card and are issued by specialist money changing companies, such as **Travelex** and **Caxton FX**. You can top up and check your balance by phone, online and sometimes by text.

Traveller's cheques (TCs)

TCs issued by reputable companies (eg **Thomas Cook, American Express**) are widely accepted. They can be easily exchanged at small local travel agents and tourist internet cafés but are rarely used directly for payment. Try to avoid changing at banks, where the process can be time consuming; opt for hotels and agents instead, take large denomination cheques and change enough to last for some days.

Changing money

The **State Bank of India** and several others in major towns are authorized to deal in foreign exchange. Some give cash against Visa/MasterCard (eg **ANZ**). American Express cardholders can use their cards to get either cash or TCs in Delhi. The larger cities have licensed money changers with offices usually in the commercial sector. Changing money through unauthorized dealers is illegal. Premiums on the currency black market are very small and highly risky. Large hotels change money 24 hrs a day for guests, but banks often give a substantially better rate of exchange. There is a bank at the airport as well as a Thomas Cook counter. Many international flights arrive during the night and it is generally far easier and less time consuming to change money at the airport than in the city. You should be given a foreign currency encashment certificate when you change money through a bank or authorized dealer; ask for one if it is not automatically given. It allows you to change Indian rupees back to your own currency on departure. It also enables you to use rupees to pay hotel bills or buy air tickets for which payment in foreign exchange may be required. The certificates are only valid for 3 months.

Opening hours
Banks are open Mon-Fri 1030-1430, Sat 1030-1230. Top hotels sometimes have a 24-hr money changing service. **Government offices** open Mon-Fri 0930-1700, Sat 0930-1300 (some open on alternate Sat only). **Post offices** open Mon-Fri 1000-1700, often shutting for lunch, and Sat mornings. **Shops** open Mon-Sat 0930-1800. Bazars keep longer hours.

Safety
Personal security
In general the threats to personal security for travellers in India are remarkably small. However, incidents of petty theft and violence directed specifically at tourists have been on the increase so care is necessary in some places, and basic common sense needs to be used with respect to looking after valuables. Follow the same precautions you would when at home. There have been much-reported incidents of severe sexual assault in Delhi, Kolkata and some more rural areas in 2013. Avoid wandering alone outdoors late at night in these places. During daylight hours be careful in remote places, especially when alone. If you are under threat, scream loudly. Be cautious before accepting food or drink from casual acquaintants, as it may be drugged – though note that Indians on a long train journey will invariably try to share their snacks with you, and balance caution with the opportunity to interact. The left-wing Maoist extremist Naxalites are active in East Central India. They have a long history of conflict with state and national authorities, including attacks on police and government officials. The Naxalites have not specifically targeted Westerners, but have attacked symbolic targets including Western companies. As a general rule, travellers are advised to be vigilant in the lead up to and on days of national significance, such as Republic Day (26 Jan) and Independence Day (15 Aug) as militants have in the past used such occasions to mount attacks.

Following a major explosion on the Delhi to Lahore (Pakistan) train in Feb 2007 and the Mumbai attacks in Nov 2008, increased security has been implemented on many trains and stations. Similar measures at airports may cause delays for passengers so factor this into your timing. Also check your airline's website for up-to-date information on luggage restrictions. In Delhi, you even find x-ray machines at the Metro stations.

That said, in the great majority of places visited by tourists, violent crime and personal attacks are extremely rare.

Travel advice
It is better to seek advice from your consulate than from travel agencies. Before you travel you can contact: **British Foreign & Commonwealth Office Travel Advice Unit**, T0845-850 2829 (Pakistan desk T020-7270 2385), www.fco.gov.uk. **US State Department's Bureau of Consular Affairs**, Overseas Citizens Services, Room 4800, Department of State, Washington, DC 20520-4818, USA, T202-647 1488, http://travel.state.gov. **Australian Department of Foreign Affairs Canberra**, Australia, T02-6261 3305, www.smartraveller.gov.au. Canadian official advice is on www.voyage.gc.ca.

Theft

Theft is not uncommon. It is best to keep TCs, passports and valuables with you at all times. Don't regard hotel rooms as being automatically safe; even hotel safes don't guarantee secure storage. Avoid leaving valuables near open windows even when you are in the room. Use your own padlock in a budget hotel when you go out. Pickpockets and other thieves operate in the big cities. Crowded areas are particularly high risk. Take special care of your belongings when getting on or off public transport.

If you have items stolen, they should be reported to the police as soon as possible. Keep a separate record of vital documents, including passport details and numbers of TCs. Larger hotels will be able to assist in contacting and dealing with the police. Dealings with the police can be very difficult and in the worst regions, even dangerous. The paperwork involved in reporting losses can be time consuming and irritating and your own documentation (eg passport and visas) may be demanded.

In some states the police occasionally demand bribes, though you should not assume that if procedures move slowly you are automatically being expected to offer a bribe. The traffic police are tightening up on traffic offences in some places. They have the right to make on-the-spot fines for speeding and illegal parking. If you face a fine, insist on a receipt. If you have to go to a police station, try to take someone with you.

If you face really serious problems (eg in connection with a driving accident), contact your consular office as quickly as possible. You should ensure you always have your international driving licence and motorbike or car documentation with you.

Confidence tricksters are particularly common around railway stations or places where budget tourists gather. A common plea is some sudden and desperate calamity; sometimes a letter will be produced in English to back up the claim. The demands are likely to increase sharply if sympathy is shown.

Telephone

The international code for India is +91. International Direct Dialling is widely available in privately run call booths, usually labelled on yellow boards with the letters 'PCO-STD-ISD'. You dial the call yourself, and the time and cost are displayed on a computer screen. Cheap rate (2100-0600) means long queues may form outside booths. Telephone calls from hotels are usually more expensive (check the price before calling), though some will allow local calls free of charge. Internet phone booths, usually associated with cybercafés, are the cheapest way of calling overseas.

A double ring repeated regularly means it is ringing; equal tones with equal pauses means engaged (similar to the UK). If calling a mobile, rather than ringing, you might hear music while you wait for an answer.

One disadvantage of the tremendous pace of the telecommunications revolution is the fact that millions of telephone numbers go out of date every year. Current telephone directories themselves are often out of date and some of the numbers given in this book will have been changed even as we go to press. **Directory enquiries**, T197, can be helpful but works only for the local area code.

Mobile phones are for sale everywhere, as are local SIM cards that allow you to make calls within India and overseas at much lower rates than using a 'roaming' service from your normal provider at home – sometimes for as little as Rs 0.5 per min. Arguably the best service is provided by the government carrier **BSNL/MTNL** but security provisions make connecting to the service virtually impossible for foreigners. Private companies such as **Airtel**, **Vodafone**, **Reliance** and **Tata Indicom** are easier to sign up with, but the deals they offer can be befuddling and are frequently changed. To connect you'll need to complete a form, have a local address or receipt showing the address of your hotel, and present photocopies of your passport and visa plus 2 passport photos to an authorized reseller – most phone dealers will be able to help, and can also sell top-up. **Univercell**, www.univercell.in, and **The Mobile Store**, www.themobilestore.in, are 2 widespread and efficient chains selling phones and SIM cards.

India is divided into a number of 'calling circles' or regions, and if you travel outside the region where your connection is based, eg from Delhi into Uttar Pradesh, you will pay higher 'roaming' charges for making and receiving calls, and any problems that may occur – with 'unverified' documents, for example – can be much harder to resolve.

Time

India doesn't change its clocks, so from the last Sun in Oct to the last Sun in Mar the time is GMT +5½ hrs, and the rest of the year it's +4½ hrs (USA, EST +10½ and +9½ hrs; Australia, EST -5½ and -4½ hrs).

Tipping

A tip of Rs 10 to a bellboy carrying luggage in a modest hotel (Rs 20 in a higher category) would be appropriate. In upmarket restaurants, a 10% tip is acceptable when service is not already included, while in places serving very cheap meals, round off the bill with small change. Indians don't normally tip taxi drivers but a small extra is welcomed. Porters at airports and railway stations often have a fixed rate displayed but will usually press for more. Ask fellow passengers what a fair rate is.

Tourist information

There are **Government of India** tourist offices in the state capitals, as well as state tourist offices (sometimes **Tourism Development Corporations**) in the Delhi and some towns and places of tourist interest. They produce their own tourist literature, either free or sold at a nominal price, and some also have lists of city hotels and paying guest options. The quality of material is improving though maps are often poor. Many offer tours of the city, neighbouring sights and overnight and regional packages. Some run modest hotels and midway motels with restaurants and may also arrange car hire and guides.

Visas and immigration

Virtually all foreign nationals, including children, require a visa to enter India. The rules regarding visas change frequently and arrangements for application and collection also vary from town to town so it is essential to check details and costs with the relevant embassy or consulate. These remain closed on Indian national holidays. Many consulates and embassies are currently outsourcing the visa process; it's best to find out in advance how long it will take. Note that visas are valid from the date granted, not from the date of entry.

Recently, the Indian government has decided to issue 'visas on arrival' for some 40 countries (including the UK, the USA, France and Germany), as well as for citizens of all countries who are over the age of 60. The exact time frame for the change is not yet clear, so check the latest situation online before travelling.

For up-to-date information on visa requirements visit www.india-visa.com.

No foreigner needs to register within the 180-day period of their tourist visa. If you have a 1-year visa or as a US citizen a 10-year visa and wish to stay longer than 180 days you will need to register with the Foreign Registration Office.

Contents

Delhi & Agra

Delhi

Delhi can take you aback with its vibrancy and growth. Less than 60 years ago the spacious, quiet and planned city of New Delhi was still the pride of late colonial British India, while to its north, the lanes of Old Delhi resonated with the sounds of a bustling medieval market. Today, both worlds have been overtaken by the rush of modernization. As Delhi's population surges, its tentacles have spread in all directions – from both the ancient core of Shahjahan's city in the north and the late British capital of New Delhi to its south.

Close to New Delhi Railway Station, the cheap hotels and guesthouses of Paharganj squeeze between cloth merchants and wholesalers. In Old Delhi, further north, with the Red Fort and Jama Masjid, the old city is still a dense network of narrow alleys and tightly packed markets and houses. Your senses are bombarded by noise, bustle, smells and apparent chaos. A 'third city' comprises the remorselessly growing squatter settlements (*jhuggies*), which provide shelter for more than a third of Delhi's population. To the south is another, newer, chrome-and-glass city, the city of the modern suburbs and urban 'farms', where the rural areas of Gurgaon have become the preserve of the prosperous, with shopping malls, banks and private housing estates. Old and new, simple and sophisticated, traditional and modern, East and West are juxtaposed. Whatever India you are looking for, the capital has it all – getting lost in warrens of crowded streets, wandering through spice markets, eating kebabs by the beautiful Jama Masjid, lazing among Mogul ruins, listening to Sufi musicians by a shrine at dusk or shopping in giant shining malls, drinking cocktails in glitzy bars and travelling on the gleaming Metro.

Arriving in Delhi

Getting there

Delhi is served by **Indira Gandhi International (IGI) Airport**, which handles both international and domestic traffic. The new T3 (International Terminal) has one of the longest runways in Asia and is connected to the city centre by Metro. It is about 23 km from the centre. During the day, it can take 30-45 minutes from the Domestic Terminal and 45-60 minutes from the International Terminal to to travel by road to the centre. With the Metro, it should take 20 minutes. A free shuttle runs between the terminals. To get to town take a pre-paid taxi (see Transport, page 64) or an airport coach, or ask your hotel to collect you.

The **Inter State Bus Terminus (ISBT)** is at Kashmere Gate, near the Red Fort, about 30 minutes by bus from Connaught Place. Local buses connect it to the other ISBTs.

There are three main railway stations. The busy **New Delhi Station**, a 10-minute walk north of Connaught Place, can be maddeningly chaotic; you need to have all your wits about you. The quieter **Hazrat Nizamuddin** (which has some south-bound trains) is 5 km southeast of Connaught Place. The overpoweringly crowded **Old Delhi Station** (2 km north of Connaught Place) has a few important train connections. ▸▸ *See Transport, page 62.*

Getting around

The new Metro is making the sprawling city very navigable: it's now possible to get from Connaught Place to Old Delhi in a cool five minutes; while Connaught Place to Qutb Minar takes about 30 minutes, and all the way down to the final stop in Gurgaon takes about one hour. It is a strange experience to go from air-conditioned high tech to the bustling streets of Chandi Chowk. There is a fine women-only carriage at the front of each train, clearly marked inside and on the platform – this prevents women from having to succumb to the crush of the other carriages. There is a fine of Rs 250 for men ignoring all the signs in pink and, in early 2011, a posse of women made men do sit-ups on the train for trespassing into the pink zone! Like any city Metro service, try and avoid rush hour if you can. At each Metro station you have to go through airport-like security and have your bag x-rayed, etc.

Auto-rickshaws and taxis are widely available, and new rate cards mean that drivers will now use their meters, even with foreigners. It's best to use pre-paid stands at stations, airport terminals and at the junction of Radial Road 1 and Connaught Place if possible. The same applies to cycle rickshaws, which ply the streets of Old Delhi. City buses are usually packed and have long queues. Be on your guard from thieves around New Delhi Station. State Entry Road runs from the southern end of Platform 1 to Connaught Place. This is a hassle-free alternative to the main Chelmsford Road during the day (gate closed at night). Also watch your change or cash interactions even at the pre-paid booths – sometimes they do a switch of a Rs 100 note for a Rs 10 for example. Fleets of Radio Taxis are the newest additions to the city's transport options. These include: **Delhi Cab** ① *T011-4433 3222;* **Easy Cab** ① *T011-4343 4343;* **Mega Cabs** ① *T011-4141 4141;* and **Quick Cab** ① *T011-4533 3333.* ▸▸ *See Transport, page 62.*

Orientation

The **Red Fort** and **Jama Masjid** are the focal point of Old Delhi, 2 km northeast of Connaught Place. Chandni Chowk, the main commercial area, heads west from the fort. Around this area are narrow lanes packed to the rafters with all different types of wares for sale. To the southeast are **New Delhi Railway Station** and the main backpackers' area, **Paharganj**, with **Connaught Place**, the notional 'centre' of New Delhi, about 1 km south.

Running due south of Connaught Place is **Janpath** with small shops selling craft products, and hotels like the **Imperial**. Janpath is intersected by **Rajpath** with all the major state buildings at its western end. Immediately south is the diplomatic enclave, **Chanakyapuri**. Most of the upmarket hotels are scattered across the wide area between Connaught Place and the airport to the southwest. As Delhi's centre of gravity has shifted southwards, a series of new markets has grown up to serve extensive housing colonies such as **South Extension**, **Greater Kailash** and **Safdarjang Enclave**. This development has brought one of the major historic sites, the **Qutb Minar**, within the limits of the city, about half an hour by taxi south of Connaught Place. **Gurgaon** which is strictly not in Delhi but in Haryana, is the new business hub with many shopping malls to boot.

Tourist information

Most tourist offices are open Monday-Friday 1000-1800. **The Government of India Tourist Office** ① *88 Janpath, T011-332 0005, Mon-Sat 0900-1800; also at the international airport*, is helpful and issues permits for visits to Rashtrapati Bhavan and gardens. There are several branches of **Delhi Tourism** ① *N-36 Connaught Pl, T011-2331 5322 (touts pester you to use one of many imposters; the correct office is directly opposite 'Competent House'), www.delhitourism.com*, the branch at **Coffee Home Annexe** ① *Baba Kharak Singh Marg, T011-336 5358*, offers hotel, transport and tour bookings (T011-2462 3782, 0700-2100). There are also branches at the airport terminals, the Inter-State Bus Terminal; **New Delhi Railway Station** ① *T011-2373 2374*; and **Nizamuddin Railway Station** ① *T011-2251 1083*. Also contact the **India Tourism Development Corporation (ITDC)** ① *L-1 Connaught Circus, T011-2332 0331*.

Best time to visit

October to March are the best months to visit, but December and January can get quite cold and foggy at night. Pollution can affect asthma sufferers – in fact a lot of people develop respiratory problems and sore throats if they spend more than a few days in Delhi; echinacea can help. Monsoon lasts from the end of June to mid-September. May and June are very hot and dry and, with the whole city switching on its air-condioning units, power cuts are suffered more frequently at this time. Even the malls in Saket were having to keep their air conditioning on low during the summer of 2012.

Background

In the modern period, Delhi has only been India's capital since 1911. It is a city of yo yo-ing fortunes and has been repeatedly reduced to rubble. There have been at least eight cities founded on the site of modern Delhi.

According to Hindu mythology, Delhi's first avatar was as the site of a dazzlingly wealthy city, Indraprastha, mentioned in the Mahabharata and founded around 2500 BC. The next five cities were to the south of today's Delhi. First was Lalkot, which, from 1206, became the capital of the Delhi Sultanate under the Slave Dynasty. The story of the first Sultan of Delhi, Qutb-ud-din Aybak, is a classic rags-to-riches story. A former slave, he rose through the ranks to become a general, a governor and then Sultan of Delhi. He is responsible for building Qutb Minar, but died before its completion.

The 1300s were a tumultuous time for Delhi, with five cities built during the century. Siri, the first of these, has gruesome roots. Legend has it that the city's founder, Ala-ud-din, buried the heads of infidels in the foundation of the fort. Siri derives its name from the

Hindi word for 'head'. After Siri came Tughlaqabad, whose existence came to a sudden end when the Sultan of Delhi, Muhammad Tughlaq, got so angry about a perceived insult from residents, he destroyed the city. The cities of Jahanpanah and Ferozebad followed in quick succession. Delhi's centre of gravity began to move northwards. In the 1500s Dinpanah was constructed by Humayun, whose wonderful tomb (1564-1573) graces Hazrat Nizamuddin. Shahjahanabad, known today as Old Delhi, followed, becoming one of the richest and most populous cities in the world. The Persian emperor Nadir Shah invaded, killing as many as 120,000 residents in a single bloody night and stealing the Kohinoor Diamond (now part of the British royal family's crown jewels).

The next destroyers of Delhi were the British, who ransacked the city in the wake of the Great Uprising/Mutiny of 1857. The resulting bloodbath left bodies piled so high that the victors' horses had to tread on them. For the next 50 years, while the port cities of Calcutta and Bombay thrived under the British, Delhi languished. Then, in 1911, King George, on a visit to India, announced that a new city should be built next to what remained of Delhi, and that this would be the new capital of India. The British architect Edwin Lutyens was brought in to design the city. You could argue that the building hasn't stopped since ...

The central part of New Delhi is an example of Britain's imperial pretensions. The government may have been rather more reticent about moving India's capital, if it had known that in less than 36 years time, the British would no longer be ruling India. Delhi's population swelled after the violence of partition, with refugees flooding to the city. In 10 years the population of Delhi doubled, and many well-known housing colonies were built during this period.

The economic boom that began in the 1990s has lead to an explosion of construction and soaring real estate prices. Delhi is voraciously eating into the surrounding countryside. It is a city changing at such breakneck speed that shops, homes and even airports seem to appear and disappear almost overnight.

Places in Delhi

The sites of interest are grouped in three main areas. In the centre is the British-built capital of **New Delhi**, with its government buildings and wide avenues. The heart of **Shahjahanabad** (Old Delhi) is about 2 km north of Connaught Circus. Ten kilometres to the south is the **Qutb Minar** complex, with the old fortress city of Tughluqabad, 8 km to its east. Across the Yamuna River is the remarkable new Akshardham Temple. You can visit each separately, or link routes together into a day-tour to include the most interesting sites.

Old Delhi → *For listings, see pages 49-65.*

Shah Jahan (ruled 1628-1658) decided to move back from Agra to Delhi in 1638. Within 10 years the huge city of **Shahjahanabad**, now known as Old Delhi, was built. The plan of Shah Jahan's new city symbolized the link between religious authority enshrined in the Jama Masjid to the west, and political authority represented by the Diwan-i-Am in the Fort, joined by Chandni Chowk, the route used by the emperor. The city was protected by rubble-built walls, some of which still survive. These walls were pierced by 14 main gates. The **Ajmeri Gate**, **Turkman Gate** (often referred to by auto-rickshaw wallahs as 'Truckman Gate'), **Kashmere Gate** and **Delhi Gate** still survive.

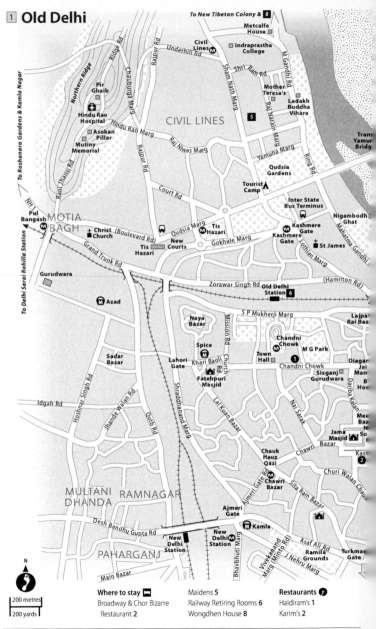

1 Old Delhi

To New Tibetan Colony & 8

Metcalfe House

Civil Lines M

Indraprastha College

Underhill Rd

Northern Ridge

Pir Ghaib

Ridge Rd

Chauburja Marg

Rajpur Rd

Sham Nath Marg

Shri Ram Rd

M Gandhi Rd

Mother Teresa's

Ladakh Buddha Vihara

Raj Narain Marg

Hindu Rao Hospital

Asokan Pillar

Mutiny Memorial

Hindu Rao Marg

Rajpur Rd

Raj Niwas Marg

CIVIL LINES

5

Yamuna Marg

Ring Rd

Trans Yamur Bridg

To Roshanara Gardens & Kamla Nagar

Rani Jhansi Rd

NH 1

Court Rd

Qudsia Gardens

Tourist Camp

Inter State Bus Terminus

Mahatma Gandhi

Nigambodh Ghat

Pul Bangash

MOTIA BAGH

Christ Church

(Boulevard Rd)

Qudsia Marg

Tis Hazari M

Gokhale Marg

Kashmere Gate

Kashmere Gate

Lothian Marg

St James

Tis Hazari

New Courts

Grand Trunk Rd

To Delhi Sarai Rohilla Station

Gurudwara

Azad

Zorawar Singh Rd

(Hamilton Rd)

Old Delhi Station 6

S P Mukherji Marg

Lajpa Rai Baz

Naya Bazar

Mission Rd

Church Rd

Chandni Chowk M

M G Park

Sadar Bazar

Spice

Khari Baoli

Lahori Gate

Fatehpuri Masjid

Town Hall

Chandni Chowk 1

Sisganj Gurudwara

Diagar Jai Man B Hos

Idgah Rd

Hoshnat Singh Rd

Jhande Walan Rd

Qutb Rd

Shraddhanand Marg

Lal Kuan Bazar

Nai Sarak

Mee Baz N Su

MULTANI DHANDA

RAMNAGAR

Chauk Hauz Qazi

Chawri Bazar

Sita Ram Bazar

Jama Masjid

Chawri

Kast

Churi Walan Chau

Ajmeri Gate Rd

Desh Bandhu Gupta Rd

Ajmeri Gate

Kamla

Asaf Ali Rd

Turkma Gate

PAHARGANJ

New Delhi Station

New Delhi Station M

Bhavbhuti Marg

Vivekanand Marg (Minto) Rd

Ramila Grounds

J Nehru Marg

Main Bazar

N

200 metres

200 yards

Where to stay 🛏
Broadway & Chor Bizarre
Restaurant **2**

Maidens **5**
Railway Retiring Rooms **6**
Wongdhen House **8**

Restaurants 🍴
Haldiram's **1**
Karim's **2**

➡ Delhi maps
1 Old Delhi, page 30
2 New Delhi, page 36
3 Connaught Place, page 41

Yamuna River

Grand Trunk Rd

Poste Restante ✉

🅿

Ring Rd

Red Fort (Lal Qila)

Vijay Ghat

Netaji Subhash Marg

Shanti Vana

al Marg

asturba

DARYAGANJ

Sunday Book Market

Aap Ki Pasand

Ansari Rd

Mahatma Gandhi Rd

Shakti Sthala

Bazar Chitli Kabar

Delhi Gate

Ansari Rd

Raj Ghat

2

Gandhi Smarak Sangrahalaya 🏛

Chandni Chowk

Shahjahanabad was laid out in blocks with wide roads, residential quarters, bazars and mosques. Its principal street, Chandni Chowk, had a tree-lined canal flowing down its centre which became renowned throughout Asia. The canal is long gone, but the jumble of shops, alleys crammed with craftsmen's workshops, food stalls, mosques and temples, cause it to retain some of its magic. A cycle rickshaw ride gives you a good feel of the place. Make sure you visit **Naughara Street**, just off Kinari Bazar; it's one of the most atmospheric streets in Delhi, full of brightly painted and slowly crumbling *havelis*.

The impressive red sandstone façade of the **Digambar Jain Mandir** (temple) standing at the eastern end of Chandni Chowk, faces the Red Fort. Built in 1656, it contains an image of Adinath. The charity bird hospital (www.charitybirdshospital. org) within this compound releases the birds on recovery instead of returning them to their owners; many remain within the temple precincts. Beyond Shahjahanabad to the north lies Kashmiri Gate, Civil Lines and the Northern Ridge. The siting of the railway line which effectively cut Delhi into two unequal parts was done deliberately. The line brought prosperity, yet it destroyed the unity of the walled city forever. The Northern Ridge was the British cantonment and Civil Lines housed the civilians. In this area the temporary capital of the British existed from 1911-1931 until New Delhi came. The Northern Ridge is a paradise for birds and trees. Follow the **Mutiny Trail** by visiting Flagstaff Tower, Pir Ghaib, Chauburj, Mutiny Memorial. Around Kashmire Gate and Civil Lines, you can discover the Old Residency, St James Church, Nicholson's Cemetery and Qudsia Bagh.

Red Fort (Lal Qila)

ⓘ *Tue-Sun sunrise to sunset, Rs 250 foreigners, Rs 10 Indians, allow 1 hr. The entrance is through the Lahore Gate (nearest the car park) with the admission kiosk opposite; keep your ticket as you will need to show it at the Drum House. There are new toilets inside, best to avoid the ones in Chatta Chowk. You must remove shoes and cover all exposed flesh from your shoulders to your legs.*

Between the new city and the River Yamuna, Shah Jahan built a fort. Most of it was built out of red *lal* (sandstone), hence the name **Lal Qila** (Red Fort), the same as that at Agra on which the Delhi Fort is modelled. Begun in 1639 and completed in 1648, it is said to have cost Rs 10 million, much of which was spent on the opulent marble palaces within. In recent years much effort has been put into improving the fort and gardens, but visitors may be saddened by the neglected state of some of the buildings, and the gun-wielding soldiers lolling around do nothing to improve the ambience. However, despite the modern development of roads and shops and the never-ending traffic, it's an impressive site.

The approach The entrance is by the Lahore Gate. The defensive barbican that juts out in front of it was built by Aurangzeb. A common story suggests that Aurangzeb built the curtain wall to save his nobles and visiting dignitaries from having to walk – and bow – the whole length of Chandni Chowk, for no one was allowed to ride in the presence of the emperor. When the emperor sat in the Diwan-i-Am he could see all the way down the chowk, so the addition must have been greatly welcomed by his courtiers. The new entrance arrangement also made an attacking army more vulnerable to the defenders on the walls.

Chatta Chowk and the Naubat Khana Inside is the **Covered Bazar**, which was quite exceptional in the 17th century. In Shah Jahan's time there were shops on both upper and lower levels. Originally they catered for the Imperial household and carried stocks of silks, brocades, velvets, gold and silverware, jewellery and gems. There were coffee shops too for nobles and courtiers.

The **Naqqar Khana** or **Naubat Khana** (Drum House or music gallery) marked the entrance to the inner apartments of the fort. Here everyone except the princes of the royal family had to dismount and leave their horses or *hathi* (elephants), hence its other name of **Hathi Pol** (Elephant Gate). Five times a day ceremonial music was played on the kettle drum, *shahnais* (a kind of oboe) and cymbals, glorifying the emperor. In 1754 Emperor Ahmad Shah was murdered here. The gateway with four floors is decorated with floral designs. You can still see traces of the original panels painted in gold or other colours on the interior of the gateway.

Diwan-i-Am Between the first inner court and the royal palaces at the heart of the fort, stood the **Diwan-i-Am** (Hall of Public Audience), the furthest point a normal visitor would reach. It has seen many dramatic events, including the destructive whirlwind of the Persian Nadir Shah in 1739 and of Ahmad Shah the Afghan in 1756, and the trial of the last 'King of Delhi', **Bahadur Shah II** in 1858.

The well-proportioned hall was both a functional building and a showpiece intended to hint at the opulence of the palace itself. In Shah Jahan's time the sandstone was hidden behind a very thin layer of white polished plaster, *chunam*. This was decorated with floral motifs in many colours, especially gilt. Silk carpets and heavy curtains hung from the canopy rings outside the building; such interiors were reminders of the Mughals' nomadic origins in Central Asia, where royal durbars were held in tents.

At the back of the hall is a platform for the emperor's throne. Around this was a gold railing, within which stood the princes and great nobles separated from the lesser nobles inside the hall. Behind the throne canopy are 12 marble panels inlaid with motifs of fruiting trees, parrots and cuckoos. Figurative workmanship is very unusual in Islamic buildings, and these panels are the only example in the Red Fort.

As well as matters of official administration, Shah Jahan would listen to accounts of illness, dream interpretations and anecdotes from his ministers and nobles. Wednesday was the day of judgement. Sentences were often swift and brutal and sometimes the punishment of dismemberment, beating or death was carried out on the spot. The executioners were close at hand with axes and whips. On Friday, the Muslim holy day, there would be no business.

Inner palace buildings Behind the Diwan-i-Am is the private enclosure of the fort. Along the east wall, overlooking the River Yamuna, Shah Jahan set six small palaces (five survive). Also within this compound are the Harem, the Life-Bestowing Garden and the Nahr-i-Bihisht (Stream of Paradise).

Life-Bestowing Gardens (Hayat Baksh Bagh) The original gardens were landscaped according to the Islamic principles of the Persian *char bagh*, with pavilions, fountains and water courses dividing the garden into various but regular beds. The two pavilions **Sawan** and **Bhadon**, named after the first two months of the rainy season (July-August), reveal something of the character of the garden. The garden used to create the effect of the monsoon and contemporary accounts tell us that in the pavilions – some of which were especially erected for the **Teej** festival, which marks the arrival of the monsoon – the royal ladies would sit in silver swings and watch the rains. Water flowed from the back wall of the pavilion through a slit above the marble shelf and over the niches in the wall. Gold and silver pots of flowers were placed in these alcoves during the day whilst at night candles were lit to create a glistening and colourful effect.

Shahi Burj From the pavilion next to the Shahi Burj (**Royal Tower**) the canal known as the **Nahr-i-Bihisht** (Stream of Paradise) began its journey along the Royal Terrace. The three-storey octagonal tower was seriously damaged in 1857 and is still unsafe. In Shah Jahan's time the Yamuna lapped the walls. Shah Jahan used the tower as his most private office and only his sons and a few senior ministers were allowed with him.

Moti Masjid To the right are the three marble domes of Aurangzeb's 'Pearl Mosque' (shoes must be removed). Bar the cupolas, it is completely hidden behind a wall of red sandstone, now painted white. Built in 1662 of polished white marble, it has some exquisite decoration. All the surfaces are highly decorated in a fashion similar to rococo, which developed at the same time as in Europe. Unusually the prayer hall is on a raised platform with inlaid outlines of individual *musallas* ('prayer mats') in black marble. While the outer walls were aligned to the cardinal points like all the other fort buildings, the inner walls were positioned so that the mosque would correctly face Mecca.

Hammam The **Royal Baths** have three apartments separated by corridors with canals to carry water to each room. The two flanking the entrance, for the royal children, had hot and cold baths. The room furthest away from the door has three basins for rose water fountains.

Diwan-i-Khas Beyond is the single-storeyed **Hall of Private Audience**, topped by four Hindu-style *chhattris* and built completely of white marble. The *dado* (lower part of the wall) on the interior was richly decorated with inlaid precious and semi-precious stones. The ceiling was silver but was removed by the Marathas in 1760. Outside, the hall used to have a marble pavement and an arcaded court. Both have gone.

This was the Mughal office of state. Shah Jahan spent two hours here before retiring for a meal, siesta and prayers. In the evening he would return to the hall for more work before going to the harem. The hall's splendour moved the 14th-century poet Amir Khusrau to write the lines inscribed above the corner arches of the north and south walls: "*Agar Firdaus bar rue Zamin-ast/Hamin ast o Hamin ast o Hamin ast*" (If there be a paradise on earth, it is here, it is here, it is here).

Royal palaces Next to the Diwan-i-Khas is the three-roomed **Khas Mahal** (Private Palace). Nearest the Diwan-i-Khas is the **Tasbih Khana** (Chamber for the Telling of Rosaries) where the emperor would worship privately with his rosary of 99 beads, one for each of the mystical names of Allah. In the centre is the **Khwabgah** (Palace of Dreams) which gives on to the octagonal **Mussaman Burj** tower. Here Shah Jahan would be seen each morning. A balcony was added to the tower in 1809 and here George V and Queen Mary appeared in their Coronation Durbar of 1911. The **Tosh Khana** (Robe Room), to the south, has a beautiful marble screen at its north end, carved with the scales of justice above the filigree grille. If you are standing with your back to the Diwan-i-Khas you will see a host of circulating suns (a symbol of royalty), but if your back is to the next building (the Rang Mahal), you will see moons surrounding the scales. All these rooms were sumptuously decorated with fine silk carpets, rich silk brocade curtains and lavishly decorated walls. After 1857 the British used the Khas Mahal as an officer's mess and sadly it was defaced.

The **Rang Mahal** (Palace of Colours), the residence of the chief *sultana*, was also the place where the emperor ate most of his meals. It was divided into six apartments. Privacy and coolness were ensured by the use of marble *jali* screens. Like the other palaces it was beautifully decorated with a silver ceiling ornamented with golden flowers to reflect the water in the channel running through the building. The north and south apartments were both known as **Sheesh Mahal** (Palace of Mirrors) since into the ceiling were set hundreds of small mirrors. In the evening when candles were lit a starlight effect would be produced.

Through the palace ran the **Life-bestowing Stream** and at its centre is a lotus-shaped marble basin which had an ivory fountain. As might be expected in such a cloistered and cosseted environment, the ladies sometimes got bored. In the 18th century the **Empress of Jahandar Shah** sat gazing out at the river and remarked that she had never seen a boat sink. Shortly afterwards a boat was deliberately capsized so that she could be entertained by the sight of people bobbing up and down in the water crying for help.

The southernmost of the palaces, the **Mumtaz Mahal** (Palace of Jewels) ① *Tue-Sun 1000-1700*, was also used by the harem. The lower half of its walls are of marble and it contains six apartments. After the Mutiny of 1857 it was used as a guardroom and since 1912 it has been a museum with exhibits of textiles, weapons, carpets, jade and metalwork as well as works depicting life in the court. It should not be missed.

Spice market

Outside the Red Fort, cycle rickshaws offer a trip to the spice market, Jama Masjid and back through the bazar. You travel slowly westwards down Chandni Chowk passing the town hall. Dismount at Church Road and follow your guide into the heart of the market on Khari Baoli where wholesalers sell every conceivable spice. Ask to go to the roof for an excellent view over the market and back towards the Red Fort. The ride back through the bazar is equally fascinating – look up at the amazing electricity system. The final excitement is getting back across Netaji Subhash Marg. Panic not, the rickshaw wallahs know what they are doing. Expect to pay about Rs 100 for a one-hour ride. The spice laden air may irritate your throat. Also ask a cycle rickshaw to take you to Naughara Street, just off Kinari Bazar, a very pretty street amidst the chaos of Old Delhi.

Jama Masjid (Friday Mosque)

ⓘ *Visitors welcome from 30 mins after sunrise until 1215; and from 1345 until 30 mins before sunset, free, still or video cameras Rs 150, tower entry Rs 20.*

The magnificent Jama Masjid is the largest mosque in India and the last great architectural work of Shah Jahan, intended to dwarf all mosques that had gone before it. With the fort, it dominates Old Delhi. The mosque is much simpler in its ornamentation than Shah Jahan's secular buildings – a judicious blend of red sandstone and white marble, which are interspersed in the domes, minarets and cusped arches.

The gateways Symbolizing the separation of the sacred and the secular, the threshold is a place of great importance where the worshipper steps to a higher plane. There are three huge gateways, the largest being to the east. This was reserved for the royal family who gathered in a private gallery in its upper storey. Today, the faithful enter through the east gate on Fridays and for **Id-ul-Fitr** and **Id-ul-Adha**. The latter commemorates Abraham's (Ibrahim's) sacrificial offering of his son Ishmael (Ismail). Islam (unlike the Jewish and Christian tradition) believes that Abraham offered to sacrifice Ishmael, Isaac's brother.

The courtyard The façade has the main *iwan* (arch), five smaller arches on each side with two flanking minarets and three bulbous domes behind, all perfectly proportioned. The *iwan* draws the worshippers' attention into the building. The minarets have great views from the top; well worth the climb for Rs 10 (women may not be allowed to climb alone). The **hauz**, in the centre of the courtyard, is an ablution tank placed as usual between the inner and outer parts of the building to remind the worshipper that it is through the ritual of baptism that one first enters the community of believers. The **Dikka**, in front of the ablution tank, is a raised platform. Muslim communities grew so rapidly that by the eighth century it sometimes became necessary to introduce a second *muballigh* (prayer leader) who stood on this platform and copied the postures and chants of the *imam* inside to relay them to a much larger congregation. With the introduction of the loudspeaker and amplification, the *dikka* and the *muballigh* became redundant. In the northwest corner of the mosque there is a small shed. For a small fee, the faithful are shown a hair from the beard of the prophet, as well as his sandal and his footprint in rock.

New Delhi → *For listings, see pages 49-65.*

Delhi's present position as capital was only confirmed on 12 December 1911, when George V announced at the Delhi Durbar that the capital of India was to move from Calcutta to Delhi. The new city, New Delhi, planned under the leadership of British architect Edwin Lutyens with the assistance of his friend Herbert Baker, was inaugurated on 9 February 1931.

The city was to accommodate 70,000 people and have boundless possibilities for future expansion. The king favoured something in form and flavour similar to the Mughal masterpieces but fretted over the horrendous expense that this would incur. A petition signed by eminent public figures such as Bernard Shaw and Thomas Hardy advocated an

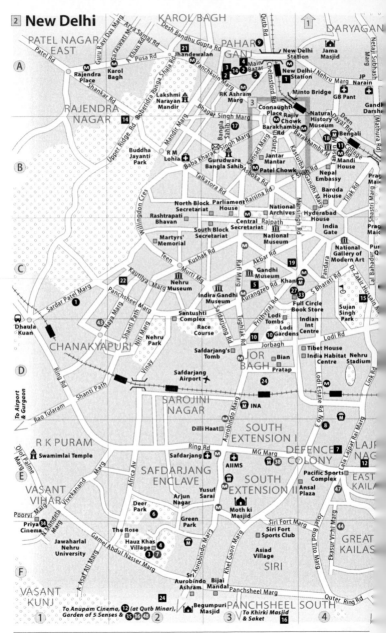

N

700 metres
700 yards

➜ **Delhi maps**
1 Old Delhi, page 30
2 New Delhi, page 36
3 Connaught Place, page 41

Where to stay 🛏

Amaraya Haveli **24** *F2*
Basera **11** *C4*
Casa Delhi **7** *E4*
Claridges **5** *C3*
Joyti Mahal **1** *A3*
K One One **28** *D4*
Life Tree **12** *E4*
Lutyens Bungalow **10** *D3*
Manor **13** *E5*
Master Guest House **14** *B2*
Metropolis Tourist Home **2** *A3*
Oberoi **15** *C4*
Prince Polonia **3** *A3*
Rak Tourist International **4** *A3*
Taj Mahal **19** *C3*
Tree of Life **16** *F3*
Yatri Paying Guest House **21** *A2*
Youth Hostel **22** *C2*

Restaurants 🍴

Baci **21** *C4*
Bukhara & Dum Pukht **1** *C1*
Café Sim Tok **2** *A3*
Diva **15** *F4*
Everest Bakery Café **5** *A3*
Grey Garden **3** *F2*
Indian Accent **13** *D5*
Kainoosh **34** *E1*
Khan Cha Cha **33** *C4*
Latitude **27** *C3*
Lodi **10** *D3*
Magique **35** *F2*
Naivedyam & Elma's **4** *F2*

Nathu's & Bengali Sweet
 House **18** *B4*
Oh! Calcutta **16** *F5*
Olive at the Qutb **12** *F2*
Park Baluchi **6** *E2*
Ploof **24** *D3*
Sagar Ratna **8** *E4*
Sakura **17** *B3*
Southern Restaurant **9** *A3*
Tadka **14** *A3*
Triveni Tea Terrace **11** *B4*
Yum Yum Tree **25** *E5*

Bars & clubs 🍸

Blue Frog **36** *F2*
Café Morrisons **38** *E3*
Living Room **/** *F2*
Pegs-n-Pints **43** *D1*
Shalom **44** *F4*
Urban Pind **47** *E4*
Zoo **48** *F2*

Metro Stops (Yellow Line) Ⓜ
Metro Stops (Videt Line) Ⓜ

Indian style and an Indian master builder. Herbert Baker had made known his own views even before his appointment when he wrote "first and foremost it is the spirit of British sovereignty which must be imprisoned in its stone and bronze". Lutyens himself despised Indian architecture. "Even before he had seen any examples of it", writes architectural historian Giles Tillotson, "he pronounced Mughal architecture to be 'piffle', and seeing it did not disturb that conviction". Yet in the end, Lutyens was forced to compromise.

India Gate and around

A tour of New Delhi will usually start with a visit to India Gate. This war memorial is situated at the eastern end of **Rajpath**. Designed by Lutyens, it commemorates more than 70,000 Indian soldiers who died in the First World War. Some 13,516 names of British and Indian soldiers killed on the Northwest Frontier and in the Afghan War of 1919 are engraved on the arch and foundations. Under the arch is the Amar Jawan Jyoti, commemorating Indian armed forces' losses in the Indo-Pakistan War of 1971. The arch (43 m high) stands on a base of Bharatpur stone and rises in stages. Similar to the Hindu *chhattri* signifying regality, it is decorated with nautilus shells symbolizing British maritime power. Come at dusk to join the picnicking crowds enjoying the evening. You may even be able to have a pedalo ride if there's water in the canal.

National Gallery of Modern Art

ⓘ *Jaipur House, near India Gate, T011-2338 4640, www.ngmaindia.gov.in, Tue-Sun 1000-1700, Rs 150 foreigners, Rs 10 Indians.*

There is now a new air-conditioned wing of this excellent gallery and select exhibits in the old building are housed in a former residence of the Maharaja of Jaipur. The '*In the Seeds of Time...*' exhibition traces the trajectory of modern Indian art. Artists include: Amrita Shergil, with over 100 exhibits, synthesizing the flat treatment of Indian painting with a realistic tone; Rabindranath Tagore (ground floor) with examples from a brief but intense spell in the 1930s; and The Bombay School or Company School (first floor) which includes Western painters who documented their visits to India. Realism is reflected in Indian painting of the early 19th century represented by the schools of Avadh, Patna, Sikkim and Thanjavur; The Bengal School (the late 19th-century Revivalist Movement) showcases artists such as Abanindranath Tagore and Nandalal Bose have their works exhibited here. Western influence was discarded in response to the nationalist movement. Inspiration derived from Indian folk art is evident in the works of Jamini Roy and YD Shukla. Prints from the gallery shop are incredibly good value – up to Rs 80 for poster-size prints of famous works.

National Museum

ⓘ *Janpath, T011-2301 9272, www.nationalmuseumindia.gov.in, daily 1000-1700, foreigners Rs 300 (including audio tour), Indians Rs 10, camera Rs 300; free guided tours 1030, 1130, 1200, 1400, films are screened every day (1430), marble squat toilets, but dirty.*

The collection was formed from the nucleus of the Exhibition of Indian Art, London (1947). Now merged with the Asian Antiquities Museum it displays a rich collection of the artistic treasure of Central Asia and India including ethnological objects from prehistoric archaeological finds to the late Medieval period. Replicas of exhibits and books on Indian culture and art are on sale. There is also a research library.

Ground floor Prehistoric: seals, figurines, toy animals and jewellery from the Harappan civilization (2400-1500 BC). **Maurya Period**: terracottas and stone heads from around the third century BC include the *chaturmukha* (four-faced) *lingam*. **Gandhara School**: stucco heads showing the Graeco Roman influence. **Gupta terracottas** (circa AD 400): including two life-size images of the river goddesses Ganga and Yamuna and the four-armed bust of Vishnu from a temple near Lal Kot. **South Indian sculpture**: from Pallava and early Chola temples and relief panels from Mysore. Bronzes from the Buddhist monastery at Nalanda. Some of Buddha's relics were placed in the Thai pavilion in 1997.

First floor Illustrated manuscripts: include the *Babur-i-nama* in the emperor's own handwriting and an autographed copy of Jahangir's memoirs. **Miniature paintings**: include the 16th-century Jain School, the 18th-century Rajasthani School and the Pahari schools of Garhwal, Basoli and Kangra. **Aurel Stein Collection** consists of antiquities recovered by him during his explorations of Central Asia and the western borders of China at the turn of the 20th century.

Second floor Pre-Columbian and Mayan artefacts: anthropological section devoted to tribal artefacts and folk arts. **Sharad Rani Bakkiwal Gallery of Musical Instruments**: displays over 300 Instruments collected by the famous *sarod* player.

Rashtrapati Bhavan and Nehru Memorial Museum
Once the Viceroy's House, Rashtrapati Bhavan is the official residence of the President of India. The Viceroy's House, New Delhi's centrepiece of imperial proportions, was 1 km around the foundations, bigger than Louis XIV's palace at Versailles. It had a colossal dome surmounting a long colonnade and 340 rooms in all. It took nearly 20 years to complete, similar to the time it took to build the Taj Mahal. In the busiest year, 29,000 people were working on the site and buildings began to take shape. The project was surrounded by controversy from beginning to end. Opting for a fundamentally classical structure, both Baker and Lutyens sought to incorporate Indian motifs, many entirely superficial. While some claim that Lutyens achieved a unique synthesis of the two traditions, Tillotson asks whether "the sprinkling of a few simplified and classicized Indian details (especially *chhattris*) over a classical palace" could be called a synthesis. The Durbar Hall, 23 m in diameter, has coloured marble from all parts of India.

To the south is **Flagstaff House**, formerly the residence of the commander-in-chief. Renamed Teen Murti Bhawan it now houses the **Nehru Memorial Museum** ① *T011-2301 4504, Tue-Sun 1000-1500, planetarium Mon-Sat 1130-1500, library Mon-Sat 0900-1900, free*. Designed by Robert Tor Russell, in 1948 it became the official residence of India's first prime minister, Jawaharlal Nehru. Converted after his death (1964) into a national memorial, the reception, study and bedroom are intact. A *Jyoti Jawahar* (torch) symbolizes the eternal values he inspired and a granite rock is carved with extracts from his historic speech at midnight on 14 August 1947; an informative and vivid history of the Independence Movement.

The **Martyr's Memorial**, at the junction of Sardar Patel Marg and Willingdon Crescent, is a magnificent 26-m-long, 3-m-high bronze sculpture by DP Roy Chowdhury. The 11 statues of national heroes are headed by Mahatma Gandhi.

Eternal Gandhi Multimedia Museum
① *Birla House, 5 Tees Jan Marg (near Claridges Hotel), T011-3095 7269, www.eternal gandhi.org, closed Mon and 2nd Sat, 1000-1700, free, film at 1500.*
Gandhi's last place of residence and the site of his assassination, Birla House has been converted into a whizz-bang display of 'interactive' modern technology. Over-attended

by young guides eager to demonstrate the next gadget, the museum seems aimed mainly at those with a critically short attention span, and is too rushed to properly convey the story of Gandhi's life. However, a monument in the garden marking where he fell is definitely worth a visit. Other museums in the city related to Gandhi include: **National Gandhi Museum** ① *opposite Raj Ghat, T011-2331 1793, www.gandhimuseum.org, Tue-Sat 0930-1730*, with five pavilions – sculpture, photographs and paintings of Gandhi and the history of the *Satyagraha* movement (the philosophy of non-violence); **Gandhi Smarak Sangrahalaya** ① *Raj Ghat, T011-2301 1480, Fri-Wed 0930-1730*, displays some of Gandhi's personal belongings and a small library includes recordings of speeches; and the **Indira Gandhi Museum** ① *1 Safdarjang Rd, T011-2301 0094, Tue-Sun 0930-1700, free*, charting the phases of her life from childhood to the moment of her death. Exhibits are fascinating, if rather gory – you can see the blood-stained, bullet-ridden sari she was wearing when assassinated.

Parliament House and around
Northeast of the Viceroy's House is the **Council House**, now **Sansad Bhavan**. Baker designed this based on Lutyens' suggestion that it be circular (173 m diameter). Inside are the library and chambers for the Council of State, Chamber of Princes and Legislative Assembly – the **Lok Sabha**. Just opposite the Council House is the **Rakabganj Gurudwara** in Pandit Pant Marg. This 20th-century white marble shrine, which integrates the late Mughal and Rajasthani styles, marks the spot where the headless body of Guru Tegh Bahadur, the ninth Sikh Guru, was cremated in 1657. West of the Council House is the **Cathedral Church of the Redemption** (1927-1935) and to its north the Italianate Roman Catholic **Church of the Sacred Heart** (1930-1934), both conceived by Henry Medd.

Connaught Place and Connaught Circus
Connaught Place and its outer ring, Connaught Circus (now officially named **Rajiv Chowk** and **Indira Chowk**, but still commonly referred to by their old names), comprise two-storey arcaded buildings, arranged radially around a circular garden that was completed after the Metro line was installed. Designed by Robert Tor Russell, they have become the main commercial and tourist centre of New Delhi. Sadly, the area also attracts bands of insistent touts.

Paharganj
Delhi's backpacker ghetto occupies a warren of lanes and dingy alleys immediately to the west of New Delhi Railway Station, a few hundred metres north of Connaught Circus. The crowded Main Bazar offers an instant immersion into the chaos of which India is capable, as stray cows and cycle rickshaws tangle with a throng of pedestrians, hotel touts, and salesmen hawking knock-off handbags, books and cheap clothing. Though there's little other than shopping to hold your interest, the hundreds of guesthouses here offer the greatest concentration of genuinely cheap accommodation in the city.

Northwest of Paharganj, the grid of streets comprising **Karol Bagh** contains what is, by some definitions, the biggest market in Asia. Conveniently linked to the city by Metro, the area is full of mid-range hotels, but mainly populated by Indians.

Lakshmi Narayan Mandir
To the west of Connaught Circus is the Lakshmi Narayan **Birla Temple** in Mandir Marg. Financed by the prominent industrialist Raja Baldeo Birla in 1938, this is one of the most

popular Hindu shrines in the city and one of Delhi's few striking examples of Hindu architecture. Dedicated to Lakshmi, the goddess of well-being, it is commonly referred to as **Birla Mandir**. The design is in the Orissan style with tall curved *sikharas* (towers) capped by large *amalakas*. The exterior is faced with red and ochre stone and white

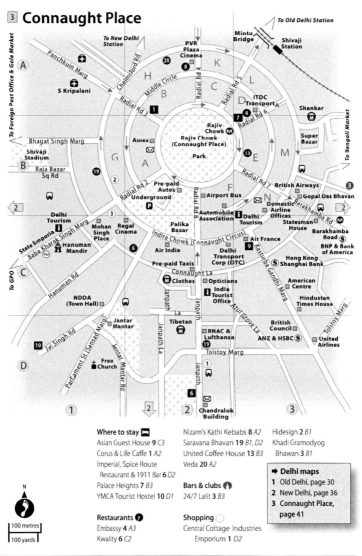

3 Connaught Place

Where to stay 🛏
Asian Guest House **9** C3
Corus & Life Caffe **1** A2
Imperial, Spice Route
  Restaurant & 1911 Bar **6** D2
Palace Heights **7** B3
YMCA Tourist Hostel **10** D1

Restaurants 🍴
Embassy **4** A3
Kwality **6** C2

Nizam's Kathi Kebabs **8** A2
Saravana Bhavan **19** B1, D2
United Coffee House **13** B3
Veda **20** A2

Bars & clubs 🍸
24/7 Lalit **3** B3

Shopping ⚪
Central Cottage Industries
  Emporium **1** D2

Hidesign **2** B1
Khadi Gramodyog
  Bhawan **3** B1

➡ **Delhi maps**
1 Old Delhi, page 30
2 New Delhi, page 36
3 Connaught Place,
  page 41

marble. Built around a central courtyard, the main shrine has images of Narayan and his consort Lakshmi while two separate cells have icons of Siva (the Destroyer) and Durga (the 10-armed destroyer of demons). The temple is flanked by a *dharamshala* (rest house) and a Buddhist *vihara* (monastery).

Gurudwara Bangla Sahib
① *Baba Kharak Singh Rd, free.*

This is a fine example of Sikh temple architecture, featuring a large pool reminiscent of Amritsar's Golden Temple. The 24-hour reciting of the faith's holy book adds to the atmosphere, and there's free food on offer, although don't be surprised if you're asked to help out with the washing up! You must remove your shoes and cover your head to enter – suitable scarves are provided if you arrive without.

Further northeast on Baba Kharak Singh Marg is **Hanuman Mandir**. This small temple was built by Maharaja Jai Singh II of Jaipur. **Mangal haat** (Tuesday Fair) is a popular market.

Jantar Mantar
Just to the east of the Hanuman Mandir in Sansad Marg (Parliament Street) is Jai Singh's **observatory** (Jantar Mantar) ① *sunrise to sunset, Rs 100 foreigners, Rs 5 Indians.* The Mughal Emperor Mohammad Shah (ruled 1719-1748) entrusted the renowned astronomer Maharaja Jai Singh II with the task of revising the calendar and correcting the astronomical tables used by contemporary priests. Daily astral observations were made for years before construction began and plastered brick structures were favoured for the site instead of brass instruments. Built in 1725 it is slightly smaller than the later observatory at Jaipur.

Memorial Ghats
Beyond Delhi Gate lies the **Yamuna River**, marked by a series of memorials to India's leaders. The river itself, a kilometre away, is invisible from the road, protected by a low rise and banks of trees. The most prominent memorial, immediately opposite the end of Jawaharlal Nehru Road, is that of Mahatma Gandhi at **Raj Ghat**. To its north is **Shanti Vana** (Forest of Peace), landscaped gardens where Prime Minister Jawaharlal Nehru was cremated in 1964, as were his grandson Sanjay Gandhi in 1980, daughter Indira Gandhi in 1984 and elder grandson, Rajiv, in 1991. To the north again is **Vijay Ghat** (Victory Bank) where Prime Minister Lal Bahadur Shastri was cremated.

South Delhi → *For listings, see pages 49-65.*

South Delhi is often overlooked by travellers. This is a real pity as it houses some of the city's most stunning sites, best accommodation, bars, clubs and restaurants, as well as some of its most tranquil parks. However be warned, South Delhi can be hell during rushhour when the traffic on the endless flyovers comes to a virtual standstill. But with the Metro, you can explore all the way down to Gurgaon with relative ease.

Lodi Gardens
These beautiful gardens, with mellow stone tombs of the 15th- and 16th-century Lodi rulers, are popular for gentle strolls and jogging. In the middle of the garden facing the east entrance from Max Mueller Road is **Bara Gumbad** (Big Dome), a mosque built in 1494. The raised courtyard is provided with an imposing gateway and *mehman khana* (guest rooms). The platform in the centre appears to have had a tank for ritual ablutions.

The **Sheesh Bumbad** (Glass Dome, late 15th century) is built on a raised incline north of the Bara Gumbad and was once decorated with glazed blue tiles, painted floral designs and Koranic inscriptions. The façade gives the impression of a two-storeyed building, typical of Lodi architecture. **Mohammad Shah's Tomb** (1450) is that of the third Sayyid ruler. It has sloping buttresses, an octagonal plan, projecting eaves and lotus patterns on the ceiling. **Sikander Lodi's Tomb**, built by his son in 1517, is also an octagonal structure decorated with Hindu motifs. A structural innovation is the double dome which was later refined under the Mughals. The 16th-century **Athpula** (Bridge of Eight Piers), near the northeastern entrance, is attributed to Nawab Bahadur, a nobleman at Akbar's court.

Safdarjang's Tomb
ⓘ *Sunrise to sunset, Rs 100 foreigners, Rs 5 Indians.*
Safdarjang's Tomb, seldom visited, was built by Nawab Shuja-ud-Daulah for his father Mirza Mukhim Abdul Khan, entitled Safdarjang, who was Governor of Oudh (1719-1748), and Wazir of his successor (1748-1754). Safdarjang died in 1754. With its high enclosure walls, *char bagh* layout of gardens, fountain and central domed mausoleum, it follows the tradition of Humayun's tomb. Typically, the real tomb is just below ground level. Flanking the mausoleum are pavilions used by Shuja-ud-Daulah as his family residence. Immediately to its south is the battlefield where Timur and his Mongol horde crushed Mahmud Shah Tughluq on 12 December 1398.

Hazrat Nizamuddin
ⓘ *Dress ultra-modestly if you don't want to feel uncomfortable or cause offence.*
At the east end of the Lodi Road, Hazrat Nizamuddin Dargah (Nizamuddin 'village') now tucked away behind the residential suburb of Nizamuddin West, off Mathura Road, grew up around the shrine of Sheikh Nizamuddin Aulia (1236-1325), a Chishti saint. This is a wonderfully atmospheric place. *Qawwalis* are sung at sunset after *namaaz* (prayers), and are particularly impressive on Thursdays – be prepared for crowds. Highly recommended.

West of the central shrine is the **Jama-at-khana Mosque** (1325). Its decorated arches are typical of the Khalji design also seen at the Ala'i Darwaza at the Qutb Minar. South of the main tomb and behind finely crafted screens is the grave of princess Jahanara, Shah Jahan's eldest and favourite daughter. She shared the emperor's last years when he was imprisoned at Agra Fort. The grave, open to the sky, is in accordance with the epitaph written by her: "Let naught cover my grave save the green grass, for grass suffices as the covering of the lowly". Pilgrims congregate at the shrine twice a year for the Urs (fair) held to mark the anniversaries of Hazrat Nizamuddin Aulia and his disciple Amir Khusrau, whose tomb is nearby.

Humayun's Tomb
ⓘ *Sunrise to sunset, Rs 250 foreigners, Rs 10 Indians, video cameras Rs 25, located in Nizamuddin, 15-20 mins by taxi from Connaught Circus, allow 45 mins.*
Eclipsed later by the Taj Mahal and the Jama Masjid, this tomb is the best example in Delhi of the early Mughal style of tomb. Superbly maintained, it is well worth a visit, preferably before visiting the Taj Mahal. Humayun, the second Mughal emperor, was forced into exile in Persia after being heavily defeated by the Afghan Sher Shah in 1540. He returned to India in 1545, finally recapturing Delhi in 1555. The tomb was designed and built by his senior widow and mother of his son Akbar, Hamida Begum. A Persian from Khurasan, after her pilgrimage to Mecca she was known as Haji Begum. She supervised the entire construction of the tomb (1564-1573), camping on the site.

The plan The tomb has an octagonal plan, lofty arches, pillared kiosks and the double dome of Central Asian origin, which appears here for the first time in India. Outside Gujarat, Hindu temples make no use of the dome, but the Indian Muslim dome had until now, been of a flatter shape as opposed to the tall Persian dome rising on a more slender neck. Here also is the first standard example of the garden tomb concept: the **char bagh** (garden divided into quadrants), water channels and fountains. This form culminated in the gardens of the Taj Mahal. However, the tomb also shows a number of distinctively Hindu motifs. Tillotson has pointed out that in Humayun's tomb, Hindu *chhattris* (small domed kiosks), complete with temple columns and *chajjas* (broad eaves), surround the central dome. The bulbous finial on top of the dome and the star motif in the spandrels of the main arches are also Hindu, the latter being a solar symbol.

The approach The tomb enclosure has two high double-storeyed gateways: the entrance to the west and the other to the south. A *baradari* occupies the centre of the east wall, and a bath chamber that of the north wall. Several Moghul princes, princesses and Haji Begum herself lie buried here. During the 1857 Mutiny Bahadur Shah II, the last Moghul emperor of Delhi, took shelter here with his three sons. Over 80, he was seen as a figurehead by Muslims opposing the British. When captured he was transported to Yangon (Rangoon) for the remaining four years of his life. The tomb to the right of the approach is that of Isa Khan, Humayun's barber.

The dome Some 38 m high, the dome does not have the swell of the Taj Mahal and the decoration of the whole edifice is much simpler. It is of red sandstone with some white marble to highlight the lines of the building. There is some attractive inlay work, and some *jalis* in the balcony fence and on some of the recessed keel arch windows. The interior is austere and consists of three storeys of arches rising up to the dome. The emperor's tomb is of white marble and quite plain without any inscription. The overall impression is that of a much bulkier, more squat building than the Taj Mahal. The cavernous space under the main tombs is home to great colonies of bats.

Hauz Khas
ⓘ *1-hr cultural show, 1845, Rs 100 (check with Delhi Tourism, see page 28).*
South of Safdarjang's Tomb, and entered off either Aurobindo Marg on the east side or Africa Avenue on the west side, is Hauz Khas. Ala-ud-din Khalji (ruled 1296-1313) created a large tank here for the use of the inhabitants of Siri, the second capital city of Delhi founded by him. Fifty years later Firoz Shah Tughluq cleaned up the silted tank and raised several buildings on its east and south banks which are known as Hauz Khas or Royal Tank.

Firoz Shah's austere tomb is found here. The multi-storeyed wings, on the north and west of the tomb, were built by him in 1354 as a *madrasa* (college). The octagonal and square *chhattris* were built as tombs, possibly to the teachers at the college. Hauz Khas is now widely used as a park for early-morning recreation – walking, running and yoga *asanas*. Classical music concerts, dance performances and a *son et lumière* show are held in the evenings when monuments are illuminated by thousands of earthen lamps and torches. Wandering the streets of Haus Khaz village, you can almost forget that you are in India. Labyrinthine alleys lead to numerous galleries, boutiques and restaurants. There are a lot of little design studios here and a more boho vibe.

Qutb Minar Complex

ⓘ *Sunrise to sunset, Rs 250 foreigners, Rs 10 Indians. The Metro goes to Qutb Minar. Bus 505 from New Delhi Railway Station (Ajmeri Gate), Super Bazar (east of Connaught Circus) and Cottage Industries Emporium, Janpath. Auto Rs 110, though drivers may be reluctant to take you. This area is also opening up as a hub for new chic restaurants and bars.*

Muhammad Ghuri conquered northwest India at the very end of the 12th century. The conquest of the Gangetic plain down to Benares (Varanasi) was undertaken by Muhammad's Turkish slave and chief general, Qutb-ud-din-Aibak, whilst another general took Bihar and Bengal. In the process, temples were reduced to rubble, the remaining Buddhist centres were dealt their death blow and their monks slaughtered. When Muhammad was assassinated in 1206, his gains passed to the loyal Qutb-ud-din-Aibak. Thus the first sultans or Muslim kings of Delhi became known as the **Slave Dynasty** (1026-1290). For the next three centuries the Slave Dynasty and the succeeding Khalji (1290-1320), Tughluq (1320-1414), Sayyid (1414-1445) and Lodi (1451-1526) dynasties provided Delhi with fluctuating authority. The legacy of their ambitions survives in the tombs, forts and palaces that litter Delhi Ridge and the surrounding plain. Qutb-ud-din-Aibak died after only four years in power, but he left his mark with the **Qutb Minar** and his **citadel**. Qutb Minar, built to proclaim the victory of Islam over the infidel, dominates the countryside for miles around. Visit the *minar* first.

Qutb Minar In 1199 work began on what was intended to be the most glorious tower of victory in the world and was to be the prototype of all *minars* (towers) in India. Qutb-ud-din-Aibak had probably seen and been influenced by the brick victory pillars in Ghazni in Afghanistan, but this one was also intended to serve as the minaret attached to the Might of Islam Mosque. From here the muezzin could call the faithful to prayer. Later every mosque would incorporate its minaret.

As a mighty reminder of the importance of the ruler as Allah's representative on earth, the Qutb Minar (literally 'axis minaret') stood at the centre of the community. A pivot of Faith, Justice and Righteousness, its name also carried the message of Qutb-ud-din's (Axis of the Faith) own achievements. The inscriptions carved in Kufi script tell that "the tower was erected to cast the shadow of God over both east and west". For Qutb-ud-din-Aibak it marked the eastern limit of the empire of the One God. Its western counterpart is the Giralda Tower built by Yusuf in Seville.

The Qutb Minar is 73 m high and consists of five storeys. The diameter of the base is 14.4 m and 2.7 m at the top. Qutb-ud-din built the first three and his son-in-law Iltutmish embellished these and added a fourth. This is indicated in some of the Persian and Nagari (North Indian) inscriptions which also record that it was twice damaged by lightning in 1326 and 1368. While repairing the damage caused by the second, Firoz Shah Tughluq added a fifth storey and used marble to face the red and buff sandstone. This was the first time contrasting colours were used decoratively, later to become such a feature of Mughal buildings. Firoz's fifth storey was topped by a graceful cupola but this fell down during an earthquake in 1803. A new one was added by a Major Robert Smith in 1829 but was so out of keeping that it was removed in 1848 and now stands in the gardens.

The original storeys are heavily indented with different styles of fluting, alternately round and angular on the bottom, round on the second and angular on the third. The beautifully carved honeycomb detail beneath the balconies is reminiscent of the Alhambra Palace in Spain. The calligraphy bands are verses from the Koran and praises to its patron builder.

Quwwat-ul-Islam Mosque The Quwwat-ul-Islam Mosque (The Might of Islam Mosque), the earliest surviving mosque in India, is to the northwest of the Qutb Minar. It was begun in 1192, immediately after Qutb-ud-din's conquest of Delhi and completed in 1198, using the remains of no fewer than 27 local Hindu and Jain temples.

The architectural style contained elements that Muslims brought from Arabia, including buildings made of mud and brick and decorated with glazed tiles, *squinches* (arches set diagonally across the corners of a square chamber to facilitate the raising of a dome and to effect a transition from a square to a round structure), the pointed arch and the true dome. Finally, Muslim buildings came alive through ornamental calligraphy and geometric patterning. This was in marked contrast to indigenous Indian styles of architecture. Hindu, Buddhist and Jain buildings relied on the post-and-beam system in which spaces were traversed by corbelling, ie shaping flat-laid stones to create an arch. The arched screen that runs along the western end of the courtyard beautifully illustrates the fact that it was Hindu methods that still prevailed at this stage, for the 16-m-high arch uses Indian corbelling, the corners being smoothed off to form the curved line.

Screens Qutb-ud-din's screen formed the façade of the mosque and, facing in the direction of Mecca, became the focal point. The sandstone screen is carved in the Indo-Islamic style, lotuses mingling with Koranic calligraphy. The later screenwork and other extensions (1230) are fundamentally Islamic in style, the flowers and leaves having been replaced by more arabesque patterns. Indian builders mainly used stone, which from the fourth century AD had been intricately carved with representations of the gods. In their first buildings in India the Muslim architects designed the buildings and local Indian craftsmen built them and decorated them with typical motifs such as the vase and foliage, tasselled ropes, bells and cows.

Iltutmish's extension The mosque was enlarged twice. In 1230 Qutb-ud-din's son-in-law and successor, Shamsuddin Iltutmish, doubled its size by extending the colonnades and prayer hall – 'Iltutmish's extension'. This accommodated a larger congregation, and in the more stable conditions of Iltutmish's reign, Islam was obviously gaining ground. The arches of the extension are nearer to the true arch and are similar to the Gothic arch that appeared in Europe at this time. The decoration is Islamic. Almost 100 years after Iltutmish's death, the mosque was enlarged again, by Ala-ud-din Khalji. The conductor of tireless and bloody military campaigns, Ala-ud-din proclaimed himself 'God's representative on earth'. His architectural ambitions, however, were not fully realized, because on his death in 1316 only part of the north and east extensions were completed.

Ala'i Minar and the Ala'i Darwaza To the north of the Qutb complex is the 26-m **Ala'i Minar**, intended to surpass the tower of the Qutb, but not completed beyond the first storey. Ala-ud-din did complete the south gateway to the building, the **Ala'i Darwaza**; inscriptions testify that it was built in 1311 (Muslim 710 AH). He benefited from events in Central Asia: since the early 13th century, Mongol hordes from Central Asia fanned out east and west, destroying the civilization of the Seljuk Turks in West Asia, and refugee artists, architects, craftsmen and poets fled east. They brought to India features and techniques that had developed in Byzantine Turkey, some of which can be seen in the Ala'i Darwaza.

The gatehouse is a large sandstone cuboid, into which are set small cusped arches with carved *jali* screens. The lavish ornamentation of geometric and floral designs in red sandstone and white marble produced a dramatic effect when viewed against the surrounding buildings.

The inner chamber, 11 sq m has doorways and, for the first time in India, true arches. Above each doorway is an Arabic inscription with its creator's name and one of his self-assumed titles – 'The Second Alexander'. The north doorway, which is the main entrance, is the most elaborately carved. The dome, raised on squinched arches, is flat and shallow. Of the effects employed, the arches with their 'lotus-bud' fringes are Seljuk, as is the dome with the rounded finial and the façade. These now became trademarks of the Khalji style, remaining virtually unchanged until their further development in Humayun's Tomb.

Iltutmish's Tomb Built in 1235, Iltutmish's Tomb lies in the northwest of the compound, midway along the west wall of the mosque. It is the first surviving tomb of a Muslim ruler in India. Two other tombs also stand within the extended Might of Islam Mosque. The idea of a tomb was quite alien to Hindus, who had been practising cremation since around 400 BC. Blending Hindu and Muslim styles, the outside is relatively plain with three arched and decorated doorways. The interior carries reminders of the nomadic origins of the first Muslim rulers. Like a Central Asian *yurt* (tent) in its decoration, it combines the familiar Indian motifs of the wheel, bell, chain and lotus with the equally familiar geometric arabesque patterning. The west wall is inset with three *mihrabs* that indicate the direction of Mecca.

The tomb originally supported a dome resting on *squinches* which you can still see. The dome collapsed (witness the slabs of stone lying around) suggesting that the technique was as yet unrefined. From the corbelled squinches it may be assumed that the dome was corbelled too, as found in contemporary Gujarat and Rajput temples. The blocks of masonry were fixed together using the Indian technology of iron dowels. In later Indo-Islamic buildings lime plaster was used for bonding.

Tughluqabad

ⓘ *Sunrise to sunset, foreigners Rs100, Indians Rs 5, video camera Rs 25, allow 1 hr for return rickshaws, turn right at entrance and walk 200 m. The site is often deserted so don't go alone. Take plenty of water.*

Tughluqabad's ruins, 7.5 km east from Qutb Minar, still convey a sense of the power and energy of the newly arrived Muslims in India. From the walls you get a magnificent impression of the strategic advantages of the site. **Ghiyas'ud-Din Tughluq** (ruled 1321-1325), after ascending the throne of Delhi, selected this site for his capital. He built a massive fort around his capital city which stands high on a rocky outcrop of the Delhi Ridge. The fort is roughly octagonal in plan with a circumference of 6.5 km. The vast size, strength and obvious solidity of the whole give it an air of massive grandeur. It was not until Babur (ruled 1526-1530) that dynamite was used in warfare, so this is a very defensible site.

East of the main entrance is the rectangular **citadel**. A wider area immediately to the west and bounded by walls contained the **palaces**. Beyond this to the north lay the **city**. Now marked by the ruins of houses, the streets were laid out in a grid fashion. Inside the citadel enclosure is the **Vijay Mandal tower** and the remains of several halls including a long underground passage. The fort also contained seven tanks.

A causeway connects the fort with the tomb of Ghiyas'ud-Din Tughluq, while a wide embankment near its southeast corner gave access to the fortresses of **Adilabad** about 1 km away, built a little later by Ghiyas'ud-Din's son Muhammad. The tomb is very well preserved and has red sandstone walls with a pronounced slope (the first Muslim building in India to have sloping walls), crowned with a white marble dome. This dome, like that of the Ala'i Darwaza at the Qutb, is crowned by an *amalaka*, a feature of Hindu architecture •

Also Hindu is the trabeate arch at the tomb's fortress wall entrance. Inside are three cenotaphs belonging to Ghiyas'ud-Din, his wife and son Muhammad.

Ghiyas'ud-Din Tughluq quickly found that military victories were no guarantee of lengthy rule. When he returned home after a victorious campaign the welcoming pavilion erected by his son and successor, Muhammad-bin Tughluq, was deliberately collapsed over him. Tughluqabad was abandoned shortly afterwards and was thus only inhabited for five years. The Tughluq dynasty continued to hold Delhi until Timur sacked it and slaughtered its inhabitants. For a brief period Tughluq power shifted to Jaunpur near Varanasi, where the Tughluq architectural traditions were carried forward in some superb mosques.

Baha'i Temple (Lotus Temple)
① 1 Apr-30 Sep 0900-1900, 1 Oct-31 Mar Tue-Sun 0930-1730, free entry and parking, visitors welcome to attend services, at other times the temple is open for silent meditation and prayer. Audio-visual presentations in English are at 1100, 1200, 1400 and 1530, remove shoes before entering. Bus 433 from the centre (Jantar Mantar) goes to Nehru Place, within walking distance (1.5 km) of the temple at Kalkaji, or take a taxi or auto-rickshaw.

Architecturally the Baha'i Temple is a remarkably striking building. Constructed in 1980-1981, it is built out of white marble and in the characteristic Baha'i temple shape of a lotus flower – 45 lotus petals form the walls – which internally creates a feeling of light and space (34 m high, 70 m in diameter). It is a simple design, brilliantly executed and very elegant in form. All Baha'i temples are nine-sided, symbolizing 'comprehensiveness, oneness and unity'. The Delhi Temple, which seats 1300, is surrounded by nine pools, an attractive feature also helping to keep the building cool. It is particularly attractive when flood-lit. Baha'i temples are "dedicated to the worship of God, for peoples of all races, religions or castes. Only the Holy Scriptures of the Baha'i Faith and earlier revelations are read or recited".

East of the Yamuna → *For listings, see pages 49-65.*

Designated as the site of the athletes' village for the 2010 Commonwealth Games, East Delhi has just one attraction to draw visitors across the Yamuna.

Swaminarayan Akshardham
① www.akshardham.com, Apr-Sep Tue-Sun 1000-1900, Oct-Mar Tue-Sun 0900-1800, temple free, Rs 170 for 'attractions', musical fountain Rs 20, no backpacks, cameras or other electronic items (bag and body searches at entry gate). Packed on Sun; visit early to avoid crowds.

Opened in November 2005 on the east bank of the Yamuna, the gleaming Akshardham complex represents perhaps the most ambitious construction project in India since the foundation of New Delhi itself. At the centre of a surreal 40-ha 'cultural complex' complete with landscaped gardens, cafés and theme park rides, the temple-monument is dedicated to the 18th-century saint Bhagwan Swaminarayan, who abandoned his home at the age of 11 to embark on a lifelong quest for the spiritual and cultural uplift of Western India. It took 11,000 craftsmen, all volunteers, no less than 300 million hours to complete the temple using traditional building and carving techniques.

If this is the first religious site you visit in India, the security guards and swarms of mooching Indian tourists will hardly prepare you for the typical temple experience. Yet despite this, and the boat rides and animatronic shows which have prompted inevitable comparisons to a 'spiritual Disneyland', most visitors find the Akshardham an inspiring, indeed uplifting, experience, if for no other reason than that the will and ability to build something of its scale and complexity still exist.

The temple You enter the temple complex through a series of intricately carved gates. The Bhakti Dwar (Gate of Devotion), adorned with 208 pairs of gods and their consorts, leads into a hall introducing the life of Swaminarayan and the activities of BAPS (Bochasanwasi Shri Akshar Purushottam Swaminarayan Sanstha), the global Hindu sect-cum-charity which runs Akshardham. The main courtyard is reached through the Mayur Dwar (Peacock Gate), a conglomeration of 869 carved peacocks echoed by an equally florid replica directly facing it.

From here you get your first look at the central monument. Perfectly symmetrical in pink sandstone and white marble, it rests on a plinth encircled by 148 elephants, each sculpted from a 20-tonne stone block, in situations ranging from the literal to the mythological: mortal versions grapple with lions or lug tree trunks, while Airavatha, the eight-trunked mount of Lord Indra, surfs majestically to shore after the churning of the oceans at the dawn of Hindu creation. Above them, carvings of deities, saints and *sadhus* cover every inch of the walls and columns framing the inner sanctum, where a gold-plated *murti* (idol) of Bhagwan Swaminarayan sits attended by avatars of his spiritual successors, beneath a staggeringly intricate marble dome. Around the main dome are eight smaller domes, each carved in hypnotic fractal patterns, while paintings depicting Swaminarayan's life of austerity and service line the walls (explanations in English and Hindi).

Surrounding the temple is a moat of holy water supposedly taken from 151 sacred lakes and rivers visited by Swaminarayan on his seven-year barefoot pilgrimage. 108 bronze *gaumukhs* (cow heads) representing the 108 names of God spout water into the tank, which is itself hemmed in by a 1-km-long *parikrama* (colonnade) of red Rajasthani sandstone.

Delhi listings

For hotel and restaurant price codes and other relevant information, see pages 13-16.

☺ Where to stay

Avoid hotel touts. Airport taxis may pretend not to know the location of your chosen hotel so give full details and insist on being taken there. Around Paharganj particularly, you might be followed around by your driver trying to eek a commission out of the guesthouse once you have checked in. It really saves a lot of hassle if you make reservations. Even if you change hotel the next day, it is good to arrive with somewhere booked especially if you are flying in late at night. Hotel prices in Delhi are significantly higher than in most other parts of the country. Smaller **$$** guesthouses away from the centre in **South Delhi** (eg Kailash, Safdarjang) or in **Sunder Nagar**, are quieter

and often good value but may not provide food. **$** accommodation is concentrated around **Janpath** and **Paharganj** (New Delhi), and **Chandni Chowk** (Old Delhi) – well patronized but basic and usually cramped yet good for meeting other backpackers. Signs in some hotels warn against taking drugs as this is becoming a serious cause for concern. Police raids are frequent.

Old Delhi and beyond *p29, map p30*
$$$$ Maidens (Oberoi), 7 Sham Nath Marg, T011-2397 5464, www.maidenshotel.com. 54 large well-appointed rooms, restaurant (slow), barbecue nights are excellent, coffee shop, old-style bar, attractive colonial style in quiet area, spacious gardens with excellent pool, friendly welcome, personal attention. One of Delhi's oldest hotels. Recommended. **$$$ Broadway**, 4/15A Asaf Ali Rd, T011-4366 3600, www.hotelbroadwaydelhi.com.

36 rooms, some wonderfully quirky. Interior designer Catherine Levy has decorated some of the rooms in a quirky kitsch style, brightly coloured with psychedelic bathroom tiles. The other rooms are classic design. **Chor Bizarre** restaurant/bar is highly regarded, as is the 'Thugs' pub. Walking tours of Old Delhi available. Easily one of the best options.
$$-$ Wongdhen House, 15A New Tibetan Colony, Manju-ka-Tilla, T011-2381 6689, wongdhenhouse@hotmail.com. Very clean rooms, some with a/c and TV, safe, cosy, convivial, good breakfast and great Tibetan meals, an insight into Tibetan culture, peacefully located by Yamuna River yet 15 mins by auto-rickshaw north of Old Delhi Station. Recommended.

Connaught Place *p40, map p41*
$$$$ Imperial, Janpath, T011-2334 1234, www.theimperialindia.com. Quintessential Delhi. 230 rooms and beautiful 'deco suites' in supremely elegant Lutyens-designed 1933 hotel. Unparalleled location, great bar, antiques and art everywhere, beautiful gardens with spa and secluded pool, amazing **Spice Route** restaurant. Highly recommended.
$$$ Hotel Corus, B-49 Connaught Pl, T011-4365 2222, www.hotelcorus.com. Comfortable hotel right at the heart of things. Good-value rooms. You get 15% discount in their onsite **Life Caffe**.
$$$ Palace Heights, D26-28 Connaught Pl, T011-4358 2610, www.hotelpalace heights.com. Recently given a complete facelift, the bright, modern rooms with good attention to detail, represent the best choice in Connaught Pl in this price bracket. There's also an attractive glass-walled restaurant overlooking the street.
$$$-$ YMCA Tourist Hostel, Jai Singh Rd, T011-2336 1915, www.newdelhiymca.org. 120 rooms, for both sexes, common areas have been recently refurbished. Prices are creeping up here. Good location. Good pool (Rs 200 extra), luggage storage, pay in advance but check bill, reserve ahead, very professional.

$ Asian Guest House, 14 Scindia House, off Kasturba Gandhi Marg, the sign is hidden behind petrol pump, T011-2331 0229, www.asianguesthouse.com. Friendly faces greet you here, although it's a bit tricky to find – call ahead for directions. Great central location. Clean basic rooms, some with a/c, some with TV.

Paharganj *p40, map p36*
Parharganj is where backpackers congregate. Sandwiched between the main sights and near the main railway station, it's noisy, dirty and a lot of hassle. Its chief virtues are economy and convenience, with plenty of shops, travel agents, budget hotels and cafés catering for Western tastes. Avoid **Hotel Bright**.
$$$$-$$$ Jyoti Mahal, 2488 Nalwa St, behind Imperial Cinema, T011-2358 0524, www.jyotimahal.net. An oasis in Paharganj with large and atmospheric rooms in a beautiful converted *haveli* and new deluxe rooms in a stylish new wing. Cool and quiet with antique pieces dotted around and bowls of floating rose petals lining the staircases. Top-notch rooftop restaurant serving Continental and Indian dishes. It's a very atmospheric place to dine. Nice boutique, **Pink Safari**, too. Highly recommended.
$$ Metropolis Tourist Home, 1634-35 Main Bazar, T011-2356 1782, www.metropolis touristhome.com. More expensive rooms have ornate heavy wooden furniture, but walls are grubby throughout. Nice rooftop restaurant, and wonderful wooden espresso bar in the lobby. Has another branch close to the Metro station.
$$ Prince Polonia, 2325-26 Tilak Gali (behind Imperial Cinema), T011-4762 6600, www.hotelprincepolonia.com. Very unusual for Paharganj in that it has a rooftop pool (small, but good for a cool down). Breezy rooftop café. Attracts a slightly more mature crowd. Safe, clean. Recently refurbished.
$ Rak International, 820 Main Bazar, Chowk Bowli, T011-2358 6508, www.hotelrak international.com. 27 basic but clean rooms.

Professionally run. Quiet, friendly hotel with a rooftop restaurant and water feature.

Karol Bagh and Rajendra Nagar

West of Paharganj on the Metro line, **Karol Bagh** is full of identikit modern hotels, albeit a degree more upmarket than Paharganj. There are plentiful good eating places, and the area is handy for Sarai Rohilla station. Nearby **Rajendra Nagar**, a residential suburb, has one of Delhi's best homestays.

$$$ Yatri Paying Guest House, corner of Panchkuin and Mandir margs, T011-2362 5563, www.yatrihouse.com. A quiet, peaceful oasis with beautiful gardens. 6 large, attractive rooms all with 42-inch televisions, nice bathrooms, Wi-Fi, fridge and a/c. Free airport pick-up or drop off. Breakfast, tea/coffee and afternoon snack included.

$$$-$$ Master Guest House, R-500 New Rajendra Nagar (Shankar Rd and GR Hospital Rd crossing), T011-2874 1089, www.masterbedandbreakfast.com. 3 beautiful rooms, a/c, Wi-Fi, rooftop for breakfast, *thalis*, warm welcome, personal attention, secure, recommended. Each room has the theme of a different god, complete with appropriate colour schemes. Very knowledgeable, caring owners run excellent tours of 'hidden Delhi'. They make Delhi feel like home. Recommended.

South Delhi *p42, map p36*

Most of the city's smartest hotels are located south of Rajpath, in a broad rectangle between Chanakyapuri and Humayun's Tomb. The southern residential suburbs are also peppered with homestays; a list is available from **Delhi Tourism**, BK Singh Marg (see page 28), or arrange with the reliable **Metropole** (see Car hire, page 63).

$$$$ Claridges, 12 Aurangzeb Rd, T011-3955 5000, www.claridges.com. 138 refurbished, classy rooms, art deco-style interiors, colonial atmosphere, attractive restaurants (**Jade Garden** is good), slick **Aura** bar, impeccable service, more atmosphere than most. Recommended.

$$$$ Manor, 77 Friends Colony, T011-2692 5151, www.themanordelhi.com. Contemporary boutique hotel with 10 stylish rooms, heavenly beds, polished stone surfaces and chrome, relaxing garden, a haven. Beautiful artwork and relaxed vibe. Acclaimed restaurant **Indian Accent**. Charming service.

$$$$ Oberoi, Dr Zakir Hussain Marg, T011-2436 3030, www.oberoihotels.com. 300 rooms and extremely luxurious suites overlooking golf club, immaculate, quietly efficient, beautiful touches, carved Tree of Life in the lobby, all 5-star facilities including 2 pools and a spa, superb business centre, good restaurants – **360°** gets rave reviews.

$$$$ Taj Mahal, 1 Mansingh Rd, T011-2302 6162, www.tajhotels.com. 1 of 3 Taj hotels in Delhi. 300 attractive rooms, comfortable, new club levels outstanding, excellent restaurants and service (**Haveli** offers a wide choice and explanations for the newcomer; **Ming House's** spicing varies; **Machan** overlooks palm trees and has a wildlife library), good Khazana shop, lavishly finished with 'lived-in' feel, friendly 1920s-style bar. There is also a **Vivanta by Taj** hotel close to Khan Market with a more business mood.

$$$$-$$$ Amarya Haveli, P5 Hauz Khas Enclave, T011-4175 9268, www.amaryagroup.com. Luxury, boutique, hip guesthouse, run by 2 Frenchmen. Unique, bright, en suite rooms, with TV, Wi-Fi. Fantastic roof garden. Great home-cooked food. Book ahead. They have a sister property, **Amarya Villa**, in Safdarjung Enclave – the decor there is inspired by *Navratna* (nine gems) – both properties are effortlessly chic. Highly recommended.

$$$$-$$$ Casa Delhi, C-56 Defence Colony, T(0)9971-425558, www.casaboutiquehotels.com. Some of the most beautiful rooms you will find in Delhi. A boutique hotel with sumptuous decor – a true oasis.

$$$ K One One, K11, Jangpura Extn, 2nd floor, T011-4359 2583, www.parigold.com. Homely guesthouse in a quiet, central residential area. Run by wonderful ex-TV chef, who also gives cooking lessons. All rooms en suite with a/c, minibar, Wi-Fi, some with balconies. Wonderful roof terrace with views of Humayan's Tomb. Rooftop room is lovely. Book ahead.

$$$ Lutyens Bungalow, 39 Prithviraj Rd, T011-2469 4523, www.lutyensbungalow. co.in. Private guesthouse in a bungalow that has been running for over 35 years – it's looking a little faded around the edges. Eccentric, rambling property with 15 a/c rooms, a wonderful pool and beautiful gardens with a garden accessory shop on-site. Free airport pickup/drop off, full services, used for long-stays by NGOs and foreign consultants.

$$$-$$ Tree of Life B&B, D-193, Saket, T(0)9810-277699, www.tree-of-life.in. Stylish B&B with beautifully decorated rooms, simple but chic. Kitchen access, excellent on-site reflexology and yoga – really good atmosphere. The owner also runs **Metropole Tourist Service** (see page 63). Close to Saket Metro station and to **PVR** cinema and malls.

$$ Life Tree, G 14 Lajpat Nagar Part II, T(0)9910-460898, lifetreebnb@gmail.com. A more simple but charming B&B from the **Tree of Life** family – well located for Khan Market and the centre.

$ Youth Hostel, 5 Naya Marg, Chanakyapuri, T011-2611 6285, www.yhaindia.org. Wide range of rooms from a/c doubles to a basic dorm (a/c dorms much better). Meals available at restaurant if ordered in advance. Soulless but clean and comfortable. Great location. You need YHA membership to stay (Rs 250 foreigners, Rs 100 Indians).

Airport
Unless you can afford a 5-star, hotels around the airport are overpriced and best avoided.
$$$-$$ Sam's Snooze at My Space, T3 IGI Airport, opposite Gate 17, T(0)8800-230013, www.newdelhiairport.in. You can book a snooze pod for US$9 per hr – only if you are flying out of T3. There's Wi-Fi, TV and DVD, work stations.

$$-$ Hotel Eurostar International, A 27/1 Street No 1, near MTNL office, Mahipalpur Extension, T011-4606 2300, www.hoteleuro star.in. Good-value option near the airport.

🍴 Restaurants

The larger hotel restaurants are often the best for cuisine, decor and ambience. Buffets (lunch or dinner) cost Rs 700 or more. Sun buffets are becoming quite the thing in the top-notch hotels. Others may only open around 1930 for dinner; some close on Sun. Alcohol is served in most top hotels, but only in some non-hotel restaurants eg Amber, Ginza and Kwality.

The old-fashioned 'tea on the lawn' is still served at the Imperial and in Claridges (see Where to stay, pages 50 and 51). Aapki Pasand, at 15 Netaji Subhash Marg, offers unusual tea-tasting in classy and extremely professional surroundings; it's quite an experience.

Old Delhi p29, map p30

In Paranthewali Gali, a side street off Chandni Chowk, stalls sell a variety of *paranthas* including *kaju badam* (stuffed with dry fruits and nuts). Other good places to try local foods like *bedmi aloo puri* with spiced potato are **Mahalaxmi Misthan Bhandhar**, 659 Church Mission St, and **Natraj Chowk**, 1396 Chandni Chowk, for *dahi balli* and *aloo tikki*. For sweets you have to seek out **Old Famous Jalebi Wala**, 1797 Dariba Corner, Chandni Chowk – as they are old and famous.

$$$-$$ Chor Bizarre, Broadway Hotel (see Where to stay, page 49), T011-4366 3600. Tandoori and Kashmiri cuisine (Wazwan, Rs 500). Fantastic food, quirky decor, including salad bar that was a vintage car. Well worth a visit.

$ Haldiram's, 1454/2 Chandni Chowk. Stand-up counter for excellent snacks and sweets on the run (try *dokhla* with coriander chutney from seller just outside), and more elaborate sit-down restaurant upstairs.

$ Karim's, Gali Kababiyan (south of Jama Masjid), Mughlai. Authentic, busy, plenty of local colour. The experience, as much as the food, makes this a must. Not a lot to tempt vegetarians though.

Connaught Place p40, map p41

$$$ Sakura, Hotel Metropolitan, Bangla Sahib Rd, T011-2334 0200. Top Japanese royal cuisine in classic, uncluttered surroundings. One of the best in the city, priced accordingly.

$$$ Sevilla, Claridges Hotel (see Where to stay, page 51). Beautiful restaurant with lots of outdoor seating serving up specialities like tapas and paella as well as wood-fired pizza and the dangerous house special sangria.

$$$ Spice Route, Imperial Hotel (see Where to stay, page 50). Award-winning restaurant charting the journey of spices around the world. Extraordinary temple-like surroundings (took 7 years to build), Kerala, Thai, Vietnamese cuisines, magical atmosphere but food doesn't always thrill.

$$$ Veda, 27-H, T011-4151 3535, www vedarestaurants.com. Owned by fashion designer Rohit Bal with appropriately beautiful bordello-style decor, done out like a Rajasthani palace with high-backed leather chairs and candles reflecting from mirror work on ceilings. Food is contemporary Indian. Great atmosphere at night. There is another branch at DLF Vasant Kunj.

$$$-$$ Life Caffe, Hotel Corus (see Where to stay, page 50), B49 Connaught Pl, T011-4365 2240. Tranquil garden, imaginative, good-value food. Perfect for when you want to escape the noise of CP.

$$ Embassy, D-11, T011-2341 6434. International food. Popular with artistic-intellectual-political crowd, good food, long-standing local favourite.

$$ Kwality, 7 Regal Building, near Park Hotel, T011-2374 2352. International. Spicy Punjabi dishes with various breads. Try *chhole bhature*.

$$ United Coffee House, E-15 Connaught Pl, T011-2341 1697. Recommended more for the colonial-era cake-icing decor than for the fairly average food. Often someone

waxing lyrical over a Casio keyboard. Always attracts a mixed crowd, well worth a visit.
$ Nathu's, and **Bengali Sweet House**, both in Bengali Market (east of Connaught Pl). Sweet shops also serving vegetarian food. Good dosa, *iddli*, *utthapam* and North Indian *chana bathura*, *thalis*, clean, functional. Try *kulfi* (hard blocks of ice cream) with *falooda* (sweet vermicelli noodles).
$ Nizam's Kathi Kebabs, H-5 Plaza, T011-2371 3078. Very good, tasty filled *parathas*, good value, clean, excellent '3-D toilets' (note the emergency button!).
$ Saravana Bhavan, P-15/90, near McDonalds, T011-2334 7755; also at 46 Janpath. Chennai-based chain, light and wonderful South Indian, superb chutneys, unmissable *kaju anjeer* ice cream with figs and nuts. Can take hours to get a table at night or at weekends. Highly recommended.
$ Street stalls, at entrance to Shankar Market. Stalls dish out *rajma chawal* (bean stew and rice) to an appreciative crowd on weekdays.
$ Triveni Tea Terrace, Triveni Kala Sangam, 205 Tansen Marg, near Mandi House Metro station (not Sun). Art galleries, an amphitheatre and this little café in quite an unusual building close to CP – the tea terrace is a bit of an institution.

Paharganj *p40, map p36*
The rooftop restaurants at **Jyoti Mahal** and **Shelton** are great locations for a bite to eat.
$$-$ Café Sim Tok, Tooti Chowk, above **Hotel Navrang**, near **Hotel Rak**, T(0)9810-386717. Tucked away little gem of a Korean restaurant. No signage, ask for **Hotel Navrang** and keep going up stairs to find delicious *kimbab* (Korean sushi), *kimchi* and all sorts of soups, in a sweet little café.
$ Everest Bakery Café, Dal Mandi, near **Star Palace Hotel**. Fantastic *momos*, cakes and pies, green teas, sociable. Recommended.
$ Southern Restaurant, opposite **Ajanta**, Arakashan Rd. Spartan but clean and very cheap café for excellent fresh *dosas*, friendly Indian clientele, atmosphere better downstairs than in fan-cooled upstairs room.

$ Tadka, off Main Bazar. Good option for tasty food in this area. Great range of all the usual Indian favourites, with nice decor, friendly staff and good hygiene levels.

South Delhi *p42, map p36*
$$$ Baci, 23 Sunder Nagar Market, near HDFC Bank, T011-4150 7445. Classy, top-quality Italian food, run by gregarious Italian-Indian owners. There are also branches of her cheaper café **Amici** springing up in Khan Market and Hauz Khas.
$$$ Bukhara, ITC Maurya Sheraton, Sardar Patel Marg, T011-2611 2233, www.itc welcomgroup.com. Stylish Northwest Frontier cuisine amidst rugged walls draped with rich rugs (but uncomfortable seating). Outstanding meat dishes and dhal. Also tasty vegetable and *paneer* dishes, but vegetarians will miss out on the best dishes.
$$$ Diva, M8, M-Block Market, Greater Kailash II, T011-2921 5673. Superb Italian in minimalist space popular with celebrity crowd. Great fish dishes, inventive starters, dedicated vegetarian section, extensive wine list. Owner Ritu Dalmia has also opened **Latitude 28** in Khan Market.
$$$ Dum Pukht, ITC Maurya Sheraton, Sardar Patel Marg, T011-2611 2233, www.itcwelcomgroup.com. Open evenings; lunch only on Sun. Voted one of the best restaurants in the world, it marries exquisite tastes and opulent surroundings.
$$$ Grey Garden, 13a Hauz Khaz Village, near the lake, T011-2651 6450. New kid on the block in the lovely Hauz Khaz village, this boho chic little number serves up a small menu but with great attention to detail. Delicious banana-wrapped fish or thin-crust pizzas, lotus stem chips and other assorted goodies. Book ahead at weekends. Highly recommended.
$$$ Indian Accent, at The Manor, 77 Friends Colony West, T011-4323 5151. With a menu designed by Manish Mehotra, who runs restaurants in Delhi and London, this acclaimed restaurant offers up Indian food with a modern twist. Your *dosas* will reveal

masala morel mushrooms, rather than the traditional Goan prawns *balchao* here you will find it with roasted scallops. Or how about toffee *chyawanprash* cheesecake with badam milk (*chyawanprash* is a health elixir from the amla fruit)? The menu reflects the changing of the seasons and there is live fusion music on Sat. Highly recommended.

$$$ Kainoosh, 122-124 DLF Promenade Mall, Vasant Kunj, T(0)9560-715544. Under the watchful eye of celebrity chef Marut Sikka, delicious *thalis* marry the traditional and modern faces of Indian food. This is *thali* with a difference – bespoke with giant morel mushrooms, sea bass mousse and chicken cooked in orange juice and saffron in a terracotta pot.

$$$ Latitude, 9 Khan Market, above Good Earth, T011-2462 1013. Like sitting in someone's very posh, very chic living room and getting served delicious Italian numbers like bruschetta, yummy salads and pastas. Topped off with top-notch coffees.

$$$ Lodi, Lodi Gardens, T011-2465 5054. Continental lunch, Indian dinner menu in pleasant, Mediterranean-style surroundings, nice terrace and garden. Come more for the setting than the food which can be mediocre.

$$$ Magique, Gate No 3, Garden of 5 Senses, Mehrauli Badarpur Rd, T(0)9717-535533. High-class quality food, in a magical setting. Sit outside among the candles and fairy lights. One of Delhi's most romantic restaurants.

$$$ Olive at the Qutb, T011-2957 4444, www.olivebarandkitchen.com. Branch of the ever popular Mumbai restaurant and some people say the Delhi version wins hands down. Serving up delicious platters of Mediterranean food and good strong cocktails. Or head to their sister restaurant in the **Diplomat Hotel** – **Olive Beach** especially for their legendary blow-out Sun brunches: for Rs 2195 you get open access to a mind-boggling buffet and as many martini's as you can drink.

$$$ Park Baluchi, inside Deer Park, Hauz Khas Village, T011-2685 9369. Atmospheric dining in Hauz Khas Deer Park. The lamb wrapped in chicken served on a flaming sword comes highly recommended. Can get crowded, book ahead.

$$$ Ploof, 13 Main Market, Lodhi Colony, T011-2463 4666. The place to come for seafood. Very popular. Bright, comfortable restaurant.

$$$ Yum Yum Tree, 1st floor, Friends Colony Community Centre (opposite Nathu Sweets), T011-4260 2020. Excellent Chinese, with an enormous menu. Very popular. Great decor.

$$ Elma's, 24/1 Hauz Khas Village, T011-2652 1020. Lovely little café serving up all manner of tea and cakes and more hearty options like shepherds pie. Mismatched china and funky furniture make this a great little hang-out. Also check out their little brother **Edwards** downstairs offering more posh deli-style food.

$$ Naivedyam, Hauz khas Village, T011-2696 0426. Very good South Indian, great service and very good value in a very beautiful restaurant. Highly recommended.

$$ Oh! Calcutta, E-Block, ground floor, International Trade Towers, Nehru Pl, T011-2646 4180. Authentic Bengali cuisine, with excellent vegetarian and fish options, somewhat odd location but not far from the Baha'i temple.

$ Khan Cha Cha, Khan Market, 75 Middle Lane. This no-frills joint serves some of the best kebabs in the city from a window in the middle lane of Khan Market. Fantastic value. You can recognize the place from the crowd clamouring at the counter.

$ Sagar Ratna, 18 Defence Colony Market, T011-2433 3110. Other branches in Vasant Kunj, Malviya Nagar and NOIDA. Excellent South Indian. Cheap and "amazing" *thalis* and coffee, very hectic (frequent queues). One of the best breakfasts in Delhi.

◐ Bars and clubs

Many national holidays are 'dry' days. Delhi's bar/club scene has exploded over the last few years. Expect to pay a lot for your drinks and, when in doubt, dress up; some clubs have strict dress codes.

Delhi's 'in' crowd is notoriously fickle; city magazines (*Time Out, First City*) will point you towards the flavour of the month. For more insight into Delhi check out the website www.bringhomestories.com.

Connaught Place *p40, map p41*

1911, Imperial Hotel (see page 50). Elegantly styled colonial bar, good snacks.
24/7, Lalit Hotel, Barakhamba Av. Boasting molecular mixology with their cocktails and regular turns by prominent DJs and more alternative acts, 24/7 is putting itself in the scene.

South Delhi *p42, map p36*

Blue Frog, near Qutb Minar, www.bluefrog.co.in. For years, Blue Frog has been the best venue in Mumbai with supreme live acts and star DJs doing a turn and now it's coming to Delhi.
Café Morrisons, Shop E-12, South Extension Part II, T011-2625 5652. Very popular rock bar. Come for live bands or to mosh to the DJ.
The Living Room, 31 Haus Khaz, T011-4608 0533, www.tlrcafe.com. Recently done-up, this place has a funky laid-back atmosphere day and night over 3 floors. By day there's cosy armchairs and sofas. By night, things kick up a gear with live music, open mics and DJs spinning electronica and dubstep, and all manner of themed nights. Recommended.
Pegs-n-Pints, Chanakya Lane, Chanakyapuri (tucked away behind Akbar Bhawan), T011-2687 8320. On Tue evenings it hosts Delhi's only gay club. Western and Indian pop. It gets packed. A lot of fun.
Rick's, Taj Mahal Hotel, 1 Mansingh Rd, T011-2302 6162, www.tajhotels.com. Suave Casablanca-themed bar with long martini list, a long-time fixture on Delhi's social scene.
Shalom, 'N' Block Market, Greater Kailash 1, T011-4163 2280. Comfortable, stylish lounge bar serving Lebanese cuisine; the resident DJ plays ambient music.
Urban Pind, N4, N-block market, GK1, T011-3951 5656. Multi-level bar, with large roof terrace, popular. Hosts a controversial expat/

journalist night on Thu with an 'all-you-can-drink' entry fee, unsurprisingly this normally features a lot of drunk foreigners.
Zoo, at Magique (see Restaurants, page 55), one of the latest and most popular places on the scene serving up big portions of beats in a beautiful location.

☺ Entertainment

Delhi *p26, maps p30, p36 and p41*
For advance notice of upcoming events see www.delhievents.com. Current listings and reviews can be found in *First City* (monthly, Rs 50), *Time Out* (fortnightly, Rs 50), *Delhi City Info* (fortnightly, free) and *Delhi Diary* (weekly). For programmes see cinema listings in the daily *Delhi Times*. Also check out www.bringhomestories.com for inspiration on what to do in Delhi.

Cinema

PVR is a multiplex chain with branches everywhere, mostly screening Hindi movies, including **PVR Plaza** in Connaught Pl. Now with the Metro, it's pretty easy to get to PVR Saket for example where as once it was extremely unlikely you would bother.

Music, dance and culture

Goethe Institute, 3 Kasturba Gandhi Marg, T011-2332 9506. Recommended for arts, film festivals, open-air cinema, plays and events.
India Habitat Centre, Lodi Rd, T011-2468 2222. Good programme of lectures, films, exhibitions, concerts, excellent restaurant.
Indian International Centre, 40 Lodhi Estate, Max Mueller Marg, T011-2461 9431, www.iicdelhi.nic.in. Some fantastic debates and performances, well worth checking the 'forthcoming programmes' section of their website.
Kingdom of Dreams, Great Indian Nautanki Company Ltd. Auditorium Complex, Sector 29, Gurgaon, Metro IFFCO, T0124-452 8000, www.kingdomofdreams.in. Ticket prices Rs 750-3000 depending on where you sit and more pricey at the weekend. The highlight is a much acclaimed all-singing,

all-dancing Bollywood style performance. A little like an Indian Disneyland showcasing Indian tastes, foods, culture, dress and dance all in one a/c capsule, but done impeccably. **Triveni Kala Sangam**, 205 Tansen Marg (near Mandi House Metro station), T011-2371 8833. Strong programme of photography and art exhibitions, plus an excellent North Indian café.

Son et lumière

Red Fort (see page 31), Apr-Nov 1800-1900 (Hindi), 1930-2030 (English). Entry Rs 50. Tickets available after 1700. Take mosquito cream.

❀ Festivals

Delhi *p26, maps p30, p36 and p41*
For exact dates consult the weekly *Delhi Diary* available at hotels and many shops and offices around town.

Muslim festivals of **Ramadan, Id-ul-Fitr, Id-ul-Zuha** and **Muharram** are celebrated according to the lunar calendar.

January
26 Jan Republic Day Parade, Rajpath. A spectacular fly-past and military march-past, with colourful pageants and tableaux from every state, dances and music. Tickets through travel agents and most hotels, Rs 100. You can see the full dress preview free, usually 2 days before; week-long celebrations during which government buildings are illuminated.
29 Jan Beating the Retreat, Vijay Chowk, a stirring display by the armed forces' bands marks the end of the Republic Day celebrations.
30 Jan Martyr's Day, Marks the anniversary of Mahatma Gandhi's death; devotional *bhajans* and Guard of Honour at Raj Ghat. **Kite Flying Festival**, Makar Sankranti above Palika Bazar, Connaught Pl.

February
2 Feb Vasant Panchami, celebrates the 1st day of spring. The Mughal Gardens are opened to the public for a month. **Thyagaraja Festival**, South Indian music and dance, Vaikunthnath Temple.

April
Amir Khusrau's Birth Anniversary, a fair in Nizamuddin celebrates this with prayers and *qawwali* singing.

August
Janmashtami, celebrates the birth of the Hindu god Krishna. Special *puja*, Lakshmi Narayan Mandir.
15 Aug Independence Day, Impressive flag-hoisting ceremony and prime ministerial address at the Red Fort.

October-November
2 Oct Gandhi Jayanti, Mahatma Gandhi's birthday; devotional singing at Raj Ghat. **Dasara**, with over 200 Ramlila performances all over the city recounting the *Ramayana* story. **Ramlila Ballet**, the ballet, which takes place at Delhi Gate (south of Red Fort) and Ramlila Ground, is performed for a month and is most spectacular. Huge effigies of Ravana are burnt on the 9th night; noisy and flamboyant. **Diwali**, the festival of lights; lighting of earthen lamps, candles and firework displays. **National Drama Festival**, Rabindra Bhavan. **Oct/Nov Dastkar Nature Bazaar**, working with over 25,000 crafts people from across India, **Dastkar's** main objective is to empower rural artisans and keep alive the traditional crafts of India. They hold many events each year, but this is the pinnacle. Knowing that shopping here will bring a difference to the lives of rural people.

December
25 Dec Christmas, Special Christmas Eve entertainments at major hotels and restaurants; Midnight Mass and services at all churches.

O Shopping

Delhi *p26, maps p30, p36 and p41*
There are several state emporia around
Delhi including the Cottage Industries
Emporium (CIE), a huge department store
of Indian handicrafts, and those along Baba
Kharak Singh Marg (representing crafts from
most states of India). In this stretch, there
are several places selling products from
women's collectives or rural artisans, like
Mother Earth and Hansiba). Shops generally
open 1000-1930 (winter 1000-1900). Food
stores and chemists stay open later. Most
shopping areas are closed on Sun.

Art galleries
Galleries exhibiting contemporary art are
listed in *First City*.
Delhi Art Gallery, Hauz Khas Village.
A newly expanded gallery with a good range
of moderately priced contemporary art.
Nature Morte, A-1 Neethi Bagh, near Kamla
Nehru College, www.naturemorte.com.
With a twin gallery in Berlin, you can
expect the most profound and inspiring
of contemporary art here.
Photo Ink, Hyundai MGF building,
1 Jhandewalan Faiz Rd, www.photoink.net.
Close to Paharganj, this gallery offers up
top notch contemporary photography.

Books and music
Serious bibliophiles should head to the
Sun book market in Daryaganj, Old Delhi,
when 2 km of pavement are piled high with
books – some fantastic bargains to be had.
Bahri & Sons, opposite Main Gate, Khan
Market. One among many in the booklovers'
heaven of Khan Market. Wide choice.
Central News Agency, P 23/90, Connaught
Pl. Carries national and foreign newspapers
and journals.
Full Circle, 5 B, Khan Market, T011-2465
5641. Helpful knowledgeable staff. Sweet
café upstairs for a quick drink – food is hit
and miss though.

Jacksons, 5106, Main Bazar, Paharganj, T011-
5535 1083. Selection in many languages,
mostly second hand at half original price
(also buys used books).
Kabaadi Bazaar, Netaji Subhash Marg,
Old Delhi. Sun market with thousands of
very cheap used books, great for browsing.
Manohar, 4753/23 Ansar Rd, Daryaganj,
Old Delhi. A real treasure trove for books on
South Asia and India especially, most helpful,
knowledgeable staff. Highly recommended.
Munshiram Manoharlal, Nai Sarak,
Chandni Chowk. Books on Indology.
New Book Depot, 18B, Connaught Pl.
Highly recommended.
Rikhi Ram, G Block Connaught Circus,
T011-2332 7685. This is the place to come
if you've wondered about how easy it
is to learn to play and travel with a sitar.
Has a range of guitars and other stringed
instruments too.

Carpets
Carpets can be found in shops in most top
hotels and a number round Connaught Pl,
not necessarily fixed price. If you are visiting
Agra, check out the prices here first.

Clothing
For designer wear, try **Ogaan** and for more
contemporary, less budget blowing try **Grey
Garden** both in Hauz Khas Village, **Sunder
Nagar Market** near the Oberoi hotel, or the
Crescent arcade near the Qutab Minar.
   For inexpensive (Western and Indian)
clothes, try shops along Janpath and
between Sansad Marg and Janpath;
you can bargain down 50%.
   The **Central Cottage Industries
Emporium** (see below) has a good selection
of clothing and fabrics. The **Khadi shop** (see
Emporia, below) has Indian-style clothing.
Fab India, 14N-Gt Kailash I (also in B-Block
Connaught Pl, Khan Market and Vasant
Kunj). Excellent shirts, Nehru jackets,
salwar kameez, linen, furnishing fabrics
and furniture. The most comprehensive
collection is in N block.

Earthenware

Unglazed earthenware *khumba matkas* (water pots) are sold round New Delhi Railway Station (workshops behind main road).

Emporia

Most open 1000-1800 (close 1330-1400).
Central Cottage Industries Emporium, corner of Janpath and Tolstoy Marg. Offers hassle-free shopping, gift wrapping, will pack and post overseas; best if you are short of time.

Dilli Haat, opposite INA Market. Rs 15, open 1100-2200. Well-designed open-air complex with rows of brick alcoves for craft stalls from different states; local craftsmen's outlets (bargaining obligatory), occasional fairs (tribal art, textiles, etc). Also good regional food – hygienic, safe, weighted towards non-vegetarian. Pleasant, quiet, clean (no smoking) and uncrowded, not too much hassle.

Khadi Gramodyog Bhawan, near the Regal building, Baba Kharak Singh Marg. For inexpensive homespun cotton *kurta pajama* (loose shirt and trousers), cotton/ silk waistcoats, fabrics and Jaipuri paintings.

Khazana, Taj Mahal and Taj Palace hotels (daily 0900-2000). High class.

Jewellery

Traditional silver and goldsmiths in Dariba Kalan, off Chandni Chowk (north of Jama Masjid). Cheap bangles and along Janpath; also at Hanuman Mandir, Gt Kailash I, N-Block. Also Sunder Nagar market. Bank St in Karol Bagh is recommended for gold.

Amrapali, Khan Market has an exceptional collection from affordable to mind-blowing.

Ashish Nahar, 1999 Naughara St, Kinari Bazaar, Chandni Chowk, T011-2327 2801. On quite possibly the prettiest street in Delhi, full of brightly painted and slowly crumbling *havelis*, you will find a little gem of a jewellery shop.

Leather

Cheap sandals from stalls on Janpath (Rs 100).
Yashwant Place Market next to Chanakya Cinema Hall, Chanakyapuri. **Khan Market** (see below) sells leather goods and shoes.
Da Milano, South Extension and Khan Market.
Hidesign, G49, Connaught Pl. High class.

Markets and malls

Beware of pickpockets in markets and malls.
Hauz Khas village, South Delhi. Authentic, old village houses converted into designer shops selling handicrafts, ceramics, antiques and furniture in addition to luxury wear. Many are expensive, but some are good value. A good place to pick up old Hindi film posters with many art galleries and restaurants.

Khan Market, South Delhi. Great bookshops, cafés, restaurants and boutiques. Full of expats so expect expat prices.

Sarojini Nagar, South Delhi. Daily necessities as well as cheap fabric and clothing. Come for incredible bargains. This is where a lot of the Western brands dump their export surplus or end-of-line clothes. Haggle hard.

Select City Walk, Saket. An enormous, glitzy mall for the ultimate in upmarket shopping. Lots of chains, cinemas, etc.

Shahpur Jat, is a new up and coming shopping area, south of **South Extension**.

Tibetan Market, North Delhi. Stalls along Janpath have plenty of curios – most are new but rapidly aged to look authentic.

Souvenirs

Aap ki Pasand, opposite Golcha cinema, Netaji Subhash Marg, Old Delhi. Excellent place to taste and buy Indian teas.

Dastkari Haat, 39 Khan Market, www.indian craftsjourney.in. Charming selection of conscious crafts from around India working with rural artisans and women's collectives.

Gulabsingh Johrimal Perfumers, 467 Chandni Chowk, T011-2326 3743. Authentic *attars* (sandalwood based perfumes), perfumes and incense. High-quality oils are used.

Haldiram's, Chandni Chowk near Metro.
Wide selection of sweet and salty snack foods.
Khazana India, 50A Hauz Khaz Village.
Little treasure trove of Bollywood posters,
old photographs and all sorts of interesting
bric-a-brac.
People Tree, 8 Regal Building, Connaught
Pl. Handmade clothing, mostly T-shirts with
arty and people conscious slogans. Great
posters made up of all those weird signs
that you see around India and wide-range
of ecological books. A real find.
Playclan, F51 Select Citywalk, Saket, www.
theplayclan.com. Fantastic shop selling
all manner of clothes, notebooks, lighters
and pictures with great colourful cartoon
designs created by a collective of animators
and designers – giving a more animated
view of India's gods, goddesses, gurus,
Kathakali dancers and the faces of India.
Purple Jungle, 16 Hauz Khaz Village,
T(0)9650-973039, www.purple-jungle.com.
Offering up kitsch India with bollywood
pictures and curious road signs refashioned
onto bags, clothes, cushions, etc.

⚙ What to do

Body and soul
The Yoga Studio, Hauz Khaz, www.the
yogastudio.info. Regular yoga classes
with Seema Sondhi, author of several
yoga books, and her team
Integral Yoga, Sri Aurobindo Ashram,
Aurobindo Marg, T011-2656 7863. Regular
yoga classes (Tue-Thu and Sat 0645-0745 and
1700-1800) in *asana* (postures), *pranayama*
(breathing techniques) and relaxation.
Laughter Club of Delhi, various locations,
T011-2721 7164. Simple yogic breathing
techniques combined with uproarious
laughter. Clubs meet early morning in
parks throughout the city.
Sari School, Jangpura Extension, near Lajpat
Nagar, T011-4182 3297. Author of *Saris in
India*, Rta Christi Kapur holds classes every
Sat in different styles of sporting a sari.

Tree of Life Reflexology, T(0)9810-356677.
Reflexology with acclaimed teacher Suruchi.
She also does private and group yoga
classes on the roof and in the park.
Yogalife, Shapur Jat main market, T(0)9811-
863332, www.yogalife.org. Closed Mon.
Bright, friendly centre.

Sport
Members only clubs, but maybe you
can find a willing member to take you.
Delhi Gymkhana Club, 2 Safdarjang Rd,
T011-2301 5533. Mostly for government
and defence personnel, squash, tennis,
swimming, bar and restaurant.
Pacific Sports Complex, next to Central
School, Andrews Ganj, T011-6507 9552.
Can be hard to find – it's near Lady Sri
Ram College.
Siri Fort Club, August Kranti Marg, New
Delhi, near Siri Fort Auditorium, T011-2649
7482. You can get temporary membership –
wonderful outdoor swimming pool
(summer only), tennis, squash, basketball,
reiki, taekwando, etc.

Tours and tour operators
Delhi Tourism tours
Departs from **Delhi Tourism**, Baba Kharak
Singh Mg near State Govt Emporia, T011-
2336 3607, www.delhitourism.nic.in. Book
a day in advance. Check time.
Evening Tour (Tue-Sun 1830-2200):
Rajpath, India Gate, Kotla Firoz Shah, Purana
Qila, *son et lumière* (Red Fort). Rs 150.
New Delhi Tour (0900-1400): Jantar Mantar,
Qutb Minar, Lakshmi Narayan Temple, Baha'i
Temple (Safdarjang's Tomb on Mon only).
Old Delhi Tour (1415-1715): Jama Masjid,
Red Fort, Raj Ghat, Humayun's Tomb. Both
Rs 100 plus entry fees.

ITDC Tours
Guides are generally good but tours are
rushed, T011-2332 0331. Tickets booked
from **Hotel Indraprastha**, T011-2334 4511.
New Delhi Tour: departs from L-1
Connaught Circus and **Hotel Indraprastha**

(0800-1330), Rs 125 (a/c coach): Jantar Mantar, Lakshmi Narayan Temple, India Gate,Nehru Pavilion, Pragati Maidan (closed Mon), Humayun's Tomb, Qutb Minar.
Old Delhi Tour: departs Hotel Indraprastha. (1400-1700), Rs 100: Kotla Firoz Shah, Raj Ghat, Shantivana, Jama Masjid and Red Fort.

Taj Mahal tours
Many companies offer coach tours to Agra (eg ITDC, from L1 Connaught Circus, Sat-Thu 0630-2200, Rs 600, a/c coach). However, travelling by road is slow and uncomfortable; by car, allow at least 4 hrs each way. Train is a better option: either *Shatabdi* or *Taj Express*, but book early.

Walking tours
Chor Bizarre, Hotel Broadway, T011-2327 3821. Special walking tours of Old Delhi, with good lunch, 0930-1330, 1300-1630, Rs 350 each, Rs 400 for both.
Delhi Metro Walks, T(0)9811-330098, www. delhimetrowalks.com. With the charismatic Surekha Narain guiding your every step, informative heritage walks around Delhi.
Master Guest House (see Where to stay, page 51). Highly recommended walking tours for a more intimate experience.
Salaam Baalak Trust, T(0)9873-130383, www.salaambaalaktrust.com. NGO-run tours of New Delhi station and the streets around it, guided by Javed, himself a former street child. Your Rs 200 goes to support the charity's work with street children.

Tour operators
There are many operators offering tours, ticketing, reservations, etc, for travel across India. Many are around Connaught Circus, Parharganj, Rajendra Pl and Nehru Pl. Most belong to special associations (IATA, PATA) for complaints.
Ibex Expeditions, 30 Community Centre East of Kailash, New Delhi, T011-2646 0244, www.ibexexpeditions.com. Offers a wide range of tours and ticketing, all with an eco pledge. Recommended.
Kunzum Travel Café, T-49 Hauz Khaz Village, T011-2651 3949. Unusual travel centre and meeting place for travellers. Free Wi-Fi, walls lined with photos, magazines, and buzzing with people. Also hosts photography workshops and travel writing courses.
Namaste Voyages, I-Block 28G/F South City, 2 Gurgaon, 122001, T0124-221 9330, www. namastevoyages.com. Specializes in tailor-made tours, tribal, treks, theme voyages.
Paradise Holidays, 312 Ansal Classique Tower, J block, Rajouri Garden, T011-4552 0736, www.paradiseholidays.com. Value for money. Highly recommended.
Royal Expeditions, 26 Community Center (2nd floor), East of Kailash, New Delhi 110065, T011-2623 8545, www.royalexpeditions.com. Specialist staff for customized trips, knowledgeable about options for senior travellers. Owns luxury 4WD vehicles for escorted self-drive adventures in Himalaya, offers sightseeing in classic cars in Jaipur.

Shanti Travel, F-189/1A Main Rd Savitri Nagar, T011-4607 7800, www.shantitravel.com. Tailor-made tours throughout India.

☉ Transport

Air

All international flights arrive at the shiny new terminal of **Indira Gandhi International Airport**, 20 km south of Connaught Pl. Terminal 1 (Domestic) enquiries T011-2567 5126, www.newdelhiairport.in; Terminal 3 (International) T0124-377 6000. At check-in, be sure to tag your hand luggage, and make sure it is stamped after security check, otherwise you will be sent back at the gate to get it stamped.

The domestic air industry is in a period of massive growth, so check a 3rd-party site such as www.cleartrip.com or www.makemytrip.com for the latest flight schedules and prices.

The most extensive networks are with **Indian Airlines**, T140/T011-2562 2220, www.airindia.com; and **Jet Airways**, T011-3989 3333, airport T011-2567 5404, www.jetairways.com. **Indigo**, T(0)9910-383838, www.goindigo.in, has the best record for being on time etc, and **Spicejet**, T(0)9871-803333, www.spicejet.com.

For a complete list of international airline offices see *First City* magazine.

Transport to and from the airport

The **Metro** us up and running and it is now possible to travel from New Delhi train station to the airport in 20 mins. There is a booth just outside 'Arrivals' at the International and Domestic terminals for the **bus** services. It is a safe, economical option. A free **shuttle** runs between the 2 terminals every 30 mins during the day. Some hotel buses leave from the Domestic terminal. **Bus 780** runs between the airport and New Delhi Railway Station.

The International and Domestic terminals have **pre-paid taxi** counters outside the baggage hall (3 price categories) which ensure that you pay the right amount (give your name, exact destination and number of items of luggage). Most expensive are white 'DLZ' **limousines** and then white 'DLY' **luxury taxis**. Cheapest are 'DLT' **ordinary Delhi taxis** (black with yellow top Ambassador/Fiat cars and vans, often very old). 'DLY' taxis charge 3 times the DLT price. A 'Welcome' desk by the baggage reclamation offers expensive taxis only. Take your receipt to the ticket counter outside to find your taxi and give it to the driver when you reach the destination; you don't need to tip, although they will ask. From the International terminal DLT taxis charge about Rs 240 for the town centre (Connaught Pl area); night charges double 2300-0500.

Bus
Local

The city bus service run by the **Delhi Transport Corporation** (DTC) connects all important points in the city and has more than 300 routes. Information is available at www.dtc.nic.in, at DTC assistance booths and at all major bus stops. Don't be afraid to ask conductors or fellow passengers. Buses are often hopelessly overcrowded so only use off-peak.

Long distance

Delhi is linked to most major centres in North India. Services are provided by **Delhi Transport Corporation** (DTC) and State Roadways of neighbouring states from various **Inter-State Bus Termini** (ISBT). Allow at least 30 mins for buying a ticket and finding the right bus. If any of the numbers below have changed since writing check www.delhitourism.gov.in.

Kashmere Gate, north of Old Delhi, T011-2296 0290 (general enquiries), is the main terminus, with a restaurant, left luggage, bank (Mon-Fri 1000-1400; Sat 1000-1200), post office (Mon-Sat 0800-1700) and telephones (includes international calls). The following operators run services to neighbouring states from here: **Delhi**

Transport Corp, T011-2386 5181; **Haryana Roadways**, T011-2296 1262; daily to **Agra** (5-6 hrs, quicker by rail), **Chandigarh** (5 hrs), **Jaipur** (6½ hrs, again quicker by rail), **Mathura**, etc, Himachal Roadways, T011-2296 6725; twice daily to **Dharamshala** (12 hrs), **Manali** (15 hrs), **Shimla** (10 hrs), etc. J&K Roadways, T011-2332 4511; Punjab Roadways, T011-2296 7892, to **Amritsar**, **Chandigarh**, **Jammu**, **Pathankot**. UP Roadways, T011-2296 8709, city office at Ajmeri Gate, T011-2323 5367; to **Almora** (5 hrs), **Dehradun**, **Haridwar**, **Mussoorie**, **Gorakhpur**, **Kanpur**, **Jhansi**, **Lucknow**, **Nainital**, **Varanasi**.

Sarai Kale Khan Ring Rd, smaller terminal near Nizamuddin Railway Station, T011-2469 8343 (general enquiries), for buses to Haryana, Rajasthan and UP: **Haryana Roadways**, T011-2296 1262. Rajasthan Roadways, T011-2291 9537. For **Agra**, **Mathura** and **Vrindavan**; **Ajmer**; **Alwar**; **Bharatpur** (5 hrs); **Bikaner** (11 hrs); **Gwalior**; **Jaipur**; **Jodhpur**; **Pushkar**; **Udaipur**, etc.

Anand Vihar, east side of Yamuna River, T011-2215 2431, for buses to Uttar Pradesh, Uttarakhand and Himachal Pradesh.

Bikaner House, Pandara Rd (south of India Gate), T011-2338 1884; for several 'Deluxe' a/c buses to **Jaipur** (6 hrs, Rs 300); ask for 'direct' bus (some buses stop at Amber for a tour of the fort). Also to **Udaipur** via **Ajmer**, and to **Jodhpur**.

HPTDC, Chandralok Bldg, 36 Janpath, T011-2332 5320, hptdcdelhi@hub.nic.in, runs a/c Volvo and Sleeper buses to **Manali** and **Dharamshala**. Of the myriad private bus operators, **Raj National Express** has by far the best buses, and highest prices.

Car hire
The main roads out of Delhi are very heavily congested; the best time to leave is in the very early morning.

Hiring a car is an excellent way of getting about town either for sightseeing or if you have several journeys to make.

Full day local use with driver (non a/c) Rs 900 and for (a/c) is about Rs 13-1600, 80 km/8 hrs, driver overnight *bata* Rs 150 per day; to Jaipur, about Rs 6 to 8000 depending on size of car. The Government of India tourist office (see page 28), 88 Janpath, has a list of approved agents. We highly recommend **Metropole**, see below.

Cozy Travels, N1 BMC House, Middle Circle, Connaught Pl, T011-4359 4359, cozytravels@vsnl.net.com.

Metropole Tourist Service, 224 Defence Colony Flyover Market (Jangpura side), New Delhi, T011-2431 2212, T(0)9810-277699, www.metrovista.co.in. Car/jeep (US$45-70 per day), safe, reliable and recommended, also hotel bookings and can help arrange homestays around Delhi. Highly recommended.

Metro
The sparkling new Metro system (T011-2436 5202, www.delhimetrorail.com) is set to revolutionize transport within Delhi. For travellers, the yellow line is the most useful as it stops Chandni Chowk, Connaught Pl and Qutb Minar. The blue line connects to Parhaganj; the violet line runs to Khan Market; and the orange line links the airport with New Delhi train station.
Line 1 (Red) Running northwest to east, of limited use to visitors; from Rithala to Dilshad Garden.
Line 2 (Yellow) Running north–south through the centre from Jahangipuri to Huda City via Kashmere Gate, Chandni Chowk, New Delhi Station, Connaught Pl (Rajiv Chowk), Hauz Khaz, Qutb Minar and Saket – probably the most useful line for visitors.
Line 3 (Blue) From Dwarka 21 to Vaishall or City Centre (splits after Yamuna Bank) Intersecting with Line 2 at Rajiv Chowk and running west through Paharganj (RK Ashram station) and Karol Bagh.
Line 4 (Orange) Just 4 stations for now including I.G.I Airport to New Delhi Train Station.

Line 5 (Green) From Mundka to Inderlok.
Line 6 (Violet) From Central Secretariat to Badarpur, including Khan Market and Lajpat Nagar. Useful.

Trains run 0600-2200. Fares are charged by distance: tokens for individual journeys cost Rs 6-19. **Smart Cards**, Rs 100, Rs 200 and Rs 500, save queuing and money. **Tourist Cards** valid for 1 or 3 days (Rs 70/200) are useful if you plan to make many journeys. Luggage is limited to 15 kg; guards may not allow big backpacks on board. Look out for the women-only carriages at the front of each train, clearly marked in pink. For an insight into the construction of the Metro, there is a Metro museum at **Patel Chowk** on the yellow line.

Motorcycle hire
Chawla Motorcycles, 1770, Shri Kissan Dass Marg, Naiwali Gali, T(0)9811-888918. Very reliable, trustworthy, highly recommended for restoring classic bikes.
Ess Aar Motors, Jhandewalan Extn, west of Paharganj, T011-2367 8836, www.ess aarmotors.com. Recommended for buying Enfields, very helpful.

For scooter rentals try **U Ride**, T(0)9711-701932, find them on facebook.

Rickshaw
Auto-rickshaws Widely available at about half the cost of taxis. Normal capacity for foreigners is 2 people (3rd person extra); the new fare system is encouraging rickshaw wallahs to use the meter. Expect to pay Rs 30 for the shortest journeys. Allow Rs 150 for 2 hrs' sightseeing/shopping. It is best to walk away from hotels and tourist centres to look for an auto.
Cycle-rickshaws Available in the Old City. Be prepared to bargain. They are not allowed into Connaught Pl.

Taxi
Yellow-top taxis, which run on compressed natural gas, are readily available at taxi stands or you can hail one on the road. Meters

should start at Rs 13; ask for the conversion card. Add 25% at night (2300-0500) plus Rs 5 for each piece of luggage over 20 kg.
Easy Cabs, T011-4343 4343. Runs clean a/c cars and claim to pick up anywhere within 15 mins; Rs 20 per km (night Rs 25 per km). Waiting charges Rs 50/30 mins.

Train
Delhi stations from which trains originate have codes: **OD** – Old Delhi, **ND** – New Delhi, **HN** – Hazrat Nizamuddin, **DSR** – Delhi Sarai Rohilla. The publication *Trains at a Glance'* (Rs 30) lists important trains across India, available at some stations, book shops and newsagents,

New Delhi Railway Station and
Hazrat Nizamuddin Station (500 m north and 5 km southeast of Connaught Pl respectively) connect Delhi with most major destinations. The latter has many important southbound trains. **Old Delhi Station**, 6 km north of the centre, has broad and metre-gauge trains. **Delhi Sarai Rohilla**, northeast of CP, serves Rajasthan.

Train enquiries T131. Reservations T1330. Each station has a computerized reservation counter where you can book any Mail or Express train in India.

International Tourist Bureau (ITB), 1st floor, Main Building, New Delhi Station, T011-2340 5156, Mon-Fri 0930-1630, Sat 0930-1430, provides assistance with planning and booking journeys, for foreigners only; efficient and helpful if slow. You need your passport; pay in US$, or rupees (with an encashment certificate/ ATM receipt). Those with **Indrail** passes should confirm bookings here. At the time of writing the station was under renovation, so the layout may change, but be wary of rickshaw drivers/travel agents who tell you the ITB has closed or moved elsewhere. (There are also counters for foreigners and NRIs at **Delhi Tourism**, N-36 Connaught Pl, 1000-1700, Mon-Sat, and at the airport; quick and efficient.)

New Delhi and Hazrat Nizamuddin stations have pre-paid taxi and rickshaw counters with official rates per km posted: expect to pay around Rs 25 for 1st km, Rs 8 each km after. Authorized *coolies* (porters), wear red shirts and white *dhotis;* agree the charge, there is an official rate, before engaging one. For left luggage, you need a secure lock and chain.

Some principal services are: **Agra**: *Shatabdi Exp 12002,* ND, 0600, 2 hrs; *Taj Exp 12280,* HN, 0710, 2¾ hrs. **Ahmedabad**: *Rajdhani Exp 12958, ND, 1935,* 14½ hrs. **Amritsar**: *Shatabdi Exp 12013,* ND, 1630, 6 hrs; *New Delhi-Amritsar Exp 12459,* ND, 1340, 8 hrs; *Shan-e-Punjab Exp 12497,* ND, 0650, 7½ hrs. **Bengaluru (Bangalore)**: *Ktk Smprk K Exp 12650,* Mon, Tue, Sat, Sun, HN, 0645, 36 hrs; **Chandigarh**: *Shatabdi Exp 12011,* ND, 0740, 3½ hrs; *Shatabdi Exp 12005,* ND, 1715, 3 hrs. **Chennai**: *GT Exp 12616,* ND, 1840, 35¼ hrs; *Tamil Nadu Exp 12622,* ND, 2230, 33½ hrs. **Dehradun**: *Shatabdi Exp 12017,* ND, 0655, 5¾ hrs same train stops at **Haridwar**. **Jaipur**: *Shatabdi Exp 12015,* Jp Double Dcker 12986, DSR, 1735, 4½ hrs goes onto **Ajmer Jhansi**: *Shatabdi Exp 12002,* ND, 0600, 4½ hrs; *Lakshadweep Exp 12618,* HN, 0920, 6 hrs. **Jodhpur**: *Mandore Exp 12461,* OD, 2115, 1½ hrs. **Kolkata**: *Rajdhani Exp 12314,* ND, 1630, 17½ hrs. **Madgaon** (Goa): *Mngla Lksdp Exp 12618,* HN, 0920, 35 hrs, goes onto **Ernakulum**. **Mumbai (Central)**: *Rajdhani Exp 12954,* ND, 1655, 17½ hrs; *Golden Temple Mail 12904,* ND, 0750, 22 hrs. **Udaipur**: *Mewar Exp 12963,* HN, 1900, 12 hrs; *Chetak Exp 12981,* DSR, 1940,12 hrs. **Varanasi**: *Swatantrta S Ex 12562,* ND, 2040, 12 hrs.

For special diesel *Palace on Wheels* and other tours, see page 8.

see page 8.

● Directory

Delhi *p26, maps p30, p36 and p41*
Embassies and consulates Most are in the diplomatic enclave/Chanakyapuri. **Australia**, 1/50-G Shantipath, T011-4139 9900. **Canada**, 7-8 Shantipath, T011-4178 2000. **France**, 2/50-E Shantipath, T011-2419 6100. **Ireland**, 230 Jor Bagh, T011-2462 6733. **New Zealand**, 50-N Nyaya Marg, T011-688 3170. **South Africa**, B/18 Vasant Marg, T011-2614 4911. **UK**, Shantipath, T011-2419 2100. **USA**, Shantipath, T011-2419 8000.
Medical services Ambulance (24 hrs): T102. **Hospitals**: Embassies and high commissions have lists of recommended doctors and dentists. Doctors approved by IAMAT (International Association for Medical Assistance to Travellers) are listed in a directory. Casualty and emergency wards in both private and government hospitals are open 24 hrs. Ram Manohar Lohia, Willingdon Crescent, T011-2336 5525, 24-hr A&E. Bara Hindu Rao, Sabzi Mandi, T011-2391 9476. JP Narayan, J Nehru Marg, Delhi Gate, T011-2323 2400. Safdarjang General, Sri Aurobindo Marg, T011-2616 5060. S Kripalani, Panchkuin Rd, T011-2336 3728. Chemists: Many hospitals have 24-hr services: Hindu Rao Hospital, Sabzi Mandi; Ram Manohar Lohia Hospital, Willingdon Crescent; S Kripalani Hospital, Panchkuin Rd. In Connaught Pl: Nath Brothers, G-2, off Marina Arcade; Chernico, H-45. **Post** Head post offices at Sansad Marg, Mon-Sat 1000-1830, Eastern Court, Janpath, 24 hrs, Connaught Pl, A-Block, Mon-Sat 1000-1700 (parcel packing service outside). New Delhi GPO at Ashoka Pl, southwest of Connaught Pl, 24 hrs, **Useful contacts** Fire: T101. Foreigners' Registration Office: East Block-VIII, Level 2, Sector 1, RK Puram, T011-2671 1443. Police: T100.

Agra and around

The romance of what is arguably the world's most famous building still astonishes in its power. In addition to the Taj Mahal, Agra also boasts the great monuments of the Red Fort and the I'timad-ud-Daulah, but to experience their beauty you have to endure the less attractive sides of one of India's least prepossessing towns. A big industrial city, the monuments are often covered in a haze of polluted air, while visitors may be subjected to a barrage of high-power selling. Despite it all, the experience is unmissable. The city is also the convenient gateway to the wonderful, abandoned capital of Fatehpur Sikri, the beautifully serene Akbar's Mauseuleum and some of Hinduism's most holy sites.

Arriving in Agra

Getting there By far the best way to arrive is on the *Shatabdi Express* train from Delhi, which is much faster than travelling by car and infinitely more comfortable than the frequent 'express' buses, which can take five tiring hours.

Getting around Buses run a regular service between the station, bus stands and the main sites. See Entrances, page 69. Cycle-rickshaws, autos and taxis can be hired to venture further afield, or hire a bike if it's not too hot. ▸▸ *See Transport, page 82.*

Tourist information Government of India tourist office ① *191 The Mall, T0562-222 6378, guides available (Rs 100)*, helpful and friendly. **UPTDC** ① *64 Taj Rd, T0562-236 3377, also at Agra Cantt, T0562-242 1204*, and **Tourist Bungalow** ① *Raja-ki-Mandi, T0562-285 0120*. **UP Tours** ① *Taj Khema, Taj East Gate, T0562-233 0140*.
　　Note that there is an **Agra Development Authority Tax** of Rs 500 levied on each day you visit the Taj Mahal, which includes the Red Fort, Fatehpur Sikri and other attractions. This is in addition to the individual entry fees to the monuments.

Climate The best time to visit is between November and March.

Background

With minor interruptions Agra alternated with Delhi as the capital of the Mughal Empire. **Sikander Lodi** seized it from a rebellious governor and made it his capital in 1501. He died in Agra but is buried in Delhi (see page 43). Agra was Babur's capital. He is believed to have laid out a pleasure garden on the east bank of the River Yamuna and his son Humayun built a mosque here in 1530. **Akbar** lived in Agra in the early years of his reign. Ralph Fitch, the English Elizabethan traveller, described a "magnificent city, with broad streets and tall buildings". He also saw Akbar's new capital at Fatehpur Sikri, 40 km west, describing a route lined all the way with stalls and markets. Akbar moved his capital again to Lahore, before returning to Agra in 1599, where he spent the last six years of his life. **Jahangir** left Agra for Kashmir in 1618 and never returned. Despite modifying the Red Fort and building the Taj Mahal, **Shah Jahan** also moved away in 1638 to his new city Shah Jahanabad in Delhi, though he returned in 1650, taken prisoner by his son Aurangzeb and left to spend his last days in the Red Fort. It was **Aurangzeb**, the last of the Great Mughals, who moved the seat of government permanently to Delhi. In the 18th century Agra suffered at the hands of the Jats, was taken, lost and retaken by the Marathas who, in turn, were ousted by the British in 1803. It was the centre of much fighting in the 'Uprising' and was the administrative centre of the Northwest Provinces and Oudh until that too was transferred to Allahabad in 1877.

Taj Mahal → For listings, see pages 80-82.

ⓘ *Sat-Thu sunrise to sunset (last entry 1700), foreigners Rs 750 (including Development Tax), Indians Rs 20, cash only, includes still camera, video cameras, tripods, other electronic items eg mobile phones not allowed, lockers at East and West Gates Rs 1. No photos inside the tomb (instant fines). Allow at least 1 hr. Full moon viewing 2 nights either side of full moon (see www.stardate.org/nightsky/moon for full moon dates), 2030-0030, separate entry fee of foreigners Rs 750, Indians Rs 510, book tickets day before at Architectural Survey of India, 22 The Mall, T0562-222 7261. The Archaeological Survey of India explicitly asks visitors not to make donations to anyone including custodians in the tomb.*

Of all the world's great monuments, the Taj Mahal is one of the most written about, photographed, televized and talked about. To India's Nobel Laureate poet, Tagore, the Taj was a "tear drop on the face of humanity", a building to echo the cry "I have not forgotten, I have not forgotten, O beloved" and its mesmerizing power is such that despite the hype, no one comes away disappointed.

Shah Jahan, the fifth of the Great Mughals, was so devoted to his favourite wife, Mumtaz Mahal (Jewel of the Palace) that he could not bear to be parted from her and insisted that she always travel with him, in all states of health. While accompanying him on a military campaign, she died at the age of 39 giving birth to their 14th child. On her deathbed, it is said, she asked the emperor to show the world how much they loved one another.

The grief-stricken emperor went into mourning for two years. He turned away from the business of running the empire and dedicated himself to architecture, resolving to build his wife the most magnificent memorial on earth. On the right bank of the River Yamuna in full view of his fortress palace, it was to be known as the Taj-i-Mahal (Crown of the Palace).

According to the French traveller Tavnier, work on the Taj commenced in 1632 and took 22 years to complete, employing a workforce of 20,000. The red sandstone was available locally but the white marble was quarried at Makrana in Rajasthan and transported 300 km by a fleet of 1000 elephants. Semi-precious stones for the inlay came from far and wide: red carnelian from Baghdad; red, yellow and brown jasper from the Punjab; green jade and crystal from China; blue lapis lazuli from Ceylon and Afghanistan; turquoise from Tibet; chrysolite from Egypt; amethyst from Persia; agates from the Yemen; dark green malachite from Russia; diamonds from Central India and mother-of-pearl from the Indian Ocean. A 3-km ramp was used to lift material up to the dome and, because of the sheer weight of the building; boreholes were filled with metal coins and fragments to provide suitable foundations. The resemblance of the exquisite double dome to a huge pearl is not coincidental; a saying of the Prophet describes the throne of God as a dome of white pearl supported by white pillars.

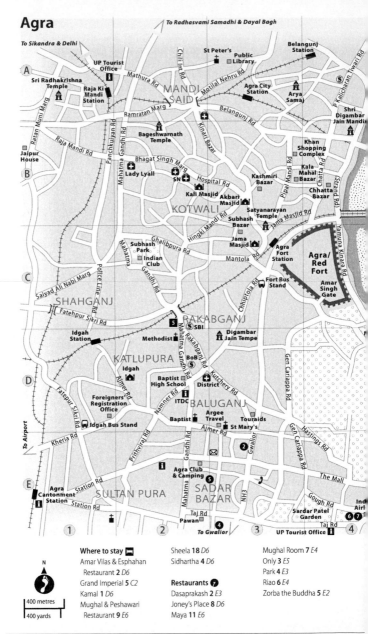

Agra

To Radhasvami Samadhi & Dayal Bagh

To Sikandra & Delhi

A

- UP Tourist Office
- Sri Radhakrishna Temple
- Raja Ki Mandi Station
- Mathura Rd
- Chhipi Rd
- St Peter's
- Public Library
- Motilal Nehru Rd
- MANDI SAID
- Agra City Station
- Arya Samaj
- Belangunj Station
- Shri Digambar Jain Mandir

B

- Ratan Muni Marg
- Jaipur House
- Raja Mandi Rd
- Panchkuyan Rd
- Mahatma Gandhi Rd
- Ramratan Marg
- Bageshwarnath Temple
- Bhagat Singh Marg
- Lady Lyall
- SN
- Belangunj Rd
- Kinari Bazar
- Hospital Rd
- Kali Masjid
- Akbari Masjid
- Kashmiri Bazar
- Khan Shopping Complex
- Kala Mahal Bazar
- Chhatta Rd
- Strand Rd
- Chhatta Bazar
- Pipal Mandi Rd

KOTWALI

- Satyanarayan Temple
- Subhash Bazar
- Jama Masjid Rd
- Hingki Mandi Rd

C

- Saiyad Ali Nabi Marg
- Police Line
- Mahatma Gandhi Rd
- SHAHGANJ
- Fatehpur Sikri Rd
- Subhash Park
- Indian Club
- Ghalibpura Rd
- Jama Masjid
- Mantola
- Chhipitola Rd
- Fort Bus Stand
- Agra Fort Station
- Agra/Red Fort
- Yamuna Kinara Rd
- Amar Singh Gate

D

- To Airport
- Kheria Rd
- Fatepur Sikri Rd
- Idgah Station
- KATLUPURA
- Idgah
- Ajmer Rd
- Foreigners Registration Office
- Idgah Bus Stand
- Namner Rd
- Baptist High School
- District
- Baptist
- Prithviraj Rd
- Mahatma Gandhi Rd
- RAKABGANJ
- SBI
- Methodist
- BoB
- Digambar Jain Tempe
- Kutchery Rd
- BALUGANJ
- Argee Travel
- St Mary's
- Touraids
- Ajmer Rd
- Gwalior
- Gen Cariappa Rd
- Hastings Rd

E

- To Gwalior
- Agra Cantonment Station
- Station Rd
- SULTAN PURA
- Pawan
- Taj Rd
- Agra Club & Camping
- SADAR BAZAR
- NH3
- The Mall
- Gough Rd
- Sardar Patel Garden
- Indi Airli
- UP Tourist Office

1 2 3 4

N
400 metres
400 yards

Where to stay
Amar Vilas & Esphahan Restaurant 2 *D6*
Grand Imperial 5 *C2*
Kamal 1 *D6*
Mughal & Peshawari Restaurant 9 *E6*

Sheela 18 *D6*
Sidhartha 4 *D6*

Restaurants
Dasaprakash 2 *E3*
Joney's Place 8 *D6*
Maya 11 *E6*

Mughal Room 7 *E4*
Only 3 *E5*
Park 4 *E3*
Riao 6 *E4*
Zorba the Buddha 5 *E2*

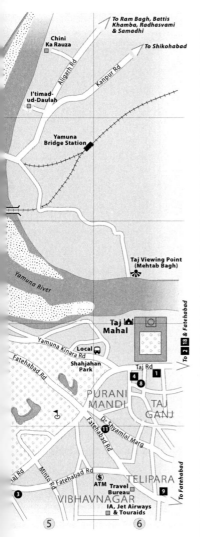

Myths and controversy surround the Taj Mahal. On its completion it is said that the emperor ordered the chief mason's right hand to be cut off to prevent him from repeating his masterpiece. Another legend suggests that Shah Jahan intended to build a replica for himself in black marble on the other side of the river, connected to the Taj Mahal by a bridge built with alternate blocks of black and white marble. Some have asserted that architects responsible for designing this mausoleum must have come from Turkey, Persia or even Europe (because of the pietra dura work on the tomb). In fact, no one knows who drew the plans. What is certain is that in the Taj Mahal, the traditions of Indian Hindu and Persian Muslim architecture were fused together into a completely distinct and perfect art form.

Viewing

The white marble of the Taj is extraordinarily luminescent and even on dull days seems bright. The whole building appears to change its hue according to the light in the sky. In winter (December to February), it is worth being there at sunrise. Then the mists that often lie over the River Yamuna lift as the sun rises and casts its golden rays over the pearl-white tomb. Beautifully lit in the soft light, the Taj appears to float on air. At sunset, the view from across the river is equally wonderful.

Entrances

To reduce damage to the marble by the polluted atmosphere, local industries now have to comply with strict rules, and vehicles emitting noxious fumes are not allowed within 2 km of the monument. Visitors are increasingly using horse-drawn carriages or walking. You can approach the Taj from three directions. The western entrance is usually used by those arriving from the fort and is an easy 10-minute walk along a pleasant garden road. At the eastern entrance, rickshaws and camel drivers offer to take visitors to the gate for up to Rs 100 each; however, an official battery bus ferries visitors from the car park to the gate for a small fee.

The approach

In the unique beauty of the Taj, subtlety is blended with grandeur and a massive overall design is matched with immaculately intricate execution. You will already have seen the dome of the tomb in the distance, looking almost like a miniature, but as you go into the open square, the Taj itself is so well hidden that you almost wonder where it can be. The glorious surprise is kept until the last moment, for wholly concealing it is the massive red sandstone gateway of the entrance, symbolizing the divide between the secular world and paradise.

The gateway was completed in 1648, though the huge brass door is recent. The original doors (plundered by the Jats) were solid silver and decorated with 1100 nails whose heads were contemporary silver coins. Although the gateway is remarkable in itself, one of its functions is to prevent you getting any glimpse of the tomb inside until you are right in the doorway itself. From here only the tomb is visible, stunning in its nearness, but as you move forward the minarets come into view.

The garden

The Taj garden, well kept though it is, is nothing compared with its former glory. The guiding principle is one of symmetry. The *char bagh*, separated by the watercourses (rivers of heaven) originating from the central, raised pool, were divided into 16 flower beds, making a total of 64. The trees, all carefully planted to maintain the symmetry, were either cypress (signifying death) or fruit trees (life). The channels were stocked with colourful fish and the gardens with beautiful birds. It is well worth wandering along the side avenues for not only is it much more peaceful but also good for framing photos of the tomb with foliage. You may see bullocks pulling the lawnmowers around.

The mosque and its jawab

On the east and west sides of the tomb are identical red sandstone buildings. On the west (left-hand side) is a mosque. It is common in Islam to build one next to a tomb. It sanctifies the area and provides a place for worship. The replica on the other side is known as the **Jawab** (answer). This can't be used for prayer as it faces away from Mecca.

The tomb

There is only one point of access to the **plinth** and tomb, where shoes must be removed (socks can be kept on; remember the white marble gets very hot) or cloth overshoes worn (Rs 2, though strictly free).

The **tomb** is square with bevelled corners. At each corner smaller domes rise while in the centre is the main dome topped by a brass finial. The dome is actually a double dome and this device, Central Asian in origin, was used to gain height. The resemblance of the dome to a huge pearl is not coincidental. The exterior ornamentation is calligraphy (verses of the Koran), beautifully carved panels in bas relief and superb inlay work.

The **interior** of the mausoleum comprises a lofty central chamber, a *maqbara* (crypt) immediately below this, and four octagonal corner rooms. The central chamber contains replica tombs, the real ones being in the crypt. The public tomb was originally surrounded by a jewel-encrusted silver screen. Aurangzeb removed this, fearing it might be stolen, and replaced it with an octagonal screen of marble carved from one block of marble and inlaid with precious stones. It is an incredible piece of workmanship. This chamber is open at sunrise, but may close during the day.

Above the tombs is a **Cairene lamp** whose flame is supposed never to go out. This one was given by Lord Curzon, Governor General of India (1899-1905), to replace the original which was stolen by Jats. The tomb of Mumtaz with the 'female' slate, rests immediately beneath the dome. If you look from behind it, you can see how it lines up centrally with the main entrance. Shah Jahan's tomb is larger and to the side, marked by a 'male' pen-box, the sign of a cultured or noble person. Not originally intended to be placed there but squeezed in by Aurangzeb, this flaws the otherwise perfect symmetry of the whole complex. Finally, the acoustics of the building are superb, the domed ceiling being designed to echo chants from the Koran and musicians' melodies.

The **museum** ① *above the entrance, Sat-Thu 1000-1700,* has a small collection of Mughal memorabilia, photographs and miniatures of the Taj through the ages but has no textual information. Sadly, the lights do not always work.

Agra Fort (Red Fort) → *For listings, see pages 80-82.*

① *0600-1800, foreigners Rs 300 (Rs 250 if you've been to the Taj on the same day), Indians Rs 15, video Rs 25; allow a minimum of 1½ hours for a visit. The best route round is to start with the building on your right before going through the gate at the top of the broad 100 m ramp; the gentle incline made it suitable for elephants.*

On the west bank of the River Yamuna, Akbar's magnificent fort dominates the centre of the city. Akbar erected the walls and gates and the first buildings inside. **Shah Jahan** built the impressive imperial quarters and mosque, while Aurangzeb added the outer ramparts. The outer walls, just over 20 m high and faced with red sandstone, tower above the outer moat. The fort is crescent-shaped with a long, nearly straight wall facing the river, punctuated at regular intervals by bastions. The main entrance used to be in the centre of the west wall, the **Delhi Gate**, facing the bazar. It led to the Jami Masjid in the city but is now permanently closed. You can only enter now from the **Amar Singh Gate** in the south. Although only the southern third of the fort is open to the public, this includes nearly all the buildings of interest. At the gate you will have to contend with vendors of cheap soapstone boxes and knick-knacks. If you want to buy something, bargain hard. Guides will offer their services – most are not particularly good.

Fortifications

The fortifications tower above the 9-m-wide, 10-m-deep moat (still evident but containing stagnant water) formerly filled with water from the Yamuna River. There is an outer wall on the riverside and an imposing 22-m-high inner main wall, giving a feeling of great defensive power. Although it served as a model for Shah Jahan's Red Fort in Delhi, its own model was the Rajput Fort built by Raja Man Singh Tomar of Gwalior in 1500. If an aggressor managed to get through the outer gate they would have to make a right-hand turn and thereby expose their flank to the defenders on the inner wall. The inner gate is solidly powerful but has been attractively decorated with tiles. The similarities with Islamic patterns of the tilework are obvious, though the Persian blue was also used in the Gwalior Fort and may well have been imitated from that example. The incline up to this point and beyond was suitable for elephants and as you walk past the last gate and up the broad brick-lined ramp with ridged slabs, it is easy to imagine arriving on elephant back. At the top of this 100-m ramp is a gate with a map and description board on your left.

Jahangiri Mahal Despite its name, this was built by Akbar (circa 1570) as women's quarters. It is all that survives of his original palace buildings. In front is a large **stone bowl**, with steps both inside and outside, which was probably filled with fragrant rose water for bathing. Almost 75 m sq, the palace has a simple stone exterior. Tillotson has pointed out that the blind arcade of pointed arches inlaid with white marble which decorate the façade is copied from 14th-century monuments of the Khaljis and Tughluqs in Delhi. He notes that they are complemented by some features derived from Hindu architecture, including the *jarokhas* (balconies) protruding from the central section, the sloping dripstone in place of *chajja* (eaves) along the top of the façade, and the domed *chhattris* at its ends. The presence of distinctively Hindu features does not indicate a synthesis of architectural styles at this early stage of Mughal architecture, as can be seen much more clearly from inside the Jahangiri Mahal. Here most of the features are straightforwardly Hindu; square-headed arches and extraordinarily carved capitals and brackets illustrate the vivid work of local Hindu craftsmen employed by Akbar without any attempt either to curb their enthusiasm for florid decoration and mythical animals nor to produce a fusion of Hindu and Islamic ideas. Tillotson argues that the central courtyard is essentially Hindu, in significant contrast with most earlier Indo-Islamic buildings. In these, an Islamic scheme was modified by Hindu touches. He suggests, therefore, that the Jahangiri Mahal marks the start of a more fundamental kind of Hinduization, typical of several projects during Akbar's middle period of rule, including the palace complex in Fatehpur Sikri. However, it did not represent a real fusion of ideas – something that only came under Shah Jahan – simply a juxtaposition of sharply contrasting styles.

Jodh Bai's Palace On the south side, this is named after one of Jahangir's wives. On the east the hall court leads onto a more open yard by the inner wall of the fort. In contrast to other palaces in the fort, this is quite simple. Through the slits in the wall you can see the Taj.

Shah Jahan's palace buildings
Turn left through to Shah Jahan's Khas Mahal (1636). The open tower allows you to view the walls and see to your left the decorated Mussaman Burj tower. The use of white marble transforms the atmosphere, contributing to the new sense of grace and light.

Anguri Bagh (Vine Garden) The formal, 85-m-sq, geometric gardens are on the left. In Shah Jahan's time the geometric patterns were enhanced by decorative flower beds. In the middle of the white marble platform wall in front is a decorative water slide. From the pool with its bays for seating and its fountains, water would drain off along channels decorated to mimic a stream. The surface was scalloped to produce a rippling waterfall, or inlaid to create a shimmering stream bed. Behind vertical water drops, there are little cusped arch niches into which flowers would be placed during the day and lamps at night. The effect was magical.

Golden Pavilions The curved *chala* roofs of the small pavilions by the Khas Mahal are based on the roof shape of Bengali village huts constructed out of curved bamboo, designed to keep off heavy rain. The shape was first expressed in stone by the Sultans of Bengal. Originally gilded, these were probably ladies' bedrooms, with hiding places for jewellery in the walls. These pavilions are traditionally associated with Shah Jahan's daughters, Roshanara and Jahanara.

Khas Mahal This was the model for the Diwan-i-Khas at the Red Fort in Delhi. Some of the original interior decoration has been restored (1895) and gives an impression of how splendid the painted ceiling must have been. The metal rings were probably used for *punkhas*. Underneath are cool rooms used to escape the summer heat. The Khas Mahal illustrates Shahs' original architectural contribution.

The buildings retain distinctively Islamic Persian features – the geometrical planning of the pavilions and the formal layout of the gardens, for example. Tillotson points out that here "Hindu motifs are treated in a new manner, which is less directly imitative of the Hindu antecedents. The temple columns and corbel capitals have been stripped of their rich carving and turned into simpler, smoother forms ... the *chhattris* have Islamic domes. Through these subtle changes the indigenous motifs have lost their specifically Hindu identity; they therefore contrast less strongly with the Islamic components, and are bound with them into a new style. The unity is assisted by the use of the cusped arch and the *Bangladar* roof". Seen in this light, the Khas Mahal achieves a true synthesis which eluded Akbar's designs.

Mussaman Burj On the left of the Khas Mahal is the Mussaman Burj (Octagonal Tower, though sometimes corrupted into Saman Burj, then translated as Jasmine Tower). It is a beautiful octagonal tower with an open pavilion. With its openness, elevation and the benefit of cooling evening breezes blowing in off the Yamuna River, this could well have been used as the emperor's bedroom. It has been suggested that this is where Shah Jahan lay on his deathbed, gazing at the Taj. Access to this tower is through a magnificently decorated and intimate apartment with a scalloped fountain in the centre. The inlay work here is exquisite, especially above the pillars. In front of the fountain is a sunken courtyard which could be filled by water carriers, to work the fountains in the pool.

Sheesh Mahal (Mirror Palace) Here are further examples of decorative water engineering in the *hammams*; the water here may have been warmed by lamps. The mirrors, which were more precious than marble, were set into the walls, often specially chiselled to accommodate their crooked shape. The defensive qualities of the site and the fortifications are obvious. In the area between the outer rampart and the inner wall gladiatorial battles were staged pitting man against tiger, or elephant against elephant. The tower was the emperor's grandstand seat.

Diwan-i-Khas (Hall of Private Audience, 1637) This is next to the Mussaman Burj, approached on this route by a staircase which brings you out at the side. The interior of the Diwan-i-Khas, a three-sided pavilion with a terrace of fine proportions, would have been richly decorated with tapestries and carpets. The double columns in marble inlaid with semi-precious stones in delightful floral patterns in pietra dura have finely carved capitals.

Terrace and Machhi Bhavan
In front of the Diwan-i-Khas are two throne 'platforms' on a **terrace**. Gascoigne recounts how Shah Jahan tried to trick a haughty Persian ambassador into bowing low as he approached the throne by erecting a fence with a small wicket gate so that his visitor would have to enter on hands and knees. The ambassador did so, but entered backwards, thus presenting his bottom first to the Emperor. The **black marble throne** at the rear of the terrace was used by Jahangir when claiming to be Emperor at Allahabad. The emperor sat on the white marble platform facing the **Machhi Bhavan** (Fish Enclosure), which once contained pools and fountains, waiting to meet visiting dignitaries.

Diwan-i-Am Go down an internal staircase and you enter the Diwan-i-Am from the side. The clever positioning of the pillars gives the visitor arriving through the gates in the right- and left-hand walls of the courtyard an uninterrupted view of the throne. On the back wall of the pavilion are *jali* screens to enable the women of the court to watch without being seen. The open-sided, cusped arched hall built of plaster on red stone, is very impressive. The throne alcove of richly decorated white marble completed in 1634 after seven years' work used to house the Peacock Throne. Its decoration made it extraordinary: "the canopy was carved in enamel work and studded with individual gems, its interior was thickly encrusted with rubies, garnets and diamonds, and it was supported on 12 emerald covered columns" writes Tillotson. When Shah Jahan moved his capital to Delhi he took the throne with him to the Red Fort, only for it to be taken back to Persia as loot by Nadir Shah in 1739.

Nagina Masjid From the corner opposite the Diwan-i-Khas two doorways lead to a view over the small courtyards of the *zenana* (harem). Further round in the next corner is the Nagina Masjid. Shoes must be removed at the doorway. Built by Shah Jahan, this was the private mosque of the ladies of the court. Beneath it was a *mina* bazar for the ladies to make purchases from the marble balcony above. Looking out of the Diwan-i-Am you can see the domes of the **Moti Masjid** (Pearl Mosque, 1646-1653), an extremely fine building closed to visitors because of structural problems. Opposite the Diwan-i-Am are the barracks and **Mina Bazar**, also closed to the public. In the paved area in front of the Diwan-i-Am is a large well and the **tomb of Mr John Russell Colvin**, the Lieutenant Governor of the Northwest Provinces who died here during the 1857 'Uprising'. Stylistically it is sadly out of place. The yellow buildings date from the British period.

Jama Masjid
The mosque built in 1648, near the fort railway, no longer connected to the fort, is attributed to Shah Jahan's dutiful elder daughter Jahanara. In need of repair and not comparable to buildings within the fort, its symmetry has suffered since a small minaret fell in the 1980s. The fine marble steps and bold geometric patterns on the domes are quite striking.

I'timad-ud-Daulah and Sikandra → *For listings, see pages 80-82.*

I'timad-ud-Daulah
① *Sunrise-sunset, foreigners Rs 100 plus Rs 10 tax, Indians Rs 10, video Rs 25.*
The tomb of I'timad-ud-Daulah (or 'Baby Taj'), set a startling precedent as the first Mughal building to be faced with white marble inlaid with contrasting stones. Unlike the Taj it is small, intimate and has a gentle serenity, but is just as ornate. The tomb was built for **Ghiyas Beg**, a Persian who had obtained service in Akbar's court, and his wife. On Jahangir's succession in 1605 he became *Wazir* (chief minister). Jahangir fell in love with his daughter, **Mehrunissa**, who at the time was married to a Persian. When her husband died in 1607, she entered Jahangir's court as a lady-in-waiting. Four years later Jahangir married her. Thereafter she was known first as **Nur Mahal** (Light of the Palace), later being promoted to **Nur Jahan** (Light of the World). Her niece Mumtaz married Shah Jahan.

Nur Jahan built the tomb for her father in the *char bagh* that he himself had laid out. It is beautifully conceived in white marble, mosaic and lattice. There is a good view from the roof of the entrance. Marble screens of geometric lattice work permit soft lighting of the inner chamber. The yellow marble caskets appear to have been carved out of wood. On the engraved walls of the chamber is the recurring theme of a wine flask with snakes as handles – perhaps a reference by Nur Jahan, the tomb's creator, to her husband Jahangir's excessive drinking. Stylistically, the tomb marks a change from the sturdy and masculine buildings of Akbar's reign to softer, more feminine lines. The main chamber, richly decorated in pietra dura with mosaics and semi-precious stones inlaid in the white marble, contains the tomb of I'timad-ud-Daulah (Pillar of the Goverment) and his wife. Some have argued that the concept and skill must have travelled from its European home of 16th-century Florence to India. However, Florentine pietra dura is figurative whereas the Indian version is essentially decorative and can be seen as a refinement of its Indian predecessor, the patterned mosaic.

Sikandra (Akbar's Mausoleum)

ⓘ *Sunrise-sunset, foreigners Rs 100, Indians Rs 10, includes camera, video Rs 25. Morning is the quietest time to visit.*

Following the Timurid tradition, Akbar (ruled 1556-1605) had started to build his own tomb at Sikandra. He died during its construction and his son **Jahangir** completed it in 1613. The result is an impressive, large but architecturally confused tomb. A huge gateway, the **Buland Darwaza**, leads to the great garden enclosure, where spotted deer run free on the immaculate lawns. The decoration on the gateway is strikingly bold, with its large mosaic patterns, a forerunner of the pietra dura technique. The white minarets atop the entrance were an innovation which reappear, almost unchanged, at the Taj Mahal. The walled garden enclosure is laid out in the *char bagh* style, with the mausoleum at the centre.

A broad paved path leads to the 22.5-m-high tomb with four storeys. The lowest storey, nearly 100 m sq and 9 m high, contains massive cloisters. The entrance on the south side leads to the tomb chamber. Shoes must be removed or cloth overshoes worn (hire Rs 2). In a niche opposite the entrance is an alabaster tablet inscribed with the 99 divine names of Allah. The sepulchre is in the centre of the room, whose velvety darkness is pierced by a single slanting shaft of light from a high window. The custodian, in expectation of a donation, makes "Akbaaarrrr" echo around the chamber.

Some 4 km south of Sikandra, near the high gateway of the ancient **Kach ki Sarai** building, is a sculptured horse, believed to mark the spot where Akbar's favourite horse died. There are also *kos minars* (marking a *kos*, about 4 km) and several other tombs on the way.

Fatehpur Sikri → For listings, see pages 80-82.

The red sandstone capital of Emperor Akbar, one of his architectural achievements, spreads along a ridge. The great mosque and palace buildings, deserted after only 14 years are still a vivid reminder of his power and vision. Perfectly preserved, it conjures up the lifestyle of the Mughals at the height of their glory.

Background

The first two Great Mughals, Babur (ruled 1526-1530) and his son Humayun (ruled 1530-1540, 1555-1556) both won (in Humayun's case, won back) Hindustan at the end of their lives, and they left an essentially alien rule. Akbar, the third and greatest of the Mughals, changed that. By marrying a Hindu princess, forging alliances with the Rajput leaders and making the administration of India a partnership with Hindu nobles and princes rather than armed foreign minority rule, Akbar consolidated his ancestors' gains, and won widespread loyalty and respect. Akbar had enormous magnetism. Though illiterate, he had great wisdom and learning as well as undoubted administrative and military skills. Fatehpur Sikri is testimony to this remarkable character.

Although he had many wives, the 26-year-old Akbar had no living heir; the children born to him had all died in infancy. He visited holy men to enlist their prayers for a son and heir. **Sheikh Salim Chishti**, living at Sikri, a village 37 km southwest of Agra, told the emperor that he would have three sons. Soon after, one of his wives, the daughter of the Raja of Amber, became pregnant, so Akbar sent her to live near the sage. A son Salim was born, later to be known as **Jahangir**. The prophecy was fulfilled when in 1570 another wife gave birth to Murad, and in 1572 to Daniyal. Salim Chishti's tomb is here.

Akbar, so impressed by this sequence of events, resolved to build an entirely new capital at Sikri in honour of the saint. The holy man had set up his hermitage on a low hill of hard reddish sandstone, an ideal building material, easy to work and yet very durable. The building techniques used imitated carvings in wood, as well as canvas from the Mughal camp (eg awnings). During the next 14 years a new city appeared on this hill – 'Fatehpur' (town of victory) added to the name of the old village, 'Sikri'. Later additions and alterations were made and debate continues over the function and dates of the various buildings. It is over 400 years old and yet perfectly preserved, thanks to careful conservation work carried out by the Archaeological Survey of India at the turn of the century. There are three sections to the city: the 'Royal Palace', 'Outside the Royal Palace' and the 'Jami Masjid'.

When Akbar left, it was slowly abandoned to become ruined and deserted by the early 1600s. Some believe the emperor's decision was precipitated by the failure of the water supply, whilst local folklore claims the decision was due to the loss of the court singer Tansen, one of the 'nine gems' of Akbar's court. However, there may well have been political and strategic motives. Akbar's change in attitude towards orthodox Islam and his earlier veneration of the Chishti saints supplanted by a new imperial ideology, may have influenced his decision. In 1585 he moved his court to Lahore and when he returned south again, it was to Agra. But it was at Fatehpur Sikri that Akbar spent the richest and most productive years of his 49-year reign.

The entrance

ⓘ *40 km from Agra. Sunrise to sunset, foreigners Rs 250, Indians Rs 5. It is best to visit early, before the crowds. Official guides are good (Rs 100; Rs 30 off season) but avoid others. Avoid the main entrance (lots of hawkers); instead, take the right-hand fork after passing through Agra gate to the hassle-free 2nd entrance. Allow 3 hrs and carry plenty of drinking water.*

Entry to Fatehpur Sikri is through the **Agra Gate**. The straight road from Agra was laid out in Akbar's time. If approaching from Bharatpur you will pass the site of a large lake, which provided one defensive barrier. On the other sides was a massive defensive wall with nine gates (clockwise): Delhi, Lal, Agra, Bir or Suraj (Sun), Chandar (Moon), Gwaliori, Tehra (Crooked), Chor (Thief's) and Ajmeri. Sadly there are men with 'performing' bears along the road from Agra – they should be discouraged – avoid stopping to photograph or tip.

From the Agra Gate you pass the sandstone **Tansen's Baradari** on your right and go through the triple-arched **Chahar Suq** with a gallery with two *chhattris* above which may have been a **Nakkar khana** (Drum House). The road inside the main city wall leading to the entrance would have been lined with bazars. Next on your right is the square, shallow-domed **Mint** with artisans' workshops or animal shelters, around a courtyard. Workmen still chip away at blocks of stone in the dimly lit interior.

Royal Palace

The **Diwan-i-Am** (Hall of Public Audience) was also used for celebrations and public prayers. It has cloisters on three sides of a rectangular courtyard and to the west, a pavilion with the emperor's throne, with *jali* screens on either side separating the court ladies. Some scholars suggest that the west orientation may have had the added significance of Akbar's vision of himself playing a semi-divine role.

This backed onto the private palace. In the centre of the courtyard behind the throne is the **Pachisi Board** or Chaupar. It is said that Akbar had slave girls dressed in yellow, blue and red, moved around as 'pieces'!

The **Diwan-i-Khas** (Hall of Private Audience) to your right, is a two-storey building with corner kiosks. It is a single room with a unique circular throne platform. Here Akbar would spend long hours in discussion with Christians, Jains, Buddhists, Hindus and Parsis. They would sit along the walls of the balcony connected to the **Throne Pillar** by screened 'bridges', while courtiers could listen to the discussions from the ground floor. Decorative techniques and metaphysical labels are incorporated here – the pillar is lotus shaped (a Hindu and Buddhist motif), the Royal Umbrella (*chhattri*) is Hindu, and the Tree of Life, Islamic. The bottom of the pillar is carved in four tiers: Muslim, Hindu, Christian and Buddhist designs. The Throne Pillar can be approached by steps from the outside although there is no access to the upper floor. The design of the hall deliberately followed the archaic universal pattern of establishing a hallowed spot from which spiritual influence could radiate. In his later years, Akbar developed a mystical cult around himself that saw him as being semi-divine.

An Archaeological Survey of India team recently discovered an 'air-conditioned palace' built for Akbar, while digging up steps leading down to a water tank set in the middle of the main palace complex. The subterranean chambers were found under the small quadrangle in sandstone, set in the middle of a water tank and connected on all four sides by narrow corridors. It's not yet open to the public.

In the **Treasury** in the northwest corner of the courtyard is the **Ankh Michauli** (Blind Man's Buff), possibly used for playing the game, comprising three rooms each protected by a narrow corridor with guards. The *makaras* on brackets are mythical sea creatures who guard the treasures under the sea. Just in front of the Treasury is the **Astrologer's Seat**, a small kiosk with elaborate carvings on the Gujarati 'caterpillar' struts which may have been used by the court astrologer or treasurer.

The **Turkish Sultana's House** or Anup Talao Pavilion is directly opposite, beyond the Pachisi Board. Sultana Ruqayya Begum was Akbar's favourite and her 'house', with a balcony on each side, is exquisitely carved with Islamic decorations. Scholars suggest this may have been a pleasure pavilion. The geometrical pattern on the ceiling is reminiscent of Central Asian carvings in wood while the walls may have been set originally with reflecting glass to create a Sheesh Mahal (Mirror Palace). In the centre of this smaller south courtyard is the **Anup Talao** where the Emperor may have sat on the platform, surrounded by perfumed water. The *Akbarnama* mentions the emperor's show of charity when he filled the Talao with copper, silver and gold coins and distributed them over three years.

Dawlatkhana-i-Khas, the emperor's private chambers, are next to the rose-water fountain in the corner. There are two main rooms on the ground floor. One housed his library – the recesses in the walls were for manuscripts. Although unable to read or write himself, Akbar enjoyed having books read to him. Wherever he went, his library of 50,000 manuscripts accompanied him. The larger room behind was his resting area. On the first floor is the **Khwabgah** (Palace of Dreams) which would have had rich carpets, hangings and cushions. This too was decorated with gold and ultramarine paintings. The southern window (Jharokha Darshan) was where the emperor showed himself to his people every morning.

Leaving the Dawlatkhana-i-Khas you enter another courtyard which contained the **Ladies' Garden** for the *zenana*, and the **Sunahra Makan** or the Christian wife **Maryam's** House, a two-storeyed affair for the emperor's mother, which was embellished with golden murals in the Persian style. The inscriptions on the beams are verses by Fazl, Akbar's poet laureate, one of the *'Navaratna'* (Nine Jewels) of the Court. Toilets in the corner of the garden are quite clean.

The **Panch Mahal** is an elegant, airy five-storeyed pavilion just north of this, each floor smaller than the one below, rising to a single domed kiosk on top. The horizontal line of this terraced building is emphasized by wide overhanging eaves (for providing shade), parapets broken by the supporting pillars of which there are 84 on the ground floor (the magic number of seven planets multiplied by 12 signs of the zodiac). The 56 carved columns on the second floor are all different and show Hindu influence. Originally dampened scented *khuss* (grass screens) which were hung in the open spaces, provided protection from the heat and sun, as well as privacy for the women who used the pavilion.

Jodh Bai, the daughter of the Maharaja of Amber, lived in Raniwas. The spacious **palace** in the centre, assured of privacy and security by high walls and a 9-m-high guarded gate to the east. Outside the north wall is the 'hanging' **Hawa Mahal** (Palace of Winds) with beautiful *jali* screens facing the *zenana* garden which was once enclosed, and the bridge (a later addition) led to the Hathipol. Through the arch is the small **Nagina Masjid**, the mosque for the ladies of the court. The *hammams* (baths) are to the south of the palace. The centre of the building is a quadrangle around which were the harem quarters, each section self-contained with roof terraces. The style, a blend of Hindu and Muslim (the lotus, chain and bell designs being Hindu, the black domes Muslim), is strongly reminiscent of Gujarati temples, possibly owing to the craftsmen brought in (see *jarokha* windows, niches, pillars and brackets). The upper pavilions north and south have interesting ceiling structure (imitating the bamboo and thatch roof of huts), here covered with blue glazed tiles, adding colour to the buildings of red sandstone favoured by Akbar. Jodh Bai's vegetarian kitchen opposite the palace has attractive chevron patterns.

Raja Birbal's Palace is a highly ornamented house to the northwest of Jodh Bai's Palace. It has two storeys – four rooms and two porches with pyramidal roofs below, and two rooms with cupolas and screened terraces above. Birbal, Akbar's Hindu prime minister, was the brightest of Akbar's 'Nine Jewels'. Again the building combines Hindu and Islamic elements (note the brackets, eaves, *jarokhas*). Of particular interest is the insulating effect of the double-domed structure of the roofs and cupolas which kept the rooms cool, and the diagonal positioning of the upper rooms which ensured a shady terrace. Some scholars believe that this building, Mahal-i-Ilahi, was not for Birbal, but for Akbar's senior queens.

South of the Raja's house are the **stables**, a long courtyard surrounded by cells which probably housed zenana servants rather than the emperor's camels and horses, though the rings suggest animals may have been tied there.

Jami Masjid

Leaving the Royal Palace you proceed across a car park to the Jami Masjid and the sacred section of Fatehpur Sikri. The oldest place of worship here was the **Stone Cutters' Mosque** (circa 1565) to the west of the Jami Masjid. It was built near Sheikh Salim Chishti's cell which was later incorporated into it by stonecutters who settled on the ridge when quarrying for the Agra Fort began. It has carved monolithic 'S' brackets to support the wide sloping eaves.

The **Badshahi Darwaza** (King's Gate) is the entrance Akbar used. Shoes must be left at the gate but there are strips of carpet cross the courtyard to save burning your feet. The porch is packed with aggressive salesmen. The two other gates on the south and north walls were altered by subsequent additions. Built in 1571-1572, this is one of the largest mosques in India. Inside is the congregational courtyard (132 m by 111 m). To your right in the corner is the **Jamaat Khana Hall** and next to this the **Tomb of the Royal Ladies** on the north wall. The square nave carries the principal dome painted in the Persian style, with pillared aisles leading to side chapels carrying subsidiary domes. The **mihrab** in the centre of the west wall orientates worshippers towards Mecca. The sanctuary is adorned with carving, inlay work and painting.

The **Tomb of Sheikh Salim Chishti**, a masterpiece in brilliant white marble, dominates the northern half of the courtyard. The Gujarati-style serpentine 'S' struts, infilled with *jali*, are highly decorative while the carved pillar bases and lattice screens are stunning pieces of craftsmanship. The canopy over the tomb is inlaid with mother of pearl. On the cenotaph is the date of the saint's death (1571) and the date of the building's completion (1580); the superb marble screens enclosing the veranda were added by Jahangir's foster brother in 1606. Around the entrance are inscribed the names of God, the Prophet and the four Caliphs of Islam. The shrine inside, on the spot of the saint's hermitage, originally had a red sandstone dome, which was marble veneered around 1806. Both Hindu and Muslim women pray at the shrine, tying cotton threads, hoping for the miracle of parenthood that Akbar was blessed with.

Next to it, in the courtyard, is the larger, red, sandstone tomb of **Nawab Islam Khan**, Sheikh Salim's grandson, and other members of the family.

Buland Darwaza (Triumphal Gate) dominates the south wall but it is a bit out of place. Built to celebrate Akbar's brilliant conquest of Gujarat (circa 1576), it sets the style for later gateways. The high gate is approached from the outside by a flight of steps which adds to its grandeur. The decoration shows Hindu influence, but is severe and restrained, emphasizing the lines of its arches with plain surfaces. You see an inscription on the right of a verse from the Qur'an:

> *Said Jesus Son of Mary (on whom be peace):*
> *The world is but a bridge; pass over it but build no houses on it.*
> *He who hopes for an hour, hopes for Eternity.*
> *The world is an hour. Spend it in prayer, for the rest is unseen.*

Outside the Royal Palace

Between the Royal Palace and the Jami Masjid, a paved pathway to the northwest leads to the **Hathipol** (Elephant Gate). This was the ceremonial entrance to the palace quarters, guarded by stone elephants, with its *nakkar khana* and bazar alongside. Nearby are the **waterworks**, with a deep well which had an ingenious mechanism for raising water to the aqueducts above ridge height. The **caravanserai** around a large courtyard fits on the ridge side, and was probably one of a series built to accommodate travellers, tradesmen and guards. Down a ramp immediately beyond is the **Hiran Minar**, an unusual tower studded with stone tusks, thought to commemorate Akbar's favourite elephant, Hiran. However, it was probably an *akash diya* (lamp to light the sky) or the 'zero point' for marking road distances in *kos*. You can climb up the spiral staircase inside it but take care as the top has no rail. This part of Fatehpur Sikri is off the main tourist track, and though less well preserved it is worth the detour to get the 'lost city' feeling, away from the crowds.

Agra and around listings

For hotel and restaurant price codes and other relevant information, see pages 13-16.

⊖ Where to stay

Agra *p66, map p68*

It's a mixed bag in Agra. Some of the cheap hotels have great rooftop views in Taj Ganj but little else going for them. The only upscale place with a view is the **Amar Vilas**. Most of the upscale hotels are along Fatehabad Rd, a rather charmless strip of pricey restaurants, international fast-food outlets and handicrafts emporia.

$$$$ Amar Vilas, near Taj East Gate, T0562-223 1515, www.amarvilas.com. 102 rooms, all Taj-facing – the only place in Agra with such superlative views – designed in strict adherence to the Mughal style. Beautiful rooms, the best feature being the view. Stunning swimming pool, lovely gardens, extraordinary ambience. Guests are entertained at sunset with traditional dancing and musicians. If you can splash out on your trip, this is the place to do it. A magical experience.

$$$$ Grand Imperial, Mahatma Gandhi Rd, T0562-225 1190, www.hotelgrandimperial. com. Agra's first bid at a genuine heritage hotel, with 30 opulent rooms, some still displaying their original red brickwork, arcaded around a pleasant lawn in a 100-year-old neoclassical mansion, all modern facilities, smart international restaurant with live classical Indian music at dinner. Swimming pool and small spa. Charming staff. The only drawback is the distance from the Taj and the proximity to a loud main road. Recommended.

$$$$ The Mughal, Fatehabad Rd, T0562-233 1701, www.itchotels.in. Stunning suites, beautiful gardens, lovely pool. The new wing is particularly food. They have the award-winning **Kaya Kalp** spa. Low-rise construction means only rooftop observatory offers good views of the Taj. Excellent restaurant.

$$-$ Hotel Kamal, South Gate, near Taj Ganj police station, T0562-233 0126, www. hotelkamal.com. Good option in this area – variety of rooms, some with more mod cons and a/c. Great view from the rooftop restaurant although food fairly mediocre.

$ Sidhartha, Western Gate, T(0)9719-456998, www.hotelsidharta.com. One of the best in this Taj Ganj area. Clean and basic rooms and close proximity to the Taj Mahal.

$ Sheela, East Gate, 2 mins' walk from the Taj, T0562-329 3437, www.hotelsheela agra.com. Popular although fairly basic rooms. Friendly place – good for meeting other travellers. Pleasant garden, good restaurant. Very helpful manager. Good location in low pollution area.

⊖ Restaurants

Agra *p66, map p68*

$$$ Esphahan, Amar Vilas (see Where to stay). Outstanding, rich Avadhi food in high-class setting, but non-residents will find it hard to get a table.

$$$ Mughal Room, Hotel Clarks Shiraz, 54 Taj Rd. Standard 5-star fare, rich and meaty, mainly distinguished by glassed-in rooftop setting with great views over the city.

$$$ Peshawari, The Mughal (see Where to stay). Regarded as the city's best, refined North Indian cuisine, smart surroundings, vegetarian offerings less inspired.

$$ Only, 45 Taj Rd, T0562-236 4333. Interesting menu, attractive outside seating, popular with tour groups, live entertainment.

$$ Riao, next to Clarks Shiraz, 44 Taj Rd, T(0)9412-154311. Good North Indian food, puppet shows and live music, great garden and atmosphere.

$ Joney's Place, near South Gate, Taj Ganj. The original and, despite numerous similarly named imitators, still the best. Tiny place but the food is consistently good. Can produce Israeli and Korean specialities. Recommended.

$ Maya, 18 Purani Mandi Circle, Fatehabad Rd. Varied menu, good Punjabi *thalis*, pasta, 'special tea', friendly, prompt service, hygienic, tasty, Moroccan-style decor. Recommended.
$ Zorba the Buddha, E-19 Sadar Bazaar, T0562-222 6091, zorbaevergreen@yahoo.com. Open 1200-1500, 1800-2100. Run by disciples of Osho, one of India's more popular, and most libidinous, gurus. Unusual menu (in a good way), naan breads a speciality, very clean, undersize furniture gives doll's house feel, an enjoyably quirky experience.

✸ Festivals

Agra *p66, map p68*
18-27 Feb Taj Mahotsav, a celebration of the region's arts, crafts, culture and cuisine.
Aug/Sep A fair at Kailash (14 km away). A temple marks the spot where Siva is believed to have appeared in the form of a stone lingam.

◯ Shopping

Agra *p66, map p68*
Agra specializes in jewellery, inlaid and carved marble, carpets and clothes. The main shopping areas are Sadar Bazaar (closed Tue), Kinari Bazaar, Gwalior Rd, Mahatma Gandhi Rd and Pratap Pura. Beware, you may order a carpet or an inlaid marble piece and have it sent later but it may not be what you ordered. Never agree to any export 'deals' and take great care with credit card slips (scams reported). Many rickshaws, taxi drivers and guides earn up to 40% commission by taking tourists to shops. Insist on not being rushed away from sights and shop independently. To get a good price you have to bargain hard anyway.

Carpets
Silk/cotton/wool mix hand-knotted carpets and woven *dhurries* are all made in Agra. High quality and cheaper than in Delhi.
Kanu Carpet Factory, Purani Mandi, Fetehabad Rd, T0562-233 0167. A reliable source.

Mughal Arts Emporium, Shamshabad Rd. Also has marble. Artificial silk is sometimes passed off as pure silk.

Marble
Delicately inlaid marble work is a speciality. Sometimes cheaper alabaster and soapstone is used and quality varies.
Akbar International, Fatehabad Rd. Good selection, inlay demonstration, fair prices.
Handicrafts Inn, 3 Garg Niketan, Fatehabad Rd, Taj Ganj.
Krafts Palace, 506 The Mall. Watch craftsmen working here.
UP Handicrafts Palace, 49 Bansal Nagar. Wide selection from table tops to coasters, high quality and good value.

◐ What to do

Agra *p66, map p68*
Tour operators
Mercury, Hotel Clarks Shiraz, 54 Taj Rd, T0562-222 6531. Helpful and reliable.
Travel Bureau, near Taj View Hotel, T0562-233 0245, www.travelbureauagra.com. Long-established local company, highly experienced (handle ground arrangements for most foreign travel agents), helpful, can arrange anything. Recommended.
UP Tours, Taj Khema (5 mins' walk from Taj East Gate), T0562-233 0140, tajkhema@up-tourism.com. Coach tours: Fatehpur Sikri–Taj Mahal–Agra Fort (full day), 1030-1830, Rs 1700 (Indian Rs 400) including guide and entry fees; half-day Fatehpur Sikri tour ends at 1300 which only gives 45 mins at the site, not worthwhile, better take a taxi if you can afford it. Sikandra–Fatehpur Sikri (half day), 0930-1400, Rs 100 (excludes entry fees); Sikandra–Fatehpur Sikri–Taj Mahal–Agra Fort (full day), 1030-1830. Tours start and finish at Agra Cantt Railway Station and tie in with arrival/departure of *Taj Express* (see Transport); check times. Pick-up also possible from India Tourism office on The Mall.

World Ways, Taj East Gate, T(0)9358-499616, worldways@mail.com. Arrangements for budget travellers.

⊖ Transport

Agra *p66, map p68*

Air Kheria Airport is 7 km from city centre. Only charter flights and in theory it's quicker by train anyway.

Auto rickshaw Pre-paid stand at Agra Cantt Station has prices clearly listed for point-to-point rates and sightseeing. Expect to pay Rs 80-100 to Fatehabad Rd or Taj Ganj.

Cycle rickshaw Negotiate (pay more to avoid visiting shops); Taj Ganj to Fort Rs 5; Rs 80-200 for visiting sights.

Local bus City Bus Service covers most areas and main sights. Plenty leave from the Taj Mahal area and the Fort Bus Stand.

Long-distance bus Most long-distance services leave from the Idgah Bus Stand, T0562-242 0324, including to: **Delhi** (4-5 hrs) via **Mathura** (1 hr); **Fatehpur Sikri** (40 km, 1 hr); **Bharatpur** (2 hrs); **Khajuraho** (10 hrs). Agra Fort Stand, T0562-236 4557, has additional buses to **Delhi**. Deluxe buses for **Jaipur** arrive and depart from a stop near Hotel Sakura: closer to most hotels and where there is less hassle from touts. **Delhi** from tourist office, 0700, 1445, deluxe, 4 hrs.

Taxi/car hire Tourist taxis from travel agents, remarkably good value for visiting nearby sights. Full day Rs 1500 (100 km), half day Rs 950 (45 km); a/c rates and more luxury cars are pricier; to Fatehpur Sikri Rs 2300 again can be pricier depending on car). **Travel Bureau**, T0562-233 0230; **UP Tours**, T0562-233 0140.

Train To/from **Delhi** train is the quickest and most reliable way. Most trains use **Agra Cantonment Railway Station**, 5 km west of Taj Mahal, enquiries T131, reservations T0562-242 1039, open 0800-2000. Foreigners' queue at Window 1. Pre-paid taxi/auto-rickshaw kiosk outside the station. Some trains to Rajasthan from quieter **Agra Fort Station**, T132, T0562-236 9590. Trains mentioned arrive and depart from **Agra Cantt** unless specified. To **Delhi**: *Shatabdi Exp 12001* (**ND**), 2040, 2½ hrs; *Taj Exp 12279*, (**HN**), 1855, 3¼ hrs (CC/II); *Intercity Exp 11103*, (**HN**), 0600, 3½ hrs (2nd class only). To **Jaipur**: *Intercity Exp 12307*, 1645, 6 hrs (from Agra Fort); *Marudhar Exp 14853/63*, 0715, 6¾ hrs. **Jhansi** (via Gwalior): *Taj Express 12280*, 1015, 3 hrs (Gwalior 1¾ hrs), **Sawai Madhopur** (for Ranthambore) at 0600, 0900, 1800.

Fatehpur Sikri *p75*

Bus Frequent buses from Agra Idgah Bus Stand (1 hr) Rs 17.

Taxi Taxis from Agra include the trip in a day's sightseeing (expect to pay around 2300 return depending on car).

❶ Directory

Agra *p66, map p68*

Medical services Ambulance: T102. District Hospital, Chhipitola Rd/Mahatma Gandhi Rd, T0562-236 2043. Dr VN, Kaushal, opposite Imperial Cinema, T0562-236 3550. Recommended. **Police** T100. **Post** GPO opposite India Tourist Office.

Contents

Footprint features

Rajasthan

The state of Rajasthan exceeds even the most far-fetched fantasies of what India might be: women dazzle in swathes of brilliant bright fabrics; luxuriously mustachioed men drive camels over dunes; tigers and leopards prowl through ancient forests; and princely forts and palaces loom up from the crushingly hot sweep of the Thar Desert.

Over the centuries, and in testament to their tradition of chivalry and independence, Rajasthan's rulers have built scores of evocative forts and palaces, such as those at Samode, Deogarh and Udaipur. In Jodhpur, the majestic Mehrangarh sits high above a moat of iridescent blue houses, while the far-flung wonder of Jaisalmer rises proudly from the surrounding sands. But much of Rajasthan's more recent architectural bounty – and its predilection for pomp – is due to British imperial policy towards the state's then maharajas. The colonial regime allowed them great wealth but little power, thus creating a civilization characterized by great extravagance. It is this surfeit of opulence that you'll see everywhere so sadly but atmospherically crumbling into decay.

Rajasthan's people are as theatrical as their architectural backdrop, and in today's cities and villages you'll encounter an eye-popping cast of characters: everyone from suave polo-playing Rajputs to tall, peasant camel-drivers in incandescent turbans with a gold hoop in each ear, and tribal women whose thick, gathered skirts are a shock of colour against the sands.

Although it is synonymous with desert dunes, Rajasthan has landscape beyond the Thar: it holds some of the world's oldest mountains; has green, rolling hills; and dense jungle that hides Rathambhore's famous tigers, along with monkeys, leopards, deer and hyenas.

Tourism is one of the main engines of Rajasthan's economy, and some of the local colour can seem correspondingly stage-managed. Yet the state remains a sumptuous feast for the senses with many corners almost entirely untouched by tourist development.

Jaipur

The sandstone 'pink city' of Jaipur, Rajasthan's capital, is the heady gateway to the state. The city is on the popular 'Golden Triangle' route (Delhi–Agra–Jaipur–Delhi) which for many short-haul visitors is their only experience of Rajasthan. The steady stream of tourists means the city has to make little effort to attract visitors; as a result its pastel-hued buildings are not what they used to be and many of the sights are poorly maintained. Nonetheless it's a worthwhile stopover in itself, as well as a staging post for visiting the surrounding area. The old city, with its bazars, palaces and *havelis*, along with a couple of forts and the ancient city of Amber nearby, are well worth a wander. Knotted, narrow streets hold cupboard-sized workshops where elderly women dash out clothes on rusty Singers; men energetically stuff mattresses with piles of rags; boys mend bicycles next to old men rolling pellets of paste into sweets; whole families carve table legs or hammer bed headboards out of sheet metal; and 'gold men' leave the old city's textile houses sprinkled with metallic pigment from a day's work rubbing the powder into fabric patterned with resin glue. Escape the bustle and head up to the Tiger Fort (Nahargarh) for sunset, where proud peacocks pick among the ruins and monkeys scamper about in the twilight against the backdrop of Man Sagar Lake and its Jal Mahal (Water Palace). Outside the city lies a tranquil agrarian landscape, in which there are many hunting lodges, palaces and forts.

Arriving in Jaipur

Getting there Sanganer Airport, 15 km south of town, has flights from Ahmedabad, Chennai, Delhi, Jodhpur, Mumbai, Rajkot and Udaipur. Airport buses, taxis and auto-rickshaws take 30 minutes to the centre. The railway station has links with most major cities. The **Main Bus Terminal** at Sindhi Camp is used by state and private buses. Buses from Delhi use the dramatically improved NH8; the journey now takes under four hours by car. The alternative Gurgaon–Alwar–Jaipur route is more interesting but much slower. Most hotels are a short auto-rickshaw ride away from the station and bus terminal.

Getting around The walled Old City, to the northeast of town, holds most of the sights and the bazar. Take a rickshaw to the area, then explore on foot. What few attractions

the new town holds are spread out so it's best explored by rickshaw, bus or taxi. There is also a new metro system under construction which should ease the traffic above ground.
▶▶ *See Transport, page 98.*

Tourist information Government of India Tourism ① *Hotel Khasa Kothi, T0141-511 0598*, also has counters at the **Railway Station** ① *T0141-231 5714*, and **Central Bus Stand** ① *T0141-506 4102*. Guides for four to eight hours cost Rs 250-400 (Rs 100 extra for French, German, Japanese, Spanish). *'Jaipur for Aliens'*, a free miniature guidebook created by the owner of the **Hotel Pearl Palace**, has regularly updated information on transport and attractions; available at the hotel (see Where to stay, page 94).

Background

Jaipur ('City of Victory') was founded in 1727 by **Maharaja Jai Singh II**, a Kachhawaha Rajput, who ruled from 1699 to 1744. He had inherited a kingdom under threat not only from the last great Mughal Emperor Aurangzeb, but also from the Maratha armies of Gujarat and Maharashtra. Victories over the Marathas and diplomacy with Aurangzeb won back the favour of the ageing Mughal, so that the political stability that Maharaja Jai Singh was instrumental in creating was protected, allowing him to pursue his scientific and cultural interests. Jaipur is very much a product of his intellect and talent. A story relates an encounter between the **Emperor Aurangzeb** and the 10-year-old Rajput prince. When asked what punishment he deserved for his family's hostility and resistance to the Mughals, the boy answered "Your Majesty, when the groom takes the bride's hand, he confers lifelong protection. Now that the Emperor has taken my hand, what have I to fear?" Impressed by his tact and intelligence, Aurangzeb bestowed the title of *Sawai* (one and a quarter) on him, signifying that he would be a leader.

Jai Singh loved mathematics and science, and was a keen student of astronomy, via Sanskrit translations of Ptolemy and Euclid. A brilliant Brahmin scholar from Bengal, Vidyadhar Bhattacharya, helped him to design the city. Work began in 1727 and it took four years to build the main palaces, central square and principal roads. The layout of streets was based on a mathematical grid of nine squares representing the ancient Hindu map of the universe, with the sacred Mount Meru, home of Siva, occupying the central square. In Jaipur the royal palace is at the centre. The three-by-three square grid was modified by relocating the northwest square in the southeast, allowing the hill fort of Nahargarh (Tiger Fort) to overlook and protect the capital. At the southeast and southwest corners of the city were squares with pavilions and ornamental fountains. Water for these was provided by an underground aqueduct with outlets for public use along the streets. The main streets are 33 yds wide (33 is auspicious in Hinduism). The pavements were deliberately wide to promote the free flow of pedestrian traffic and the shops were also a standard size. Built with ancient Hindu rules of town planning in mind, Jaipur was advanced for its time. Yet many of its buildings suggest a decline in architectural power and originality. The architectural historian Giles Tillotson argues that the "traditional architectural details lack vigour and depth and are also flattened so that they become relief sculpture on the building's surface, and sometimes they are simply drawn on in white outline".

In addition to its original buildings, Jaipur has a number of examples of late 19th-century buildings which marked an attempt to revive Indian architectural skills. A key figure in this movement was Sir Samuel Swinton Jacob. A school of art was founded in 1866 by a group of English officers employed by Maharaja Sawai Madho Singh II to encourage an interest in Indian tradition and its development. In February 1876 the Prince of Wales visited Jaipur, and work on the Albert Hall, now the Central Museum, was begun to a design of Jacob. It was the first of a number of construction projects in which Indian craftsmen and designers were employed in both building and design. This ensured that the Albert Hall was an extremely striking building in its own right. The opportunities for training provided under Jacob's auspices encouraged a new school of Indian architects and builders. One of the best examples of their work is the Mubarak Mahal (1900), now Palace Museum, designed by Lala Chiman Lal.

Places in Jaipur → *For listings, see page 93-98.*

Hawa Mahal

ⓘ *Enter from Tripolia Bazar, Sat-Thu 0900-1630, foreigners Rs 50, Indians Rs10 – audio tours possible; for the best views accept invitations from shop owners on upper floors across the street.*
The 'Palace of the Winds' (circa 1799) forms part of the east wall of the City Palace complex and is best seen from the street outside. Possibly Jaipur's most famous building, this pink sandstone façade of the palace was built for the ladies of the harem by Sawai Pratap Singh. The five storeys stand on a high podium with an entrance from the west. The elaborate façade contains 953 small casements in a huge curve, each with a balcony and crowning arch. The windows enabled *hawa* (cool air) to circulate and allowed the women who were secluded in the *zenana* to watch processions below without being seen. The museum has second-century BC utensils and old sculpture. It's a magical place.

City Palace

ⓘ *0930-1700 (last entry 1630). Foreigners Rs 300 (includes still camera and a good audio guide), Indians Rs 75 (camera Rs 50 extra); includes Sawai Man Singh II Museum and Jaigarh Fort, valid for 1 week. Video (unnecessary) Rs 200; doorkeepers expect tips when photographed. Photography in galleries prohibited.*
The City Palace (1728-1732) occupies the centre of Jaipur, covers one seventh of its area and is surrounded by a high wall – the Sarahad. Its style differs from conventional Rajput fort palaces in its separation of the palace from its fortifications, which in other Rajput buildings are integrated in one massive interconnected structure. In contrast the Jaipur Palace has much more in common with Mughal models, with its main buildings scattered in a fortified campus. To find the main entrance, from the Hawa Mahal go north about 250 m along the Sireh Deori Bazar past the Vidhan Sabha (Town Hall) and turn left through an arch – the Sireh Deori (Boundary Gate). Pass under a second arch – the Naqqar Darwaza (Drum Gate) – into Jaleb Chowk, the courtyard which formerly housed the palace guard. Today it is where coaches park. This is surrounded by residential quarters which were modified in the 19th century under Sawai Ram Singh II. A gateway to the south leads to the Jantar Mantar, the main palace buildings and museum and the Hawa Mahal.

Mubarak Mahal The main entrance leads into a large courtyard at the centre of which is the Mubarak Mahal, faced in white marble. Built in 1890, originally as a guesthouse for the Maharaja, the Mubarak Mahal is a small but immaculately conceived two-storeyed building, designed on the same cosmological plan in miniature as the city itself – a square divided into a three by three square grid.

The **Textile and Costume Museum** on the first floor has fine examples of fabrics and costumes from all over India, including some spectacular wedding outfits, as well as musical instruments and toys from the royal nursery. In the northwest corner of the

Jaipur

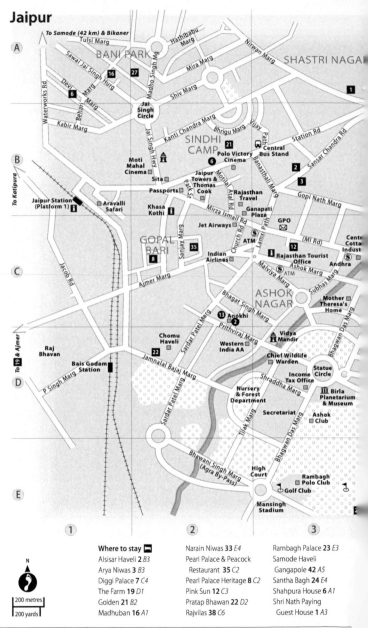

Where to stay

Alsisar Haveli 2 B3
Arya Niwas 3 B3
Diggi Palace 7 C4
The Farm 19 D1
Golden 21 B2
Madhuban 16 A1
Narain Niwas 33 E4
Pearl Palace & Peacock
  Restaurant 35 C2
Pearl Palace Heritage 8 C2
Pink Sun 12 C3
Pratap Bhawan 22 D2
Rajvilas 38 C6
Rambagh Palace 23 E3
Samode Haveli
  Gangapole 42 A5
Santha Bagh 24 E4
Shahpura House 6 A1
Shri Nath Paying
  Guest House 1 A3

To Gaitor & Path to Nahargarh (Tiger) Fort

To 42, Jaigarh Fort & Amber via Man Sarobar

Tal Katora

KANWAR NAGAR

Subash Chowk

Motikatra Bazar

Jai Niwas Gardens

PURANI BASTI

andpol Gate

Nahargarh Rd

Gangauri Bazar

Govind Deo Temple

Jaleb Chowk

Chandpol Bazar

Chhoti Chaupar

City Palace

Jantar Mantar

Town Hall

RAMACHANDRA COLONY

Kishanpol Bazar

Tripolia Bazar

Hawa Mahal

Sireh Deori Bazar

Hawa Mahal Rd

To Galta & Surya Mandir

Khajane Walonka Rasta

Badi Chaupar

Gopalji ka Rasta

Jama Masjid

Ramganj Bazar

TOPKHANADESH

Chaura Rasta

Haldiyon ka Rasta

Indra Bazar

MODIKHANA

BISESWARJI

Chhati Bazar

GHAT DARWAZA

To Galta & Surya Mandir

Singhpol Gate

Itlahn Pol

Nehru Bazar

Bapu Bazar

ATM

Ghat ki Darwaza Bazar

To Sisodia Palace & Garden

vali urs

Ajmeri Gate

Mirza Ismail Rd

Siva Pol

Clock Tower

(MI Rd)

New Gate

Sanganeri Gate

Rajasthali

Ghat Darwaza

Thomas Cook

Ram Niwas Gardens

Gem Cinema & Gem Testing Laboratory

Raj Mandir Cinema

Ashok Marg

Agra Marg

To 38, Sisodia Palace & Garden

Zoo

Zoo

Modern Art Gallery

Maharani's College

Raj Lalit Kala Akademi

Shivaji Marg

Central Museum & Art Gallery

Museum Rd

JANTA COLONY

vekananda Rd

Maharaja's College

Moti Dungri Rd

FATEH TIBA

ospital Rd

SMS Hospital

Nehru Marg

Cremation Ground

viraj Marg

ADARSH NAGAR

Sawai Ram Singh Marg

Adarshnagar Marg

SRC Museum of Indology

24

Catholic

Narain Singh Rd

33

Industrial Rd

GURU NANAK PURA

Ram Mandir

Govind Marg

Tonk, ner & t (15 km)

4

To Ganesh Temple

To University & Birla Mandir (500m)

5

6

To Agra

Umaid Bhawan **27** *A2*

courtyard is the **Armoury Museum** containing an impressive array of weaponry – pistols, blunderbusses, flintlocks, swords, rifles and daggers, as well as some fascinating paintings on the way in. This was originally the common room of the harem. From the north-facing first-floor windows you can get a view of the Chandra Mahal (see below). Just outside the Armoury Museum is **Rajendra Pol**, a gate flanked by two elephants, each carved from a single block of marble, which leads to the inner courtyard. There are beautifully carved alcoves with delicate arches and *jali* screens and a fine pair of patterned brass doors.

Diwan-i-Khas (Sarbato Bhadra) The gateway leads to the courtyard known variously as the Diwan-i-Am, the Sarbato Bhadra or the Diwan-i-Khas Chowk. Today, the building in its centre is known as the Diwan-i-Khas (circa 1730). Originally the Diwan-i-Am, it was reduced to the hall of private audience (Diwan-i-Khas) when the new Diwan-i-Am was built to its southeast at the end of the 18th century. The courtyard itself reflects the overwhelming influence of Mughal style, despite the presence of some Hindu designs, a result of the movement of Mughal-trained craftsmen from further north in search of opportunities to practise their skills. In the Diwan-i-Khas (now known by the Sanskrit name Sarbato Bhadra) are two huge silver urns – ratified by Guinness as being the largest pieces of silver in the world – used by Sawai Madho Singh for carrying Ganga water to England.

Diwan-i-Am (Diwan Khana) Art Gallery With its entrance in the southeast corner of the Diwan-i-Am courtyard, the 'new' Hall of Public Audience built by Maharaja Sawai Pratap Singh (1778-1803) today houses a fine collection of Persian and Indian miniatures, some of the carpets the maharajas had made for them and an equally fine collection of manuscripts. To its north is the **Carriage Museum**, housed in a modern building. In the middle of the west wall of the Diwan-i-Am courtyard, opposite the art gallery, is the **Ganesh Pol**, which leads via a narrow passage and the Peacock Gate into **Pritam Niwas Chowk**. This courtyard has the original palace building 'Chandra Mahal' to its north, the *zenana* on its northwest, and the Anand Mahal to its south. Several extremely attractive doors, rich and vivid in their peacock blue, aquamarine and amber colours, have small marble Hindu gods watching over them.

Chandra Mahal Built between 1727 and 1734 the Moon Palace is the earliest building of the palace complex. Externally it appears to have seven storeys, though inside the first and second floors are actually one high-ceilinged hall. The top two floors give superb views of the city and Tiger Fort. On the ground floor (north) a wide veranda – the **Pritam Niwas** (House of the Beloved) – with Italian wall paintings, faces the formal Jai Niwas garden. The main section of the ground floor is an Audience Hall. The palace is not always open to visitors.

The hall on the first and second floors, the **Sukh Niwas** (House of Pleasure), underwent a Victorian reconstruction. Above it are the **Rang Mandir** and the **Sobha Niwas**, built to the same plan. The two top storeys are much smaller, with the mirror palace of the **Chavi Niwas** succeeded by the small open marble pavilion which crowns the structure, the **Mukat Niwas**.

In the northeast corner of the Pritam Niwas Chowk, leading into the *zenana*, is the **Krishna door**, its surface embossed with scenes of the deity's life. The door is sealed in the traditional way with a rope sealed with wax over the lock.

Jantar Mantar (Observatory)
ⓘ *0900-1630, foreigners Rs 200, Indians Rs 40.*
Literally 'Instruments for measuring the harmony of the heavens', the Jantar Mantar was built between 1728 and 1734. Jai Singh wanted things on a grand scale and chose stone with a

marble facing on the important planes. Each instrument serves a particular function and each gives an accurate reading. Hindus believe that their fated souls move to the rhythms of the universe, and the matching of horoscopes is still an essential part in the selection of partners for marriage. Astrologers occupy an important place in daily life and are consulted for all important occasions and decision-making. The observatory is fascinating. It is best to hire a guide who will explain the functions of the instruments. There is little shade so avoid the middle of the day. Moving clockwise the *yantras* (instruments) are as follows:

Small 'Samrat' is a large sundial (the triangular structure) with flanking quadrants marked off in hours and minutes. The arc on your left shows the time from sunrise to midday, the one on the right midday to sundown. Read the time where the shadow is sharpest. The dial gives solar time, so to adjust it to Indian Standard Time (measured from Allahabad) between one minute 15 seconds and 32 minutes must be added according to the time of year and solar position as shown on the board.

'Dhruva' locates the position of the Pole Star at night and those of the 12 zodiac signs. The graduation and lettering in Hindi follows the traditional unit of measurement based on the human breath, calculated to last six seconds. Thus: four breaths = one *pala* (24 seconds), 60 *palas* = one *gati* (24 minutes), 60 *gatis* = one day (24 hours).

'Narivalya' has two dials: south facing for when the sun is in the southern hemisphere (21 September-21 March) and north facing for the rest of the year. At noon the sun falls on the north–south line.

The Observer's Seat was intended for Jai Singh.

Small 'Kranti' is used to measure the longitude and latitude of celestial bodies.

'Raj' (King of Instruments) is used once a year to calculate the Hindu calendar, which is based on the Jaipur Standard as it has been for 270 years. A telescope is attached over the central hole. The bar at the back is used for sighting, while the plain disk is used as a blackboard to record observations.

'Unnathamsa' is used for finding the altitudes of the celestial bodies. Round-the-clock observations can be made and the sunken steps allow any part of the dial to be read.

'Disha' points to the north.

'Dakshina', a wall aligned north–south, is used for observing the position and movement of heavenly bodies when passing over the meridian.

Large 'Samrat' is similar to the small one (see above) but 10 times larger and thus accurate to two seconds instead of 20 seconds. The sundial is 27.4 m high. It is used on a particularly holy full moon in July/August, to predict the length and heaviness of the monsoon for the local area.

'Rashivalayas' has 12 sundials for the signs of the zodiac and is similar to the Samrat yantras. The five at the back (north to south), are Gemini, Taurus, Cancer, Virgo and Leo. In front of them are Aries and Libra, and then in the front, again (north to south), Aquarius, Pisces, Capricorn, Scorpio and Sagittarius. The instruments enable readings to be made at the instant each zodiacal sign crosses the meridian.

'Jai Prakash' acts as a double check on all the other instruments. It measures the rotation of the sun, and the two hemispheres together form a map of the heavens. The small iron plate strung between crosswires shows the sun's longitude and latitude and which zodiacal sign it is passing through.

Small 'Ram' is a smaller version of the Jai Prakash Yantra (see above).

Large 'Ram Yantra' Similarly, this finds the altitude and the azimuth (arc of the celestial circle from Zenith to horizon).

'Diganta' also measures the azimuth of any celestial body.

Large 'Kranti' is similar to the smaller Kranti (see above).

Nahargarh (Tiger Fort)

ⓘ 1000-1630, foreigners Rs 30, Indians Rs 5, camera Rs 30, video Rs 70. Rickshaw for sunset Rs 400-500 return. Snacks and drinks are available at the Durg Café. It is an incredibly atmospheric place after dark.

The small fort with its immense walls and bastions stands on a sheer rock face. The city at its foot was designed to give access to the fort in case of attack. To get there on foot you have to first walk through some quiet and attractive streets at the base of the hill, then 2 km up a steep, rough winding path to reach the top. Alternatively, it can also be reached by road via Jaigarh Fort. Beautifully floodlit at night, Tiger Fort dominates the skyline by day. Much of the original fort (1734) is in ruins but the walls and 19th-century additions survive, including rooms furnished for maharajas. This is a 'real fort', quiet and unrushed, and well worth visiting for the breathtaking views, to look inside the buildings and to walk around the battlements. However, it is an active fort used as a training ground for soldiers; women alone may feel quite vulnerable here. You can combine this visit with Jaigarh Fort (see page 100), 7 km away along the flat-topped hill, which is part of the same defensive network.

Central Museum and Modern Art Gallery

ⓘ Museum Sat-Thu 1000-1630, foreigners Rs 150, Indians Rs 20; gallery 1000-1700, free, closed 2nd Sat of month and Sun; garden 0900-1700, foreigners Rs 100, Indians Rs 10.

Within the Ram Niwas Gardens you can visit the museum, gallery and a zoological garden. Housed in the beautiful Albert Hall is the **Central Museum**, displaying mainly excellent decorative metalware, miniature portraits and other art pieces. It also features Rajasthani village life – including some gruesome torture techniques – displayed through costumes, pottery, woodwork, brassware, etc. The first floor displays are covered in dust and poorly labelled. **Modern Art Gallery**, Ravindra Rang Manch, has an interesting collection of contemporary Rajasthani art. Finally, outside is the **Zoological Garden** containing lions, tigers, panthers, bears, crocodiles and deer, plus a bird park opposite.

SRC Museum of Indology

ⓘ 24 Gangwal Park, 0800-1600, foreigners Rs 40, Indians Rs 20.

Further south, along J Nehru Marg, is the extraordinarily eclectic, and not a little quirky, SRC Museum of Indology. It houses a collection of folk and tantric art including all manner of manuscripts, textiles, paintings, Hindi written on a grain of rice, Sanskrit on a rabbit hair, fossils, medals, weapons and so on.

Surya Mandir

ⓘ Galta Pol can be reached by taking a bus or by walking 2 km east from the Hawa Mahal; from there it is about 600 m uphill and then downhill.

From Galta Pol take a walk to the 'Valley of the Monkeys' to get a view of the city from the Surya Mandir (Sun Temple), which is especially impressive at sunset. It is not on the tourist circuit and so you are less likely to get hassled here. There are plenty of monkeys on the way up to the temple and you can buy bags of nuts to feed them. Walk down the steps from the top of the ridge to the five old temples, with impressive wall paintings, dedicated to Rama-Sita and Radha-Krishna. Hundreds of monkeys can be seen playing in the water tank below.

Jaipur listings

For hotel and restaurant price codes and other relevant information, see pages 13-16.

🛏 Where to stay

Jaipur *p85, map p88*

The city's popularity has meant that foreigners are targeted by hotel and shop touts, many of whom drive rickshaws, so be on your guard. Under construction at the time of writing was the stunning floating Jal Mahal, www.jalmahal.com.

$$$$ The Farm, Prithvisinghpura, Dhankiya Rd, 30 km outside of Jaipur, off Ajmer Rd. T(0)9828-023030, www.thefarmjaipur.com. This is a place to escape to. Although named The Farm, this place is urban and quirky. The rooms are large and the furniture is recycled and put together with effortless chic. There is a beautiful large communal lounge and a stunning swimming pool surrounded by gazebos.

$$$$ Rajvilas (Oberoi), 8 km from town on Goner Rd, T0141-268 0101, www.oberoi hotels.com. This award-winning hotel is housed in a low-lying recreated fort-palace within large, exquisitely landscaped gardens with orchards, pools and fountains. There are 71 rooms including 13 'tents' and 3 private villas with their own pools. Room interiors are not especially imaginative, but the safari-style 'tents' in a desert garden area are delightful. There is also an Ayurvedic spa in a restored *haveli*.

$$$$ Rambagh Palace (Taj), Bhawani Singh Rd, T0141-221 1919, www.tajhotels. com. 90 luxuriously appointed rooms and extraordinary suites arranged around a courtyard in the former maharaja's palace, still feels like the real thing. Set in 19 ha of beautifully maintained garden, larger groups are invited to participate in elephant polo on the back lawn! Stunning indoor pool and a tented spa, but the real pièce de résistance is the spectacular dining hall, reminiscent of Buckingham Palace. Pleasant, relaxed

atmosphere, good food and friendly staff. Extremely pricey but unforgettable.

$$$$ Samode Havell Gangapole, T0141-263 2407, www.samode.com. 150-year-old, beautifully restored *haveli* with a leafy courtyard and gardens. 30 rooms and 2 suites (the spectacular Maharaja and Maharani suites have original mirrored mosaics, faded wall paintings, pillars, lamp-lit alcoves, cushions and carved wooden beds). Evening meals are served in the peaceful, atmospheric courtyard or in the magnificent, somewhat over-the-top dining room. Large pool with bar. Excellent food. Highly recommended.

$$$$-$$$ Diggi Palace, SMS Hospital Rd, T0141-237 3091, www.hoteldiggipalace. com. 43 attractive rooms in a charming 125-year-old building. Not as glitzy as some but wonderfully chic. Lovely open restaurant, great home-grown food, peaceful garden, enthusiastic, helpful owners who host the Jaipur Literature and Heritage Festival. Craft and cookery workshops available, as well as trips to their organic farm. Highly recommended.

$$$$-$$$ Narain Niwas, Kanota Bagh, Narain Singh Rd, T0141-256 1291, www.hotelnarainniwas.com. The well-presented rooms pale in comparison to the suites in this characterful old mansion. There's a great dining room and lounge area, and clean pool in beautiful gardens with roaming peacocks, lots of room to sit around the pool (which is rare). You can also pay to use the pool as a non-resident. The beautiful boutique Hot Pink is in the grounds and offers designer names.

$$$ Alsisar Haveli, Sansar Chandra Rd, T0141-236 8290, www.alsisarhaveli.com. 36 intricately painted a/c rooms, modern frescoes, excellent conversion of 1890s house, heaps of character, attractive courtyards, beautiful pool, but average food and below par service can be frustrating, village safaris available.

$$$ Shahpura House, Devi Marg, Bani Park, T0141-220 2293, www.shahpurahouse.com. The only genuine 'heritage' option in the area, this 1950s maharaja's residence is still run by the family and has with many original features including mirrored *thekri* ceilings, comfortable individually decorated suites, old-fashioned bathrooms, lovely canopied rooftop restaurant (pricey meals), and a pool. Recommended.

$$$-$$ Pratap Bhawan Bed & Breakfast, A-4 Jamnalal Bajaj Marg, C-Scheme, T(0)9829-074354, www.pratapbhawan.com. Run by delightful couple, this is a lovely homestay with delicious food. Rooms are decorated with wildlife photography. Excellent cookery lessons available. Highly recommended.

$$ Arya Niwas, Sansar Chandra Rd (behind Amber Tower), T0141-407 3546, www.arya niwas.com. 95 very clean, simple rooms but not always quiet, modernized and smart, good very cheap vegetarian food, pleasant lounge, travel desk, tranquil lawn, friendly, helpful, impressive management, book ahead (arrive by 1800), great value.

$$ Madhuban, D237 Behari Marg, Bani Park, T0141-220 0033, www.madhuban.net. Elegant, characterful hotel, 25 beautifully furnished rooms, small courtyard pool, pleasant garden, helpful staff, good food. Recommended.

$$ Pearl Palace Heritage, 54 Gopal Bari Lane 2, T0141-237 5242, www.pearl palaceheritage.com. An amazing new heritage-style property from the charming owner of the extremely popular **Hotel Pearl Palace**. Beautiful stone carvings line the walls, while each room is themed: the desert room has golden stone from Jaisalmer; there is a mirrored Udaipur room; and a Victoriana room. The rooms are large here with big sitting areas, TVs and beautifully tiled bathrooms. Exceptionally good value. There is a swimming pool on the way. Whole-heartedly recommended.

$$ Umaid Bhawan, D1-2A Bani Park, T0141-231 6184, www.umaidbhawan.com.

28 beautifully decorated and ornately furnished rooms, many with balconies, one of the most charming *haveli*-style guesthouses with a lovely pool and friendly, knowledgeable owners. Recommended.

$$ Santha Bagh, Kalyan Path, Narain Singh Rd, T0141-256 6790. 12 simple, comfortable rooms (a/c or air-cooled), very friendly, helpful and charming staff, excellent meals, lawn, quiet location. Recommended.

$$-$ Golden Hotel, 5, Kanti Nagar, opposite Polovictory Cinema, T(0)9351-484055. New cheap hotel in good location – it has modern business style, Wi-Fi and a/c. Good value.

$ Hotel Pearl Palace, Hari Kishan Somani Marg, Hathroi Fort, Ajmer Rd, T0141-237 3700, www.hotelpearlpalace.com. A real gem. Rooms are quirky and decorated with art pieces collected by the charming owner; some have a/c and Wi-Fi but all are modern, comfortable and have lots of character. The **Peacock** restaurant on the roof has great views and serves excellent food. Great value. Advance booking essential. Whole-heartedly recommended.

$ Hotel Pink Sun, Chameliwala market, off Mirza Ismail Rd, T0141-237 6753. Clean, simple rooms in busy location, right at the heart of things. Good rooftop restaurant.

$ Shri Sai Nath Paying Guest House, 1233 Mali Colony, outside Chandpol Gate, T0141-230 4975. 10 clean, quiet rooms, meals on request, very hospitable, helpful and warm.

🍴 Restaurants

Jaipur *p85, map p88*

$$$ Rambagh Palace (see Where to stay, page 93). Royal Indian cuisine from 4 regions in the beautiful **Suvarna Mahal** restaurant, attractive light-filled coffee shop, popular for lunch, pricey (Rs 2500 minimum for non-residents) but generous.

$$$-$$ Chokhi Dhani, 19 km south on Tonk Rd, T0141-277 0555, www.chokhi dhani.com. Enjoyable 'village' theme park with camel and elephant rides, traditional dancing and puppet shows popular with families from Delhi. If you are only coming to Jaipur, this gives you a Disney view of the rest of Rajasthan, but it is done very well.

$$ Anokhi Café, KK Square Shopping Complex, Prithviraj Rd, C-Scheme, T0141-400 7244. Great café offering up international tastes like Thai green bean salad, quiches and sandwiches. Try the pomegranate and pineapple juice, great filter coffee and an array of cakes and biscuits. A little oasis and right next door to the beautiful **Anokhi** shop with handblock prints galore.

$$ Diggi Palace (see Where to stay, page 93). Many of the ex-pats who call Jaipur home head to **Diggi Palace** for food. Some produce comes from their organic farm near Ramgarh and they offer up all types of Indian fare. They even have their own cookbook – *Tastes of Diggi*.

$$ Four Seasons, D-43A2 Subhash Mg, C-Scheme, T0141-227 5450. High-quality vegetarian Indian and Chinese, with an extensive menu, pleasantly smart ambience and good staff. A worthwhile detour.

$$ LMB, Johari Bazar. Rajasthani vegetarian in slightly confused contemporary interior matched by upbeat dance tunes. Tasty (if a little overpriced) *thalis*; (*panchmela saaq* particularly good). Popular sweet shop and egg-free bakery attached. During Diwali, this is a feast for the senses.

$$ Niros, Mirza Ismail Rd, T0141-237 4493. International. This is a characterful restaurant serving up good Indian and the obligatory Chinese and Continental dishes.

$$-$ Peacock, on roof of **Hotel Pearl Palace** (see Where to stay, page 94). Excellent Indian and Continental dishes plus backpacker fare, with vegetarian and non-vegetarian food prepared in separate kitchens. Superb views by day and night from this 2-tiered restaurant, eclectic collection of quirky furniture designed by the owner. Very atmospheric – highly recommended.

$ Kanji, opposite Polo Victory Cinema, Station Rd. Clean and extremely popular sweets-and-snacks joint, a good place to experiment with exotica such as *Raj kachori* or *aloo tikki*, both of which come smothered in yoghurt and mild sweet chutney. Stand-up counters downstairs, a/c seating upstairs.

$ Lassiwala, Mirza Ismail Rd, opposite Niro's. The unrivalled best *lassis* in the city, served in rough clay cups and topped off with a crispy portion of milk skin. Of the 3 'original' *lassiwalas* parked next to each other, the genuine one is on the left, next to the alley. Come early; they run out by afternoon.

⊕ Entertainment

Jaipur *p85, map p88*
Raj Mandir Cinema, off Mirza Ismail Rd. 'Experience' a Hindi film in shell pink interior. Recommended.
Ravindra Rang Manch, Ram Niwas Garden. Hosts cultural programmes and music shows.

⊕ Festivals

Jaipur *p85, map p88*
Jan Jaipur Literary Festival (17-21 Jan 2014) at Diggi Palace. International Literary Festival hosted by William Dalrymple, with live music in the evenings. **14 Jan** Makar Sankranti The kite-flying festival is spectacular. Everything closes down in the afternoon and kites are flown from every rooftop, street and even from bicycles. The object is to bring down other kites to the deafening cheers of huge crowds.
Feb/Mar Elephant Festival (16 Mar 2014, 5 Mar 2015) at Chaugan Stadium, procession, elephant polo, etc.
Mar/Apr Gangaur Fair (2-3 Apr 2014, 22-23 Mar 2015) about a fortnight after **Holi**, when a colourful procession of women starts from the City Palace with the idol of Goddess Gauri. They travel from the Tripolia Gate to Talkatora, and these areas of the city are closed to traffic during the festival.
Jul/Aug Teej (30-31 Jul 2014, 17-18 Aug 2015). The special celebrations in Jaipur have elephants, camels and dancers joining in the processions.

O Shopping

Jaipur *p85, map p88*

Jaipur specializes in printed cotton, handicrafts, razia (fine quilts) carpets and *durries* (thick handloomed rugs); also embroidered leather footwear and blue pottery. You may find better bargains in other cities in Rajasthan.

Antiques and art

Art Palace, Chomu Haveli. Specializes in 'ageing' newly crafted items – alternatives to antiques. Also found around Hawa Mahal.
Mohan Yadav, 9 Khandela House, behind Amber Gauer, SC Rd, T0141-378009. Visit the workshop to see high-quality miniatures produced by the family.

Bazars

Traditional bazars and small shops in the Old City are well worth a visit; cheaper than Mirza Ismail Rd shops but may not accept credit cards. Most open Mon-Sat 1030-1930.
Bapu Bazar specializes in printed cloth.
Chaupar and **Nehru Bazars** for textiles.
Johari Bazar for jewellery.
Khajanewalon-ka-Rasta, off Chandpol bazar, for marble and stoneware.
Maniharon-ka-Rasta for lac bangles which the city is famous for.
Ramganj Bazar has leather footwear while opposite Hawa Mahal you will find the famous featherweight Jaipuri *rezais* (quilts).
Tripolia Bazar (3 gates), inexpensive jewellery.

Blue pottery

Blue Pottery Art Centre, Amer Rd, near Jain Mandir. For unusual pots.
Kripal Kumbha, B-18, Shiv Marg, Bani Park, T0141-220 0127. Gives lessons by appointment. Recommended.

Carpets

Channi Carpets and Textiles, Mount Rd opposite Ramgarh Rd. Factory shop, watch carpets being hand-knotted, then washed, cut and quality checked with a blow lamp.

Maharaja, Chandpol (near Samode Haveli). Watch carpet weavers and craftsmen, good value carpets and printed cotton.
The Reject Shop, Bhawani Singh Rd. For 'Shyam Ahuja' *durrie* collections.

Clothing and lifestyle

Hot Pink, Narain Niwas (see Where to stay, page 93), Kanota Bagh, Narain Singh Rd, T0141-510 8932, www.hotpink india.com. Beautiful boutique in the grounds of Narain Niwas Palace in the south of city with pieces from Indian designers including Manish Arora (the master of Kitsch chic), Abraham & Thakore (for true elegance) and Tarun Tahliani (for Bollywood style). Homeware also available. There is also a lovely small branch in Amber Fort.

Handicrafts

Anokhi, KK Shopping Complex, Prithviraj Rd, C-Scheme, T0141-400 7244. Beautifully crafted clothes, great designs. Some mens and childrens clothes, attractive block-printed homeware and bags. Recommended.
Rajasthali, Government Handicrafts, Mirza Ismail Rd, 500 m west of Ajmeri Gate.
Ratan Textiles, Papriwal Cottage, Ajmer Rd, T0141-408 0444, www.ratantextiles.com. Great array of textiles, homeware, clothing and unique souvenirs. Well crafted.

Jewellery

Jaipur is famous for gold, jewellery and gem stones (particularly emeralds, rubies, sapphires and diamonds; the latter require special certification for export). Semi-precious stones set in silver are more affordable (but check for loose settings, catches and cracked stones); sterling silver items are rare in India and the content varies widely. **Johari Bazar** is the scene of many surreptitious gem deals, and has backstreet factories where you may be able to see craftsmen at work. Bargaining is easier on your own so avoid being taken by a 'guide'. For about Rs 40 you can have gems authenticated and valued at the **Gem**

Testing Laboratory, off Mirza Ismail Rd, near New Gate, T0141-256 8221 (reputable jewellers should not object).

Do not use credit cards to buy these goods and never agree to 'help to export' jewellery. There have been reports of misuse of credit card accounts at **Apache Indian Jewellers** (also operating as **Krishna Gems** or **Ashirwad Gems & Art**) opposite Samodia Complex, Loha Mandi, SC Rd; and **Monopoli Gems**, opposite Sarga Sooli, Kishore Niwas (1st floor) Tripolia Bazar.

Reputable places include **Beg Gems**, Mehdi-ka-Chowk, near Hawa Mahal. **Bhuramal Rajmal Surana**, 1st floor, between Nos 264 and 268, Haldiyon-ka-Rasta. Highly recommended. **Dwarka's**, H20 Bhagat Singh Marg. Crafts high-quality gemstones in silver, gold and platinum in modern and traditional designs. **Gem Palace**, Mirza Ismail Rd, opposite Natraj and Niros, T0141-237 4175, www.gempalacejaipur.com. Exceptional range of jewellery in diverse styles, from traditional Indian bridal to chic modern pieces. It's a great place to see the unique styles of Indian jewellery from tribal regions to high society. Recommended. **Pearl Palace Silver Shop**, at Hotel Pearl Palace (see Where to stay, page 94). Great value jewellery and bits and pieces of traditional crafts from Jaipur from a trusted source.

⏱ What to do

Jaipur *p85, map p88*
Some hotels (such as the **Rambagh Palace**, see Where to stay, page 93) will arrange golf, tennis, squash, or elephant polo.

Body and soul
Kerala Ayurveda Kendra, T(0)93146-435574, www.keralaayurvedakendra.com. Great place to reinvigorate after a long day looking at the sites. There are a whole range of massages available and if you are interested in more long-term treatment, a great doctor on-site offering consultations and panchakarma. Phone for free pick-up. **Vipassana Centre**, Dhammathali, Galta, 3 km east of centre, T0141-268 0220. Meditation courses for new and experienced students.

City tours
RTDC City Sightseeing Half day: 0800-1300, Rs 150; Central Museum, City Palace, Amber Fort and Palace, Gaitore, Laxmi Narayan Temple, Jantar Mantar, Jal Mahal, Hawa Mahal. Full day: 0900-1800, Rs 200; including places above, plus Jaigarh Fort, Nahargarh Fort, Birla Planetarium, Birla Temple and Kanak Vrindavan. Pink City by Night: 1830-2230, Rs 250. Includes views of Jai Mahal, Amber Fort, etc, plus dinner at Nahargarh Fort. Call T0141-220 3531 or book at railway station, **Gangaur Hotel** or **Tourist Hotel**. Fantastic range of walks and tours designed to show you the 'real' Jaipur. Walks include 'Bazars, Crafts & Cuisines', where you can watch local artisans at work and try the best samosas in town; and 'Havelis & Temples' which visits hidden temples. You will hear fascinating stories about the buildings and families that populate the labyrinthine lanes of the old town. Cookery lessons available. Highly recommended.

General tours
Aravalli Safari, opposite Rajputana Palace Hotel, Palace Rd, T0141-236 5344, aravalli2@datainfosys.net. Very professional. **Forts & Palaces Tours Ltd**, S-1, Prabhakar Apartment, Vaishali Nagar, T0141-235 4508, www.palaces-tours.com. A very friendly, knowledgeable outfit offering camel safaris, sightseeing tours, hotel reservations, etc. **Pepper Tours**, T0484-405 8886/(0)9847-322802, www.peppertours.com. Creates memorable journeys in Kerala, Rajasthan and Goa.

⊖ Transport

Jaipur *p85, map p88*
Air Sanganer Airport, T0141-272 1333, has good facilities. Transport to town: taxi, 30 mins, Rs 250-300; auto-rickshaw Rs 150. Air India, Nehru Pl, Tonk Rd, T0141-274 3500; airport, T0141-272 1333, flies to **Delhi**, **Mumbai**, **Udaipur**, **Ahmedabad**, **Kolkata**. Jet Airways, T1800-225 522; airport T0141-2725 025, flies to **Delhi**, **Mumbai** and **Udaipur**.

Auto-rickshaw Avoid hotel touts and use the pre-paid auto-rickshaw counter to get to your hotel. Persistent auto-rickshaw drivers at railway station may quote Rs 10 to anywhere in town, then overcharge for city tour.

Station to city centre hotel, about Rs 50; sightseeing 3-4 hrs, Rs 200; 6-7 hrs, Rs 360. From railway and bus stations, drivers (who expect to take you to shops for commission) offer whole-day hire including Amber for Rs 150; have your list of sights planned and refuse to go to shops.

Local bus Unless you have plenty of time and a very limited budget, the best way to get around the city is by auto-rickshaw. To **Amber**, buses originate from Ajmeri Gate, junction with Mirza Ismail Rd, so get on there if you want a seat.

Long-distance bus Central Bus Stand, Sindhi Camp, Station Rd. Enquiries: *Deluxe*, Platform 3, T0141-511 6031, *Express*, T0141-511 6044 (24 hrs). Left luggage, Rs 10 per item per day. When arriving, particularly from Agra, you may be told to get off at Narain Singh Chowk, a bus stand some distance south of the centre; to avoid paying an inflated auto-rickshaw fare, insist on staying on until you reach the bus stand. Private buses will drop you on Station Rd but are not allowed inside the terminal. State and private Deluxe buses are very popular so book 2 days in advance. To **Agra**, 12 buses a day 0600-2400, 6½ hrs with 1 hr stop; **Ajmer** (131 km), regular service 0400-2330, 3 hrs;

Bharatpur 5 buses a day, but all deluxe and a/c buses to Agra go through Bharatpur but you have to pay Agra fare; **Delhi** (261 km), half hourly, 5½ hrs, almost hourly service with deluxe, Pink Line and Volvo buses running Rs 400/700 for a/c; **Jaisalmer** (654 km), 2145, 13 hrs via Jodhpur. **Jodhpur** (332 km), frequent, 7 hrs around Rs 400; **Udaipur** (374 km), 12 hrs; **Kota** via Bundi (7 daily), 4-5 hrs.

Cycle rickshaw These are often pretty rickety. From the station to the central hotels costs Rs 30.

Taxi Unmetered taxis; 4 hrs costs Rs 450 (40 km), 8 hrs costs Rs 750 (city and Amber). Extra hill charge for Amber, Raigarh, Nahargarh. Out of city Rs 5-8 per km; **Marudhar Tours** recommended; or try RTDC, T0141-220 3531. Also **Pink City Cabs**, T0141-405 4824, excellent radio cab service.

Train Enquiry, T131, T0141-220 4536, reservation T135. Computerized booking office in separate building to front and left of station; separate queue for foreigners. Use pre-paid rickshaw counter. **Abu Rd** (for **Mount Abu**): *Aravali Exp 19708* (goes on to Mumbai), 0845, 8 hrs; **Agra Cantt**: *Marudhar Exp 14854/14864*, 1550, 7 hrs. **Ajmer**: *Aravali Exp 19708*, 0845, 2½ hrs. **Bikaner**: *Bikaner Exp 14710*, 1600, 7 hrs. **Chittaurgarh**: *Jp Udz Exp 12992*, 1400, 5 hrs. **Delhi**: *Shatabdi 12016*, 1745, 4 hrs 25 mins, *Dee Double Dcke 12985*, DSR, 0600, 4½ hrs. **Jodhpur**: *Ranthambhore Exp 12465*, 1705, 5½ hrs; **Mumbai** (C): *Jaipur BCT Superfast 12956*, 1410, 17½ hrs; **Udaipur** *Jp Udz Sf Spl 09721*, 0645, 7 hrs.

ⓘ Directory

Jaipur *p85, map p88*
Banks Several on Mirza Ismail Rd and Ashok Marg. **Medical services** Ambulance: T102. Santokba Durlabhji Hospital, Bhawani Singh Rd, T0141-256 6251. SMS Hospital, Sawai Ram Singh Marg, T0141-256 0291.

Around Jaipur

Amber Fort is one of Jaipur's biggest draws, with an elephant ride to the top a priority on many people's 'to do' list. It's still an impressive building but has been poorly maintained in recent years. In the backstreets of Amber, you will also find the Anokhi Museum of Handprinting in a beautifully converted *haveli*. Bagru offers good opportunities to see handicrafts in production, while Samode is perhaps the last word in elegant living.

Amber (Amer) → For listings, see pages 101-102.

Today there is no town to speak of in Amber, just the palace clinging to the side of the rocky hill, overlooked by the small fort above, with a small village at its base. In the high season this is one of India's most popular tourist sites, with a continuous train of colourfully decorated elephants walking up and down the ramp to the palace. One penalty of its popularity is the persistence of the vendors.

Background

Amber, which takes its name from Ambarisha, a king of the once-famous royal city of Ayodhya, was the site of a Hindu temple built by the Mina tribes as early as the 10th century. Two centuries later the Kachhawaha Rajputs made it their capital, which it remained until Sawai Jai Singh II moved to his newly planned city of Jaipur in 1727. Its location made Amber strategically crucial for the Mughal emperors as they moved south, and the Maharajahs of Amber took care to establish close relations with successive Mughal rulers. The building of the fort palace was begun in 1600 by Raja Man Singh, a noted Rajput general in Akbar's army, and Mughal influence was strong in much of the subsequent building.

The approach

ⓘ *Rs 900 per elephant carrying 2 people, no need to tip, though the driver will probably ask, takes 10 mins. Jeeps Rs 200 each way. It can be quite a long wait in a small garden with little shade and you will be at the mercy of the hawkers. If you do want to buy, wait until you reach the steps when the price will drop dramatically.*

From the start of the ramp you can either walk or ride by elephant; the walk is quite easy and mainly on a separate path. Elephants carry up to four people on a padded seat. The ride can be somewhat unnerving when the elephant comes close to the edge of the road, but it is quite safe. You have to buy a 'return ticket' even if you wish to walk down later. The elephants get bad tempered as the day wears on. If you are interested in finding out more about the welfare of Amber's elephants, or indeed any of Jaipur's street animals, contact **Help in Suffering** ⓘ *T0141-276 0803, www.his-india.org.au.*

The Palace

ⓘ *0900-1630 (it's worth arriving at 0900), foreigners Rs 200, Indians Rs 25 (tickets in the chowk, below the steps up to Shila Mata). Take the green bus from the Hawa Mahal.*

Auto-rickshaw Rs 100 (Rs 250 for return, including the wait). Guides are worth hiring, Rs 400 for a half day (group of 4), find one with a government guide licence.

After passing through a series of five defensive gates, you reach the first courtyard of the **Raj Mahal** built by Man Singh I in 1600, entered through the **Suraj Pol** (Sun Gate). Here you can get a short ride around the courtyard on an elephant, but bargain very hard. There are some toilets near the dismounting platform. On the south side of this Jaleb Chowk with the flower beds, is a flight of steps leading up to the **Singh Pol** (Lion Gate) entrance to the upper courtyard of the palace.

A separate staircase to the right leads to the green marble-pillared **Shila Mata Temple** (to Kali as Goddess of War), which opens at certain times of the day and then only allows a limited number of visitors at a time (so ask before joining the queue). The temple contains a black marble image of the goddess that Man Singh I brought back from Jessore (now in Bangladesh; the chief priest has always been Bengali). The silver doors with images of Durga and Saraswati were added by his successor.

In the left-hand corner of the courtyard, the **Diwan-i-Am** (Hall of Public Audience) was built by Raja Jai Singh I in 1639. Originally, it was an open pavilion with cream marble pillars supporting an unusual striped canopy-shaped ceiling, with a portico with double red sandstone columns. The room on the east was added by Sawai Ram Singh II. **Ganesh Pol** (circa 1700-1725), south of the chowk, colourfully painted and with mosaic decoration, takes its name from the prominent figure of Ganesh above the door. It separates the private from the public areas.

This leads onto the **Jai Singh I** court with a formal garden. To the east is the two-storeyed cream-coloured marble pavilion **Jai Mandir** (Diwan-i-Khas or Hall of Private Audience), below, and **Jas Mandir** (1635-1640) with a curved Bengali roof, on the terrace above. The former, with its marble columns and painted ceiling, has lovely views across the lake. The latter has colourful mosaics, mirrors and marble *jali* screens which let in cooling breezes. Both have **Shish Mahals** (Mirror Palaces) faced with mirrors, seen to full effect when lit by a match. To the west of the chowk is the **Sukh Niwas**, a pleasure palace with a marble water course to cool the air, and doors inlaid with ivory and sandalwood. The Mughal influence is quite apparent in this chowk.

Above the Ganesh Pol is the **Sohag Mandir**, a rectangular chamber with beautiful latticed windows and octagonal rooms to each side. From the rooftop there are stunning views over the palace across the town of Amber, the long curtain wall surrounding the town and further north, through the 'V' shaped entrance in the hills, to the plains beyond. Beyond this courtyard is the **Palace of Man Singh I**. A high wall separates it from the Jai Singh Palace. In the centre of the chowk which was once open is a *baradari* (12-arched pavilion), combining Mughal and Hindu influences. The surrounding palace, a complex warren of passages and staircases, was turned into *zenana* quarters when the newer palaces were built by Jai Singh. Children find it great fun to explore this part.

Old Palace and Anokhi Museum

Old Palace of Amber (1216) lies at the base of **Jaigarh Fort**. A stone path (currently being restored) from the Chand Pol in the first courtyard of Amber Palace leads to the ruins. Though there is little interest today, nearby are several worthwhile temples. These include the **Jagatsiromani Temple**, dedicated to Krishna, with carvings and paintings; it is associated with Mira Bai. Take time to visit the fantastic **Anokhi Museum of Hand Printing** ⓘ *www.anokhi.com*, which has a great textile collection and you can even try your hand at handblock printing.

Ramgarh Lake and Jamwa Sanctuary

The 15-sq-km lake of Jamwa Ramgarh attracts large flocks of waterfowl in winter, and lies within a game sanctuary with good boating and birdwatching. Built to supply Jaipur with water, it now provides less than 1% of the city's needs and in years of severe drought may dry up completely. The 300-sq-km Jamwa Sanctuary, which once provided the Jaipur royal family with game, still has some panthers, nilgai and small game. Contact the tourist office in Jaipur (see page 86) for details of public buses. It is about a 45-minute drive.

Samode

At the head of the enclosed valley in the dry rugged hills of the northern Aravallis, Samode stands on a former caravan route. The sleepy village, with its local artisans producing printed cloth and glass bangles, nestles within a ring of old walls. The painted *havelis* are still full of character. Samode is well worth the visit from Jaipur, and makes a good stop en route to the painted towns of Shekhawati (see page 198). Both the palace and the *bagh* are wonderful, peaceful places to spend a night.

The **palace** ⓘ *now a heritage hotel, Rs 500 for non-residents includes tea/coffee,* which dominates the village, is fabulously decorated with 300-year-old wall paintings (hunting scenes, floral motifs, etc) which still look almost new. Around the first floor of the Darbar Hall are magnificent alcoves, decorated with mirrors like *shish mahal* and *jali* screens through which the royal ladies would have looked down into the grand jewel-like Darbar Hall.

Towering immediately above the palace is **Samode Fort**, the maharajah's former residence, reached in times of trouble by an underground passage. The old stone zigzag path has been replaced by 300 steps. Though dilapidated, there are excellent views from the ramparts; a caretaker has the keys. The main fort gate is the starting point of some enticing walks into the Aravallis. A paved path leads to a shrine about 3 km away. There are two other powerful forts you can walk to, forming a circular walk ending back in Samode. Allow three hours, wear good shoes and a hat, and carry water.

Samode Bagh, a large 400-year-old Mughal-style formal garden with fountains and pavilions, has been beautifully restored. It is 3 km southeast of Samode, towards the main Jaipur–Agra road. Within the grounds are modest-sized but elaborately decorated tents.

Around Jaipur listings

For hotel and restaurant price codes and other relevant information, see pages 13-16.

🍴 Where to stay

Amber *p99*

$$ Mosaics Guesthouse, Sirayam Ki Doongri, Amber, T0141-253 0031, www.mosaicsgueshouse.com. With lovely views of Amber Fort, this place has just 4 rooms packed full of art and curiosities. A welcome change to staying in Jaipur.

Ramgarh Lake and Jamwa Sanctuary
p101

$$$$ Ramgarh Lodge (Taj), overlooking the lake, T01426-252217, www.tajhotels.com. 18 elegant a/c rooms (3 enormous suites) in a former royal hunting lodge. There's a museum and library, furnished appropriately with various hunting trophies on display. The restaurant is limited but there are delightful walks, fishing and boating, plus the ruins of old Kachhawaha Fort are nearby. **$$$** in summer.

$ Jheel Tourist Village (RTDC), Mandawa Choraha, T01426-252170. Pleasant surroundings for 10 not especially well-maintained village-style rustic huts.

Samode *p101*

$$$$ Samode Bagh, 3 km from the palace, T01423-240235, www.samode.com. 44 luxury a/c tents decorated in the Mughal style, each with a beautiful modern bathroom and its own veranda. *Darbar* tent, al fresco meals, pool with slide, tennis, volleyball, badminton, lovely setting in peaceful walled Mughal gardens, plenty of birdwatching, safaris to sand dunes, amazing. Reservations essential.

$$$$ Samode Palace, T01423-240014, www.samode.com. Reservations essential. Half price 1 May-30 Sep. Contact **Samode Haveli**, T0141-263 2407, to reserve and arrange taxi from Jaipur. Magical place to indulge your fantasies of being a maharajah or maharani for a night. 42 a/c rooms, tastefully modernized without losing any of the charm. The setting is magnificent, with 2 pools and a garden. There is a traditional buffet restaurant and an International boutique-style restaurant. Good shop with textiles, camel rides around the village and to Samode Bagh. Really remarkable for its setting and atmosphere, generally friendly and exceptional service. Well worth a visit even if not staying. Very romantic. Highly recommended.

$$$$ The Treehouse Resort, 35th Kilometer stone on NH-8, 35 km out of Jaipur, T(0)9001-797422, www.treehouseresort.in. Unique property inspired by naturalist Jim Corbett's treehouses, Sunil Mehta has built what they call 'deluxe nests' in the trees. If you like nature and creature comforts, such as a/c, then these are the treehouses for you. It has great eco credentials and a back-to-nature vibe. There is a good restaurant and stunning **Peacock Bar** reconstructed from a 400-year-old heritage building. Recommended.

$ Prem Devi Artist's Homestay, CB Mugal Art Galary, Shilp Colony, Samode T(0)9828-643924, sureshmdw1983@ yahoo.com. Simple, friendly homestay run by a lovely family of artists – the ever cheerful Prem Devi, her husband and 2 grown-up children. 5 sparse but very clean rooms with attached bathrooms. The exterior and lobby of the house are beautifully decorated with traditional art and miniature paintings. 3 home-cooked vegetarian meals per day available for an extra Rs 250 (no restaurants in Samode); free art classes.

⊖ Transport

Samode *p101*

Samode is a 1-hr drive from **Jaipur**. Buses from Chandpol Gate go to Chomu where you can pick up a local bus to Samode.

Udaipur

Enchanting Udaipur, set in the Girwa Valley in the Aravalli hills of south Rajasthan, must be one of the most romantic cities in India, with white marble palaces, placid blue lakes, attractive gardens and green hills that are a world away from the surrounding desert. High above the lake towers the massive palace of the Maharanas. From its rooftop gardens and balconies, you can look over Lake Pichola, the Lake Palace "adrift like a snowflake" in its centre. The monsoons that deserted the city earlier in the decade have returned – though water shortage remains a threat – to replenish the lakes and ghats, where women thrash wet heaps of washing with wooden clubs, helped by splashing children. The houses and temples of the old city stretch out in a pale honeycomb, making Udaipur an oasis of colour in a stark and arid region. Sunset only intensifies the city's beauty, turning the city palace's pale walls to gold, setting the lake to shimmer in silvery swathes against it, while mynah birds break out into a noisy twilight chorus. Ochre and orange skies line the rim of the westernmost hills while countless roof terraces light up and the lake's islands appear to float on waters dancing in the evening breeze and turning purple in the fading light.

Arriving in Udaipur
Getting there The airport, about 30-45 minutes by taxi or city bus, is well connected to the rest of the country. The main bus stand is east of Udai Pol, 2-3 km from most hotels, while Udaipur City Railway Station is another 1 km south. Both have auto-rickshaw stands outside as well as pushy hotel touts.

Getting around The touristy area around the Jagdish Temple and the City Palace, the main focus of interest, is best explored on foot but there are several sights further afield. Buses, shared tempos, auto-rickshaws and taxis cover the city and surrounding area; some travellers prefer to hire a scooter or bike. ▶▶ *See Transport, page 114.*

Tourist information Be prepared for crowds, dirt and pollution and persistent hotel touts who descend on new arrivals. It is best to reserve a hotel in advance or ask for a particular street or area of town. Travellers risk being befriended by someone claiming to show you the city for free. If you accept, you run the risk of visiting one shop after

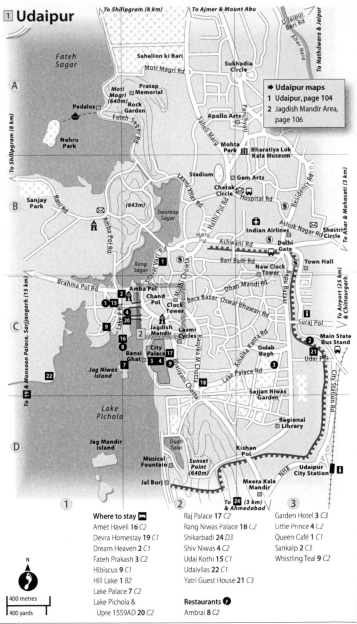

1 Udaipur

To Shillpgram (8 km)

To Ajmer & Mount Abu

To Nathdwara & Jaipur

Fateh
Sagar

Sahelion ki Bari

Moti Magri Rd

Sukhadia
Circle

Udaipur
Bari Rd

Ahar Nala

➡ Udaipur maps
1 Udaipur, page 104
2 Jagdish Mandir Area,
page 106

Moti
Magri
(640m)
Rock
Garden

Pratap
Memorial

Pedalos

Nehru
Park

Fateh Sagar Rd

Apollo Arts

Panchwati

Mohta
Park

Bharatiya Lok
Kala Museum

To Shillpgram (8 km)

Sanjay
Park

Rani Rd

Amba Pol Rd

(643m)

Swaroop
Sagar

Stadium

Gem Arts

Laxmi Vilas Rd

Chetak
Circle

Hospital Rd

Residency Rd

Ashok Nagar Rd

Shastri
Circle

To Ahar & Mahasati (3 km)

Rang
Sagar

Sukhar Vari Rd

Hathi
Pol

Ashwani Rd

Indian Airlines

Delhi
Gate

Town Hall

Brahma Pol Rd

Amba Pol

Chand
Pol

Clock
Tower

Bari Badi Rd

New Clock
Tower

Bapu Bazaar

Motti Chowk

Bara Bazaar

Dhan Mandi Rd

Oswal Bhawan Rd

Suraj Pol

To Airport (25 km)
& Chittaurgarh

To Monsoon Palace, Sarjiangarh (15 km)

Jagdish
Mandir

Laxmi
Cycles

Bajika M Chotta

City
Palace

Gulab
Bagh

Main State
Bus Stand

Udai Pol

Bansi
Ghat

Lake Amalka Kanta Rd

Lake Palace Rd

City Station Rd

Jag Niwas
Island

Bhatiyani Chotta

Lake
Pichola

Sajjan Niwas
Garden

Jag Mandir
Island

Dudh
Talai

Regional
Library

Kishan
Pol

Musical
Fountain

Sunset
Point
(640m)

Jal Burj

Meera Kala
Mandir

NH8

Udaipur
City Station

To 24 (3 km)
& Ahmedabad

N

400 metres

400 yards

104 • Rajasthan Udaipur

Where to stay 🛏
Amet Haveli **16** *C2*
Devra Homestay **19** *C1*
Dream Heaven **2** *C1*
Fateh Prakash **3** *C2*
Hibiscus **9** *C1*
Hill Lake **1** *B2*
Lake Palace **7** *C2*
Lake Pichola &
  Upre 1559AD **20** *C2*

Raj Palace **17** *C2*
Rang Niwas Palace **18** *C2*
Shikarbadi **24** *D3*
Shiv Niwas **4** *C2*
Udai Kothi **15** *C1*
Udaivilas **22** *C1*
Yatri Guest House **21** *C3*

Restaurants 🍴
Ambrai **8** *C2*

Garden Hotel **3** *C3*
Little Prince **4** *C2*
Queen Café **1** *C1*
Sankalp **2** *C3*
Whistling Teal **9** *C2*

another with your 'friend'. **Rajasthan Tourism Development Corporation (RTDC)**
① *Tourist Reception Centre, Fateh Memorial, Suraj Pol, T0294-241 1535, 1000-1700, guides 4-8 hrs, Rs 250-400.*

Background

The legendary **Ranas of Mewar** who traced their ancestry back to the Sun, first ruled the region from their seventh-century stronghold Chittaurgarh. The title 'Rana', peculiar to the rulers of **Mewar**, was supposedly first used by Hammir who reoccupied Mewar in 1326. In 1568, **Maharana Udai Singh** founded a new capital on the shores of Lake Pichola and named it Udaipur (the city of sunrise) having selected the spot in 1559. On the advice of an ascetic who interrupted his rabbit hunt, Udai Singh had a temple built above the lake and then constructed his palace around it.

In contrast to the house of Jaipur, the rulers of Udaipur prided themselves on being independent from other more powerful regional neighbours, particularly the Mughals. In a piece of local princely one-upmanship, **Maharana Pratap Singh**, heir apparent to the throne of Udaipur, invited Raja Man Singh of Jaipur to a lakeside picnic. Afterwards he had the ground on which his guest had trodden washed with sacred Ganga water and insisted that his generals take purificatory baths. Man Singh reaped appropriate revenge by preventing Pratap Singh from acceding to his throne. Udaipur, for all its individuality, remained one of the poorer princely states in Rajasthan, a consequence of being almost constantly at war. In 1818, Mewar, the Kingdom of the Udaipur Maharanas, came under British political control but still managed to avoid almost all British cultural influence.

Places in Udaipur

Old City

Udaipur is a traditionally planned fortified city. Its bastioned rampart walls are pierced by massive gates, each studded with iron spikes as protection against enemy war elephants. The five remaining gates are: **Hathi Pol** (Elephant Gate – north), **Chand Pol** (Moon Gate – west), **Kishan Pol** (south), the main entrance **Suraj Pol** (Sun Gate – east) and **Delhi Gate** (northeast). On the west side, the city is bounded by the beautiful Pichola Lake and to the east and north, by moats. To the south is the fortified hill of Eklingigarh. The main street leads from the Hathi Pol to the massive City Palace on the lakeside.

The walled city is a maze of narrow winding lanes flanked by tall whitewashed houses with doorways decorated with Mewar folk art, windows with stained glass or *jali* screens, majestic *havelis* with spacious inner courtyards and shops. Many of the houses here were given by the Maharana to retainers – barbers, priests, traders and artisans – while many rural landholders (titled jagirdars) had a *haveli* conveniently located near the palace.

The **Jagdish Mandir** ① *150 m north of the palace, 0500-1400, 1600-2200*, was built by Maharana Jagat Singh in 1651. The temple is a fine example of the Nagari style, and contrasts with the serenity of Udaipur's predominantly whitewashed buildings, surrounded as it often is by chanting Sadhus, gambolling monkeys and the smell of incense. A shrine with a brass Garuda stands outside and stone elephants flank the entrance steps; within is a black stone image of Vishnu as Jagannath, the Lord of the Universe.

A quiet, slightly eccentric museum, including what they claim is the world's largest turban, now lies in the lovely 18th-century **Bagore ki Haveli** ① *1000-1900, Rs 25, camera Rs 10*. The *haveli* has 130 rooms and was built as a miniature of the City Palace. There are cool shady courtyards containing some peacock mosaics and fretwork, and carved pillars made from granite, marble and the local blueish-grey stone. A slightly forlorn but funny puppet show plays several times a day on the ground floor.

City Palace
① *0930-1730, last entry 1630. From Ganesh Deori Gate: Rs 50 (more from near Lake Palace Ghat). Camera Rs 100, video Rs 300. From 'Maharajah's gallery', you can get a pass for Fateh Prakash Palace, Shiv Niwas and Shambu Niwas, Rs 75. Guided tour, 1 hr, Rs 100 each. Guides hang around the entrance; standards vary wildly and they can cause a scene if you have already hired a guide. Ask at the ticket office. Rs 25 gets you access to the complex and a nice walk down to the jetty.*

This impressive complex of several palaces is a blend of Rajput and Mughal influences. Half of it, with a great plaster façade, is still occupied by the royal family. Between the **Bari Pol** (Great Gate, 1608, men traditionally had to cover their heads with a turban from this point on) to the north, and the **Tripolia Gate** (1713), are eight *toranas* (arches), under which the rulers were weighed against gold and silver on their birthdays, which was then distributed to the poor. One of the two domes on top of the Tripolia originally housed a water clock; a glass sphere with a small hole at the base was filled with water and would take exactly one hour to empty, at which point a gong would be struck and the process repeated. The gate has three arches to allow the royal family their private entrance, through the middle, and then a public entry and exit gate to either side. Note the elephant to the far left (eastern) end of the gate structure; they were seen as bringers of good fortune and appear all over the palace complex. The Tripolia leads in to the **Manak Chowk**, originally a large courtyard which was converted in to a garden only in 1992. The row of lumps in the surface to the left are original, and demarcate elephant parking bays! Claiming descent from Rama, and therefore the sun, the Mewars always insured that there was an image of the sun available for worship even on a cloudy day, thus the beautiful example set in to the exterior wall of the palace. The large step in front of the main entrance was for mounting horses, while those to the left were for elephants. The family crest above the door depicts a Rajput warrior and one of the Bhil tribesmen from the local area whose renowned archery skills were much

2 Jagdish Mandir area

➡ **Udaipur maps**
1 Udaipur, page 104
2 Jagdish Mandir Area, page 106

Where to stay 🛏
Jagat Niwas 6
Jheel Guest House 7
Kankarwa Haveli 16
Lake Ghat 8
Lal Ghat Haveli 17
Lalghat Guest House 3
Minerva 14
Nayee Haveli 4
Nukkad Guest House 9
Poonam Haveli 12
The Tiger 11
Udai Garh 15
Udai Niwas 13

Restaurants 🍴
Café Edelweiss 1
Papu's Juice Bar 5
Savage Garden 2

used in the defence of the Mewar household. The motto translates as 'God protects those who stand firm in upholding righteousness'.

As you enter the main door, a set of stairs to the right leads down to an armoury which includes an impressive selection of swords, some of which incorporate pistols into their handles. Most people then enter the main museum to the right, although it is possible to access the government museum from here (see below). The entrance is known as **Ganesh Dori**, meaning 'Ganesh's turn'; the image of the elephant god in the wall as the steps start to turn has been there since 1620. Note the tiles underneath which were imported from Japan in the 1930s and give even the Hindu deities an oriental look to their eyes. The second image is of Laxmi, bringer of good fortune and wealth.

The stairs lead in to **Rai Angan**, 'Royal Court' (1559). The temple to the left is to the sage who first advised that the royal palace be built on this side. Opposite is a display of some of Maharana Pratap Singh's weapons, used in some of his many battles with the Mughals, as well as his legendary horse, Chetak. The Mughals fought on elephants, the Mewars on horses; the elephant trunk fitted to Chetak's nose was to fool the Mughal elephants in to thinking that the Mewar horses were baby elephants, and so not to be attacked. A fuller version of this nosepiece can be seen in one of the paintings on the walls, as indeed can an elephant wielding a sword in its trunk during battle.

The stairs to the left of the temple lead up to **Chandra Mahal**, featuring a large bowl where gold and silver coins were kept for distribution to the needy. Note that the intricately carved walls are made not from marble but a combination of limestone powder, gum Arabic, sugar cane juice and white lentils. From here steps lead up in to **Bari Mahal** (1699-1711), situated on top the hill chosen as the palace site; the design has incorporated the original trees. The cloisters' cusped arches have wide eaves and are raised above the ground to protect the covered spaces from heavy monsoon rain. This was an intimate 'playground' where the royal family amused themselves and were entertained. The painting opposite the entrance is an aerial view of the palace; the effect from the wall facing it is impressive. The chair on display was meant for Maharana Fateh Singh's use at the Delhi Darbar, an event which he famously refused to attend. The chair was sent on and has still never been used.

The picture on the wall of two elephants fighting shows the area that can be seen through the window to the left; there is a low wall running from the Tripolia Gate to the main palace building. An elephant was placed either side of the wall, and then each had to try to pull the other until their opponent's legs touched the wall, making them the victor.

The next room is known as **Dil Kushal Mahal** ('love entertainment room'), a kind of mirrored love nest. This leads on to a series of incredibly intricate paintings depicting the story of life in the palace, painted 1782-1828. The **Shiv Vilas Chini ki Chatar Sali** incorporates a large number of Chinese and Dutch tiles in to its decoration, as well as an early petrol-powered fan. Next is the Moti Mahal, the ladies' portion of the men's palace, featuring a changing room lined with mirrors and two game boards incorporated into the design of the floor.

Pritam Niwas was last lived in by Maharana Gopal Singh, who died in 1955 having been disabled by polio at a young age. His wheel armchair and even his commode are on display here. This leads on to **Surya Chopar**, which features a beautiful gold-leaf image of the sun; note the 3D relief painting below. The attractive **Mor Chowk** court, intended for ceremonial darbars, was added in the mid-17th century, and features beautiful late 19th-century peacock mosaics. The throne room is to its south, the **Surya Chopar**, from which the Rana (who claimed descent from the Sun) paid homage to his divine ancestor.

The **Manak Mahal** (Ruby Palace) was filled with figures of porcelain and glass in the mid-19th century. To the north, the **Bari Mahal** or Amar Vilas (1699-1711) was added on top of a low hill. It has a pleasant garden with full grown trees around a square water tank in the central court.

A plain, narrow corridor leads in to the **Queen's Palace**, featuring a series of paintings, lithographs and photographs, and leading out in to **Laxmi Chowk**, featuring two cages meant for trapping tigers and leopards. The entrance to the **Government Museum** ① *Sat-Thu 1000-1600, Rs 3,* is from this courtyard. The rather uncared for display includes second-century BC inscriptions, fifth- to eighth-century sculptures and 9000 miniature paintings of 17th- and 19th-century Mewar schools of art but also a stuffed kangaroo and Siamese twin deer.

On the west side of the Tripolia are the **Karan Vilas** (1620-1628) and **Khush Mahal**, a rather grotesque pleasure palace for European guests, whilst to the south lies the **Shambhu Niwas Palace** the present residence of the Maharana.

Maharana Fateh Singh added to this the opulent **Shiv Niwas** with a beautiful courtyard and public rooms, and the **Fateh Prakash Palace**. Here the Darbar Hall's royal portrait gallery displays swords still oiled and sharp. The Bohemian chandeliers (1880s) are reflected by Venetian mirrors, the larger ones made in India of lead crystal. Both, now exclusive hotels (see Where to stay, page 109), are worth visiting.

On the first floor is the **Crystal Gallery** ① *0900-2000, Rs 500 for a guided tour with a talk on the history of Mewar, followed by a cup of tea (overpriced with a cold reception according to some; avoid the cream tea as the scones are so hard they will crack your teeth).* The gallery has an extensive collection of cut-crystal furniture, vases, etc, made in Birmingham (England) in the 1870s, supplemented by velvet, rich 'zardozi' brocade, objects in gold and silver and a precious stone-studded throne.

'The Legacy of honour', outlining the history of the Mewar dynasty, is a good **Son et Lumière** show, the first privately funded one in India. There are two shows daily at 1930 and 2030, Rs 100 for ground seating, Rs 300 on terrace; book at the City Palace ticket office.

Lake Pichola

Fringed with hills, gardens, *havelis*, ghats and temples, Lake Pichola is the scenic focus of Udaipur though parts get covered periodically with vegetation, and the water level drops considerably during the summer. Set in it are the Jag Niwas (Lake Palace) and the Jag Mandir palaces.

Jag Mandir, built on an island in the south of the lake, is notable for the Gul Mahal, a domed pavilion started by Karan Singh (1620-1628) and completed by Jagat Singh (1628-1652). It is built of yellow sandstone inlaid with marble around an attractive courtyard. Maharajah Karan Singh gave the young Prince Khurram (later Shah Jahan), refuge here when he was in revolt against his father Jahangir in 1623, cementing a friendly relationship between the Mewar Maharaja and the future Mughal emperor. Refugee European ladies and children were also given sanctuary here by Maharana Sarap Singh during the Mutiny. There is a lovely pavilion with four stone elephants on each side (some of the broken trunks have been replaced with polystyrene!). You get superb views from the balconies. It's possible to take an enjoyable **boat trip** ① *Apr-Sep 0800-1100, 1500-1800, Oct-Mar 1000-1700, on the hour, Rs 300 for 1-hr landing on Jag Mandir, Rs 200 for boat ride without stop,* from Rameshwar Ghat, south of the City Palace complex. It's especially attractive in the late afternoon light. Rates from the boat stand at Lal Ghat may be slightly cheaper. There is a pricey bar/restaurant on the island but it's worth stopping for the stunning views.

Jag Niwas Island (Lake Palace) ① *it is no longer possible to go to the Lake Palace for lunch or dinner unless you are a resident at Lake Palace, Leela or Oberoi*, is entirely covered by the Dilaram and Bari Mahal palaces, which were built by **Maharana Jagat Singh II** in 1746. Once the royal summer residences and now converted into a hotel, they seem to float like a dream ship on the blue waters of the lake.

On the hill immediately to the east of Dudh Talai, a pleasant two-hour walk to the south of the city, is **Sunset Point** which has excellent free views over the city. The path past the café (good for breakfast) leads to the gardens on the wall; a pleasant place to relax. Although it looks steep it is only a 30-minute climb from the café.

Fateh Sagar and around

This lake, north of Lake Pichola, was constructed in 1678 during the reign of Maharana Jai Singh and modified by Maharana Fateh Singh. There is a pleasant lakeside drive along the east bank but, overall, it lacks the charm of the Pichola. **Nehru Park** on an island (accessible by ferry) has a restaurant.

Overlooking the Fateh Sagar is the **Moti Magri (Pearl Hill)** ① *0900-1800, Rs 20, camera free.* There are several statues of local heroes in the attractive rock gardens including one of Maharana Pratap on his horse Chetak, to which he owed his life. Local guides claim that Chetak jumped an abyss of extraordinary width in the heat of the battle of Haldighati (1576) even after losing one leg. For more information, read *Hero of Haldighati* by Kesri Singh.

Sahelion ki Bari (Garden of the Maids of Honour) ① *0900-1800, Rs 10, plus Rs 2 for 'fountain show',* a little north from Moti Magri, is an ornamental pleasure garden; a great spot, both attractive and restful. There are many fountains including trick ones along the edge of the path which are operated by the guide clapping his hands! In a pavilion in the first courtyard, opposite the entrance, a children's museum has curious exhibits including a pickled scorpion, a human skeleton and busts of Einstein and Archimedes.

Udaipur listings

For hotel and restaurant price codes and other relevant information, see pages 13-16.

● Where to stay

Udaipur *p103, maps p104 and p106*
Frenzied building work continues to provide more hotels, while restaurants compete to offer the best views from the highest rooftop. The area around the lake is undeniably the most romantic place to stay, but also the most congested. The hotels on Lake Palace Rd and on the hilltop above Fateh Sagar Lake offer more peaceful surroundings, while Swaroop Sagar offers a good compromise between calmness and convenience. **Tourist Reception Centre**, Fateh Memorial, has a list of accommodation.

$$$$ Fateh Prakash (HRH), City Palace, T0294-252 8016, www.hrhindia.com. Well-appointed lake-facing rooms in the modern 'Dovecote' wing and 7 superb suites in the main palace building. Original period furniture, great views from the **Sunset Terrace** restaurant, good facilities and service (residents may ask for a pass at the City Palace entrance for a short cut to the hotel).

$$$$ Lake Palace (Taj), Lake Pichola, T0294-252 8800, www.tajhotels.com. 84 rooms, most with lake view, in one of the world's most spectacularly located hotels; quite an experience. Standard rooms are tasteful but unremarkable, suites are outstanding and priced to match. There's a spa and a small pool, but service can be slightly abrupt. It was the location for the

1980s Bond film *Octopussy*. Be aware that unless you are staying here or at **Fateh Prakash**, **Shiv Niwas** or the **Leela** you cannot come over to **Lake Palace** to eat.

$$$$ Shiv Niwas (HRH), City Palace (turn right after entrance), T0294-252 8016, www.hrhindia.com. 19 tasteful rooms, 17 luxurious suites including those stayed in by Queen Elizabeth II and Roger Moore, some with superb lake views, very comfortable, good restaurant, very pleasant outdoor seating for all meals around a lovely marble pool (non-residents pay Rs 300 to swim), tennis, squash, excellent service, beautiful surroundings, reserve ahead in high season. This place will have you feeling like a Maharani. Recommended.

$$$$ Udaivilas (Oberoi), Lake Pichola, T0294-243 3300, www.oberoihotels.com. The elegant but monochrome exterior of this latter-day palace does nothing to prepare you for the opulence within; the stunning entry courtyard sets the scene for staggeringly beautiful interiors. The 87 rooms are the last word in indulgence; some have one of the hotel's 9 swimming pools running alongside their private balcony. The setting on the lake, overlooking both the Lake and City palaces, is superb, as are the food and service. This is probably one of the most perfect hotels in India. Outstanding. Highly recommended.

$$$ Amet Haveli, outside Chandpole, T0294-243 1085, amethaveli@sify.com. Enviable location on the lakefront. Beautiful rooms – some with unparalleled views across the lake. The highly recommended **Ambrai** restaurant is on site.

$$$ Devra Homestay, Sisarma–Bujra Rd, Kalarohi, T0294-2431049, www.devra udaipur.com. This lovely place is on the other side of the lake from the City Palace and inland near the small village of Kalarohi, so it has beautiful views of the rolling hills around Udaipur. There are 9 rooms. It's peaceful and quiet, with abundant birdlife. Activities include yoga, village walks and birdwatching.

$$$ The Tiger, 33 Gangaur Ghat, T0294-242 0430, www.thetigerudaipur.com. Stylish new rooms, funky decor (lots of animal print) and vibe. Fantastic in-house spa with steam room, sauna, jacuzzi and traditional massage. Great sunset view from the rooftop restaurant. Recommended.

$$$-$$ Jagat Niwas, 24-25 Lal Ghat, T0294-242 0133, www.jagatniwaspalace.com. 30 individual, very clean rooms in a beautifully restored 17th-century 'fairy tale' *haveli*. Good restaurant (see Restaurants, page 112), helpful staff, good travel desk, excellent service. Lots of groups, though, so book well in advance.

$$$-$$ Kankarwa Haveli, 26 Lal Ghat, T0294-241 1457, www.kankarwahaveli.com. Wide range of rooms in a renovated 250-year-old *haveli* on the lakeshore, some rooms have views and beautiful original artwork. Each room is unique. 2 new stunning suites have been built – modern glass-fronted design but fitting in seamlessly with this classic building – one suite has possibly the best view of the lake in this area. The roof terrace has also had a revamp and you can sample some great home cooking. Lots of cosy nooks to sit in. You will be welcomed warmly by Janardan Singh and his family. Very atmospheric. Highly recommended.

$$$-$$ Udai Garh, 21 Lal Ghat, behind Jagdish Temple, T0294-242 1239, www.udaigarhudaipur.in. Beautiful rooms with classic furniture, but the crowning glory here is the rooftop swimming pool with great views across the lake. Seductive rooftop restaurant too.

$$ Hibiscus Guest House, 190 Naga Nagri, Chandpol, follow signs to **Leela Palace Hotel**, T0294-280 3490, www.hibiscus inudaipur.com. Tucked away on the Chandpol side of the lake, this lovely guesthouse has a relaxed vibe. Beautifully decorated rooms, lovely dining room, pretty garden, massive dog!

$$ Hotel Hill Lake, Purohit Ji Ka Khurra, inside Chandpole, T0294-320 4820, www.hotelhilllake.com. Stylish rooms in a new build, but with exceptional views across both Fateh Sagar Lake and across to the City Palace and Lake Pichola from the atmospheric rooftop restaurant. In a quieter area.

$$ Lake Pichola, Hanuman Ghat, overlooking the lake, T0294-243 1197, www.lakepicholahotel.com. 32 rooms, some a/c, fantastic views with lots of beautiful window seats overlooking the lake, boat rides, friendly. Home to the rather lovely Upre restaurant and chic rooftop bar. The swimming pool is ill thoughtout though.

$$ Rang Niwas Palace, Lake Palace Rd, T0294-252 3890, www.rangniwaspalace.com. 20 beautifully renovated a/c rooms in a 200-year-old building, some with charming balconies facing the garden, some with beautiful window seats. There's a restaurant, pool, pretty gardens, helpful staff. Plenty of old-world charm. Good location, but some road noise.

$$-$ Jheel Guest House, 56 Gangaur Ghat (behind temple), T0294-242 1352, www.jheelguesthouse.com. Friendly owner and fantastic views. Don't be deceived by the unremarkable entrance, one room in particular practically hangs over the ghats with a spectacular view towards the Lake Palace hotel. The new extension has 6 pleasant rooms with bath and hot water; 8 rooms in the older part, good rooftop restaurant. There is the Ginger café downstairs, too. Recommended.

$$-$ Raj Palace, 103 Bhatiyani Chotta, T0294-241 0364, www.hotelrajpalaceudaipur.com. 26 beautiful rooms arranged around a pleasant courtyard garden, lovely rooftop restaurant, excellent service with views of the City Palace.

$ Dream Heaven, just over Chandpol, on the edge of the lake, T0294-243 1038, www.dreamheaven.co.in. 6 clean, simple rooms with bath, family-run, no frills but an excellent rooftop restaurant – exceptional overflowing *thalis* and very good lasagne. Great views.

$ Krishna Ranch, Badi Village, 8 km northwest of Udaipur, T(0)9828-059506, www.krishnaranch.com. Run by a Dutch-Indian couple, there are a few cottages here as well as an organic vegetable garden and lots of opportunities to be close to nature. The focus of this retreat is horse safaris – they have 14 Marwari horses and a whole host of other animals. They also own the Kumbha Palace Guest House in the centre of Udaipur – www.hotelkumbhapalace.com. Recommended.

$ Lake Ghat Guest House, 4/13 Lalghat, 150 m behind Jagdish Mandir, T0294-252 1636. 13 atmospheric, well-decorated rooms, friendly, lots of greenery cascading down the inner staircase, light and airy, great views from the terraces, good food.

$ Lal Ghat Haveli, 4 Lal Ghat, T0294-241 3666. 8 well-maintained rooms, particularly charming lower down, cheap but with character. Disappointing restaurant.

$ Lalghat Guest House, 33 Lal Ghat, T0294-252 5301, www.lalghat.com. The best dorm in town (good clean beds with curtains). Some of the 24 rooms have lake views. Very relaxed and sociable, good place to meet people, but indifferent management. Some travellers report that upon arrival the great room with a view they were promised has already been taken.

$ Minerva, 5/13 Gadiya Devra, Gangaur Ghat (behind temple), T0294-252 34/1. Good range of rooms for many budgets, decorative touches. Atmospheric rooftop restaurant. Good, speedy internet.

$ Nayee Haveli, 55 Gangaur Marg, T(0)9829-511573, www.nayeehaveli.blogspot.co.uk. This is a really sweet little place – very welcoming. 5 clean, basic rooms in a friendly family home with home-cooked food. Great value. Recommended.

$ Nukkad Guest House, 56 Ganesh Chowk (signposted from Jagdish Temple), T0294-241 1403, nukkad_raju@yahoo.com. 10 small, simple rooms, some with bath, in a typical family house, home-cooked meals, rooftop, very friendly and helpful, clean. There is morning yoga and afternoon cookery classes.

$ Poonam Haveli, 39 Lal Ghat, T0294-241 0303, www.hotelpoonamhaveli.com. 16 modern, attractive, clean rooms all with nice touches of Rajasthani decor, plus there's a large roof terrace. The restaurant serves good food from around the globe. Recommended.

$ Udai Niwas, near Jagdish Temple, Gangaur Marg, T0294-512 0789, www.hoteludainiwas.com. 14 renovated rooms in a friendly hotel with a pleasant rooftop and good views, even a 'penthouse' with lake view and a 4-poster bed, all are well decorated with Rajasthani touches.

Restaurants

Udaipur *p103, maps p104 and p106*
Note it is no longer possible to go for lunch or dinner at the Lake Palace Hotel unless you are a guest at the hotel itself or staying at the Leela or the Oberoi.

$$$ Ambrai, Lake Pichola Rd. Magical garden restaurant with tables under trees by lake shore, superb views of the City Palace, good at sunset. Recommended by everyone you speak to in Udaipur.

$$$ Savage Garden, up an alley near the east end of Chandpol bridge. Good in the evenings: striking blue interior and superior food including Indian-style pasta dishes, fish dishes, risottos and great mezze. Recommended.

$$$ Shiv Niwas, Jagat Niwas Hotel, see Where to stay, page 110. Wonderful buffet followed by disappointing desserts, eat in the bar, or dine in luxury by the pool listening to live Indian classical music; the bar is expensive but the grand surroundings are worth a drink.

$$$ Upre by 1559AD, Lake Pichola Hotel, Hanuman Ghat, T0294-243 1197, www.1559AD.com. Run by Arwan Shaktawat, this is a stunning chic rooftop restaurant and lounge with great Udaipur views – best at night. There's an interesting menu of Indian classics and European treats.

$$ Sankalp, outside Suraj Pol, City Station Rd, T0294-510 2686. Upmarket South Indian, modern, great range of chutneys.

$$ Whistling Teal, Jhadol Haveli, 103 Bhattiyana Chohatta, T0294-242 2067. Delicious traditional Rajasthani food as well as a bit of everything from around the globe in lovely garden restaurant.

$ Café Edelweiss, 73 Gangaur Ghat, opposite The Tiger. Great coffee. Small patisserie – sometimes you just have to sit on the side of the road – but the coffee is that good. Recommended.

$ Dream Heaven (see Where to stay, page 111). Excellent, never-ending *thalis* on the rooftop. "Watch the sun go down over the lake listening to the drums from the Jagdish Mandir".

$ Garden Hotel, opposite Gulab Bagh. Excellent Gujarati/Rajasthani vegetarian *thalis*, Rs 50, served in the former royal garage of the Maharanas of Mewar, an interesting circular building. The original fuel pumps can still be seen in the forecourt where 19 cars from the ancestral fleet have been displayed. Packed at lunch, less so for dinner, elderly Laurel-and-Hardyesque waiters shout at each other and forget things, food may arrive cold, but worth it for the experience. Recommended.

$ The Little Prince, Hanuman Ghat, near the footbridge. At this charming little café you can sit right at water's edge and get big portions of the usual travellers fare from around the globe. Very popular.

$ Papu's Juice Stand, by the footbridge. Extremely popular hole-in-the-wall juice stand serving up great juice combos and fantastic fruit salads.

$ Queen Café, 14 Bajrang Marg. Fantastic menu of unusual curries (mango, pumpkin and irresistible chocolate balls. Also offers cooking lessons. Highly recommended.

🎭 Entertainment

Udaipur *p103, maps p104 and p106*
Bagore-ki-Haveli, T0294-242 3610
(after 1700). Daily cultural shows 1900-
2000. Foreigners Rs 100, Indians Rs 60
(museum Rs 30). Enjoyable music and
dance performances, including traditional
dances with women balancing pots of
fire on their heads. No need to book.
Bharatiya Lok Kala Museum,
T0294-252 5077. The 20-min puppet
demonstrations during the day are
good fun. Evening puppet show and
folk dancing Sep-Mar 1800-1900, Rs 30,
camera Rs 50. Recommended.

🎉 Festivals

Udaipur *p103, maps p104 and p106*
Mar/Apr Mewar Festival (2-4 Apr 2014,
22-24 Mar 2015).

🛍 Shopping

Udaipur *p103, maps p104 and p106*
The local handicrafts are wooden toys,
colourful portable temples (*kavad*),
Bandhani tie-dye fabrics, embroidery and
Pichchwai paintings. Paintings are of 3 types:
miniatures in the classical style of courtly
Mewar; *phads* or folk art; and *pichchwais*
or religious art (see Nathdwara, page 118).
The more expensive ones are 'old'
(20-30 years) and are in beautiful dusky
colours; the cheaper ones are brighter.
    The main shopping centres are: Chetak
Circle, Bapu Bazar, Hathipol, Palace Rd, clock
tower, Nehru Bazar, Shastri Circle, Delhi Gate,
Sindhi Bazar, Bada Bazar.

Books
BA Photo and Books, 708 Palace Rd.
Very good selection in several languages,
also has internet access.
Mewar International, 35 Lalghat. A wide
selection of English books, exchange, films.

Handicrafts and paintings
Some shops sell old pieces of embroidery
turned into bags, cushion covers, etc.
Others may pass off recent work as antique.
Apollo Arts, 28 Panchwati; **Ashoka Arts**
and **Uday Arts** on Lake Palace Rd, for
paintings on marble paper and 'silk';
bargain hard. Hathipol shop has good
silk scarves (watch batik work in progress).
Ganesh Handicraft Emporium, City Palace
Rd, T0294-252 3647, ganeshemporium@
yahoo.com. Through the dull entrance of
Ganesh on the main road, you disappear
down an alley and come out at a huge old
haveli spilling with traditional Udaipur and
Gujarati embroideries, wooden horses and all
manner of textiles. Maybe not the cheapest
place, but great selection and ask for a tour
of the exceptionally beautiful building.
Honest Art Gallery, inside Chandpol 18,
www.honestart.org. Honest Art supports
Indian artists who receive 60% for each
piece – find unique artworks.
Modern Art Gallery, outside Chandpol,
near the footbridge. Beautiful collection
of artwork by local artists, including
Sharmila Rathore, who runs the shop.
Sadhna Women's Collective, Jagdish
Temple Rd, www.sadhna.org. Sadhna
started in 1988 with 15 women and has
grown to include the work of 600 women
today as artisans and co-owners. On offer
is a beautiful variety of clothes, *kurtas* and
scarves as well as a homeware range with
traditional appliqué, tanka and patchwork.
The patterns incorporated in the pieces
reflect rural life in Rajasthan. Recommended.

⏱ What to do

Udaipur *p103, maps p104 and p106*
Art, cooking and Hindi classes
Ashoka Arts, 339 'Ashoka Haveli' Gangaur
Ghat. In the courtyard of Gangaur Palace,
art classes are available.
Hare Krishna Arts, City Palace Rd, T0294-
242 0304. Rs 450 per 2-hr art lesson,

miniature techniques a speciality. Cooking classes, too.

Queen Café, 14 Bajrang Marg, T0294-243 0875. Rs 2000 for 5-hr introductory class in the basics of Indian cooking: tiny kitchen but a very good class. Also Hindi lessons. Both are highly recommended.

Body and soul
Bharti Guesthouse, Lake Pichola Rd, T0294-243 3469. Therapeutic, Swedish-style massage.
The Tiger, 33 Gangaur Ghat, T0294-242 0430. Great spa, with real sauna and steam rooms, jacuzzi and a range of traditional massages on offer. Recommended.

Elephant, camel and horse riding
Travel agencies (eg **Namaskar, Parul** in Lalghat) arrange elephant and camel rides, but need sufficient notice. Horse riding through **Krishna Ranch**, or **Princess Trails**, T(0)9829-042012, www.princesstrails.com, a German-Indian company that has Marwari horses for everything from half-day treks to 9-day horse safaris. Experience a totally different side of Rajasthan from horseback – see village life and be a part of nature.

Sightseeing tours
Offered by **RTDC Fateh Memorial**, Suraj Pol. City sightseeing: half day (0830-1300) Rs 90 (reported as poor). Excursion: half day (1400-1900), Haldighati, Nathdwara, Eklingji, Rs 130. Chittaurgarh (0830-1800), Rs 350 (with lunch); Ranakpur, Kumbhalgarh (0830-1900) Rs 330; Jagat–Jaisamand–Chavand–Rishabdeo (0830-1900) Rs 330 (with lunch).

In addition to sightseeing tours, some of the following tour operators offer accommodation bookings and travel tickets.
Parul, Jagat Niwas Hotel, Lalghat, T0294-242 1697, parul_tour@rediffmail.com. Air/train, palace hotels, car hire, exchange. Highly recommended.
People & Places, 34-35 Shrimal Bhawan, Garden Rd, T0294-241 7359, www.palaces-tours.com.

Shree Ji Tours, Hotel Minerva, Ghangor Ghat, T0294-2427052, www.shreejitours udaipur.com. Reliable and friendly company for all travel and sightseeing options.
Virasat Experiences, www.virasat experiences.com. The great team at Virasat offer interesting heritage walks and city tours, but also an outback walk into the villages around Udaipur meeting the Bhil tribe.

Swimming
Some hotel pools are open to non-residents: Lakshmi Vilas (Rs 175); Mahendra Prakash (Rs 125); Rang Niwas (Rs 100); Shiv Niwas (Rs 300). Also at Shilipgram Craft Village, Rs 100.

⊖ Transport

Udaipur *p103, maps p104 and p106*
Air Dabok Airport is 25 km east, T0294-265 5453. Security check is thorough; no batteries allowed in hand luggage. Transport to town: taxis, Rs 190. **Air India**, Delhi Gate, T0294-241 0999, open 1000-1315, 1400-1700; airport, T0294-265 5453, enquiry T142. Reserve well ahead. Indian Airlines flights to **Delhi**, via **Jodhpur** and **Jaipur**; **Mumbai**. Jet Airways, T0294-256 1105, airport T0294-265 6192: **Delhi** via **Jaipur, Mumbai**.
Auto-rickshaw Agree rates: about Rs 40 from bus stand to Jagdish Mandir.
Bicycle Laxmi Bicycles, halfway down Bhatiyani Chotta, charges Rs 30 per day for hire, well maintained and comfortable. Also shops near Kajri Hotel, Lalghat and Hanuman Ghat area, which also have scooters (Rs 200 per day).
Long-distance bus Main State Bus Stand, near railway line opposite Udai Pol, T0294-248 4191; reservations 0700-2100. State RTC buses to **Agra**, 15 hrs; **Ahmedabad**, 252 km, 6 hrs; **Ajmer**, 274 km, 7 hrs; **Bikaner**, 500 km, 13 hrs; **Chittaurgarh**, 2½ hrs; **Delhi**, 635 km, 17 hrs; **Jaipur**, 405 km, 9 hrs; **Jaisalmer**, 14 hrs; **Jodhpur**, 8 hrs (uncomfortable, poorly maintained

but scenic road); **Mount Abu**, 270 km, 0500-1030, 6 hrs; **Mumbai**, 802 km, very tiring, 16 hrs; **Pushkar**, tourist bus, 7 hrs; **Ujjain**, 7 hrs. Private buses and luxury coaches run mostly at night; ticket offices offices on City Station Rd, from where most buses depart. Try **Shrinath**, T0294-645 0503, www.shrinath.biz, or a reliable firm for booking bus tickets in the city is **Shree Ji Tours**, Hotel Minerva, Ghangor Ghat, T0294-242 7052, www.shreejitoursudaipur.com.

Motorbike Scooters and bikes can be hired from **Heera Tours & Travels** in a small courtyard behind Badi Haveli (Jagdish Temple area), Rs 250-500 per day depending on size of machine.

Taxi RTDC taxis from Fateh Memorial, Suraj Pol. Private taxis from airport, railway station, bus stands and major hotels; negotiate rates. **Taxi Stand**, Chetak Circle, T0294-252 5112. **Tourist Taxi Service**, Lake Palace Rd, T0294-252 4169.

Train Udaipur City station, 4 km southeast of centre, T0294-252 7390, T131, reservations T135. **Ahmedabad**: *Ahmedabad Exp 19943*, 1745, 10½ hrs. **Chittaurgarh**: 5 local trains daily. **Delhi** (**HN**): *Mewar Exp 12964*, 1815, 12 hrs, via Chittaurgarh, Kota and Bharatpur. **Jaipur**: *Udz Kurj Express 19666*, 2220, 7½ hrs, and on to **Agra** (12 hrs) and **Gwalior** (14 hrs) and **Khajuraho**; **Mumbai Bandra**: *Udz Bdts Sf Exp 12966*, 2135, 16½ hrs.

O Directory

Udaipur *p103, maps p104 and p106*
Medical services Ambulance: T102. General Hospital, Chetak Circle. **Aravali Hospital** (private), 332 Ambamata Main Rd, opposite **Charak Hostel**, T0294-243 0222, very clean, professional. Recommended. **Chemist** on Hospital Rd. **Post** The GPO is at Chetak Circle. **Police**: T100. **Tourist Assistance Force**: T0294-241 1535.

Around Udaipur

The area around Udaipur is dotted with a wide range of attractions, from some of the grandest of Rajasthan's heritage hotels to some of its cosiest castles, from secluded forest lakes, surrounded by wildlife, to one of the largest reservoirs in Asia. It's also home to some ancient temples and perhaps the most evocative of Rajasthan's plentiful palaces, the Juna Mahal near Dungarpur.

Getting around

Most of the sights in this area are a little isolated and so not well connected by train. However, the quality of the region's roads has greatly improved recently, making travel either by bus or taxi both quick and convenient. ▶▶ *See Transport, page 120.*

Monsoon Palace

ⓘ *15 km west. In order to reach the Monsoon Palace, you enter into Sajjangarh: foreigners Rs 160, Indians Rs 20, car Rs 130. Allow about 3 hrs for the round trip. Rickshaws cannot make it up the steep hill to the palace, so expect a good hike up or get a taxi.*

There are good views from this deserted palace on a hilltop. The unfinished building on **Sajjangarh**, at an altitude of 335 m, which looks picturesque from the west-facing battlements, was named after Sajjan Singh (1874-1884) and was planned to be high enough to see his ancestral home, Chittaurgarh. Normally, you need a permit from the police in town to enter, though many find a tip to the gateman suffices. It offers panoramic views of Udaipur (though the highest roof is spoilt by radio antennas); the windows of the Lake Palace can be seen reflecting the setting sun. The palace itself is very run down but the views from the hill top are just as good. The views to the other sides of the rolling hills are equally as sublime. A visit in the late afternoon is recommended – sunset is spectacular. Take binoculars.

Jaisamand Lake

Before the building of huge modern dams in India, Jaisamand was the second largest artificial lake in Asia, measuring 15 km by 10 km. Dating from the late 17th century, it is surrounded by the summer palaces of the Ranis of Udaipur. The two highest surrounding hills are topped by the **Hawa Mahal** and **Ruti Rani palaces**, now empty but worth visiting for the architecture and views. A small sanctuary nearby has deer, antelope and panther. Tribals still inhabit some islands on the lake while crocodiles, keelback water snakes and turtles bask on others.

Bambora

The imposing 18th-century hilltop fortress of Bambora has been converted to a heritage hotel by the royal family of Sodawas, at an enormous restoration cost, and has retained its ancient character. The impressive fort is in Mewari style with domes, turrets and arches. To get here from Udaipur, go 12 km east along the airport road and take the right turn towards Jaisamand Lake passing the 11th-century Jagat Temple (38 km) before reaching Bambora.

Sitamata Wildlife Sanctuary

The reserve of dense deciduous forests covers over 400 sq km and has extensive birdlife (woodpeckers, tree pies, blue jays, jungle fowl). It is one of the few sanctuaries between the Himalaya and the Nilgiris where giant brown flying squirrels have been reported. Visitors have seen hordes of langur monkey, nilgai in groups of six or seven, four-horned antelope, jackal and even panther and hyena, but the thick forests make sightings difficult. There are crocodiles in the reservoirs.

Rishabdeo

Rishabdeo, off the highway, has a remarkable 14th-century Jain temple with intricate white marble carving and black marble statuary, though these are not as fine as at Dilwara or Ranakpur. Dedicated to the first Jain Tirthankar, Adinath or Rishabdev, Hindus, Bhils as well as Jains worship there. An attractive bazar street leads to the temple, which is rarely visited by tourists. Special worship is conducted several times daily when Adinath, regarded as the principal focus of worship, is bathed with saffron water or milk. The priests are friendly; a small donation (Rs 10-20) is appreciated.

Dungarpur

Dungarpur (City of Hills) dates from the 13th century. The district is the main home of the Bhil tribal people. It is also renowned for its stone masons, who in recent years have been employed to build Hindu temples as far afield as London. The attractive and friendly village has one of the most richly decorated and best-preserved palaces in Rajasthan, the Juna Mahal. Surrounded on three sides by Lake Gaibsagar and backed by picturesque hills, the more recent **Udai Bilas Palace** (now a heritage hotel, see page 119) was built by Maharawal Udai Singhji in the 19th century and extended in 1943. The huge courtyard surrounds a 'pleasure pool' from the centre of which rises a four-storeyed pavilion with a beautifully carved wooden chamber.

The **Juna Mahal**, above the village, dates from the 13th century when members of the Mewar clan at Chittaur moved south to found a new kingdom after a family split. It is open to guests staying at Udai Bilas and by ticket (Rs 150) for non-residents, obtainable at the hotel. The seven-storeyed fortress-like structure with turrets, narrow entrances and tiny windows has colourful and vibrant rooms profusely decorated over several centuries with miniature wall paintings (among the best in Rajasthan), and glass and mirror inlay work. There are some fine *jarokha* balconies and sculpted panels illustrating musicians and dancers in the local green-grey parava stone which are strikingly set against the plain white walls of the palace to great effect. The steep narrow staircases lead to a series of seven floors giving access to public halls, supported on decorated columns, and to intimate private chambers. There is a jewel of a Sheesh Mahal and a cupboard in the Maharawal's bedroom on the top floor covered in miniatures illustrating some 50 scenes from the *Kama Sutra*. Windows and balconies open to the breeze command lovely views over the town below. Perhaps nowhere else in Rajasthan gives as good an impression of how these palaces must have been hundreds of years ago; it is completely unspoilt and hugely impressive. It is amazing, but not very accessible to people with limited mobility. There is no actual path.

Some interesting temples nearby include the 12th-century Siva temple at **Deo Somnath**, 12 km away, and the splendid complex of temple ruins profusely decorated with stone sculptures.

Khempur

This small, attractive village is conveniently located midway between Udaipur and Chittaurgarh. To find it turn off the highway, 9 km south of Mavli and about 50 km from Udaipur. The main reason for visiting is to eat or stay in the charming heritage hotel (see Where to stay, page 120).

Eklingji and Nagda

① *0400-0700, 1000-1300 and 1700-1900. No photography.*

The white marble **Eklingji Temple** has a two-storey mandapa to Siva, the family deity of the Mewars. It dates from AD 734 but was rebuilt in the 15th century. There is a silver door and screen and a silver Nandi facing the black marble Siva. The evenings draw crowds of worshippers and few tourists. Many smaller temples surround the main one and are also worth seeing. Nearby is the large but simple **Lakulisa Temple** (AD 972), and other ruined semi-submerged temples. The back-street shops sell miniature paintings. It is a peaceful spot attracting many waterbirds. Occasional buses go from Udaipur to Eklingji and Nagda which are set in a deep ravine containing the Eklingji Lake. The **RTDC** (see page 105) run tours from Udaipur, 1400-1900.

At Nagda, are three temples: the ruined 11th-century Jain temple of **Adbhutji** and the **Vaishnavite Sas-Bahu** (Mother-in-law/Daughter-in-law) temples. The complex, though comparatively small, has some very intricate carving on pillars, ceiling and mandapa walls. You can hire bicycles in Eklingji to visit them. There are four 14th-century Jain temples at **Delwara**, about 5 km from Eklingji, which also boast the **Devi Garh**, one of India's most luxurious hotels.

Nathdwara

This is a centre of the Krishna worshipping community of Gujarati merchants who are followers of Vallabhacharya (15th century). Non-Hindus are not allowed inside the temple, which contains a black marble Krishna image, but the outside has interesting paintings. **Shrinathji Temple** is one of the richest Hindu temples in India. At one time only high caste Hindus (Brahmins, Kshatriyas) were allowed inside, and the *pichhwais* (temple hangings) were placed outside, for those castes and communities who were not allowed into the sanctum sanctorum, to experience the events in the temple courtyard and learn about the life of lord Krishna. You can watch the 400-year-old tradition of *pichhwai* painting which originated here. The artists had accompanied the Maharana of Mewar, one of the few Rajput princes who still resisted the Mughals, who settled here when seeking refuge from Aurangzeb's attacks. Their carriage carrying the idol of Shrinathji was stuck at Nathdwara in Mewar, 60 km short of the capital Udaipur. Taking this as a sign that this was where God willed to have his home, they developed this into a pilgrim centre for the worship of lord Krishna's manifestation, Shrinathji. Their paintings, *pichhwais*, depict Lord Krishna as Shrinathji in different moods according to the season. The figures of lord Krishna and the *gopis* (milkmaids) are frozen on a backdrop of lush trees and deep skies. The bazar sells *pichhwais* painted on homespun cloth with mineral and organic colour often fixed with starch.

Rajsamand Lake

At **Kankroli** is the Rajsamand Lake. The **Nauchoki Bund**, the embankment which contains it, is over 335 m long and 13 m high, with ornamental pavilions and *toranas*, all of marble and exquisitely carved. Behind the masonry bund is an 11-m-wide earthen embankment, erected in 1660 by Rana Raj Singh who had defeated Aurangzeb on several occasions. He also commissioned the longest inscription in the world, "Raj Prashasthi Maha Kavyam", which tells the story of Mewar on 24 granite slabs in Sanskrit. Kankroli and its beautiful temple are on the southeast side of the lake.

Deogarh

Deogarh (Devgarh) is an excellent place to break the journey between Udaipur and Jaipur or Pushkar. It is a very pleasant, little frequented town with a dusty but interesting bazar (if you are interested in textiles, visit **Vastra Bhandar** ℗ *T02904-252187*, for reasonably priced and good-quality textiles). Its elevation makes it relatively cool and the countryside and surrounding hills are good for gentle treks. There is an old fort on a hill as well as a magnificent palace on a hillock in the centre with murals illustrating the fine local school of miniature painting. **Raghosagar Lake**, which is very pleasant to walk around, has an island with a romantic ruined temple and centotaphs (poor monsoons leave the lake dry). It attracts numerous migratory birds and is an attractive setting for the charming 200-year-old palace, **Gokal Vilas**, the home of the present Rawat Saheb Nahar Singhji and the Ranisahiba. Their two sons have opened the renovated 17th-century **Deogarh Mahal Palace** to guests (see Where to stay, page 120). The Rawat, a knowledgeable historian and art connoisseur, has a private collection of over 50 paintings which guests may view, advance notice required. The shop at the hotel has good modern examples to buy. There is plenty to do here including an excellent 45-minute train journey from Deogarh to Phulud which winds down through the Aravalli hills to the plain below through tunnels and bridges.

Around Udaipur listings

For hotel and restaurant price codes and other relevant information, see pages 13-16.

◯ Where to stay

Bambora *p116*
$$$$-$$$ Karni Fort, Bambora, T0291-251 2101, www.karnihotels.com. Heritage hotel with 30 beautifully decorated rooms (circular beds) in a large, imposing fort, with marble bathrooms, modern facilities, impressive interiors and an enthusiastic and friendly manager. There's an exceptional marble pool, folk concerts, great beer bar and delicious food. All hugely enjoyable. They also have a 10-room colonial manor, **Karni Kot**, with art deco-style rooms. Recommended.

Sitamata Wildlife Sanctuary *p117*
$$$-$$ Fort Dhariyawad, at the sanctuary, T02950-220050, www.fortdhariyawad.com. 14 rooms and 4 suites in a restored and converted, mid-16th-century fort (founded by one of Maharana Pratap's sons) and some rooms in a contemporary cottage cluster. Period decor and a medieval flavour. Meals available (international menu), great location by the sanctuary (flying squirrels, langur monkeys in garden, crocodiles in reservoir), tribal village tours, jeeps to park, horse safaris, treks.

$$ Forest Lodge, at the sanctuary, Dhariyawad, contact District Forest Officer, Chittorgarh, T01472-244915. Rather expensive considering the lack of amenities, but it has a fantastic location and views, and it's a paradise for birders.

Dungarpur *p117*
$$$$-$$$ Udai Bilas Palace, 2 km from Dungarpur, T02964-230808, www.udaibilas palace.com. 22 unique a/c rooms (including 16 suites of which 6 are vast 'grand suites') mirror mosaics, some dated with art deco furniture, marble bathrooms. With quite possibly the most stunning restaurant in India, charming host Harshvardhan Singh has built a beautiful restaurant around a central water feature. He has also created a very eccentric bar to appeal to every car fanatic

which compliments his great vintage car collection. There is a lovely relaxing pool area too. Highly recommended.
$ Vaibhav, Saghwara Rd, T02964-230244. Simple rooms, tea stall/restaurant, owner very friendly and helpful.

Khempur *p118*
$$$-$$ Ravla Khempur, T02955-237154, www.ravlakhempur.com. The former home of the village chieftain, this is a charming, small-scale heritage property. The rooms have been sensitively renovated with modern bathrooms, pleasant lawns, horse rides a speciality. With a UK management team, this is a slick operation.

Eklingji and Nagda *p118*
$$$$ Devi Garh, Delwara, 5 km from Eklingji, T02953-289211, www.lebua.com/devigarh. For the ultimate in luxury. **Devi Garh** is spectacular – this is not a typical palace renovation, it is chic and super stylish with amazing attention to detail. The rooms are themed, so you might find yourself in the Lapis Lazuli room or the Marigold room. The original paintings in the restaurant are exquisite. Recently taken over by the **Lebua** group so there might be changes afoot. Stunning.

Nathdwara *p118*
$$-$ Gokul (RTDC), near Lalbagh, 2 km from the bus stand, Nathdwara, T02953-230917, www.rtdc.in. 6 rooms and dorm, restaurant.

Deogarh *p119*
$$$$-$$$ Deogarh Mahal, T(0)9928-834777, www.deogarhmahal.com. This labyrinthine fort dates back to 1617 and boasts 50 beautifully restored rooms, including atmospheric suites furnished in traditional style with good views, the best have balconies with private jacuzzis, but not all are up to the same standard. Fabulous lotus flower-shaped pool, Keralan massage, Mewari meals, home-grown produce, bar, great gift shop, log fires, folk entertainment, boating, birdwatching, jeep safaris, audio tour by William Dalrymple, talks on art history, hospitable and delightful hosts. They can organize romantic dinners in private courtyards around the mahal or out in abandoned forts in the surrounding countryside or gala dinners with camel cart rides and fireworks. Stunning.
$$$ Deogarh Khayyam, 4 km from Deogarh, T(0)9928-834777, www.deogarhmahal.com. These stunning tents are perched on a jungle plateau – you are utterly surrounded by nature. The 16 luxurious tents are fairly spread out so you feel the birds and wildlife are your neighbours not your fellow guests. Log fires and starry skies in the evening and the same amazing food as **Deogarh Mahal**. Camping has never been so exciting.

☸ Festivals

Dungarpur *p117*
Feb Baneshwar Fair (10-14 Feb 2014, 30-31 Jan 2015). The tribal festival at the Baneshwar Temple, 70 km from Dungarpur, is one of Rajasthan's largest tribal fairs when Bhils gather at the temple in large numbers for ritual bathing at the confluence of rivers. There are direct buses to Baneshwar during the fair. The temporary camp during the fair is best avoided. **Vagad Festival** in Dungarpur offers an insight into local tribal culture. Both are uncommercialized and authentic. Details from **Udai Bilas Palace**, see Where to stay, page 119.

☻ Transport

Around Udaipur *p116*
Bus For **Nathdwara**, several buses from Udaipur from early morning. Buses also go to **Nagda**, **Eklingji** and **Rajsamand**. Private transport only for Khempur and Deogarh. From Dungarpur buses travel to/from **Udaipur** (110 km), 2 hrs, **Ahmedabad** (170 km), 4 hrs. You will need to hire a taxi to get to the other destinations.

Kumbhalgarh, Ranakpur and around

Little-known Kumbhalgarh is one of the finest examples of defensive fortification in Rajasthan. You can wander around the palace, the many temples and along the walls – 36 km in all – to savour the great panoramic views. It is two hours north (63 km) of Udaipur through the attractive Rajasthani countryside. The small fields are well kept and Persian wheels and 'tanks' are dotted across the landscape. In winter, wheat and mustard grow in the fields, and the journey itself is as magical as the fort.

The temples of Ranakpur are incredibly ornate and amazingly unspoilt by tourism, having preserved a dignified air which is enhanced by the thick green forests that surround them. There are a number of interesting villages and palaces in the nearby area; if time allows this is a great region to explore at leisure, soaking in the unrushed, rural way of life.

Kumbhalgarh → *For listings, see pages 124-125.*

Kumbhalgarh Fort
ⓘ *Foreigners Rs 100, Indians Rs 5.*
Kumbhalgarh Fort, off the beaten tourist track, was the second most important fort of the Mewar Kingdom after Chittaurgarh. Built mostly by Maharana Kumbha (circa 1485), it is situated on a west-facing ridge of the Aravalli hills, commanding a great strategic position on the border between the Rajput kingdoms of Udaipur (Mewar) and Jodhpur (Marwar). It is accessible enough to make a visit practicable and getting there is half the fun. There are superb views over the lower land to the northwest, standing over 200 m above the pass leading via Ghanerao towards Udaipur.

The approach Passing though charming villages and hilly terrain, the route to the fort is very picturesque. The final dramatic approach is across deep ravines and through thick scrub jungle. Seven gates guarded the approaches while seven ramparts were reinforced by semicircular bastions and towers. The 36-km-long black walls with curious bulbous towers exude a feeling of power as they snake their way up and down impossibly steep terrain. They were built to defy scaling and their width enabled rapid deployment of forces – six horses could walk along them side by side. The walls enclose a large plateau containing the smaller Katargarh Fort with the decaying palace of Fateh Singh, a garrison, 365 temples and shrines, and a village. The occupants (reputedly 30,000) could be self-sufficient in food and water, with enough storage to last a year. The fort's dominant location enabled defenders to see aggressors approaching from a great distance. Kumbhalgarh is believed to have been taken only once and that was because the water in the ponds was poisoned by enemy Mughals during the reign of Rana Pratap.

The gates The first gate **Arait Pol** is some distance from the main fort; the area was once thick jungle harbouring tigers and wild boar. Signals would be flashed by mirror in times of emergency. **Hulla Pol** (Gate of Disturbance) is named after the point reached by invading Mughal armies in 1567. **Hanuman Pol** contains a shrine and temple. **Bhairava Pol**, records the 19th-century chief minister who was exiled. The fifth gate, **Paghra** (Stirrup) **Pol**, is where the cavalry assembled; the star tower nearby has walls 8 m thick. The **Top-Khana** (Cannon Gate) is alleged to have a secret escape tunnel. The last, **Nimbu** (Lemon) **Pol** has the Chamundi temple beside it.

The palace It is a 30-minute walk (fairly steep in parts) from the car park to the roof of the Maharana's darbar hall. Tiers of inner ramparts rise to the summit like a fairytale castle, up to the appropriately named Badal Mahal (19th century) or 'palace in the clouds', with the interior painted in pastel colours. Most of the empty palace is usually unlocked (a *chaukidar* holds the keys). The views over the walls to the jungle-covered hillsides (now a wildlife reserve) and across the deserts of Marwar towards Jodhpur, are stunning. The palace rooms are decorated in a 19th-century style and some have attractive coloured friezes, but are unfurnished. After the maze-like palace at Udaipur, this is very compact. The Maharana's palace has a remarkable blue darbar hall with floral motifs on the ceiling. Polished *chunar* (lime) is used on walls and window sills, but the steel ceiling girders give away its late 19th-century age. A gap separated the *mardana* (men's) palace from the *zenana* (women's) palace. Some of the rooms in the *zenana* have an attractive painted frieze with elephants, crocodiles and camels. A circular Ganesh temple is in the corner of the *zenana* courtyard. A striking feature of the toilets was the ventilation system which allowed fresh air into the room while the toilet was in use.

Kumbhalgarh Wildlife Sanctuary
① *Foreigners Rs 100, Indians Rs 10, car Rs 65, open sunrise to sunset.*
The sanctuary to the west of the fort covering about 600 sq km has a sizeable wildlife population but you have to be extremely lucky to spot any big game in the thick undergrowth. Some visitors have seen bear, panther, wolf and hyena but most have to be contented with seeing nilgai, sambhar deer, wild boar, jackal, jungle cat and birds. Crocodiles and water fowl can be seen at **Thandi Beri Lake**. Jeep and horse safaris can be organized from hotels in the vicinity including **Aodhi**, **Ranakpur**, **Ghanerao** and **Narlai**. The rides can be quite demanding as the tracks are very rough. There is a 4WD jeep track and a trekking trail through the safari area can be arranged through **Shivika Lake Hotel**, www.shivikalakehotel.com, in Ranakpur.

The tribal Bhils and Garasias – the latter found only in this belt – can be seen here, living in their traditional huts. The Forest Department may permit an overnight stay in their Rest House in **Kelwara**, the closest town, 6 km from sanctuary. With steep, narrow streets devoid of cars it is an attractive little place.

Ghanerao and Rawla Narlai → *For listings, see pages 124-125.*

Ghanerao was founded in 1606 by Gopal Das Rathore of the Mertia clan, and has a number of red sandstone *havelis* as well as several old temples, *baolis* and marble *chhatris*, 5 km beyond the reserve. The village lay at the entrance to one of the few passes through the Aravallis between the territories held by the Rajput princes of Jodhpur and Udaipur. The beautiful 1606 **royal castle** has marble pavilions, courtyards, paintings, wells, elephant stables and walls marked with canon balls. The present Thakur Sajjan Singh has opened his castle to guests (see Where to stay, page 124), and organizes two- to three-day treks to Kumbhalgarh Fort, 50 km by road (4WD only), and Ranakpur.

The **Mahavir Jain Temple**, 5 km away, is a beautiful little 10th-century temple. It is a delightful place to experience an unspoiled rural environment.

Rawla Narlai, 25 km from Kumbhalgarh Fort, and an hour's drive from Ranakpur, is a Hindu and Jain religious centre. It has a 17th-century fort with interesting architecture, right in the heart of the village, which is ideal for a stopover.

Ranakpur → *For listings, see pages 124-125.*

ⓘ *Daily, non-Jains are only allowed to visit the Adinatha 1200-1700, free. Photos with permission from Kalyanji Anandji Trust office next to the temple, camera Rs 50, video Rs 150, photography of the principal Adinatha image is prohibited. Shoes and socks must be removed at the entrance. Black clothing and shorts are not permitted. No tips, though unofficial 'guides' may ask for baksheesh.*

One of five holy Jain sites and a popular pilgrimage centre, it has one of the best-known Jain temple complexes in the country. Though not comparable in grandeur to the Dilwara temples in Mount Abu, it has very fine ornamentation and is in a wonderful setting with peacocks, langurs and numerous birds. The semi-enclosed deer park with spotted deer, nilgai and good birdlife next to the temple, attracts the occasional panther! You can approach Ranakpur from Kumbhalgarh through the wildlife reserve in 1½ hours although you will need to arrange transport from the Sanctuary entrance. A visit is highly recommended.

The **Adinatha** (1439), the most noteworthy of the three main temples here, is dedicated to the first Tirthankar. Of the 1444 engraved pillars, in Jain tradition, no two are the same and each is individually carved. The sanctuary is symmetrically planned around the central shrine and is within a 100-sq-m raised terrace enclosed in a high wall with 66 subsidiary shrines lining it, each with a spire; the gateways consist of triple-storey porches. The sanctuary, with a clustered centre tower, contains a *chaumukha* (four-fold) marble image of Adinatha. The whole complex, including the extraordinary array of engraved pillars, carved ceilings and arches are intricately decorated, often with images of Jain saints, friezes of scenes from their lives and holy sites. The lace-like interiors of the corbelled domes are a superb example of western Indian temple style. The **Parsvanatha** and **Neminath** are two smaller Jain temples facing this, the former with a black image of Parsvanatha in the sanctuary and erotic carvings outside. The star-shaped **Surya Narayana Temple** (mid-15th century) is nearby.

There is a beautiful 3.7-km trek around the wildlife sanctuary, best attempted from November to March; contact the sanctuary office next to the temples for information.

Kumbhalgarh, Ranakpur and around listings

For hotel and restaurant price codes and other relevant information, see pages 13-16.

Where to stay

Kumbhalgarh *p121*

$$$$ Aodhi (HRH), 2 km from the fort gate, T02954-242341, www.eternalmewar.in. The closest place to the fort, great location set into the rock face. 27 rooms in modern stone 'cottages' decorated in colonial style to good effect with attached modern bathrooms. Beautiful restaurant and coffee shop, pool, relaxing atmosphere, very helpful staff, fabulous views, very quiet, superb horse safaris (US$200 per night), trekking, tribal village tours. Highly recommended.

$$ Dera, Kelwara, T02954-242400, www.derakumbhalgarh.com. Great array of tents in 3 categories – some with a/c. Some of the tents are semi-permanent so are beautifully furnished, others are a fabulous purple inside rather than the standard white. Great views. Recommended.

$$-$ Ratnadeep, Kelwara, in the middle of a bustling village, T02954-242217, hotelratnadeep@yahoo.co.in. 14 basic rooms, some deluxe with cooler and marble floors, Western toilets, small lawn, restaurant, camel, horse and jeep safaris, friendly, well run.

$ Forest Department Guest House, near the Parsram Temple, about 3 km from **Aodhi** by road then 3 km by 4WD jeep or on foot. Basic facilities but fantastic views over the Kumbalgarh sanctuary towards the drylands of Marwar.

Ghanerao and Rawla Narlai *p123*

$$$$ Fort Rawla Narlai, Rawla Narlai, T(0)9928-754913, www.rawlanarlai.com. Overlooked by a huge granite boulder, this place is rather special. The energy of the boulder and the temples and caves that are dotted around it, plus the beautifully renovated fort create a very serene place

to hideaway. 20 rooms (11 a/c) individually decorated with antiques, new showers, plus 5 luxurious, well-appointed 'tents', good simple meals under the stars, helpful, friendly staff, attractive garden setting, good riding.You can wander up to the Shiva temple on top of the boulder by scaling 700 steps. Check out the special dinner they host at a candlelit stepwell – so romantic. Highly recommended.

$$$ Ghanerao Jungle Lodge, Ghanerao, T02934-284035, www.ghaneraoroyalcastle. com. Formerly **Bagha-ka-Bagh** (Tiger's Den). Spartan hunting lodge among tall grass jungle near the wildlife sanctuary gate. 8 basic rooms, but atmospheric location. Great for birdlife and wildlife. There is an organic farm under the guidance of Vandana Shiva's Navdanya – her project involves tribal participation and conserving local seeds to create an Organic Seed Bank. Guests can volunteer. Recommended.

$$$ Ghanerao Royal Castle, Ghanerao, T02934-284035, www.ghaneraoroyalcastle. com. Suites and a restaurant serving simple food, slightly run-down but has the nostalgic appeal of faded glory, charming hosts. Activities include local walks, jeep rides and camping trips.

Ranakpur *p123*

$$$$-$$$ The Mana Hotel, Ranakpur– Sadri Rd, Ranakpur Rd, T011-4808 0000 (Delhi), www.manahotels.in. Innovative contemporary design in rural Rajasthan – quite unexpected and pulled off successfully. Lovely common areas, large glass and steel villas and a variety of rooms.

$$$ Maharani Bagh (WelcomHeritage), Ranakpur Rd, T02934-285105, www.welcom heritagehotels.in. 18 well-furnished modern bungalows with baths in a lovely 19th-century walled orchard of the Jodhpur royal family, full of bougainvillea and mangos, outdoor Rajasthani restaurant (traditional Marwari meals Rs 400), pool, jeep safaris,

horse riding. Your wake-up call is care
of the peacocks or langur monkeys tap
dancing on the roof.

$$$-$$ Ranakpur Hill Resort, Ranakpur
Rd, T02934-286411, www.ranakpurhillresort.
com. 16 good-sized, well-appointed rooms,
5 a/c, in a new construction, pleasant dining
room, there are some royal tents as well,
clean pool.

$ Dharamshala, T02934-285119. Some
comfortable rooms, simple and extremely
cheap vegetarian meals.

$ Roopam, Ranakpur Rd, T02934-285321.
12 well-maintained rooms, some a/c,
pleasant restaurant, attractive lawns.

⊘ Transport

While most of the places in this section do
have bus links, a private car is indispensable
and makes the most of the scenic drives on
offer. A round-trip from Udaipur could also
take in Eklingji, Nagda and Nathdwara.

Kumbhalgarh *p121*

Bus and taxi For the fort: buses (irregular
times) from Chetak Circle, Udaipur go to
Kelwara, Rs 20, 3 hrs (cars take 2 hrs); from
there a local bus (Rs 6) can take you a further
4 km up to a car park; the final 2-km climb
is on foot; the return is a pleasant downhill
walk of 1 hr. Jeep taxis charge Rs 50-100
from Kelwara to the fort (and say there are
no buses). Return buses to Udaipur from
Kelwara until 1730. Buses to **Saira** leave in
the afternoon.
From Udaipur, a taxi for 4 costs about
Rs 2600-3500, depending on the car.
An 11-hr trip will cover the fort and
Ranakpur; very worthwhile.

Ranakpur *p123*

Bus From Udaipur, there are 6 buses
daily (0530-1600), slow, 3 hrs. Also buses
from **Jodhpur** and **Mount Abu**. To get to
Kumbhalgarh, take Udaipur bus as far as
Saira (20 km, 45 mins), then catch a bus
or minibus to the Kumbhalgarh turn-off
(32 km, 1 hr).
Taxi For taxi options, see above.
Train The nearest railway line is
Falna Junction on the Ajmer–Mount
Abu line, 39 km away.

Mount Abu and around

Mount Abu, Rajasthan's only hill resort, stretches along a 20-km plateau. Away from the congestion and traffic of the tourist centres on the plains, Mount Abu is surrounded by well-wooded countryside filled with flowering trees, numerous orchids during the monsoon and a good variety of bird and animal life. Many of the rulers from surrounding princely states had summer houses built here and today it draws visitors from Rajasthan and neighbouring Gujarat who come to escape the searing heat of summer (and Gujarat's alcohol prohibition) and also to see the exquisite Dilwara Jain temples. In the hot months between April and June, and around Diwali, it's a great place to see Indian holidaymakers at play: softy ice creams, portrait sketchers and pedaloes on Nakki Lake abound. There are some fabulous heritage hotels in the area, well off the beaten track and worthwhile experiences in themselves.

Arriving in Mount Abu

Getting there and around The nearest railway station is at Abu Road, 27 km away. It is usually quicker to take a bus directly to Mount Abu, instead of going to Abu Road by train and then taking a bus up the hill. The compact area by Nakki Lake, with hotels, restaurants and shops, is pedestrianized. Taxis are available at a stand nearby. A form of transport unique to Mount Abu is the *baba gari*, a small trolley generally used to pull small children up the steepest of Mount Abu's hills. ▸▸ *See Transport, page 131.*

Tourist information RTDC ① *opposite the bus stand, T02974-238944, 0800-1100, 1600-2000*. Guides available, four to eight hours, Rs 250-400.

Mount Abu → *For listings, see pages 130-132.*

Mount Abu was the home of the legendary sage Vasishtha. One day Nandini, his precious wish-fulfilling cow, fell into a great lake. Vasishtha requested the gods in the Himalaya to save her so they sent Arbuda, a cobra, who carried a rock on his head and dropped it into the lake, displacing the water, and so saved Nandini. The place became known as Arbudachala, the 'Hill of Arbuda'. Vasishtha also created the four powerful 'fire-born' Rajput tribes, including the houses of Jaipur and Udaipur at a ritual fire ceremony on the mount. Nakki Talao (Lake), sacred to Hindus, was, in legend, scooped out by the *nakki* (fingernails) of gods attempting to escape the wrath of a demon. Abu was leased by the British government from the Maharao of Sirohi and was used as the headquarters for the Resident of Rajputana until 1947, and as a sanatorium for troops.

Dilwara Jain Temples

ⓘ *Free (no photography), shoes and cameras, mobile phones, leather items and backpacks (Rs 1 per item) are left outside, tip expected; 1200-1800 for non-Jains; some guides are excellent, it's a 1-hr uphill walk from town, or share a jeep, Rs 5 each.*

Set in beautiful surroundings of mango trees and wooded hills, 5 km from the town centre, the temples have superb marble carvings. The complex of five principal temples is surrounded by a high wall, dazzling white in the sunlight. There is a resthouse for pilgrims on the approach road, which is also lined with stalls selling a collection of tourist kitsch lending a carnival atmosphere to the sanctity of the temples. It would be beautiful and serene here, but noisy guides and visitors break the sanctity of the magnificent temples.

Chaumukha Temple The grey sandstone building is approached through the entrance on your left. Combining 13th- and 15th-century styles, it is generally regarded as inferior to the two main temples. The colonnaded hall (ground floor) contains four-faced images of the Tirthankar Parsvanatha (hence *chaumukha*), and figures of *dikpalas* and *yakshis*.

Adinatha Temple (Vimala Shah Temple) This temple lies directly ahead; the oldest and most famous of the Dilwara group. Immediately outside the entrance to the temple is a small portico known as the Hastishala (elephant hall), built by Prithvipal in 1147-1159 which contains a figure of the patron, Vimala Shah, the chief minister of the Solanki king, on horseback. Vimala Shah commissioned the temple, dedicated to Adinatha, in 1031-1032. The riders on the 10 beautifully carved elephants that surround him were removed during Alauddin Khilji's reign. Dilwara belonged to Saivite Hindus who were unwilling to part with it until Vimala Shah could prove that it had once belonged to a Jain community. In a dream, the goddess Ambika (Ambadevi or Durga) instructed him to dig under a champak tree where he found a huge image of Adinatha and so won the land. To the southwest, behind the hall, is a small shrine to Ambika, once the premier deity. In common with many Jain temples the plain exterior conceals a wonderful ornately carved interior, remarkably well preserved given its age. It is an early example of the Jain style in West India, set within a rectangular court lined with small shrines and a double colonnade. The white marble of which the entire temple is built was brought not from Makrana, as some suggest, but from the relatively nearby marble quarries of Ambaji in Gujarat, 25 km south of Abu Road. Hardly a surface is left unadorned. Makaras guard the entrance, and below them are conches. The cusped arches and ornate capitals are beautifully designed and superbly made.

Lining the walls of the main hall are 57 shrines. Architecturally, it is suggested that these are related to the cells which surround the walls of Buddhist monasteries, but in the Jain temple are reduced in size to house simple images of a seated Jain saint. Although the carving of the images themselves is simple, the ceiling panels in front of the saints' cells are astonishingly ornate. Going clockwise round the cells, some of the more important ceiling sculptures illustrate: cell 1, lions, dancers and musicians; cells 2-7, people bringing offerings, birds, music-making; cell 8, Jain teacher preaching; cell 9, the major auspicious events in the life of the Tirthankars; and cell 10, Neminath's life, including his marriage, and playing with Krishna and the *gopis*. In the southeast corner of the temple between cells 22 and 23 is a large black idol of Adinath, reputedly installed by Vimal Shah in 1031.

Cell 32 shows Krishna subduing Kaliya Nag, half human and half snake, and other Krishna scenes; cell 38, the 16-armed goddess Vidyadevi (goddess of knowledge); cells 46-48, 16-armed goddesses, including the goddess of smallpox, Shitala Mata; and cell

49, Narasimha, the 'man-lion' tearing open the stomach of the demon Hiranya-Kashyapa, surrounded by an opening lotus.

As in Gujarati Hindu temples, the main hall focuses on the sanctum which contains the 2.5-m image of Adinatha, the first Tirthankar. The sanctum with a pyramidal roof has a vestibule with entrances on three sides. To its east is the Mandapa, a form of octagonal nave nearly 8 m in diameter. Its 6-m-wide dome is supported by eight slender columns; the exquisite lotus ceiling carved from a single block of marble, rises in 11 concentric circles, carved with elaborately repeated figures. Superimposed across the lower rings are 16 brackets carved in the form of the goddesses of knowledge.

Risah Deo Temple Opposite the Vimala Visahi, this temple is unfinished. It encloses a huge brass Tirthankar image weighing 4.3 tonnes and made of *panchadhatu* (five metals) – gold, silver, copper, brass and zinc. The temple was commenced in the late 13th century by Brahma Shah, the Mewari Maharana Pratap's chief minister. Building activity was curtailed by war with Gujarat and never completed.

Luna Vasihi or Neminatha Temple (1231) To the north of the Adinatha Temple, this one was erected by two wealthy merchants Vastupala and Tejapala, and dedicated to the 22nd Tirthankar; they also built a similar temple at Girnar. The attractive niches on either side of the sanctum's entrance were for their wives. The craftsmanship in this temple is comparable to the Vimala Vasahi; the decorative carving and *jali* work are excellent. The small domes in front of the shrine containing the bejewelled Neminatha figure, the exquisitely carved lotus on the sabhamandapa ceiling and the sculptures on the colonnades are especially noteworthy.

There is a fifth temple for the Digambar ('Sky-Clad') Jains which is far more austere.

Spiritual University, Art Gallery and State Museum and Spiritual Museum
The headquarters of the Spiritual University movement of the Brahma Kumaris is **Om Shanti Bhavan** ① *T02974-238268*, with its ostentatious entrance on Subhash Road. You may notice many residents dressed in white taking a walk around the lake in the evening. It is possible to stay in simple but comfortable rooms with attached baths and attend discourses, meditation sessions, yoga lessons, and so on. The charitable trust runs several worthy institutions including a really good hospital.

Walks around Mount Abu
Trevor's Tank ① *50 m beyond the Dilwara Jain temples, Rs 5, car/jeep taken up to the lake Rs 125*, is the small wildlife sanctuary covering 289 sq km with the lake which acts as a watering hole for animals including sloth bear, sambhar, wild boar, panther. Most of these are nocturnal but on your walk you are quite likely to see a couple of crocodiles basking on the rocks. The birdlife is extensive with eagles, kites, grey jungle fowl, red spurfowl, francolin, flycatchers, bulbuls and more seen during walks on the trails in the sanctuary. There are superb views from the trails.

Adhar Devi, 3 km from town, is a 15th-century Durga temple carved out of a rock and approached by 220 steep steps. There are steep treks to Anandra point or to a Mahadev temple nearby for great views.

To the west of Nakki Lake, **Honeymoon Point** and **Sunset Point** afford superb views across the plains. They can both be reached by a pleasant walk from the bus stand (about 2 km). You can continue from Honeymoon Point to **Limbdi House**. If you have another

1½ hours, walk up to **Jai Gurudev's meditation eyrie**. If you want to avoid the crowds at Sunset Point, take the **Bailey's Walk** from the Hanuman Temple near Honeymoon Point to **Valley View Point**, which joins up with the Sunset Point walk. You can also walk from the Ganesh temple to the Crags for some great views. Note only do this walk, and others in the area, when there are other people around as attacks by animals and robberies do occur.

Around Mount Abu → *For listings, see pages 130-132.*

Bera
The large panther population in the surrounding hills of Bera and the Jawai River area draws wildlife photographers. Antelopes and jackals also inhabit the area. Visit the **Jawai Dam**, 150 km from Mount Abu towards Jodhpur, to see historic embankments, numerous birds and basking marsh crocodiles. A bed for the night is provided by **Leopard's Lair** in a colourful Raika village near the lake and jungle (see Where to stay, page 130).

Jalor
Jalor is a historic citadel. In the early 14th century, during court intrigues, the Afghani Diwan of Marwar, Alauddin Khilji, took over the town and set up his own kingdom. Later, the Mughal emperor Akbar captured it and returned the principality to his allies, the Rathores of Marwar by means of a peaceful message to the Jalori Nawabs, who moved south to Palanpur in Gujarat. The medieval fort straddles a hill near the main bazar and encloses Muslim, Hindu and Jain shrines. It is a steep climb up but the views from the fort are rewarding. The old Topkhana at the bottom of the fortified hill has a mosque built by Alauddin Khilji using sculptures from a Hindu temple. Of particular interest are the scores of domes in different shapes and sizes, the symmetry of the columns and the delicate arches. Jalor bazar is good for handicrafts, silver jewellery and textiles, and is still relatively unaffected by tourist pricing.

Bhenswara
Bhenswara is a small, colourful village on the Jawai River. It has another Rajput country estate whose 'castle' has been converted into an attractive hotel. The jungles and the impressive granite Esrana hills nearby have leopard, nilgai, chinkara, blackbuck, jungle cat, porcupines, jackals and spiny-tailed lizards. It's a good place to stay for a couple of nights.

Bhinmal
Bhinmal has some important archaeological ruins, notably one of the few shrines in the country to Varaha Vishnu. It is also noted for the quality of its leather embroidered *mojdis*. Nearby, at **Vandhara**, is one of the few marble *baolis* (step wells) in India, while the historic **Soondha Mata Temple** is at a picturesque site where the green hills and barren sand dunes meet at a freshwater spring fed by a cascading stream.

Daspan
Daspan is a small village where the restored 19th-century castle built on the ruins of an old fort provides a break between Mount Abu and Jaisalmer.

Mount Abu and around listings

For hotel and restaurant price codes and other relevant information, see pages 13-16.

🛏 Where to stay

Mount Abu *p126*

Touts can be a nuisance to budget travellers at the bus stand. Prices shoot up during Diwali, Christmas week and summer (20 Apr-20 Jun) when many **$** hotels triple their rates; meals, ponies and jeeps cost a lot more too. Off-season discounts of 30-50% are usual, sometimes up to 70% in mid-winter (when it can get very cold). For a list of families receiving paying guests visit the tourist office.

$$$$ Cama Rajputana Club Resort, Adhar Devi Rd, T02974-238205, www. camahotelsindia.com. Refurbished old club house (1895) for Mt Abu's royal and British residents, guests become temporary members, 42 rooms in split-level cottages with views and modern decor, 2 period suites, lounge with fireplaces and old club furniture, average restaurant, eco-friendly (recycled water, alternative energy, drip irrigation), beautifully landscaped gardens, billiards, tennis, etc, efficient service, immaculate pool.

$$$ The Jaipur House, above Nakki Lake, T02974-235176. 9 elegant rooms and 14 new cottages in the Maharaja of Jaipur's former summer palace, unparalleled hilltop location, fantastic views, especially from the terrace restaurant, friendly, professional staff. Recommended.

$$$-$$ Hilltone, set back from the road near the petrol pump, T02974-238391, www.hotelhilltone.com. 66 tastefully decorated rooms (most a/c), attractive Handi (a style of cooking using baking/steaming in covered pots) restaurant, pool, garden, quiet, most stylish of Mt Abu's hotels, helpful staff. Recommended.

$$$-$$ Sunrise Palace, Bharatpur Kothi, T02974-235573. 20 large, sparsely furnished rooms, great bathrooms, in a grand, slightly unloved converted mansion, good small restaurant, open-air BBQ, elevated with excellent views from the restaurant.

$$ Lake Palace, facing lake, T02974-237154, www.savshantihotels.com. 13 rooms (some a/c), garden restaurant, beautifully situated with great lake views from terrace, rear access to hill road for Dilwara, well run and maintained. Recommended.

$ Lake View, on a slope facing the lake, T02974-238659. Beautiful location, 15 basic rooms, Indian WC, helpful staff.

$ Panghat, overlooking Nakki Lake, T02974-238886. Great location, 10 small but adequate rooms and friendly staff.

$ Shri Ganesh, west of the polo ground, uphill behind Brahma Kumari, T02974-237292, lalit_ganesh@yahoo.co.in. 23 clean, simple rooms, plenty of solar-heated hot water, very quiet, cookery classes, wildlife walks in morning and afternoon, one of the few places catering specifically for foreigners.

Around Mount Abu *p129*

$$$ Leopard's Lair, in a colourful Raika village, Bera, T(0)8003-979964, www. leopardslairresort.com. Well-designed stone cottages, 6 a/c rooms modern amenities, delicious meals included (fresh fish from the lake), bar, pool, garden, riding, birdwatching, panther-viewing 'safaris' with the owner.

$$$-$$ Ravla Bhenswara (Rajput Special Hotel), Bhenswara, T02978-282187, www. hotelravlabhenswara.com. 40 rooms with bath, painted exterior, inspired decor ('Badal Mahal' with cloud patterns, 'Hawa Mahal' with breezy terrace, etc), delicious Marwari meals. Courtyard lawns with a lovely swimming pool. Walk to parakeet-filled orchards and a pool at the nearby Madho Bagh. The hospitable family are very knowledgeable and enterprising. Visits to Rabari herdsmen, Bhil tribal hamlets, night safaris for leopards, camping safaris including the Tilwara cattle fair or even treks to Mt Abu. Recommended.

🍴 Restaurants

Mount Abu *p126*
Small roadside stalls sell tasty local vegetarian food. You can also get good *thalis* (Rs 30-40) at simple restaurants.
$$ Sankalp, opposite Samrat International, excellent South Indian chain restaurant with amazing chutneys.
$$ Shere-e-Punjab, near the taxi stand. One of the best in town for vegetarian/non-vegetarian Indian (some Chinese/Western).
$ Maharaja, near the bus stand. Gujarati. Simple, clean, produces excellent value *thalis*.
$ Veena, near the taxi stand. Brews real coffee, serves traditional Indian meals and a few Western favourites, very clean, outdoors, loud music, best of many on the same strip.

✹ Festivals

Mount Abu *p126*
Diwali is especially colourful here.
May An annual Summer Festival (12-14 May 2014, 2-4 May 2015) features folk music, dancing, fireworks, etc.
29-31 Dec Winter Festival.

Around Mount Abu *p129*
Sep The Navratri Festival is held in Bhinmal. Despan also holds special Navratri celebrations.

♦ What to do

Mount Abu *p126*
Mountain sports
For rock climbing and rapelling, contact the Mountaineering Institute, near Gujarat Bhawan Hostel. Equipment and guide/instructors are available.

Polo
Occasional matches and tournaments have begun to take place at the long-abandoned polo ground in the town centre. Entry is free, with local investors keen to generate income from 'polo tourism'. Ask the tourist office for information on upcoming matches.

Swimming, tennis and billiards
Non-residents can use facilities at the Cama Rajputana and Bikaner House Palace hotels.

⊖ Transport

Mount Abu *p126*
Toll on entering town, Rs 10 per head. Frequent rockfalls during the monsoon makes the road from Mount Abu hazardous; avoid night journeys. The nearest airport is Udaipur.
Bus Local buses go to **Dilwara** and **Achalgarh** at 1100 and 1500, go early if doing a day-trip. **State Bus Stand**, Main Rd (opposite tourist office, T02974-235434); **Private Bus Stand**, south of Govt Bus Stand on Petrol Pump road. Many 'direct' long-distance buses involve a change at Abu Rd bus stand, T02974-222323. To **Abu Rd**: every 30 mins (45 mins-1 hr), Rs 20. **Ahmedabad**: several (7 hrs) via Palanpur (3 hrs, change here for Bhuj, Gujarat); **Delhi**: overnight. **Jaipur** (overnight, 9 hrs), **Jodhpur** morning and afternoon (7 hrs). **Mumbai, Pune**: early morning (18 hrs). **Udaipur**: 0830, 1500, 2200 (5-6 hrs). **Vadodara**: 0930, 1930 (5 hrs). Gujarat Travels, T02974-235564, www.gujarattravels.co.in, run private buses.
Taxi and jeep Posted fares for sightseeing in a jeep; about Rs 800 per day, but open to negotiation; anywhere in town Rs 40; to Sunset Point Rs 70. Taxi (for sharing) Abu Rd Rs 300; shared taxis for Jain Temples from Dilwara stand near the bazar opposite Chacha Museum (from Rs 5).
Train Western Railway Out Agency, Tourist Reception Centre, has a small reservation quota, Mon-Sat 0900-1600, Sun 0900-1230. Book well in advance; you may have to wait 2-3 days even in

the off-season. Abu Rd, T02974-222222, is the railhead with frequent buses to Mt Abu. To **Ahmedabad**: *Aravalli Exp 19708*, 1655, 5 hrs (continues to **Mumbai**, further 8½ hrs). **Jaipur**: *Aravalli Exp 19707*, 1010, 9 hrs, via **Ajmer**, 6 hrs; **Jodhpur**: *Adi Jat Express 19223*, 1525, 4½ hrs. **Delhi**: *Ashram Exp 12915*, 2205, 12 hrs.

Around Mount Abu *p129*
Train/bus To Bera from **Mumbai** and **Ajmer** via Abu Rd (*Aravalli* and *Ranakpur Exp*) stop at Jawai Dam and Mori Bera. For **Bhenswada**, trains and buses from Abu Rd. For **Bhinmal**, trains from **Jodhpur**. From **Ahmedabad**, 2130 (12 hrs); to Ahmedabad, 1940.

Chittaurgarh and around

This is a relatively undiscovered corner of Rajasthan but it's home to some of the state's oldest and most interesting treasures. Chittaurgarh's 'Tower of Victory' has become well known in recent years, but the whole of this ancient, historically important city is worth exploring. Kota and the area around Jhalawar contain some of the oldest and most impressive temples and cave paintings in India, while nowhere takes you back in time as far as Bundi, which has been seemingly untouched for centuries. There are limited rail connections in this area, but a new highway is being constructed pretty much across the whole of southern Rajasthan. Limited transport links mean that a visit to this region does require a little more time and effort than to other areas in Rajasthan, but also that the region has remained uncrowded, unspoilt and hugely hospitable.

Arriving in Chittaurgarh
Getting there All of the region's major towns are served by the railway, but often by branch lines some way off the main routes. Buses starting from all the major cities surrounding the area give quick access to the main towns; from Udaipur to Chittaurgarh takes 2½ hours.

Getting around Most of the principal sights are fairly close together, making travel by road a convenient option. Frequent buses criss-cross the area, but a private taxi might be worth considering as some of the sights and most interesting places to stay are somewhat off the beaten track. ▸▸ *See Transport, page 141.*

Tourist infortmation Tourist office ⓘ *Janta Avas Grih, Station Rd, T01472-241089.*

Chittaurgarh → *For listings, see pages 139-141.*

The hugely imposing Chittaurgarh Fort stands on a 152-m-high rocky hill, rising abruptly above the surrounding plain. The walls, 5 km long, enclose the fascinating ruins of an ancient civilization, while the slopes are covered with scrub jungle. The modern town lies at the foot of the hill with access across a limestone bridge of 10 arches over the Gambheri River.

Background
One of the oldest cities in Rajasthan, Chittaurgarh was founded formally in AD 728 by Bappu Rawal, who according to legend was reared by the Bhil tribe. However, two sites near the River Berach have shown stone tools dating from half a million years ago and Buddhist relics

from a few centuries BC. From the 12th century it became the centre of Mewar. Excavations in the Mahasati area of the fort have shown four shrines with ashes and charred bones, the earliest dating from about the 11th century AD. This is where the young Udai Singh was saved by his nurse Panna Dai; she sacrificed her own son by substituting him for the baby prince when, as heir to the throne, Udai Singh's life was threatened.

Chittaurgarh Fort

① 0600-1800, entry Rs 100. Visiting the fort on foot means a circuit of 7 km; allow 4 hrs. The views from the battlements and towers are worth the effort.

The fort dominates the city. Until 1568 the town was situated within the walls. Today the lower town sprawls to the west of the fort. The winding 1.5-km ascent is defended by seven impressive gates: the **Padal Pol** is where Rawat Bagh Singh, the Rajput leader, fell during the second siege; the Bhairon or **Tuta Pol** (broken gate) where Jaimal, one of the heroes of the third siege, was killed by Akbar in 1567 (chhatris to Jaimal and Patta); the **Hanuman Pol** and **Ganesh Pol**; the **Jorla** (or Joined) **Pol** whose upper arch is connected to the **Lakshman Pol**; finally the **Ram Pol** (1459) which is the main gate. Inside the walls is a village and ruined palaces, towers and temples, most of which are out in the open and so easy to explore.

Rana Kumbha's Palace, on the right immediately inside the fort, are the ruins of this palace (1433-1468), originally built of dressed stone with a stucco covering. It is approached by two gateways, the large Badi Pol and the three-bay deep Tripolia. Once there were elephant and horse stables, zenanas (recognized by the jali screen), and a Siva temple. The jauhar committed by Padmini and her followers is believed to have taken place beneath the courtyard. The north frontage of the palace contains an attractive combination of canopied balconies. Across from the palace is the Nau Lakha Bhandar (The Treasury). The temple to Rana Kumbha's wife **Mira Bai** who was a renowned poetess is visible from the palace and stands close to the Kumbha Shyama Temple (both circa 1440). The older 11th-century Jain **Sat Bis Deori** with its 27 shrines, is nearby. The **Shringara Chauri Temple** (circa 1456), near the fort entrance, has sculptured panels of musicians, warriors and Jain deities.

Rana Ratan Singh's Palace is to the north by the Ratneshwar Lake. Built in stone around 1530 it too had stucco covering. Originally rectangular in plan and enclosed within a high wall, it was subsequently much altered. The main gate to the south still stands as an example of the style employed.

The early 20th-century **Fateh Prakash Palace** built by Maharana Fateh Singh (died 1930) houses an interesting **museum** ① Sat-Thu 0800-1630, Rs 3. To the south is the **Vijay Stambha** (1458-1468), one of the most interesting buildings in the fort, built by Rana Kumbha to celebrate his victory over Mahmud Khilji of Malwa in 1440. Visible for miles around, it stands on a base 14 sq m and 3 m high, and rises 37 m. The nine-storeyed sandstone tower has been restored; the upper section retains some of the original sculpture. For no extra charge you can climb to the top. Nearby is the Mahasati terrace where the ranas were cremated when Chittaurgarh was the capital of Mewar. There are also numerous sati stones. Just to the south is the **Samdhishvara Temple** to Siva (11th and 15th centuries), which still attracts many worshippers and has some good sculptured friezes. Steps down lead to the deep Gomukh Kund, where the sacred spring water enters through a stone carved as a cow's mouth (hence its name).

Of the two palaces of **Jaimal** and **Patta**, renowned for their actions during the siege of 1567, the latter, based on the zenana building of Rana Kumbha's palace, is more interesting. You then pass the Bhimtal before seeing the **Kalika Mata Temple** (originally an eighth-century Surya temple, rebuilt mid-16th century) with exterior carvings and the ruins of Chonda's House with its three-storey domed tower. Chonda did not claim the title when his father, Rana Lakha, died in 1421.

Padmini's Palace (late 13th century, rebuilt end of the 19th century) is sited in the middle of the lake surrounded by pretty gardens. Ala-ud-din Khilji is said to have seen Padmini's beautiful reflection in the water through a mirror on the palace wall. This striking vision convinced him that she had to be his.

You pass the deer park on your way round to the **Suraj Pol** (Sun Gate) and pass the **Adbhutanatha Temple** to Siva before reaching the second tower, the **Kirti Stambha**, a Tower of Fame (13th and 15th centuries). Smaller than the Vijay Stambha (23 m) with only seven storeys, but just as elegant, it is dedicated to Adinath, the first Jain Tirthankar. Naked figures of Tirthankars are repeated several hundred times on the face of the tower. A narrow internal staircase goes to the top.

Of particular interest are the number of tanks and wells in the fort that have survived the centuries. Water, from both natural and artificial sources, was harnessed to provide an uninterrupted supply to the people.

Chittaurgarh to Kota → *For listings, see pages 139-141.*

Bassi, 28 km from Chittaurgarh, is famous for handicrafts and miniature wooden temples painted with scenes from the epics. The palace, a massive 16th-century fort, has been opened as a hotel (see Where to stay, page 139).

Bijaipur is a feudal village with a 16th-century **castle**, set among the Vindhya hills and also now open as a hotel (see Where to stay, page 139). It has a splendid location near the **Bassi-Bijaipur Wildlife Sanctuary**, which is home to panther, antelope and other wildlife. The forests are interspersed with lakes, reservoirs, streams and waterfalls with good birdlife in the winter months. The ruined **Pannagarh Fort** facing a lily covered lake is believed to be one of the oldest in Rajasthan.

Menal, further east, has a cluster of Siva temples believed to date from the time of the Guptas. They are associated with the Chauhans and other Rajput dynasties. Though neglected the temples have some fine carvings and a panel of erotic sculptures somewhat similar to those at Khajuraho in Madhya Pradesh. Behind is a deep, wooded ravine with a seasonal waterfall.

Kota

Kota's attractive riverside location and decent hotels make it a comfortable place to stay. The town itself is of no special appeal, but can be used as a base from which to visit nearby Bundi if you're short on time. There's a **tourist office** ① *Hotel Chambal, T0744-232 6257,* for information.

At the south end of the town, near the barrage, is the vast, strongly fortified **City Palace** (1625) which you enter by the south gate having driven through the bustling but quite charming old city. There are some striking buildings with delicate ornamental stonework on the balconies and façade, though parts are decaying. The best-preserved murals and carved marble panels are in the chambers upstairs and in the Arjun Mahal. These murals feature motifs characteristic of the Kota School of Art, including portraiture (especially profiles), hunting scenes, festivals and the Krishna Lila.

The 15th-century **Kishore Sagar** tank between the station and the palace occasionally has boats for hire. **Jag Mandir Island Palace**, closed to visitors, is in the centre of the lake.

The **Chambal Gardens** by Amar Niwas, south of the fort, is a pleasant place for a view of the river, although the rare fish-eating gharial crocodiles with which the pond was stocked are rarely seen these days. A variety of birds, occasionally including flamingos, can be seen at the river and in nearby ponds.

The **Umed Bhawan** (1904), 1 km north of town, was built for the Maharao Umaid Singh II and designed by Sir Samuel Swinton Jacob in collaboration with Indian designers. The buff-coloured stone exterior with a stucco finish has typical Rajput detail. The interior, however, is Edwardian with a fine drawing-room, banquet hall and garden. It has now been converted into a heritage hotel (see Where to stay, page 139).

Bundi → For listings, see pages 139-141.

Bundi lies in a beautiful narrow valley with Taragarh Fort towering above. The drive into the town is lovely as the road runs along the hillside overlooking the valley opposite the fort. You might feel 'forted out' by the time you reach Bundi, but this beautiful old town nestles under the palace and fort and offers spectacular views and a unique charm. Much less developed than the other fort towns, Bundi is starting to blossom – now more classic *havelis* are being 'boutiqued', and there are plenty of more down-home family guesthouses springing up too. Popular with backpackers and now increasingly tour buses, Bundi is relaxed and friendly and still a long way off the bazar bustle of Pushkar and the speed and hustle of the more developed fort towns of Jodhpur and Jaisalmer, but good cafés serving cappuccinos cannot be too far along the line. It is well worth spending a day or two here to soak in the atmosphere. Bundi is especially colourful and interesting during the many festivals (see Festivals, page 141). **Tourist office** ① *Circuit House, near Raniji ki Baori, T0747-244 3697.*

Background

Formerly a small state founded in 1342, Bundi's fortunes varied inversely with those of its more powerful neighbours. Neither wealthy nor powerful, it nevertheless ranked high in the Rajput hierarchy since the founding family belonged to the specially blessed Hada Chauhan clan. After Prithviraj Chauhan was defeated by Muhammad Ghuri in 1193, the rulers sought refuge in Mewar. However, adventurous clan members overran the Bhils and Minas in the Chambal valley and established the kingdom of Hadavati or **Hadoti** which covers the area around Bundi, Kota and Jhalawar in southeastern Rajasthan. It prospered under the guidance of the able 19th-century ruler Zalim Singh, but then declined on his death. The British reunited the territory in 1894.

Places in Bundi

Taragarh Fort (1342) ① *0600-1800, foreigners Rs 100, Indians Rs 20, camera Rs 50, video Rs 100,* stands in sombre contrast to the beauty of the town and the lakes below. There are excellent views but it is a difficult 20-minute climb beset in places by aggressive monkeys; wear good shoes and wield a big stick. The eastern wall is crenellated with high ramparts while the main gate to the west is flanked by octagonal towers. The **Bhim Burj** tower dominates the fort and provided the platform for the Garbh Ganjam ('Thunder from the Womb'), a huge cannon. A pit to the side once provided shelter for the artillery men, and there are several stepped water tanks inside. Cars can go as far as the TV tower then it is 600 m along a rough track.

The **Palace Complex** ① *below Taragarh, 0900-1700, foreigners Rs 100, Indians Rs 20,* which was begun around 1600, is at the northern end of the bazar, and was described by Kipling as "such a palace as men build for themselves in uneasy dreams – the work of goblins rather than of men". The buildings, on various levels, follow the shape of the hill. A steep, rough stone ramp leads up through the **Hazari Darwaza** (Gate of the Thousand) where the garrison lived; you may need to enter through a small door within the *darwaza*. The palace entrance is through the **Hathi Pol** (Elephant Gate, 1607-1631), which has two carved elephants with a water clock. Steps lead up to **Ratan Daulat** above the stables, the unusually small Diwan-i-Am which was intended to accommodate a select few at public

Bundi

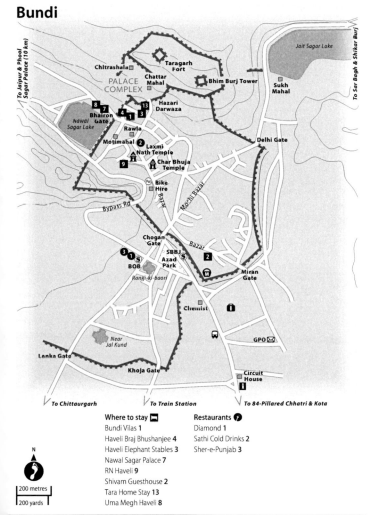

To Jaipur & Phool Sagar Palace (10 km)

Jait Sagar Lake

To Sar Bagh & Shikar Burj

Chitrashala

Taragarh Fort

PALACE COMPLEX

Chattar Mahal

Bhim Burj Tower

Sukh Mahal

Hazari Darwaza

8 7 4 13
1 3

Bhairon Gate

Nawal Sagar Lake

Rawla

Motimahal 2

Laxmi Nath Temple

Char Bhuja Temple

Delhi Gate

9

Bike Hire

Bypass Rd

Bazar

Mochi Bazar

Chogan Gate

Bazar

3 1 $
BOB

SBBJ
$
Azad Park

2

Ranji-ki-baori

Miran Gate

Chemist

Near Jal Kund

GPO

Lanka Gate

Khoja Gate

Circuit House

To Chittaurgarh

To Train Station

To 84-Pillared Chhatri & Kota

Where to stay
Bundi Vilas **1**
Haveli Braj Bhushanjee **4**
Haveli Elephant Stables **3**
Nawal Sagar Palace **7**
RN Haveli **9**
Shivam Guesthouse **2**
Tara Home Stay **13**
Uma Megh Haveli **8**

Restaurants
Diamond **1**
Sathi Cold Drinks **2**
Sher-e-Punjab **3**

N

200 metres
200 yards

audience. A delicate marble balcony overhangs the courtyard giving a view of the throne to the less privileged, who stood below. The **Chattar Mahal** (1660), the newer palace of green serpentine rock, is pure Rajput in style and contains private apartments decorated with wall paintings, glass and mirrors. The **Badal Mahal** bedroom has finely decorated ceilings. The **Chitrashala** ① *0900-1700, Rs 20*, a cloistered courtyard with a gallery running around a garden of fountains, has a splendid collection of miniatures showing scenes from the Radha Krishna story. Turquoise, blues and greens dominate (other pigments may have faded with exposure to sunlight) though the elephant panels on the dado are in a contrasting red. The murals (circa 1800) are some of the finest examples of Rajput art but are not properly maintained. There is supposedly a labyrinth of catacombs in which the state treasures are believed to have been stored. Each ruler was allowed one visit but when the last guide died in the 1940s the secret of its location was lost. At night, the palace is lit up and thousands of bats pour out of its innards. There are several 16th- to 17th-century step wells and 'tanks' (*kunds*) in town. The 46-m-deep **Raniji-ki-baori** ① *Mon-Sat 1000-1700, closed 2nd Sat each month, free, caretaker unlocks the gate*, with beautiful pillars and bas relief sculpture panels of Vishnu's 10 *avatars*, is the most impressive. No longer in use, the water is stagnant. **Sukh Mahal**, a summer pleasure palace, faces the **Jait Sagar** lake; Kipling spent a night in the original pavilion. Further out are the 66 royal memorials at the rarely visited **Sar Bagh**, some of which have beautiful carvings. The caretaker expects Rs 10 tip. The square artificial **Nawal Sagar** lake has in its centre a half-submerged temple to Varuna, the god of water. The lake surface beautifully reflects the entire town and palace, but tends to dry up in the summer months. A dramatic tongue-slitting ceremony takes place here during Dussehra. West of the Nawal Sagar, 10 km away, is **Phool Sagar Palace**, which was started in 1945 but was left unfinished. Prior permission is needed to view.

South of Kota → *For listings, see pages 139-141.*

Jhalawar, 85 km southeast of Kota, was the capital of the princely state of the Jhalas, which was separated from Kota by the British in 1838. It lies in a thickly forested area on the edge of the Malwa plateau with some interesting local forts, temples and ancient cave sites nearby. The **Garh Palace** in the town centre, now housing government offices, has some fine wall paintings which can be seen with permission. The **museum** ① *Sat-Thu 1000-1630, Rs 3*, established in 1915, has a worthwhile collection of sculptures, paintings and manuscripts. **Bhawani Natyashala** (1921) was known for its performances ranging from Shakespearean plays to Shakuntala dramas. The stage with a subterranean driveway allowed horses and chariots to be brought on stage during performances. The **tourist office** ① *T07432-230081*, is at the **Hotel Chandravati**.

The small walled town of **Jhalarapatan**, 7 km south of Jhalawar, has several fine 11th-century Hindu temples, the **Padmanath Sun Temple** on the main road being the best. The **Shantinath Jain** temple has an entrance flanked by marble elephants. There are some fine carvings on the rear façade and silver polished Idols inside the shrines.

About 7 km away, **Chandrawati**, on the banks of the Chandrabhaga River, has the ruins of some seventh-century Hindu temples with fragments of fine sculpture.

Chittaurgarh and around listings

For hotel and restaurant price codes and other relevant information, see pages 13-16.

⊜ Where to stay

Chittaurgarh *p133*
$$$ Padmini Haveli, Anna Poorna Temple Rd, Shah Chowk, T01472-241 251, www.thepadminihaveli.com. This newly restored *haveli* within the fort walls provides a rare opportunity to stay within Chittaurgarh Fort. 9 beautifully furnished rooms built around a central courtyard. Home-cooked meals available.
$$ Pratap Palace (Rajput Special Hotels), Sri Gurukul Rd, near GPO, T01472-240099, www.hotelpratappalacechittaugarh.com. Clean, well-maintained rooms, some a/c, 2 with ornately painted walls, good fun, good food in restaurant or in the pleasant garden, jeep and horse safaris visiting local villages. Recommended.
$ Ganesh Guest House, New Fort Rd, opposite Sukhadiya Park, T01472-248240. 20 basic and yet still overpriced rooms, Indian and Western toilets.
$ Meera, near railway station, Neemuch Rd, T01472-240466. Modern, 24 a/c and non-a/c rooms with TV and phone, Gujarati/Punjabi restaurant, bar, laundry, car rental, travel assistance, internet, characterless but efficient.

Chittaurgarh to Kota *p135*
$$$-$$ Castle Bijaipur (Rajput Special Hotels), Bijaipur, T01472-240099, www.castlebijaipur. com. 25 simple rooms in traditional style with comfortable furniture and modern bathrooms in castle and a new wing. Lawns and gardens, hill views from breezy terrace, superb pool, delicious Rajasthani meals, also tea on the medieval bastion, jeep/horse safaris with camping and jungle trekking. Popular with yoga groups.
$$ Bassi Fort Palace, Bassi, T01472-225321, www.bassifortpalace.com. 16 unpretentious rooms in a family-run 16th-century fort.

The same family runs an abandoned fort on the top of the nearby hill (where dinner can be arranged) and a hunting lodge 6 km away accessible by boat or horse. Safaris to this lodge and local tribal villages can be arranged. Refreshingly informal. Recommended.

Kota *p135*
$$$ Umed Bhawan (WelcomHeritage), Palace Rd, T0744-232 5262, www.welcom heritagehotels.in. 32 large, comfortable rooms, impressive building and interesting memorabilia and billiards rooms with more stuffed animals than you can shake a stick at, it's not such a great surprise that there are so few tigers left in the wild when you come to some of these Raj-era establishments. Elegant dining room, great beer bar, sunny terraces, behind woods (langurs, deer, parakeets, peacocks), tennis, attentive staff.
$$ Palkiya Haveli, Mokha Para (in walled city), near Suraj Pol, T0744-238 7497, www.palkiyahaveli.com. A beautifully restored *haveli*, with a nice family vibe. 6 traditionally furnished a/c rooms with bath (tubs), carved wood furniture, exquisite murals, very good fixed meals, peaceful courtyard garden (full of birds). Recommended.
$$ Sukhdham Kothi, Civil Lines, T0744-232 0081, www.sukhdhamkothi.com. 15 elegant rooms (size varies), 10 a/c, in a 19th-century British residence with sandstone balconies and screens, good home-made Rajasthani food, large, private garden well set back from the road, family-run, friendly. Peacocks in the garden. Recommended.

Bundi *p136, map p137*
$$$-$$ Bundi Vilas, below the palace, behind **Haveli Braj Bhushanjee**, T(0)9414-175280, www.bundivilas.com. Wander up a beautiful atmospheric alleyway and you find yourself at a super-stylish, newly restored *haveli* with good views from the

rooftop. Great attention to detail, rose petals everywhere scenting the way, Wi-Fi, stylishly furnished. Good tasty food – brown bread is brought daily from Delhi, jams from the Himalaya and the lady of the house makes a great sesame dessert. Highly recommended.
$$$-$ Haveli Braj Bhushanjee, below the fort, opposite the Ayurvedic Hospital, T0747-244 2322, www.kiplingsbundi.com. 16 quaint rooms with clean bath (hot showers), in a 19th-century 4-storey *haveli* covered in frescos, plenty of atmosphere and memorabilia but a bit stuffy and overpriced, although some of the cheaper rooms are good value. Home-cooked vegetarian meals (no alcohol), pleasant terrace, good fort views, pick-up from station on request, good craft shop below, mixed reports on service. Also offers modern rooms in attached, newly restored 17th-century **Badi Haveli**.
$$-$ Nawal Sagar Palace, Balchandpada, T0747-230 0644, nawalsagarpalace@ hotmail.com. Through an imposing door, you find charming, comfortable rooms. Beautifully decorated. New restaurant planned in adjacent wing. Friendly owner, friendly dog.
$ Haveli Elephant Stables, at the base of the palace near gate, T(0)9928-154064, elephantstable_guesthouse@hotmail.com. Formerly used to house royal elephants, the 4 simple but huge rooms have mosquito nets and basic Indian toilets, beneath a huge peepal tree in a dusty courtyard. Good home cooking, relaxed.
$ Lake View Paying Guest House, Bohra Meghwan Ji Ki Haveli, Balchand Para, below the palace, by Nawal Sagar, T0747-244 2326, lakeviewbundi@yahoo.com. 7 simple clean rooms (3 in a separate, basic garden annexe with shared bath) in a 150-year-old *haveli* with wall paintings, private terrace shared with monkeys and peacocks, lovely views from the rooftop, warm welcome, popular, very friendly hosts.
$ R N Haveli, behind Laxmi Nath Temple, T0747-512 0098, rnhavelibundi@yahoo.co.in.

5 rooms in a friendly family home – home cooking is good. Recommended.
$ Shivam Guesthouse, outside the walls near the Nawal Sagar, T0747-244 7892, www.shivam-bundi.co.in. Simple, comfortable rooms around a shaded blue courtyard, exceptionally friendly, come for food even if you're not staying. Recommended.
$ Tara Home Stay, near Elephant Stables, T(0)9829-718554, tarahomestay@gmail.com, Only a couple of rooms, but exceptional views of the palace.
$ Uma Megh Haveli, Balchand Para, T0747-244 2191. Very atmospheric, 11 unrestored rooms, 7 with basic attached bathrooms, plus a pleasant garden and restaurant.

🍴 Restaurants

Kota *p135*
$ Hariyali, Bundi Rd. Good Punjabi, some Chinese/Continental. Pleasant garden restaurant, outdoors or under a small shelter, very popular but some way out of town.
$ Jodhpur Sweets, Ghumanpura Market. Saffron *lassis* and flavoured milks.
$ Palace View, outdoor meals/snacks. Handy for visitors to the City Palace.

Bundi *p136, map p137*
Several of the hotels have pleasant rooftop restaurants, see Where to stay.
$ Diamond, Suryamahal Chowk. Very popular locally for cheap vegetarian meals, handy when visiting step wells.
$ Sathi Cold Drinks, Palace Rd. Excellent *lassis* (saffron, spices, pistachio and fruit), pleasant.
$ Sher-e-Punjab, near Diamond. Non-vegetarian.

🎉 Festivals

Chittaurgarh *p133*
Oct/Nov Mira Utsav, 2 days of cultural evening programmes and religious songs in the fort's Mira temple.

Kota *p135*
Mar/Apr Colourful Gangaur.
Jul/Aug Teej.
Sep/Oct Dasara Mela (1-3 Oct 2014, 21-22 Oct 2015). Great atmosphere, with shows in lit up palace grounds.

Bundi *p136, map p137*
Aug Kajli Teej (12-13 Aug 2014, 31 Aug-1 Sep 2015), and **Bundi Utsav**, which takes place 3 days after the Pushkar fair has finished (see box, page 189).
Nov Jhalawar sees the Chandrabhaga Fair (5-7 Nov 2014, 24-26 Nov 2015) a cattle and camel fair with all the colour and authenticity of Pushkar but less commercialization. Animals are traded in large numbers, pilgrims come to bathe in the river as the temples become the centre of religious activity and the town is abuzz with all manner of vendors.

⊖ Transport

Chittaurgarh *p133*
Bicycle hire By railway station, Rs 5 per hr.
Bus Enquiries, T01472-241177. Daily buses to **Bundi** (4 hrs), **Kota** (5 hrs), **Ajmer** (5 hrs) and frequent buses to **Udaipur**.
Train Enquiries, T01472-240131. A 117-km branch line runs from Chittaurgarh to **Udaipur**. At **Mavli Junction** (72 km) another branch runs down the Aravalli scarp to **Marwar Junction** (150 km). The views along this line are very picturesque, though trains are slow, with hard seats. By taking this route you can visit Udaipur, Ajmer and Jodhpur in a circular journey. Call for times as services have been scaled back in recent years.
Jaipur: *Udz Jp Exp 1299*, 0820, 5 hrs.

Kota *p135*
Bus At least hourly to **Bundi** (45 mins) and a few daily to **Ajmer**, **Chittaurgarh**, **Jhalarapatan** (2½ hrs) and Udaipur; also to **Gwalior**, **Sawai Madhopur** and **Ujjain**.
Train From Kota Junction: **Bharatpur**: *Golden Temple Mail 12903*, 1105, 4 hrs (continues to **Mathura**, 5 hrs). **Mumbai** (**Central**): *Jp Bct Supfast 12956*, 1730, 14 hrs; **New Delhi**: *Rajdhani Exp 12951*, 0330, 5½ hrs; *Golden Temple Mail 12903*, 1105, 7½ hrs, all via **Sawai Madhopur**, 1½ hrs.

Bundi *p136, map p137*
Bus Enquiries: T0747-244 5422. To **Ajmer** (165 km), 5 hrs; **Jaipur**, several daily, 4 deluxe, 4-5 hrs; **Kota** (37 km), 45 mins; **Chittaurgarh** (157 km), 5 hrs; **Udaipur** (120 km), 3 hrs. For **Jhalarapatan** catch a bus from **Kota** to **Jhalawar**; then auto-rickshaw or local bus for sights. The Ujjain–Jhalawar road is appalling.
Train Enquiries: T0747-244 3582. The station south of town has a train each way between **Kota** and **Neemuch** via **Chittaurgarh**. A direct Delhi service may be running, but involves hours waiting in Kota; better to take the bus to Kota and board trains there.

ⓘ Directory

Kota *p135*
Medical services MBS Hospital, T0744-232 3261. **Police** T0744-245 0066.

Bundi *p136, map p137*
Medical services City Hospital, T0747-244 2333.

Jodhpur and around

Rajasthan's second largest city, Jodhpur is entirely dominated by its spectacular Mehrangarh fort, towering over proceedings below with absolute authority. You could spend most of a day wandering this grand stone edifice on its plinth of red rock, pausing in the warm shafts of sunlight in its honey-coloured courtyards and strolling its chunky, cannon-lined ramparts high above the moat of blue buildings which make up the old city. Up there, birds of prey circle on the thermals, close to eye level, while the city hums below, its rickshaw horns and occasional calls to prayer still audible. Jodhpur's fascinating old city is a hive of activity, the colourful bazars, narrow lanes, and bustling Sardar Market frequented by equally colourful tribal people from the surrounding areas. South of the railway line, things are altogether more serene, and nowhere more so than the impressive Umaid Bhawan Palace, its classic exterior belying the art deco extravaganza within. There are also some remarkable sights around Jodhpur: the temples of Osian and Nagaur are well worth a visit and there are some great heritage hotels set in quiet nearby villages.

Arriving in Jodhpur
Getting there Jodhpur has good air, rail and road links with the other major cities of Rajasthan as well as Delhi and Mumbai. Many visitors stop here either on the way to or from Jaisalmer, or on their way down to Udaipur.

Getting around The train and bus stations are conveniently located close to the old city, with most hotels a Rs 20-30 rickshaw ride away, while the airport is 5 km south of town. The old city is small enough to walk around, although many people find a rented bicycle the best way to get about. ▸▸ See Transport, page 155.

Tourist information The government tourist office is on the grounds of the RTDC ① Hotel Ghoomar, High Court Rd, T0291-254 4010. As well as the usual supply of maps and pamphlets, it organizes half-day city tours and village safaris. Also, **Tourist Assistance Force** has a presence at the railway station bus stand and clock tower.

Background
The **Rathore** Rajputs had moved to **Marwar** – the 'region of death' – in 1211, after their defeat at Kanauj by Muhammad Ghori. In 1459, Rao Jodha – forced to leave the Rathore

capital at Mandore, 8 km to the north – chose this place as his capital because of its strategic location on the edge of the Thar Desert. The Rathores subsequently controlled wide areas of Rajasthan. Rao Udai Singh of Jodhpur (died 1581) received the title of Raja from Akbar, and his son, Sawai Raja Sur Singh (died 1595), conquered Gujarat and part of the Deccan for the emperor. Maharaja Jaswant Singh (died 1678), having supported Shah Jahan in the Mughal struggle for succession in 1658, had a problematic relationship with the subsequent Mughal rule of Aurangzeb, and his son Ajit Singh was only able to succeed him after Aurangzeb's own death in 1707. In addition to driving the Mughals out of Ajmer he added substantially to the Mehrangarh Fort in Jodhpur. His successor, Maharaja Abhai Singh (died 1749) captured Ahmedabad, and the state came into treaty relations with the British in 1818.

Jodhpur lies on the once strategic Delhi–Gujarat trading route and the Marwaris managed and benefited from the traffic of opium, copper, silk, sandalwood, dates, coffee and much more besides.

Jodhpur → *For listings, see pages 149-155.*

The Old City
The Old City is surrounded by a huge 9.5-km-long wall which has 101 bastions and seven gates, above which are inscribed the names of the places to which the roads underneath them lead. It comprises a labyrinthine maze of narrow streets and lively markets, a great place to wander round and get lost. Some of the houses and temples are of richly carved stone, in particular the red sandstone buildings of the Siré (Sardar) Bazar. Here the **Taleti Mahal** (early 17th century), one of three concubines' palaces in Jodhpur, has the unique feature of *jarokhas* decorated with temple columns.

Mehrangarh
ⓘ *T0291-254 8790, 0900-1700, foreigners Rs 400, students Rs 300, Indians Rs 60, includes excellent MP3 audio guide and camera fee, video Rs 200, allow at least 2 hrs, there is a pleasant restaurant on the terrace near the ticket office. For a novel way of viewing the fort, try ziplining with Flying Fox, www.flyingfox.asia.*
The 'Majestic Fort' sprawls along the top of a steep escarpment with a sheer drop to the south. Originally started by Rao Jodha in 1459, it has walls up to 36 m high and 21 m wide, towering above the plains. Most of what stands today is from the period of Maharajah Jaswant Singh (1638-1678). On his death in 1678, Aurangzeb occupied the fort. However, after Aurangzeb's death Mehrangarh returned to Jaswant Singh's son Ajit Singh and remained the royal residence until the Umaid Bhavan was completed in 1943. It is now perhaps the best preserved and presented palace in Rajasthan, an excellent example which the others will hopefully follow.

The summit has three areas: the palace (northwest), a wide terrace to the east of the palace, and the strongly fortified area to the south. There are extensive views from the top. One approach is by a winding path up the west side, possible by rickshaw, but the main approach and car park is from the east. The climb is quite stiff; those with walking difficulties may use the elevator (Rs 15 each way).

The gateways There were originally seven gateways. The first, the **Fateh Gate**, is heavily fortified with spikes and a barbican that forces a 45° turn. The smaller **Gopal Gate** is followed by the **Bhairon Gate**, with large guardrooms. The fourth, **Toati Gate**, is now missing but the fifth, **Dodhkangra Gate**, marked with cannon shots, stands over a turn in the path and has loopholed battlements for easy defence. Next is the **Marti Gate**, a long passage flanked by guardrooms. The last, **Loha (Iron) Gate**, controls the final turn into the fort and has handprints (31 on one side and five on the other) of royal *satis*, the wives of

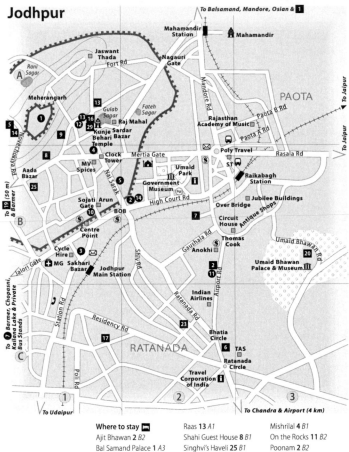

Jodhpur

Where to stay 🛏

Ajit Bhawan **2** *B2*
Bal Samand Palace **1** *A3*
Cosy Guest House **5** *A1*
Devi Bhavan **6** *C2*
Durag Niwas Guest
  House **7** *B2*
Hare Krishna Guest
  House **9** *A1*
Haveli Inn Pal **16** *A1*
Inn Season **17** *C1*
Juna Mahal **19** *B1*
Pal Haveli **29** *A1*

Raas **13** *A1*
Shahi Guest House **8** *B1*
Singhvi's Haveli **25** *B1*
Umaid Bhawan Palace **20** *B3*
Yogi's Guest House **14** *A1*

Mishrilal **4** *B1*
On the Rocks **11** *B2*
Poonam **2** *B2*
Sankalp **7** *C1*
Softy & Softy **14** *B2*

Restaurants 🍴

Café Sheesh Mahal **12** *A1*
Chokelao **1** *A1*
Hotel Priya **5** *B1*
Jhankar **13** *A1*
Jodhpur Coffee House **10** *B1*
Kalinga **3** *B1*

maharajas. It is said that six queens and 58 concubines became *satis* on Ajit Singh's funeral pyre in 1724. *Satis* carried the Bhagavad Gita with them into the flames and legend has it that the holy book would never perish. The main entrance is through the **Jay (Victory) Pol**.

The palaces From the Loha Gate the ramp leads up to the Suraj (Sun) Pol, which opens onto the Singar Choki Chowk, the main entrance to the museum, see below. Used for royal ceremonies such as the anointing of rajas, the north, west and southwest sides of the Singar Choki Chowk date from the period immediately before the Mughal occupation in 1678. The upper storeys of the chowk were part of the *zenana*, and from the **Jhanki Mahal** (glimpse palace) on the upper floor of the north wing the women could look down on the activities of the courtyard. Thus the chowk below has the features characteristic of much of the rest of the *zenana*, *jarokhas* surmounted by the distinctive Bengali-style eaves and beautifully ornate *jali* screens. These allowed cooling breezes to ventilate rooms and corridors in the often stiflingly hot desert summers.

Also typical of Mughal buildings was the use of material hung from rings below the eaves to provide roof covering, as in the columned halls of the **Daulat Khana** and the **Sileh Khana** (armoury), which date from Ajit Singh's reign. The collection of Indian weapons in the armoury is unequalled, with remarkable swords and daggers, often beautifully decorated with calligraphy. Shah Jahan's red silk and velvet tent, lavishly embroidered with gold thread and used in the Imperial Mughal campaign, is in the **Tent Room**. The **Jewel House** has a wonderful collection of jewellery, including diamond eyebrows held by hooks over the ears. There are also palanquins, howdahs and ornate royal cradles, all marvellously well preserved.

The **Phool Mahal** (Flower Palace), above the Sileh Khana, was built by Abhai Singh (1724-1749) as a hall of private audience. The stone *jali* screens are original and there are striking portraits of former rulers, a lavishly gilded ceiling and the Jodhpur coat of arms displayed above the royal couch; the murals of the 36 musical modes are a late 19th-century addition.

The **Umaid Vilas**, which houses Rajput miniatures, is linked to the **Sheesh Mahal** (Mirror Palace), built by Ajit Singh between 1707 and 1724. The room has characteristic large and regularly sized mirror work, unlike Mughal 'mirror palaces'. Immediately to its south, and above the Sardar Vilas, is the **Takhat Vilas**. Added by Maharajah Takhat Singh (1843-1873), it has wall murals of dancing girls, love legends and Krishna Lila, while its ceiling has two unusual features: massive wooden beams to provide support and the curious use of colourful Belgian Christmas tree balls.

The **Ajit Vilas** has a fascinating collection of musical instruments and costumes. On the ground floor of the Takhat Vilas is **Sardar Vilas**, and to its south the **Khabka** and **Chandan Mahals** (sleeping quarters). The **Moti Vilas** wings to the north, east and south of the Moti Mahal Chowk, date from Jaswant Singh's reign. The women could watch proceedings in the courtyard below through the *jali* screens of the surrounding wings. Tillotson suggests that the **Moti Mahal (Pearl Palace)** ① *Rs 150 for 15 mins*, to the west, although placed in the *zenana* of the fort, was such a magnificent building that it could only have served the purpose of a Diwan-i-Am (Hall of Public Audience). The Moti Mahal is fronted by excellently carved 19th-century woodwork, while inside waist-level niches housed oil lamps whose light would have shimmered from the mirrored ceiling. A palmist reads your fortune at Moti Mahal Chowk (museum area).

Mehrangarh Fort Palace Museum is in a series of palaces with beautifully designed and decorated windows and walls. It has a magnificent collection of the maharajas' memorabilia – superbly maintained and presented.

Jaswant Thada ① *off the road leading up to the fort, 0900-1700, Rs 30*, is the cremation ground of the former rulers with distinctive memorials in white marble which commemorate Jaswant Singh II (1899) and successive rulers of Marwar. It is situated in pleasant and well-maintained gardens and is definitely worth visiting on the way back from the fort.

The new city

The new city beyond the walls is also of interest. Overlooking the Umaid Sagar is the **Umaid Bhawan Palace** on Chittar Hill. Building started in 1929 as a famine relief exercise when the monsoon failed for the third year running. Over 3000 people worked for 14 years, building this vast 347-room palace of sandstone and marble. The hand-hewn blocks are interlocked into position, and use no mortar. It was designed by HV Lanchester, with the most modern furnishing and facilities in mind, and completed in 1943. The interior decoration was left to the artist JS Norblin, a refugee from Poland; he painted the frescoes in the Throne Room (East Wing). For the architectural historian, Tillotson, it is "the finest example of Indo-Deco. The forms are crisp and precise, and the bland monochrome of the stone makes the eye concentrate on their carved shapes". The royal family still occupy part of the palace.

The **Umaid Bhawan Palace Museum** ① *T0291-251 0101, 0900-1700, Rs 50*, includes the Darbar Hall with its elegantly flaking murals plus a good collection of miniatures, armour and quirky old clocks as well as a bizarre range of household paraphernalia; if it was fashionable in the 1930s, expensive and not available in India, it's in here. Many visitors find the tour and the museum in general disappointing with not much to see (most of the china and glassware you could see in your grandma's cabinets). The palace hotel which occupies the majority of the building has been beautifully restored, but is officially inaccessible to non-residents; try sneaking in for a cold drink and a look at the magnificent domed interior, a remarkable separation from the Indian environment in which it is set (see Where to stay, page 150).

The **Government Museum** ① *Umaid Park, Sat-Thu 1000-1630, Rs 3*, is a time-capsule from the British Raj, little added to since Independence, with some moth-eaten stuffed animals and featherless birds, images of Jain Tirthankars, miniature portraits and antiquities. A small zoo in the gardens has a few rare exotic species.

Just southeast of Raikabagh Station are the **Raikabagh Palace** and the **Jubilee Buildings**, public offices designed by Sir Samuel Swinton Jacob in the Indo-Saracenic style. On the Mandore Road, 2 km to the north, is the large **Mahamandir Temple**.

Excursions from Jodhpur

Taking a 'safari' to visit a **Bishnoi village** is recommended, although these trips have naturally become more touristy over the years. Most tours include the hamlets of **Guda**, famous for wildlife, **Khejarali**, a well-known Bishnoi village, **Raika** cameleers' settlement and **Salawas**. Interesting and alternative trips are run by **Virasat Experiences**. ►► *See What to do, page 154*.

The small, semi-rural village of **Jhalamand**, 12 km south of Jodhpur, is a good alternative to staying in the city, particularly if you have your own transport. It works especially well as a base from which to explore the Bishnoi and Raika communities.

Marwar, 8 km north of Jodhpur, is the old 14th-century capital of Mandore, situated on a plateau. Set around the old cremation ground with the red sandstone *chhatris* of the Rathore rulers, the gardens are usually crowded with Indian tourists at weekends. The **Shrine of the 33 Crore Gods** is a hall containing huge painted rock-cut figures of heroes and gods, although some of the workmanship is a little crude. The largest deval, a combination of temple and cenotaph, is Ajit Singh's (died 1724), though it is rather unkempt. The remains of an eighth-century Hindu temple is on a hilltop nearby.

Bal Samand Lake is the oldest artificial lake in Rajasthan, 5 km north. Dating from 1159, it is surrounded by parkland laid out in 1936 where the 19th-century **Hawa Mahal** was turned into a royal summer palace. Although the interior is European in style, it has entirely traditional red sandstone filigree windows and beautifully carved balconies. The peaceful and well-maintained grounds exude calm and tranquillity, while the views over the lake are simply majestic.

Around Jodhpur → *For listings, see pages 149-155.*

The temples of Osian are remarkable as much for their location in the middle of the desert as for their architecture, while Nagaur is one of Rajasthan's busiest but most unaffected cities. The area south of Jodhpur is refreshingly green and fertile compared to the desert landscapes of most of Western Rajasthan (although it can be very dry from March until the monsoon). Leaving the city, the landscape soon becomes agricultural, punctuated by small, friendly villages, in some of which are stunning heritage hotels.

Osian

Surrounded by sand dunes, this ancient town north of Jodhpur in the Thar Desert contains the largest group of eighth- to 10th-century Hindu and Jain temples in Rajasthan. The typical Pratihara Dynasty **temple complex** is set on a terrace whose walls are finely decorated with mouldings and miniatures. The sanctuary walls have central projections with carved panels and curved towers rising above them. The doorways are usually decorated with river goddesses, serpents and scrollwork. The 23 temples are grouped in several sites to the north, west and south of the town. The western group contains a mixture of Hindu temples, including the **Surya Temple** (early eighth century) with beautifully carved pillars. The Jain **Mahavira Temple** (eighth to 10th centuries), the best preserved, 200 m further on a hillock, rises above the town, and boasts a fantastically gaudy interior. The 11th- to 12th-century **Sachiya Mata Temple** is a living temple of the Golden Durga. Osian is well worth visiting.

Khimsar

On the edge of the desert, 80 km northeast of Jodhpur, Khimsar was founded by the Jain saint Mahavir 2500 years ago. The isolated, battle-scarred 16th-century moated castle of which a section remains, had a *zenana* added in the mid-18th century and a regal wing added in the 1940s.

Nagaur

① *Foreigners Rs 50, Indians Rs 10, camera Rs 25, video Rs 50.*

Nagaur, 137 km north of Jodhpur, was a centre of Chishti Sufis. It attracts interest as it preserves some fine examples of pre-Mughal and Mughal architecture. The dull stretch of desert is enlivened by Nagaur's fort palace, temples and *havelis*. The city walls are said to date from the 11th- to 12th-century Chauhan period. Akbar built the mosque here and there is a shrine of the disciple of Mu'inuddin Chishti of Ajmer (see page 182). **Ahhichatragarh Fort**, which dominates the city, is absolutely vast and contains palaces of the Mughal emperors and of the Marwars. It was restored with help from the Paul Getty Foundation and under the watchful eye of Maharah Gaj Singh of Jodhpur. It is quite an exceptional renovation; the Akbar Mahal is stunningly elegant and perfectly proportioned. The fort also has excellent wall paintings and interesting ancient systems of rainwater conservation and storage, ably explained by a very knowledgeable curator. It was awarded a UNESCO Heritage Award in 2000. One of the most spectacular forts in Rajasthan, it now hosts the **World Sufi Spirit Festival** every February.

Khichan

Four kilometres from Phalodi, southwest of Bikaner just off the NH15, is a lovely, picturesque village with superb red sandstone *havelis* of the Oswal Jains. Beyond the village are sand dunes and mustard fields, and a lake which attracts ducks and other waterfowl. The once quiet village has grown into a bustling agricultural centre and a prominent bird-feeding station. Jain villagers put out grain behind the village for winter visitors; up to 8000 demoiselle cranes and occasionally common eastern cranes can be seen in December and January on the feeding grounds. At present you can go along and watch without charge.

Pokaran

Pokaran, between Jaisalmer and Jodhpur, stands on the edge of the great desert with dunes stretching 100 km west to the Pakistan border. It provides tourists with a midway stopover between Bikaner/Jodhpur and Jaisalmer as it did for royal and merchant caravans in the past. The impressive 16th-century yellow sandstone **Pokaran Fort** ① *foreigners Rs 50, Indians Rs 10, camera Rs 50*, overlooking a confusion of streets in the town below, has a small museum with an interesting collection of medieval weapons, costumes and paintings. There are good views from the ramparts. Pokaran is also well known for its potters who make red-and-white pottery and terracotta horses/elephants. **Ramdeora**, the Hindu and Jain pilgrim centre nearby, has Bishnoi hamlets and is a preserve for blackbuck antelope, Indian gazelle, bustards and sand grouse. **Ramdeora Fair** (September) is an important religious event with cattle trading.

Khetolai, about 25 km northwest of Pokaran, is the site of India's first nuclear test explosion held underground on 18 March 1974, and of further tests in May 1998.

Balotra and around

The small textile town, 100 km southwest of Jodhpur, is known for its traditional weaving using pit looms and block prints, although many are now mechanized causing pollution of the Luni River. Nearby is the beautiful Jain temple with elephant murals at **Nakoda**. **Kanana**, near Balotra, celebrates **Holi** with stage shows and other entertainment. There is a *dharamshala* at Nakoda and guesthouses at Balotra.

At **Tilwara**, 127 km from Jodhpur, the annual **Mallinathji Cattle Fair** is a major event, which takes place just after **Holi** on the dry Luni riverbed. Over 50,000 animals are brought (although this has declined in recent years due to the drought), including Kapila (Krishna's) cows and Kathiawari horses, making it Rajasthan's largest animal fair. Few tourists make it this far so it is much less commercial than Pushkar. Try and go with a Rajasthani-speaking guide as the farmers and traders are very happy to allow you in on the negotiations as well as describing the key things to look for when buying a camel (the front legs should not rub against its belly, for instance). There are some interesting trade stalls including sword makers.

Salawas

Salawas, about 30 minutes' drive south from Jodhpur, is well known for its pit loom weaving. The village produces *durries*, carpets, rugs, bed covers and tents using camel hair, goat hair, wool and cotton in colourful and interesting patterns. You can visit the weavers' co-operatives such as **Roopraj** and **Salawas Durry Udhyog** (anyone on a Bishnoi village tour is normally frogmarched into one of them), where you can buy authentic village crafts, but watch out for high prices and pushy salesmen.

Luni

The tiny bustling village of Luni, 40 km from Jodhpur, sits in the shadow of the 19th-century red sandstone **Fort Chanwa** which has been converted to a hotel (see Where to stay, page 151). With its complex of courtyards, water wheels, and intricately carved façades, the fort and its village offer an attractive and peaceful alternative to the crowds of Jodhpur. The village of **Sanchean**, which you will pass through on the way, is worth exploring.

Rohet and Sardar Samand

Rohet, 50 km north of Jodhpur, was once a picturesque hamlet settled by the Bishnoi community. It is now a busy highway village although it has a busy bazar and is pleasant to wander around. At the end of the village a lake attracts numerous winter migrants in addition to resident birds. Here also are the family cenotaphs. **Rohetgarh**, a small 'castle' beside the lake, which has been converted in to a hotel (see Where to stay, page 152), has a collection of antique hunting weapons. The hotel will organize trips to the local Bishnoi villages. It is quite usual to see blue bull, black buck and other antelopes in the fields. Village life can be very hard in this arid environment but the Bishnoi are a dignified people who delight in explaining their customs. You can take part in the opium tea ceremony which is quite fun and somewhat akin to having a pint with the locals down at the pub.

The lake nearby is a beautiful setting for the royal 1933 art deco hunting lodge, **Sardar Samand Palace**. The lake attracts pelicans, flamingos, cranes, egrets and kingfishers, and the wildlife sanctuary has blackbuck, gazelle and nilgai. The water level drops substantially during summer; the lake has actually dried up from April to June in recent years. Sardar Samand is 60 km southeast of Jodhpur.

Nimaj

A small feudal town 110 km east of Jodhpur on the way to the Jaipur–Udaipur highway, the real attraction is the artificial lake, **Chhatra Sagar**, 4 km away. The ex-ruling family have recreated a 1920s-style tented hunting lodge on the lake's dam, which offers amazing views over the water and a genuine family welcome (see Where to stay, page 152).

Jodhpur and around listings

For hotel and restaurant price codes and other relevant information, see pages 13-16.

⊖ Where to stay

Jodhpur *p143, map p144*
Certain budget hotels, including some of those listed below, may quote low room prices that depend on you booking a tour or camel safari with them; some have been known to raise the price dramatically or even evict guests who refuse. Confirm any conditions before checking in.

$$$$ Raas, Tunvarji Ka Jhalra, Makrana Mohalla, www.raasjodhpur.com, T0291-263 6455. **Raas** is a gem at the heart of the city. Built from the same warm rose-red sandstone as the fort that towers above it; stunning balconies with carved stone shutters discreetly open up to reveal exceptional fort views. There is a contemporary vibe inspired by the essence of Rajasthan, rather than the traditional 'heritage-style' and yet it blends into the old city – it looks chic and stylish without looking out of place. As well as all the mod cons, you will find sumptuous fabrics and evocative photographs in every room. There are 2 restaurants, one open for non-residents as well as a very inviting pool. Recommended.

$$$$ Umaid Bhawan Palace, T0291-251 0101, www.tajhotels.com. Stunning art deco hotel, with 36 rooms and 40 beautifully appointed suites, best with garden-view balconies and unforgettable marble bathrooms, rather cool and masculine, far removed from the typical Rajasthani colour-fest, soaring domed lobbies, formal gardens and an extraordinary underground swimming pool.

$$$$-$$$ Ajit Bhawan, Circuit House Rd, T0291-251 3333, www.ajitbhawan.com. With a rather imposing palace façade, it is hard to imagine the variety of rooms, cottages and tents at this fantastic property. All luxuriously kitted out, the cottages are particularly beautiful. There is a very ornate swimming pool, several restaurants on-site, an opulent bar and heaps of character. This is India's first heritage hotel, started in 1927, and still leads the way.

$$$$-$$$ Pal Haveli, behind the clock tower in the middle of town, T0291-329 3328, www.palhaveli.com. 20 chic and atmospheric rooms in an authentic 200-year-old *haveli* with stylishly decorated drawing room/mini-museum, attractive courtyard dining area plus good views from roof bar/restaurant of both the fort and clock tower. Occasional theme nights are held. Massage available, friendly staff and chilled vibe. They are also opening a newly renovated fort property, **Pal Garh**, in a neighbouring village. Recommended.

$$ Devi Bhawan, 1 Ratanada Circle, T0291-251 1067, www.devibhawan.com. Beautiful rooms with bath, most with a/c, delightful shady garden with lovely new pool, excellent Indian dinner (set timings), Rajput family home. Popular with independent travellers, this is a very special place. Recommended.

$$ Haveli Inn Pal, T0291-261 2519, www.haveliinnpal.com. Quirkily designed rooms, some with huge windows overlooking the fort, some with lake views and unusual marble shower troughs, others with beds you need a ladder to get into, fantastic furniture, rooftop restaurant with commanding views and a rare patch of lawn, pleasant. Recommended.

$$ Juna Mahal, Ada Bazar, Daga St, T0291-244 5511, www.junamahal.com. Special little place, recently renovated 472-year-old *haveli* with bags of charm and stylish decor. The Lord Krishna room is particularly lovely.

$$ Shahi Guest House, City Police, Gandhi St, opposite Narsingh Temple, T0291-262 3802, www.shahiguesthouse.net. Enchanting 350-year-old mughal-style *haveli* with 6 quirky rooms (4 a/c, 2 with air-coolers) set around central courtyard. The building was traditionally the *janana dodi*, or women's area, of the Rajput officers' quarters. Alas, some of the modernization has detracted from its old charm. The Queen's Palace room and Honeymoon Suite are lovely. Friendly family and little rooftop restaurant with beautiful views of the old city and the fort. Charming young family hosts.

$$-$ Singhvi's Haveli, Navchokiya, Ramdevjika Chowk, T0291-262 4293, singhvi15adhaveli@hotmail.com. 11 rooms in a charming, 500-year-old *haveli* (one of the oldest), tastefully decorated, friendly family. New extra-special suite with mirror-work ceiling reminiscent of the fort that towers above. Nice chill-out area. Recommended.

$ Cosy Guest House, Novechokiya Rd, in Brahm Puri, a narrow lane full of cheap guesthouses just west of the fort, T0291-261 2066, www.cosyguesthouse.com. 6 clean and simple little rooms, good if slightly pricey home-cooked meals (other restaurants 15-min walk), outstanding roof-top views of old city, sociable atmosphere, can be good for meeting other travellers.

$ Durag Niwas Guest House, Old Public Park Lane, near Circuit House, T0291-251 2385, www.durag-niwas.com. Cheaper and more character than Durag Vilas next door. Runs a women's craft collective 'Sambhali' on-site.

$ Hare Krishna Guest House, Killi Khana, Mehron Ka Chowk, T0291-263 5307, www.harekrishnaguesthouse.net. Run by the President of the Jodhpur Guest House Association, you are definitely looked after here. Variety of rooms, lots of character and great views from the restaurant and chill-out space on the roof. They also run excellent Bishnoi village safaris. Sister guesthouse **Kesar** nearby.

$ Yogi's Guest House, Raj Purohit Ji Ki Haveli, Manak Chowk, old town, T0291-264 3436, yogiguesthouse@hotmail.com. 12 rooms, most in the 500-year-old *haveli*, clean, modern bathrooms, camel/jeep safaris, experienced management. Very popular – book ahead. Lovely atmosphere.

Excursions from Jodhpur p146

$$$ Bal Samand Palace (WelcomHeritage), T0291-257 2321, www.welcomheritage hotels.com. Essentially this is 2 properties together, the Palace and the Garden Retreat. In extensive grounds on the lake, there are 10 attractively furnished suites in an atmospheric palace and 26 'garden retreat' rooms in the imaginatively renovated stables, restaurant (mainly buffet), lovely pool, boating, pleasant orchards which attract nilgai, jackals and peacocks. Calming, tranquil atmosphere.

Osian p147

Also some **$** guesthouses in town.

$$$$ Camel Camp, on the highest sand dunes, T0291-243 7023, www.camelcamp osian.com. A beautiful complex of 50 double-bedded luxury tents with modern conveniences (attached baths, hot showers), superb restaurant and bar plus an amazing pool – quite a sight at the top of a sand dune. Tariff inclusive of meals and camel safaris, ask in advance for jeep/camel transfers to avoid a steep climb up the dunes. Recommended.

Nagaur p147

$$$$ Ranvas (Jodhana Heritage), T0291-257 2321, www.ranvasnagaur.com. Stunningly restored *havelis* within the magical fort of Nagaur. This new venture is extremely stylish and yet comfortable. With beautiful furnishings, sumptuous fabrics, rare artefacts, charming courtyards and secluded spots, **Ranvas** is effortlessly chic. The rooms are converted from the *havelis* of the 16 wives of the Royal Court. There is an amazing pool and delicious restaurant. Spectactular private tours of the fort available. Highly recommended.

$$$$ Royal Camp, T0291-257 2321, www.jodhanaheritagehotels.com. Operates Oct-Mar and during the camel fair (when prices rise). 20 delightful deluxe 2-bed furnished tents (hot water bottles, heaters, etc), flush toilets, hot water in buckets, stunning dining area, all inside the fort walls. Although you seem very secluded, Nagaur fort is right in the middle of the city and not elevated, so you do get traffic and mosque noise. An experience.

$ Mahaveer International, Vijay Vallabh Chowk, near the bus stand, T01582-243158, www.minagaur.com. 15 reasonable rooms, 7 a/c, huge dining hall, friendly knowledgeable manager.

Pokaran p148

$$ Manvar Resort, 61 km from Pokaran in Manvar, off Jodhpur–Jaisalmer highway, T02928-218911, www.manvar.com. Beautifully designed cottages with attractive interiors, some a/c, restaurant. It's a good lunch stop, though drivers get a hefty commission at both the restaurant and shop. They also run the **Manvar Camp** luxury tents in the desert.

$ Motel Pokaran (RTDC), on NH15, T02994-222275. A ramshackle building with 8 sparse rooms, plus 5 passable garden cottages.

Luni p149

$$$ Fort Chanwa, T02931-284216, www.fortchanwa.com. 47 good rooms in 200-year-old fort, not large but well furnished, individually designed, excellent Rajasthani meals in an impressive dining room, pleasant lawn for drinks, excellent pool and well managed.

$ Chhotaram Prajapat's Home Stay, Village Salawas, 20 km from Jodhpur on the way to Luni, T0291-269 6744, www. salawashomestay.com. Atmospheric taste of village life, in fact they call themselves "an initiative in reality" rather than a hotel! Simple mud hut rooms, local food, village walks and friendly atmosphere.

Rohet and Sardar Samand p149

$$$$ Mihirgarh, 1 hr from Rohet, T(0)982-902 3453, www.mihirgarh.com. The 'sun fortress' is a new venture from the team at Rohetgarh (see below) offering stunning suites with private courtyards and plunge pools. There is also an infinity pool, spa, beautiful restaurant and barbeque area and 360-degree views of the desert landscape. Breathtaking.

$$$ Rohetgarh, Rohet, T02936-268231, www.rohetgarh.com. Come here to write a book. Both William Dalrymple and Bruce Chatwin have used the inspiring Rohetgarh to put pen to paper. Dating to 1622, there are a range of rooms (avoid rooms near the outdoor restaurant). Fine Rajasthani food, ordinary architecture but in a beautiful environment, pleasant lake view terraces, lovely pool, health club, riding and safaris to Bishnoi, Raika and artisans' villages, boating on the lake, a relaxing getaway. They have also set up a **Wilderness Camp** 17 km away in the desert.

Nimaj p149

$$$$ Chhatra Sagar, 4 km from Nimaj, Pali, T02939-230118, www.chhatrasagar.com. Open 1 Oct-31 Mar. 11 beautiful colonial-style tents on the banks of a very picturesque reservoir. The ex-rulers of Nimaj have recreated the hunting lodge of their forefathers to great effect, and still live on the lake themselves, so there's a very convivial family atmosphere. You might see a peacock fly across the lake. Safaris arranged – great village safari and bird walks, all meals included in the tariff (and the food is delicious). Highly recommended.

$$$$ Lakshman Sagar, near Raipur village, Pali, T011-2649 4531, www.sewara.com. Lakeside cottages in stunning desert locale. Although super stylish, the decor borrows from classic Rajasthan village life so it has a rustic chic vibe. There are plenty of outdoor spaces to sit and gaze out into the desert and a beautiful swimming pool to lounge by. They are working on other old properties across Rajasthan so check their website for new places.

❼ Restaurants

Jodhpur p143, map p144

The best restaurants are in hotels; reserve ahead. Rooftop restaurants in most budget and mid-range hotels welcome non-residents. For *Daal-bhatti*, *lassi* and *kachoris* head for Jalori and Sojati gates. Great food at **Panorama Haveli Inn Pal** and **Hotel Haveli**.

$$$ Ajit Bhawan (see Where to stay, page 150). Evening buffet, excellent meals in the garden on a warm evening with entertainment, but lacking atmosphere if eating indoors in winter.

$$$ Bijolai, Water Habitat Retreat, Air Force Radar Rd, Kailana Lake, T(0)8104-000909, www.1559AD.com. This is another serving by the team behind **1559AD** Udaipur. There are mixed reports on the food and service, however the location and ambience is unbeatable. There is indoor dining as well as lakeside gazebos. It's 8 km from the city.

$$$ Chokelao, Mehrangarh Fort, T0291-255 5389. What a backdrop. Great Rajasthani food as you sit perched over the city of Jodhpur at the majestic Mehrengarh Fort. Breathtaking.

$$ Indique, Pal Haveli (see Where stay, page 150), Beautiful rooftop restaurant by the clocktower. They describe their food as "good, wholesome, spicy and traditional" with recipes passed down through the generations. Great views.

$$ On the Rocks, near Ajit Bhawan, T0291-510 2701. Good mix of Indian and Continental, plus a relaxing bar, patisserie, ice-cream parlour and lovely gardens.

$$ Sankalp, 12th Rd (west of the city centre). Open 1030-2300. Upmarket a/c South Indian, dosas come with a fantastic range of chutneys, good service. Recommended.

$ Café Sheesh Mahal, behind the clocktower and next to Pal Haveli. Great cappuccino and macchiato in a stylish coffee lounge. You can get sandwiches and hot chocolate brownie too.

$ Hotel Priya, 181 Nai Sarak. Fantastic special *thalis* for Rs 55 and extra quick service. Always busy.

$ Jhankar, follow signs to Ganesh Guest House or ask at Blue Guest House. This little courtyard café has great character – very pretty and a menu of all the usual traveller favourites to boot.

$ Jodhpur Coffee House, Sojati Gate. Good South Indian snacks and *thalis*.

$ Mishrilal, clocktower. The best *lassis* in town, if not the world. The saffron lassi is the way to go.

$ Poonam, High Court Rd. Pure vegetarian Indian. "Gorgeous 4-ft masala dosas".

$ Softy and Softy, High Court Rd. Excellent sweets and *namkeen*, thick shakes, fun for people-watching.

⦿ Festivals

Jodhpur *p143, map p144*
Jul/Aug Nag Panchami, when Naga (*naag*), the cobra, is worshipped. The day is dedicated to Sesha, the 1000-headed god or *Anant* (infinite) Vishnu, who is often depicted reclining on a bed of serpents. In Jodhpur, snake charmers gather for a colourful fair in Mandore.

Oct Marwar Festival (7-8 Oct 2014, 26-27 Oct 2015), held at full moon, includes music, puppet shows, turban-tying competitions, camel polo and ends with a fire dance on the dunes at Osian.

Oct Rajasthan International Folk Festival (RIFF), www.jodhpurfolkfestival.org. Coinciding with Kartik Purnima, the brightest full moon of the year, Jodhpur's annual RIFF is an eclectic mix of master musicians from local Rajasthan communities, acts from around the world and cutting-edge global dance music at Club Mehran. There are workshops and interactive daytime sessions for visitors. Some performances are around the city, while the main stage and club are in the stunning Mehrangahr Fort itself.

Nagaur *p147*
Jan/Feb The popular Cattle and Camel Fair (6-9 Feb 2014, 26-29 Jan 2015) is held just outside the town. There are camel races, cock fights, folk dancing and music. The fields become full of encampments of pastoral communities, tribal people and livestock dealers with their cattle, camels, sheep, goats and other animals.

Feb World Sufi Spirit Festival, www.world sufispiritfestival.org. Held in late Feb, this festival is hosted between the stunning Nagaur and Mehrengarh forts. Bringing together Sufi musicians from around the world – the 2013 event had artists from Iran, Kazakhstan, Afghanistan and *qawwalli* singers from Gujarat and Rajasthan, as well as whirling dervishes from Turkey. Exceptional event. Book early to stay on site.

⦿ Shopping

Jodhpur *p143, map p144*
Jodhpur is famous for its once-popular riding breeches (although it is pricey to get a pair made these days), tie-dye fabrics, lacquer work and leather shoes. Export of items over 100 years old is prohibited. The main areas are: Sojati Gate for gifts; Station Rd and Sarafa Bazar for jewellery; Tripolia Bazar for handicrafts; Khanda Falsa and Kapra Bazar for tie-dye; Lakhara Bazar for lac bangles. Raj Rani has a nice selection of more unusual designed clothes (probably from Pushkar) at Makrana Mohalla, near the clock tower. Shoes

are made in Mochi Bazar, Sardarpura and Clock Tower, *bandhanas* in Bambamola, and around Siwanchi and Jalori Gates. *Durries* are woven at Salawas, 18 km away. In most places you'll need to bargain.

Antiques
Shops on the road between Umaid and Ajit Bhawans do a flourishing trade, though are pricey.
Kirti Art Collection, T0291-251 2136. Has a good selection. Recommended.

Clothing and lifestyle
There's a new parade of shops next to Ajit Bhawan (Circuit House Road) including beautiful designer jewellery shop **Amrapali**, clothes and prints from Anokhi and Pahnava.

Handloom and handicrafts
Krishna Arts and Crafts, by Tija Mata temple on main road running west from the clocktower. There's an interesting shop by the temple, with fixed prices.
Marwar Heritage Art School, 116 Kamal, T0291-5132187. One of many shops keeping the miniature painting tradition alive.
Shriganesham, 1st floor, outside Pal Haveli, behind clock tower. Wide selection.

Jewellery
Gems & Art Plaza, Circuit House Rd. As patronized by Angelina Jolie. Some nice pieces in Kundan and Minakari styles, gaudy rings.

Spices
Mohanlal Verhomal Spices, 209-B, Kirana Merchant Vegetable Market (inside the market to the left of clocktower), T0291-261 5846, www.mvspices.com. Sought after for hand-mixed spices, but quality assured and is simply the best spice outlet in the city. Usha, along with her 6 sisters and mother, runs the shop. Insist your guide takes you here as many shops have tried to pass themselves off as the original.

Pokaran *p148*
Kashida, just outside town, Jaisalmer–Bikaner Rd, T02994-222511. Excellent handwoven crafts from the desert region, clean, well laid out, reasonably priced, profits help local self-help projects, part of the URMUL trust.

⚙ What to do

Jodhpur *p143, map p144*
Adventure Sports
Flying Fox, www.flyingfox.asia, are offering ziplining around Mehrengarh Fort and surrounds. Mayor of London Boris Johnson hailed it the best thing in Jodhpur: "the zipwire sends you like Batman around the moats and crenellations. It's stunning."

Tour operators
Many of the hotels organize village safaris, as does the tourist office, which charges Rs 1100 for 4 people including car, guide and tips given to villagers. City sightseeing, starts from tourist office at **Ghoomar Hotel**, T0291-254 5083: half day (0830-1300, 1400-1800). Fort and palaces, Jaswant Thada, Mandore Gardens, Government Museum, bazar around Old City Clock Tower.
Aravalli Safari, 4 Kuchaman House Area, Airport Rd, T0291-262 6799.
Exclusive India, Kishan Villas, Police Line Rd, Ratanada, T0291-342006, exclinjdh@datainfosys.net. Ask for Rajendra Singh Rathore who is very knowledgeable and an excellent companion.
Forts & Palaces, 15 Old Public Park, T0291-251 1207, www.palaces-tours.com.
Marwar Eco-Cultural Tours, Makrana Mohalla near Haveli Hotel, T(0)9414-916941, www.themarwarecoculturaltours.com. Working with NGO Nitigat Vikas and volunteers offering village tours and trips to Osian. Profits divided between the NGO and communities.
Virasat Experiences, www.virasatexperiences.com. Fantastic walking tours to see behind the usual tourist sites, which provides a more intimate

expereince of Jodhpur. Also runs the very interesting and non-touristy **Majestic Marwar – Rural Villages Tour**, visiting the villages around Jodhpur. The tour costs Rs 2500, but Rs 500 of that goes to the villages to create rainwater harvesting projects and improve hygiene. You are really giving something back here, unlike some of the other 'tribal tours' touted locally, which can be exploitative. Also organizes private dinners and cookery classes with local families. Highly recommended.

⊖ Transport

Jodhpur *p143, map p144*
Air Transport to town: by taxi, Rs 400; auto-rickshaw, Rs 200. **Air India**, near Bhati crossroads, T0291-251 0758, 1000-1300, 1400-1700; airport enquiries T0291-251 2617, flies to **Delhi**, **Jaipur**, **Mumbai**, **Udaipur**. Jet Airways, T0291-510 2222, airport T0291-251 5551, to **Delhi** and **Mumbai**.
Local bus Minibuses cover most of the city except Fort and Umaid Bhavan Palace. For **Mandore**, frequent buses leave from Paota Bus Stand. Also several daily buses to **Salawas**, **Luni** (40 km), **Rohet** (450 km) and **Osian** (65 km).
Long-distance bus RST Bus Stand, near Raikabagh Railway Station, T0291-254 4989. 1000-1700; bookings also at tourist office. A convenient bus route links Jodhpur with **Ghanerao** and **Ranakpur**, **Kumbhalgarh** and **Udaipur**. Other daily services include: **Abu Rd**, 6 hrs; **Ahmedabad**, 10 hrs; **Ajmer**, 5 hrs; **Jaipur**, frequent, 8 hrs; **Jaisalmer**, 0530 (depart Jaisalmer, 1400), 5-6 hrs; faster than train but scenically tedious; **Pali**, 1 hr; **Udaipur**, 7 hrs by rough road, best to book a good seat a day ahead.
     Private operators arrive at Barakuttulah Stadium west of town, to a scrum of

rickshaw drivers: pay around Rs 30 to the old city. Some companies have offices opposite railway station, eg **HR Travels**, **Sun City Tours**, and **Sethi Yatra**, or book at Govind Hotel.
Car and taxi Car hire from tourist office, **Ghoomar Hotel**, or with private firm whole day about Rs 1700; half day Rs 1200, www.clearcarrental.com.
Rickshaw Railway station to fort should be about Rs 25 (may demand Rs 50; try walking away).
Train Jodhpur Station enquiries: T131. Open 0800-2400. Reservations: T0291-263 6407. Open 0900-1300, 1330-1600. Advance reservations, next to GPO. Tourist Bureau, T0291-254 5083 (0500-2300). **International tourist waiting room** for passengers in transit (ground floor), with big sofas and showers; clean Indian toilets in 2nd-class waiting room on the 1st floor of the station Foyer. To **Agra**: *Jodhpur-Howrah Superfast 12308*, 2030, 9½ hrs, continues to **Kolkata**. **Ahmedabad** via **Abu Rd (Mount Abu)**: *Ranakpur Exp 14707*, 1445, 5½ hrs; both continue to **Mumbai** (19 hrs). **Delhi**: *Mandore Exp 12462*, 2000, 11 hrs (OD). **Jaipur**: *Inter-City Exp 12466*, 0610, 4½ hrs; *Marudhar Exp 14864*, 0945, 5½ hrs. **Jaisalmer** (via **Osian**): *Dli Jaisalmer Exp 14059*, 0530, 6 hrs; *Jaisalmer Exp 14810*, 2345, 6 hrs.

⊕ Directory

Jodhpur *p143, map p144*
Medical services Ambulance: T102. MG Hospital, T0291-636437. Dispensary: Paota, Residency. Mon-Sat 0800-1200, 1700-1900, Sun 0800-1200. **Post** GPO, south of railway station, 1000-2000, Sat 1000-1600. **Police**: T100.

Jaisalmer and around

The approach to Jaisalmer is magical as the city rises out of the vast barren desert like an approaching ship. With its crenellated sandstone walls and narrow streets lined with exquisitely carved buildings, through which camel carts trundle leisurely, it has an extraordinarily medieval feel and an incredible atmosphere. The fort inside, perched on its hilltop, contains some gems of Jain temple building, while beautifully decorated merchants' *havelis* are scattered through the town. Once inside the fort walls looking out to the desert, it's easy to imagine caravans and camels sweeping across towards you in a dream of Arabian nights, but what you actually see are growing legions of windmills flanking the dunes in the distance. Unlike the other forts you visit in Rajasthan, Jaisalmer's is fully alive with shops, restaurants and guesthouses inside its walls and labyrinthine alleyways. It's beautiful to wander the tiny streets, always finding a new nook or a great view.

The town's charm has not failed to attract the attention of mass tourism and at times Jaisalmer can feel overrun with package tourists, being swept from one shop to the next in a whirlwind of rapid consumption by insistent guides. Over the years, increased development of guesthouses and businesses within the walls has put pressure on the sewage, drainage and foundations of the fort. Three of the 99 bastions crumbled a couple of years ago and several people were killed. These bastions have now been replaced, but if you look at the fort bastions from the outside you can see signs of water discolouration (see box, page 160).

If you find Jaisalmer's magic diminished there's always the romantic desolation of the Thar Desert, easily accessible beyond the edge of the city. Many of the settlements close to the city have become well used to tourists, so it's worth venturing further out. Highlights include the remarkable ghost city of Khuldera and, of course, the chance to take it all in from on top of a camel.

Arriving in Jaisalmer

Getting there The nearest airport is at Jodhpur, 275 km away, which is connected to Jaisalmer by buses and several daily trains. Most long-distance buses arrive at the bus stand, a 15-minute walk from the fort. Your hotel may offer a pick-up. If not, have a place in mind and prepare for a barrage of competing touts.

Getting around Unmetered jeeps and auto-rickshaws can be hired at the station but they are no help inside the fort so you may have to carry your luggage some distance uphill if you choose a fort hotel. Rickshaws are allowed into the fort at certain times. You can hire a bike from Gopa Chowk (Rs 30) though the town is best explored on foot. Most hotels and restaurants are clustered around the two chowks and inside the fort. ▶ *See Transport, page 166.*

Tourist information RTDC ① *near TRC, Station Rd, Gadi Sagar Pol, T02992-252406, 0800-1200, 1500-1800.* Also has a counter at railway station.

Background

Founded by Prince Jaisal in 1156, Jaisalmer grew to be a major staging post on the trade route across the forbidding Thar Desert from India to the West. The merchants prospered and invested part of their wealth in building beautiful houses and temples with the local sandstone. The growth of maritime trade between India and the West caused a decline in trade across the desert which ceased altogether in 1947. However, the wars with Pakistan (1965 and 1971) resulted in the Indian government developing the transport facilities to the border to improve troop movement. This has also helped visitors to gain access. Today, the army and tourism are mainstays of the local economy; hotel touts and pushy shopkeepers have become a problem in recent years.

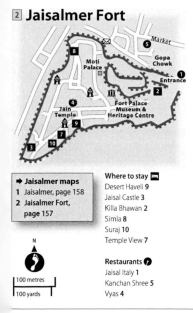

② Jaisalmer Fort

N

100 metres
100 yards

Where to stay 🛏
Desert Haveli 9
Jaisal Castle 3
Killa Bhawan 2
Simla 8
Suraj 10
Temple View 7

Restaurants 🍴
Jaisal Italy 1
Kanchan Shree 5
Vyas 4

Jaisalmer → *For listings, see pages 163-166.*

The fort

① *Best light for photography is late afternoon.* On the roughly triangular-shaped Trikuta Hill, the fort stands 76 m above the town, enclosed by a 9 km wall with 99 bastions (mostly 1633-1647). Often called the Golden Fort because of the colour of its sandstone walls, it dominates the town. You enter the fort from the east from Gopa Chowk. The inner, higher fort wall and the old gates up the ramp (Suraj Pol, Ganesh Pol, Hawa Pol and Rang Pol) provided further defences. The Suraj Pol (1594), once an outer gate, is flanked by heavy bastions and has bands of decoration which imitate local textile designs. Take a walk through the narrow streets within the fort, often blocked by the odd goat or cow, and see how even today about 1000 of the town's people live in tiny houses inside the fort often with beautiful carvings on doors and balconies. It is not difficult to get lost.

As with many other Rajput forts, within the massive defences are a series of palaces, the product of successive generations of rulers' flights of fancy. The local stone is relatively easy to carve and the dry climate has meant that the fineness of detail has been preserved through the centuries. The *jali* work and delicately ornamented balconies and windows with wide eaves break the solidity of the thick walls, giving protection from the heat, while the high plinths of the buildings keep out the sand. '**Sunset Point**', just north of the fort, is popular at sundown for views over Jaisalmer.

The entire **Fort Palace Museum and Heritage Centre** ① *0800-1800 summer, 0900-1800 winter, foreigners Rs 250 includes an excellent audio guide and camera, Indians Rs 10, video Rs 150*, has been renovated and an interesting series of displays established, including sculpture, weapons, paintings and well-presented cultural information. The view from the roof, the highest point inside the fort, is second to none. The **Juna Mahal** (circa 1500) of the seven-storey palace with its *jali* screens is one of the oldest Rajasthani palaces. The rather plain *zenana* block to its west, facing the *chauhata* (square) is decorated with false *jalis*. Next to it is the *mardana* (men's quarters) including the Rang Mahal above the Hawa Pol, built during the reign of Mulraj II (1762-1820), which has highly detailed murals

① **Jaisalmer**

To Ramgarh & Bada Bagh Chhatris

Sunset Point

Malka Pol

Khadi Showroom

Ramgarh Rd

Malka Rd

Amar Sagar Rd

Sam Rd

Crown Travels

Private Bus Stand

Amar Sagar Pol

Gandhi Chowk

Badal Mahal

Nathumal-ki Haveli

Art Exp

Taxis

Rajasthan Emporium

Bhatia News Agency

Sadar Bazar

Patwon-ki Haveli

To Lodurva (16 km), Desert National Park (40 km), Amarsagar, Airport, Sam Dunes & Khuldera

Gopa Chowk

Salim Singh-ki Haveli

Fort

Salim Singh-ki Haveli Rd

State Bus Stand

Khadi Showroom

Jaisalmer maps
1 Jaisalmer, page 158
2 Jaisalmer Fort, page 157

Raimer Rd

To Khuri & Desert National Park

N

200 metres
200 yards

Where to stay		
1st Gate Fusion 3	Oasis Haveli 17	Suryagarh 11
Killa Lodge 4	Pol Haveli 1	
Mansion 5	Residency Centre Point 9	**Restaurants**
Nachana Haveli 7	Serai 2	Desert Boys Dhani 1
	Shahi Palace 12	Dhanraj Bhatia 2

and mirror decoration. **Sarvotam Vilas** built by Akhai Singh (1722-1762) is ornamented with blue tiles and glass mosaics. The adjacent **Gaj Vilas** (1884) stands on a high plinth. Mulraj II's **Moti Mahal** has floral decoration and carved doors.

The open square beyond the gates has a platform reached by climbing some steps; this is where court was held or royal visitors entertained. There are also fascinating **Jain temples** (12th-16th centuries) ① *0700-1200, Rs 10, camera Rs 50, video Rs 100, leather shoes not permitted*, within the fort. Whilst the Rajputs were devout Hindus they permitted the practice of Jainism. The **Parsvanatha** (1417) has a fine gateway, an ornate porch and 52 subsidiary shrines surrounding the main structure. The brackets are elaborately carved as maidens and dancers. The exterior of the **Rishbhanatha** (1479) has more than 600 images as decoration whilst clusters of towers form the roof of the **Shantinatha** built at the same time. **Ashtapadi** (16th century) incorporates the Hindu deities of Vishnu, Kali and Lakshmi into its decoration. The **Mahavir Temple** ① *view 1000-1100*, has an emerald statue. The **Sambhavanatha** (1431) ① *1000-1100*, has vaults beneath it that were used for document storage. The **Gyan Bhandar** here is famous for its ancient manuscripts.

Havelis

There are many exceptional *havelis* in the fort and in the walled town. Many have beautifully carved façades, *jali* screens and oriel windows overhanging the streets below. The ground

To Mohangarh (NH15)

Kishanghat Pol

Jethwal Rd

To Jodhpur & 2 (30 km)

auto and

Gadi Sagar Pol

Desert Cultural Centre

Barmer Rd

Desert National Park Office

To Wood Fossil Park (17 km)

Tilon-ki Pol

Gadi Sagar

floor is raised above the dusty streets and each has an inner courtyard surrounded by richly decorated apartments. Further east, **Patwon-ki Haveli** (1805) ① *1030-1700, Foreginers Rs 150, Indians Rs 50 (audio tour Rs 250/camera Rs 50)*, is the best of the restored *havelis* and you get a beautiful view from the rooftop. It's a cluster of five *havelis* built for five brothers. They have beautiful murals and carved pillars. A profusion of balconies cover the front wall and the inner courtyard is surrounded by richly decorated apartments; parts have been well restored. The main courtyard and some roofs are now used as shops. The views from the decorative windows are stunning.

Inside Amar Sagar Pol, the former ruler's 20th-century palace **Badal Mahal** with a five-storeyed tower, has fine carvings. Near the fort entrance, the 17th-century **Salim Singh-ki Haveli** ① *0800-1800, Rs 10, good carvings but is being poorly restored, over-long guided tour*, is especially attractive with peacock brackets; it is often referred to as the 'Ship Palace' because of its distinctive and decorative upper portion. **Nathumal-ki Haveli** (1885), nearer Gandhi Chowk, was built for the prime minister. Partly carved out of rock by two craftsmen, each

Jaisalmer in jeopardy

Jaisalmer in Jeopardy is a UK-based charity fighting to preserve the unique historical architecture of the city. Through raising awareness and funds, it has achieved the restoration of buildings such as the Rajput Palace and Rani-ka Mahal (Maharani's Palace) and helped ensure that Jaisalmer Fort is listed on the World Monuments Fund '100 Most Endangered Sites in the World'.

Some visitors feel that it is unethical to stay in the fort guesthouses and add to the problems of water consumption and waste disposal. As far back as the late 1990s guesthouses inside the fort were offered incentives to start their businesses in new locations outside the walls, although only one, **Shahi Palace Guest House**, took up the offer. Nowadays, thanks to greater awareness, there are many beautiful guesthouses both within the walls of the fort and outside gazing up at the fairytale. Jaisalmer in Jeopardy want to ensure that the Jaisalmer Fort can be enjoyed for another 400 years. Check out www.jaisalmer-in-jeopardy.org and www.intach.org (Indian National Trust for Art and Cultural Heritage) for further information.

undertaking one half of the house, it has a highly decorative façade with an attractive front door guarded by two elephants. Inside is a wealth of decoration; notice the tiny horse-drawn carriage and a locomotive showing European influence.

Desert Cultural Centre
ⓘ *Gadisar Circle, T02992-252 188, 1000-1700, Rs 10.*
The Desert Cultural Centre was established in 1997 with the aim of preserving the culture of the desert. The museum contains a varied display of fossils, paintings, instruments, costumes and textiles which give an interesting glimpse in to life in the desert. The charismatic founder, Mr Sharma, is a fount of information and has written several books on Jaisalmer.

Around Jaisalmer → *For listings, see pages 163-166.*

Amar Sagar and Lodurva
The pleasant **Amar Sagar** ⓘ *5 km northwest of Jaisalmer, foreigners Rs 30, Indians free, camera Rs 50, video Rs 100*, was once a formal garden with a pleasure palace of Amar Singh (1661-1703) on the bank of a lake which dries up during the hot season. The Jain temple there has been restored.

A further 10 km away is **Lodurva** ⓘ *0630-1930, foreigners Rs 20, Indians free, camera Rs 50, video Rs 100*, which contains a number of Jain temples that are the only remains of a once-flourishing Marwar capital. Rising honey-coloured out of the desert, they are beautifully carved with *jali* outside and are well maintained and worth visiting. The road beyond Lodurva is unsealed.

Khuldera
This is a fascinating ghost town, and well worth stopping at on the way to Sam. The story goes that 400 or so years ago, Salim Singh, the then prime minister of Jaisalmer, took a distinct shine to a Paliwal girl from this village. The rest of the Paliwal people did not want this beautiful girl taken away from them, and so after intense pressure from the prime minister decided to abandon the village one night, with everyone dispersing in different

directions, never to return. It is remarkably well preserved, and best visited with a guide who can point out the most interesting buildings from the many still standing. **Khabha**, just south of here, is also recommended.

Sam dunes (Sain)

ⓘ *Rs 10, car Rs 20 (camera fees may be introduced), camel rates start at Rs 100 per hr.*

Sam dunes, 40 km west of Jaisalmer, is popular for sunset camel rides. It's not a remote spot in the middle of the desert but the only real large stretch of sand near town; the dunes only cover a small area, yet they are quite impressive. Right in the middle of the dunes, **Sunset View** is like a fairground, slightly tacky with lots of day-trippers – as many as 500 in the high season; the only escape from this and the camel men is to walk quite a way away.

Khuri

ⓘ *Rs 10, buses from Jaisalmer take 1½ hrs, jeep for 4 people Rs 450 for a sunset tour.*

Khuri, 40 km southwest of Jaisalmer, is a small picturesque desert village of decorated mud-thatched buildings which was ruled by the Sodha clan for four centuries. Visitors are attracted by shifting sand dunes, some 80 m high, but the peace of the village has been spoilt by the growing number of huts, tents and guesthouses which have opened along the road and near the dunes. Persistent hotel and camel agents board all buses bound for Khuri. The best months to visit are from November to February.

Thar Desert National Park

ⓘ *Rs 150 per person; car permits Rs 500; permits are required, apply 2 days in advance to Forest Department, T02992-252489, or through travel agents.*

The Thar Desert National Park is near Khuri, the core being about 60 km from Jaisalmer (the road between Sam and Khuri is passable with a high-clearance vehicle). The park was created to protect 3000 sq km of the Thar Desert, the habitat for drought resistant, endangered and rare species which have adjusted to the unique and inhospitable conditions of extreme temperatures. The desert has undulating dunes and vast expanses of flat land where the trees are leafless, thorny and have long roots. Fascinating for birdwatching, it is one of the few places in India where the **great Indian bustard** is proliferating (it can weigh up to 14 kg and reach a height of 40 cm). In winter it also attracts the migratory **houbara bustard**. You can see imperial black-bellied and common Indian sand grouse, five species of vulture, six of eagle, falcons, and flocks of larks at Sudasari, in the core of the park, 60 km from Jaisalmer. Chinkaras are a common sight, as are desert and Indian foxes. Blackbuck and desert cat can be seen at times. Close to sunset, you can spot desert hare in the bushes.

While most hotels will try to sell you a tour by 4WD vehicle, this is no longer necessary. You can hire any jeep or high-clearance car (Ambassador, Sumo) for the trip to the park. Off-the-road journeys are by camel or camel cart (park tour Rs 50 and Rs 150 respectively).

Barmer

This dusty desert town, 153 km south of Jaisalmer, is surrounded by sand dunes and scrublands. It is a major centre for wood carving, *durrie* rug weaving, embroidery and block printing (you can watch printers in Khatriyon ki galli). The 10th- to 11th-century Kiradu temples, though badly damaged, are interesting. **Someshvara** (1020), the most intact, has some intricate carving but the dome and the tower have collapsed. The town itself is surprisingly industrial and not especially charming; those interested in seeking out handicrafts are well advised to locate **Gulla**, the town's only guide. He can normally

On a camel's back

Camel safaris draw many visitors to Jaisalmer. They allow an insight into otherwise inaccessible desert interiors and a chance to see rural life, desert flora and wildlife. The 'safari' is not a major expedition into the middle of nowhere. Instead, it is often along tracks, stopping off for sightseeing at temples and villages along the way. The camel driver/owner usually drives the camel or rides alongside (avoid one sharing your camel), usually for two hours in the morning and three hours in the afternoon, with a long lunch stop in between. There is usually jeep or camel cart backup with tents and 'kitchen' close by, though thankfully out of sight. It can be fun, especially if you are with companions and have a knowledgeable camel driver.

Camel safaris vary greatly in quality with prices ranging from around Rs 500 per night for the simplest (sleeping in the open, vegetarian meals) to those costing Rs 4500 (deluxe double-bedded tents with attached Western baths). Bear in mind that it is practically impossible for any safari organizer to cover his costs at anything less than Rs 500 – if you're offered cheaper tours, assume they'll be planning to get their money back by other means, ie shopping/drug selling along the way. Safaris charging Rs 500-1000 can be adequate (tents, mattresses, linen, cook, jeep support, but no toilets). It's important to ascertain what is included in the price and what are extras.

The popular 'Around Jaisalmer' route includes **Bada Bagh**, **Ramkunda**, **Moolsagar**, **Sam dunes**, **Lodurva** and **Amar Sagar** with three nights in the desert. Some routes now include **Kuldhara**'s medieval ruins and the colourful **Kahla** village, as well as **Deda**, Jaseri lake (good birdlife) and **Khaba** ruins (with a permit). Most visitors prefer to take a two-day/one-night or three-day/two-night camel safari, with jeep transfer back to Jaisalmer.

A more comfortable alternative is to be jeeped to a tented/hut camp in the desert as a base for a night and enjoy a camel trek during the day without losing out on the evening's entertainment under the stars. A short camel ride in town up to Sunset Point (or at Sam/Khuri) is one alternative to a safari before deciding on a long haul, and also offers great views of upper levels of *havelis* – but watch out for low-slung electric wires! Pre-paid camel rides have now been introduced – Rs 80 for a 30-minute ride. For some, "half an hour is enough on a tick-ridden animal". Make sure you cover up all exposed skin and use sunscreen to avoid getting burnt.

Sunny Tours, Shahi Palace, T(0)9414-365495, www.sunnytourntravels.com, is one of the oldest tour operators in Jaisalmer. They offer fantastic camel and jeep safaris. You are in good hands with this professional team: they have separate bed rolls for sleeping (not just what you have been sitting on for sunset and dinner), they provide tents in the winter as well as delicious food, fruit and cookies and your very own camel. You can go on camel safari for half a day up to as many days as you like (or can stand). Their route takes in the usual peaceful dunes and tribal villages. If you fancy a more regal and upmarket affair try **Rajasthan Desert Safaris**, T(0)9414-140109, www.desertsafarijaisalmer.com, who have Swiss-cottage tents with attached toilets near the dunes at Rs 4500 per night. It is quite magical to be in the lap of luxury under the desert sky.

be contacted at the **KK Hotel** (see Where to stay, page 164), or emailed in advance on gulla_guide@yahoo.com. The small number of visitors to Barmer means that he doesn't get too many opportunities to practise his profession; be sure to explain exactly what you would like to see, and try to fix a price before starting the tour.

Dhorimana
The area further south of Barmer has some of the most colourful and traditional Bishnoi villages and a large population of *chinkaras* and desert fauna. The village women wear a lot of attractive jewellery but may be reluctant to be photographed so it is best to ask first. **PWD Rest house** has clean and comfortable rooms.

Jaisalmer and around listings

For hotel and restaurant price codes and other relevant information, see pages 13-16.

🛏 Where to stay

Jaisalmer *p157, maps p157 and p158*
$$$$ The Serai, near Chandan village, 30 km outside Jaisalmer, T02997-200014, www.sujanluxury.com. Already guest starring on the front cover of *Condé Nast Traveller* magazine, this luxurious resort is inspired by the colours of the desert, with warm sandstone and beautiful natural textiles. The beautiful swimming pool is based on an Indian step-well and 6 of the luxury tents have their own plunge pools. Sit by the swimming pool and get treated to sorbet and ice cold *nimbu pani*, while the restaurant serves up global fusion food. This is the most stylish way to experience desert life. It's a place for landmark moments, such as honeymoons.
$$$$ Suryagarh, Kahala Phata, Sam Rd, T02992-269269, www.suryagarh.com. Stunning heritage-style project and the outer façade of the hotel mirrors the famous Jaisalmer fort. Beautiful suites, vibey bar area and lovely indoor pool. The spa is exceptional. Attention to detail everywhere you turn.
$$$$-$$$ Mansion Hotel, Sam Rd, Mool Sagar, T(0)9829-439400, themansion11@ymail.com. Baffled by the name as this is a stunning luxury tented camp out into the desert from Jaisalmer beautifully created by

Riyaz Ahmed. You could spend your time here gazing out into the desert from the beautiful pool.
$$$ 1st Gate Fusion, Dhibba Para, T02992-254462, www.1stgate.in. Stylish Italian/Indian design with all creature comforts. Just 8 rooms here with a boutique guesthouse vibe. The attractive restaurant is getting rave reviews for its spaghetti pomodoro. Great attention to detail.
$$$ Killa Bhawan, Kotri Para, T02992-251204, www.killabhawan.com. 7 rooms, 2 a/c, in characterful old building, beautiful interiors but teeny tiny rooms, the classiest place in the fort for some margin.
$$ Killa Lodge, opposite Patwon-ki Haveli, T02992-253833, www.killabhawan.com. Small boutique hotel with only 6 rooms run by the same team as **Killa Bhawan** in the fort. Great location opposite a beautiful *haveli*. Lovely café on top and bookshop downstairs – great collection of coffee table books.
$$ Nachana Haveli, Gandhi Chowk, T02992-252110, www.nachanahaveli.com. Converted 18th-century Rajput *haveli* with carved balconies and period artefacts. Rooms are stylishly done with great bathrooms, particularly upstairs suites. Rooftop restaurant in the season, has very authentic feel overall. Friendly family. Highly recommended.
$$-$ Hotel Pol Haveli, near Geeta Ashram, Dedansar Rd, T02992-250131. New *haveli*-style building with stylish decor and chilled-out vibe. Beautiful furnishings, especially

the beds. Slightly odd area as it feels you are staying in a dusty village, but it is just a short walk from Gandhi Chowk and the heart of things. Good views of sunset point and the fort in the distance from their attractive rooftop café.

$$-$ Jaisal Castle, in the fort, T02992-252362, www.jaisalcastle.com. 11 quirky rooms in rambling, characterful old *haveli*. Room 101 is particularly lovely, ironically. Beautiful communal areas.

$$-$ Oasis, near Shahi Palace, Shiv St, T02992-250871. Another offering from the brothers at Shahi Palace (see below), Oasis boasts bigger rooms than its older sibling and some of the 7 rooms have a/c. It's beautifully decorated with sumptuous fabrics with lovely loungy diwans in the rooms. Next door, they have 6 more big rooms in Star Haveli. There's free Wi-Fi and a great ambience. Recommended.

$$-$ Shahi Palace, Shiv St, near SBBJ bank, outside the fort, T02992-255920, www.shahi palacehotel.com. 16 super-stylish rooms in a beautiful sandstone building with outstanding bathrooms. The team of 4 brothers here work hard to make everyone feel at home. Beautiful chic rooftop restaurant with lots or archways and even a wooden boat from Karnataka masquerading as a flowerpot. The view of the fort is outstanding as is their food. They provide free station pick-up and all manner of travel support. Excellent reports on their camel safaris. Wholeheartedly recommended.

$$-$ Simla, Kund Para, T02992-253061, www.simlahaveli.com. 5 clean rooms in a thoughtfully renovated 550-year-old *haveli*, attractive wall hangings, 1 large room with bath, others are minute with bath downstairs, no safari pressure, friendly management, a cut above the norm.

$$-$ Suraj, behind Jain Temple, T02992-251623, www.hotelsurajjaisalmer.webs.com. Suraj boasts beautiful rooms in this 530-year-old *haveli* overlooking the Jain temple. It may have seen better days and can get quite chilly in winter, but it's very atmospheric.

$ The Desert Haveli, near Jain Temple, T(0)7568-455656, www.deserthaveli-hostel. com. 7 characterful rooms in a charming, 400-year-old *haveli*, honest, friendly owner. Very atmospheric. Recommended.

$ Residency Centre Point, near Patwon-ki Haveli, T02992-252883. Quiet family-run hotel with 5 basic but characterful rooms, good views from the roof. Excellent value.

$ Temple View, next to Jain Temple, T02992-252832, luna_raju@yahoo.com. 7 well-decorated rooms, 3 with attached bath, attention to detail, great view of the temples from the roof, entertaining owner.

Sam dunes *p161*

$ Sam Dhani (RTDC), T02992-252392. 8 huts facing the dunes, very busy in the late afternoon and sunset but very pleasant at night and in the early morning. Includes all meals.

Khuri *p161*

$$$ The Mama's Resort and Camp, T03014-274042, www.themamasjaisalmer. com. Stay in the desert in style with luxury tents and 4-poster beds. There are also nice rooms, but the tents win. You can book packages which include a camel safari.

$ Khuri Guest House, reservations T022-240 42211, www.nivalink.com/khuri. Simple rooms or huts, friendly management. Good desert cooking too. Recommended.

Thar Desert National Park *p161*

$ Rest Huts, facing the park. Adequate. Contact the Park Director on T02992-252489.

Barmer *p161*

$$ New KK Hotel, Station Rd, T02982-221087. Close to the original cheaper KK Hotel, this has more of a modern vibe. The original KK is quite reasonable.

$ Krishna, Station Rd, a few mins' walk from the station, T(0)9783-305054. Clean rooms some with a/c, but no restaurant.

🍴 Restaurants

Jaisalmer *p157, maps p157 and p158*
$$-$ Desert Boy's Dhani, near Nagar Palika, Dhibba. Lovely garden restaurant with good range of Indian classics and traditional Rajasthani food. Folk dance and music.
$ Dhanraj Bhatia. Scrumptious Indian sweets including Jaisalmeri delights (try *godwa*).
$ Jaisal Italy, in the main fort gate. Charming, cool interiors with windows looking up the pathway to the fort: excellent bruschetta and a great meeting point before or after-fort walks. Recommended.
$ Kanchan Shree, Gopa Chowk, 250 m from Salim Singh-ki Haveli. *Lassis* (19 varieties) and ice cream floats, as well as cheap, tasty *thalis*. Many recommendations for this place.
$ Saffron, Nachana Haveli (see Where to stay, page 163). Another hotel with great views of the fort at night. Beautiful decor, lovely food and a relaxed vibe. Often with live music and dance.
$ Shahi Palace (see Where to stay, page 164). Great food from this beautiful rooftop restaurant with amazing views of the fort. Try traditional Rajasthani meals like *kej sangari* (desert beans) and *kadi pakoda* (yoghurt turmeric curry) and, if they're not busy, you can go in the kitchen and watch how they make it. And if you need a little oomph, they have a cappuccino machine. Recommended.
$ Vyas, Fort. Simple, good vegetarian *thalis*, pleasant staff.

🎭 Entertainment

Jaisalmer *p157, maps p157 and p158*
The more expensive hotels have bars.
Desert Cultural Centre, Gadisar Circle. 2 puppet shows every evening, at 1830 and 1930, Rs 30 entry, Rs 20 camera, Rs 50 video.

🎉 Festivals

Jaisalmer *p157, maps p157 and p158*
Feb/Mar Holi is especially colourful but gets riotous.

Sam dunes *p161*
Feb 3-day Desert Festival (12-13 Feb 2014, 1-3 Feb 2015) with *son et lumière* amid the sand dunes at Sam, folk dancing, puppet shows and camel races, camel polo and camel acrobatics, Mr Desert competition. You can also watch craftsmen at work. Rail and hotel reservations can be difficult.

Barmer *p161*
Mar Thar Festiva highlights desert culture and handicrafts.

🛍 Shopping

Jaisalmer *p157, maps p157 and p158*
Shops open 1000-1330 and 1500-1900. Jaisalmer is famous for its handicrafts – stone-carved statues, leather ware, brass enamel engraving, shawls, tie-dye work, embroidered and block printed fabrics, but garments are often poorly finished. Look in **Siré Bazar**, **Sonaron-ka-Bas** and shops in the narrow lanes of the old city including **Kamal Handicrafts**, **Ganpati Art Home**, and **Damodar** in the fort. In Gandhi Chowk: **Rajasthali**, closed Tue; the good, fairly priced selection at **Khadi Emporium** at the end of the courtyard just above Narayan Niwas Hotel. **Jaisalmer Art Export**, behind Patwon-ki Haveli has high-quality textiles. For textiles try **Amrit Handprint Factory**, just inside Sagar Gate on the left. **Geeta Jewellers** on Aasni Rd near Fort Gate is recommended, good value and no hard sell.

🎯 What to do

Jaisalmer *p157, maps p157 and p158*
Camel safaris
Camel safaris are big business in Jaisalmer (see box, page 162). Many guesthouses offer their own trips but the following tour operators are recommended.
Rajasthan Desert Safaris, T(0)9414-140109, www.desertsafarijaisalmer.com. One of the more upmarket options.
Sahara Travels, see under Tour operators.

Sunny Tours, see under Tour operators.
Trotters' Independent Travels, Gopa
Chowk, near Bhang Shop, T(0)9414-469292,
www.trotterscamelsafarijaisalmer.com.

Cooking
Karuna, Ishar Palace, in the fort near
the Laxminath Temple, T02992-253062,
karunaacharya@yahoo.com. Learn Indian
cookery with Karuna. Courses of any length
can be arranged. Highly recommended.

Swimming
Gorbandh Palace (non-residents Rs 350);
also **Heritage Inn** (meal plus swim deals)
and **Fort Rajwada**.

Tour operators
Rajasthan Tourism, T02992-252406.
City sightseeing: half day, 0900-1200.
Fort, *havelis*, Gadisagar Lake. Sam sand
dunes: half day, 1500-1900.
Royal Desert Safaries, Nachna Haveli,
Gandhi Chowk, T02992-252538, www.
palaces-tours.com. Experienced and efficient.
Sahara Travels, Gopa Chowk, right of the
1st Fort gate, T02992-252609. Mr (Desert)
Bissa's reliable camel safaris with good food.
Sunny Tours, Shahi Palace, T(0)9414-
365495, www.sunnytourntravels.com.
One of the oldest tour operators in
Jaisalmer they offer top notch travel
support and camel and jeep safaris.
Professional. Recommended.
Thar Safari, Gandhi Chowk, near Trio,
T02992-252722. Reliable tours.

⊖ Transport

Jaisalmer *p157, maps p157 and p158*
Jaisalmer is on NH15 (Pathankot–
Samakhiali). Transport to town from train
and bus station is by auto-rickshaws or
jeeps; police are on duty so less harassment.
Bus Touts may board buses outside town
to press you to take their jeep; it is better to
walk 10-15 mins from Amar Sagar Pol and
choose a hotel. Most hotels offer station
pick-up too so call ahead.

State Roadways buses, from near the
station, T02992-251541, and at SBBJ Bank
Government Bus Stop. There is now a
new Volvo bus running daily Jaisalmer to
Delhi, via Jodhpur and Jaipur, but takes
a whopping 18 hrs – leaves 1730 from
Jaisalmer (from Delhi to Jaisalmer starts
at 1730 too). Services to **Ajmer**, **Barmer**,
Bikaner (330 km on good road, 8 hrs,
Rs 160), **Jaipur** (638 km); Abu Rd for **Mount
Abu**. **Jodhpur** (285 km, 0500, 0600, 0630,
0730 and 2230, 5 hrs). **Udaipur** (663 km, a
tiring 14 hrs). **Bikaner** 0600 and 2130 from
Hanuman Chowk; Private deluxe coaches
from outside Amar Sagar Pol or Airforce
Circle, to a similar range of destinations.
Most hotels can reserve bus tickets.
Operators: **Marudhara Travels**, Station Rd,
T02992-252351; **National Tours**, Hanuman
Choraha, T02992-252348.
Train The military presence can make
getting tickets slow; book in advance if
possible. Foreign Tourist Bureau with
waiting room, T02992-252354, booking
office T02992-251301. *Jsm Hwh Sf Exp 12372*,
to **Bikaner** (5½ hrs) and **Delhi** (15 hrs).
Jsm Dli Express14660, 1715, 5 hrs. Can get
very cold (and dusty) try and book 3AC
where bedding is provided.

Barmer *p161*
From Barmer, the hot and dusty bus journey
to **Jaisalmer** takes 4 hrs; **Mt Abu**, 6 hrs.

❶ Directory

Jaisalmer *p157, maps p157 and p158*
Medical services Maheshwan Hospital,
Barmer Rd, T02992-250024. **Post** The GPO
is near Police Station, T02992-252407.
Police: T02992-252668.

Alwar, Sariska and around

Alwar, in northeastern Rajasthan, has fascinating monuments including the Bala Quilla fort, overlooking the town, and the Moti Doongri fort, in a garden. The former, which was never taken by direct assault, has relics of the early Rajput rulers, the founders of the fort, who had their capital near Alwar. Over the centuries it was home to the Khanzadas, Mughals, Pathans, Jats and finally the Rajputs. There are also palaces and colonial period parks and gardens. The town itself is very untouristy and spread over a large area, making navigation difficult at times, but is generally very welcoming.

The 480-sq-km Sariska reserve is a dry deciduous forest set in a valley surrounded by the barren Aravalli hills. The princely shooting reserve of the Maharajah of Alwar was declared a sanctuary in 1955. Exactly 50 years later it acquired the dubious honour of being the first Project Tiger reserve to be declared free of tigers, the last ones presumably having been poached. Nevertheless, the park still holds some wildlife, and a certain rugged appeal.

Arriving in Alwar and Sariska
Getting there and around Alwar is well connected to both Delhi and Jaipur by bus and train, and is only a three-hour drive from Delhi, or 1½ hours from Jaipur. Sariska is an easy 35-km drive from Alwar. » See Transport, page 170.

Tourist information Rajasthan Tourist Reception Centre ① *Nehru Marg, opposite railway station, Alwar, T0144-234 7348, closed weekends.*

Background
As Mughal power crumbled, Rao Pratap Singhji of Macheri founded Alwar as his capital in 1771. He shook off Jat power over the region and rebelled against Jaipur suzerainty making Alwar an independent state. His successors lent military assistance to the British in their battles against the Marathas in AD 1803, and in consequence gained the support of the colonial power. The Alwar royals were flamboyant and kept a fleet of custom-made cars (including a throne car and a golden limousine), and collected solid silver furniture and attractive walking sticks.

Alwar → For listings, see pages 169-170.

Alwar is protected by the hilltop **Bala Quilla**, which has the remains of palaces, temples and 10 tanks built by the first rulers of Alwar. It stands 308 m above the town, to the northwest, and is reached by a steep 4WD track (permission must be obtained from the police station). There are splendid views.

The City Palace, **Vinai Vilas Mahal** (1840) ⓘ *closed Mon, 1000-1700, free, museum Rs 50 foreigners, Rs 5 for Indians*, with intricate *jali* work, ornate *jarokha* balconies and courtyards, houses government offices on the ground floor, and a fine museum upstairs. The palace is impressive but is poorly maintained, with dusty galleries (you may find children playing cricket in the courtyard). The Darbar Room is closed, and the throne, miniatures and gilt-edged mirrors can only be viewed through the glass doors and windows or by prior permission of the royal family (not easily obtained). The museum is interesting, housing local miniature paintings, as well as some of the Mughal, Bundi and other schools, an array of swords, shields, daggers, guns and armour, sandalwood carvings, ivory objects, jade art, musical instruments and princely relics. Next to the city palace are the lake and royal cenotaphs. On the south side of the tank is the Cenotaph of Maharaja Bakhtawar Singh (1781-1815) which is made of marble on a red sandstone base. The gardens are alive with peacocks and other birds. To the right of the main entrance to the palace is a two-storey processional elephant carriage designed to carry 50 people and be pulled by four elephants.

The **Yeshwant Niwas**, built by Maharaja Jai Singh in the Italianate style, is also worth seeing. Apparently on its completion he disliked it and never lived in it. Instead he built the **Vijay Mandir** in 1918, a 105-room palace beside Vijay Sagar, 10 km from Alwar. Part of it is open with prior permission from the royal family or their secretary, but even without it is worth seeing from the road, with its façade resembling an anchored ship. When not in Delhi, the royal family now live in Phool Bagh, a small 1960s mansion opposite the New Stadium.

Alwar to Sariska → For listings, see pages 169-170.

Kesroli, 10 km northeast, has a seven-turreted 16th-century fort atop a rocky hillock, now sympathetically (though more modestly) restored. It is a three-hour drive from Delhi and convenient for an overnight halt. Turn left off the NH8 at Dharuhera for Alwar Road and you will find it. **Kushalgarh Fort** is en route to Sariska. Near Kushalgarh is the temple complex of **Talbraksha** (or Talvriksh) with a large population of rhesus macaque monkeys. Guides report panthers having been seen near the **Cafeteria Taal** here, probably on the prowl for monkeys near the canteen.

Sariska Tiger Reserve → For listings, see pages 169-170.

ⓘ *Rs 450 including still camera, Indians Rs 60, video Rs 200; vehicle Rs 250 per trip. Early-morning jeep trips from Sariska Palace Hotel or Tiger Den (see Where to stay, page 170) venture into the park as far as the Monkey Temple, where you can get a cup of tea and watch monkeys and peacocks. Jeep hire for non-standard trips in the reserve Rs 1050 for 3 hrs, excluding entry fees. Compulsory guide Rs 150. You need to get permit from the Forest Registry Office for early morning and late afternoon safaris (0600-1000/1500-1800). Closed Jul-Sep.*

Despite the lack of tigers, Sariska provides plenty of opportunities to see wildlife. The main rhesus monkey population lives at Talvriksh near Kushalgarh, while at Bhartri-Hari you will see many langurs. The chowsingha, or four-horned antelope, is found here, as are other deer including chital and sambar. You may see nilgai, wild boar, jackals, hyenas, hares and porcupines; leopards are present but rarely seen since the reserve is closed at night to visitors. During the monsoons many animals move to higher ground, but the place is alive with birds. There are ground birds such as peafowl, jungle fowl, spur fowl and grey partridge. Babblers, bulbuls and treepies are common round the lodges. Since 2008, a number of tigers have been relocated from Ranthambhore National Park further south, in the hope of repopulating Sariska, but only time will tell if this has been a success. The organization **Save Our Tigers** ① www.saveourtigers.com, sponsored by the communications company Aircel, has launched a big TV and billboard campaign to raise awareness. In the 2011 Tiger Census, numbers were up across the country to 1706, but only by four in Rajasthan.

Unlike most national parks, Sariska is open all year round (though it is open to pilgrims only from June until September). During the monsoon travel through the forest may be difficult. The best season to visit is between November and April. In the dry season, when the streams disappear, the animals become dependent on man-made water holes at Kalighatti, Salopka and Pandhupol.

Sariska, the gateway to the national park, is a pleasant, quiet place to stay and relax. Excursions by jeep are possible to forts and temples nearby. The **Kankwari Fort** (2 km) – where Emperor Aurangzeb is believed to have imprisoned his brother **Dara Shikoh**, the rightful heir to the Mughal throne – is within the park. The old **Bhartrihari** temple (6 km) holds a fair and six-hour dance-drama in September and October. **Neelkanth** (33 km) has a complex of sixth- to 10th-century carved temples. **Bhangarh** (55 km), on the outskirts of the reserve, is a deserted city of some 10,000 dwellings established in 1631. It was abandoned 300 years ago, supposedly after it was cursed by a magician.

Alwar, Sariska and around listings

For hotel and restaurant price codes and other relevant information, see pages 13-16.

⬤ Where to stay

Alwar *p168*
$$$$-$$$ Dadhikar Fort, Village Dadhikar, T(0)9950-449900, www.dadhikar.com. Nestling in the Aravali hills 6 km outside Alwar, is the ancient site of the Dadhikar Fort, now restored from ruin into a deluxe hotel. 11 individually styled rooms have been comfortably furnished with bespoke heavy wooden furniture and antique objets d'art, and include a rooftop suite, an underground chamber and a family duplex. Dining takes place in the cosy central courtyard (with individual bonfires in winter) and breakfast is served on the rooftop to take in unparalleled views across the colourful mustard fields and lush green hills. Highly recommended.

$$$$-$$$ Hill Fort Kesroli (Heritage Hotel), Alwar Rd, Kesroli, T01468-289352, www.neemranahotels.com. Comfortable, if eccentric, airy rooms and plush suites, set around a courtyard, delicious lunch and dinner buffet included, some of the best food in Rajasthan, relaxing, and in a lovely isolated rural location. Often overrun by groups though.
$$$$-$$$ Neemrana Fort Palace, 65 km north of Alwar, Delhi–Jaipur Highway, T01494-246 006, www.neemranahotels.com. The pinnacle of the Neemrana properties, this palace looks like it has come straight out of a fairy-tale, with many tiers and turreted rooms. There are many rooms with their own private rooftop terraces. Ziplining available
$$$-$$ Hotel Hill View, Moti Doongri, T0144-329 8111, www.hillviewalwar.com. Excellent value for money, mid-range hotel run by an enthusiastic and helpful manager.

11 very comfortable, clean rooms, all with TV and fridge. Most rooms have views across to Moti Doongri. There is internet, billiards and a small gym. small garden and rooftop; multi-cuisine restaurant. The hotel will happily arrange a tiger safari and guide.

$ Ashoka, Manu Marg, T0144-234 6780. 30 rooms, clean and comfortable, deluxe rooms have TV, running hot water and Western toilets, cheaper rooms have Indian toilets and hot water in buckets, restaurant, good value.

$ Hotel Yuvraj Kothi Rao, 31 Moti Dungri, T0144-270 0741, www.hotelkothirao.com. Dubbed a 'House Hotel' by the very charming family of owners who offer up home cooked meals and take great pride in their home-style hospitality. It's a bit shabby around the edges for the price.

Alwar to Sariska p168

$$ Burja Haveli, Burja, 7th Mile Stone Rajgarh Rd, T(0)9928-026521, www.burja-haveli.com. Atmospheric little place outside of Alwar. It's a 240-year-old *haveli* with a homely atmosphere.

Sariska Tiger Reserve p168

$$$ Alwar Bagh, T0144-288 5231, next door to Sariska Tiger Camp (see below). Extremely well run hotel in a peaceful location. 32 deluxe rooms and suites in 2 separate villas and a traditional '*haveli* style' building; all with TV, a/c and great walk-in showers; suites offer such delights as hanging beds and private rooftop terraces, most rooms overlook pretty orchard gardens and a beautiful pool,

very child friendly, great food, solar panels and an opportunity to become involved in village social projects for a day. Recommended.

$$$ Sariska Tiger Camp, 19 km towards Alwar on the main road, T0144-288 5311. Eccentric design with 20 simply furnished 'mud concept' rooms in traditional 'village style with wall paintings'; well-tended garden and swimming pool, the restaurant has a lovely terrace. Often caters for groups and feels a bit 'empty' without them.

$$$-$$ Tiger Den (RTDC), in the sanctuary, T0144-284 1342. Superbly located tourist bungalow with views of hill and park, 30 rooms with attached baths (hot showers) but shabby, dirty public areas, vegetarian restaurant (Indian buffets Rs 130-150), bar and shop sells cards and souvenirs, nice garden, friendly management.

$ Forest Rest House, Main Rd, opposite turning to Kushalgarh, T0144-284 1333. 6 simple rooms, only open during winter.

⊖ Transport

Alwar p168

Bus Regular buses to/from **Delhi** (4½-5 hrs) and **Jaipur**. Frequent service to **Bharatpur** (2½ hrs), **Deeg** (1½ hrs) and **Sariska** (1 hr).

Train **New Delhi**: *Shatabdi Exp 12016*, not Sun, 1941, 2½ hrs. **Delhi**: *Jodhpur Delhi Exp 14860*, 0835, 3 hrs; *Jaipur-JAT Exp 12413*, 1900, 3 hrs.

Sariska Tiger Reserve p168

Train The nearest station is at Alwar (36 km), with buses to the sanctuary.

Deeg, Bharatpur and around

For a typical dusty and hot North Indian market town, Deeg gained the somewhat surprising reputation as the summer resort of the Raja of Bharatpur. Located on the plains just northwest of Agra, the raja decided to develop his palace to take full advantage of the monsoon rains. The fort and the 'monsoon' pleasure palace have ingenious fountains and are of major architectural importance, their serenity in stark contrast to the barely controlled chaos of the rest of the town. One of the most popular halting places on the 'Golden Triangle', Bharatpur is best known for its Keoladeo Ghana Bird Sanctuary. Once the hunting estate of the Maharajas of Bharatpur, with daily shoots recorded of up to 4000 birds, the 29-sq-km piece of marshland, with over 360 species, is potentially one of the finest bird sanctuaries in the world, but has suffered badly in recent years from water deprivation. Lesser visited are the sights off the road which connects Agra to Jaipur, NH11, which sees huge volumes of tourist traffic. The Balaji temple is particularly remarkable.

Arriving in Deeg and Bharatpur
There are regular bus services from both Mathura and Bharatpur to Deeg, with the road from Bharatpur being by far the smoother of the two. Bharatpur, 40 km south of Deeg, has good bus and train connections from Agra, Jaipur and Delhi. Keoladeo Ghana National Park is 4 km south of Bharatpur town.

Deeg → *For listings, see pages 174-175.*

The rubble and mud walls of the square **fort** are strengthened by 12 bastions and a wide, shallow moat. It has a run-down *haveli* within, but is otherwise abandoned. The entrance is over a narrow bridge across the moat, through a gate studded with anti-elephant spikes. Negotiating the undergrowth, you can climb the ramparts which rise 20 m above the moat; some cannons are still in place on their rusty carriages. You can walk right around along the wide path on top of the walls and climb the stairs to the roof of the citadel for good views.

The **palaces** ⓘ *opposite the fort, Sat-Thu 0930-1730, Rs 200*, are flanked by two reservoirs, Gopal (west) and Rup Sagar (east), and set around a beautifully proportioned central formal garden in the style of a Mughal *char bagh*. The main entrance is from the north, through the ornamental, though unfinished, Singh (Lion) Pol; the other gates are Suraj (Sun) Pol (southwest) and Nanga Pol (northeast). The impressive main palace **Gopal Bhavan** (1763), bordering Gopal Sagar, is flanked by Sawon and Bhadon pavilions (1760), named after the monsoon months (mid-July to mid-September). Water was directed over the roof lines to create the effect of sheets of monsoon rain. The palace still retains many of the original furnishings, including scent and cigarette cases made from elephant's feet and even a dartboard. There are vegetarian and non-vegetarian dining rooms, the former particularly elegant, with floor seating around a low-slung horseshoe-shaped marble table. Outside, overlooking the formal garden, is a beautiful white marble *hindola* (swing) which was brought as booty with two marble thrones (black and white) after Suraj Mal attacked Delhi. To the south, bordering the central garden, is the single-storey marble **Suraj Bhavan** (circa 1760), a temple, and **Kishan Bhavan** with its decorated façade, five arches and fountains.

Bhandarej to Bharatpur → *For listings, see pages 174-175.*

Bhandarej, 62 km from Jaipur, south of NH11 after Dausa, is a relaxing place to stop for the night. From here the NH11 goes through a series of small towns and villages to **Sakrai** (77 km) which has a good roadside RTDC restaurant. Some 15 km after Sakrai is the turning for Balaji, home to the truly extraordinary **Balaji Temple**. People who believe themselves to have been possessed by demons come here, to have the evil spirits exorcized. The scenes on the first floor in particular are not for the faint-hearted; methods of restraining the worst afflicted include chaining them to the walls and placing them under large rocks. Most exorcisms take place on Tuesdays and Saturdays, when there are long queues to get in. From **Mahuwa** a road south leads through Hindaun to Karauli (64 km).

Noted for its pale red sandstone, **Karauli** (1348), was the seat of a small princely state which played a prominent part in support of the Mughal emperors. The impressive **City Palace** has some fine wall paintings, stone carvings and a fine Darbar Hall. Fairs are held at nearby temples lasting a week to a fortnight. Mahavirji, associated with the 24th Tirthankar Mahavir, is an important Jain pilgrimage centre.

Bharatpur → *For listings, see pages 174-175.*

Built by Suraj Mal, the **Lohagarh Fort**, which occupies the island at the centre of Bharatpur village, appears impregnable, but the British, initially repulsed in 1803, finally took it in 1825. There are double ramparts, a 46-m-wide moat and an inner moat around the palace. Much of the wall has been demolished but there are the remains of some of the gateways. Inside the fort are three palaces (circa 1730) and Jewel House and Court to their north. The **museum** ① *1000-1630, closed Fri, Rs 3,* in the Kachhari Kalan, exhibits archaeological finds from villages nearby, dating from the first to 19th centuries as well as paintings and artefacts; the armoury is upstairs.

Peharsar ① *23 km away, Rs 30 to 'headman' secures a tour,* with a carpet-weaving community, makes a very interesting excursion from Bharatpur.

Keoladeo Ghana National Park → *For listings, see pages 174-175.*

The late Maharaja Brajendra Singh converted his hunting estate into a bird sanctuary in 1956 and devoted many of his retired years to establishing it. He had inherited both his title and an interest in wildlife from his deposed father, Kishan Singh, who grossly overspent his budget – 30 Rolls Royces, a private jazz band and some extremely costly wild animals including "dozens of lions, elephants, leopards and tigers" – for Bharatpur's jungles. It has been designated a World Heritage Site, and can only be entered by bicycle or cycle rickshaw, thus maintaining the peaceful calm of the park's interior. In 2010, a tiger wandered out of Ranthambhore Park, took a wander around, went via Mathura oil refinery and ended up in Keoloadeo Ghana National Park, which could make the rickshaw wallah cycling you around the park peddle a little faster!

Tragically, at the end of 2004 the state government bowed to pressure from local farmers and diverted 97% of the park's water supply for irrigation projects. The catastrophic damage to its wetlands has resulted in the loss of many of the migratory birds on which Bharatpur's reputation depends and potentially they will lose their UNESCO status. The battle goes on and in recent years the Chief Minister Ashok Gehlot has released water from the nearby Panchna Dam to help restore the park's natural habitat. It's an ongoing story but certainly the nature of the park is changing.

Arriving in Keoladeo Ghana National Park

Getting around Official cycle-rickshaws at the entrance are numbered and work in rotation, Rs 50 per hour for two people (drivers may be reluctant to take more than one). This is well worthwhile as some rickshaw-wallahs are very knowledgeable and can help identify birds (and know their location): a small tip is appropriate. The narrower paths are not recommended as the rough surface makes rickshaws too noisy. It is equally feasible to just walk or hire a bike, particularly once you're familiar with the park. If there's any water, a boat ride is highly recommended for viewing.

Tourist information The official website for the park is www.knpark.org. Entry costs Rs 400, video Rs 200, professional video Rs 1500, payable each time you enter. The park is closed May and June. There are cafés inside the park, or ask your hotel to provide a packed lunch. Information and guides are available from **RTDC** ① *Hotel Saras, T05644-222542*, and **Wildlife Office** ① *Forest Rest House, T05644-222777*. Good naturalist guides (costing Rs 70-100 per hour, depending on group size) are also available at the Bird Sanctuary gate, or contact **Nature Bureau** ① *Haveli SVP Shastri, Neemda Gate, T05644-225498*. It is worth buying the well-illustrated *Collins Handguide to the Birds of the Indian Sub-continent* (available at the reserve and in bookshops in Delhi, Agra, Jaipur, etc). *Bharatpur: Bird Paradise* by Martin Ewans (Lustre Press, Delhi) is extremely good.

Best time to visit Winters can be very cold and foggy, especially in the early morning. It is traditionally best November to February when it is frequented by northern hemisphere migratory birds. To check in advance whether there is any water, try contacting the tourist information numbers above, or use the contact form on www.keoladeonationalpark.itgo.com.

Wildlife
The handful of rare Siberian cranes that used to visit Bharatpur each year have been missing since 2003. The ancient migratory system, some 1500 years old, may have been lost completely, since young cranes must learn the route from older birds (it is not instinctive). These cranes are disappearing worldwide – eaten by Afghans and sometimes employed as fashionable 'guards' to protect Pakistani homes (they call out when strangers approach). The Sarus crane can still be seen in decent numbers.

Other birds that can be spotted include Asian openbills, Ferruginous ducks, spoonbills, storks, kingfishers, a variety of egrets, ducks and coots, as well as birds of prey including Laggar falcon, greater-spotted eagle, marsh harrier, Scops owl and Pallas' eagle. There are also chital deer, sambar, nilgai, feral cattle, wild cats, hyenas, wild boar and monitor lizards, whilst near Python Point, there are usually some very large rock pythons.

Birds, accustomed to visitors, can be watched at close range from the road between the boat jetty and Keoladeo temple, especially at Sapan Mori crossing. Dawn (which can be very cold) and dusk are the best times; trees around Keoladeo temple are favoured by birds for roosting, so are particularly rewarding. Midday may prove too hot so take a book and find a shady spot. Carry a sun hat, binoculars and plenty of water.

Deeg, Bharatpur and around listings

For hotel and restaurant price codes and other relevant information, see pages 13-16.

🛏 Where to stay

Deeg *p171*
If you have to spend a night there are a couple of very basic options near the bus stand.

Bhandarej to Bharatpur *p172*
$$$-$$ Bhanwar Vilas Palace (Heritage Hotel), Karauli, T07464-220024, www.karauli. com. 29 comfortable rooms, including 4 a/c suites in a converted palace, most air-cooled, cheaper in cottage, Rajasthani restaurant, pool, tours, camping, amazingly ornate lounge and dining halls, real air of authenticity. Recommended.
$$$-$$ Chandra Mahal, Peharsar, Jaipur–Agra Rd, Nadbai, Peharsar, T05643-264336. 23 rooms in simply furnished, 19th-century Shia Muslim *haveli* with character, quality set meals (from Rs 250), jeep hire and good service.

Bharatpur *p172*
Most of Bharatpur's accommodation is out of town, close to the bird sanctuary. However, there is a great budget choice in the old city.
$ Shagun Guest House, just inside Mathura Gate, T05644-232455. Has 6 basic rooms, 1 with attached bathroom, all under Rs 100, bicycle and binocular hire. Friendly, welcoming and knowledgeable manager.

Keoladeo Ghana National Park *p172*
Inside the park
$$$ Bharatpur Forest Lodge (Ashok), 2.5 km from gate, 8 km from railway and bus stand, T05644-222760, www. bharatpurforestlodge.in. Book in advance. 17 comfortable a/c rooms with balconies, pricey restaurant and bar, very friendly staff, peaceful, boats for birdwatching, animals (eg wild boar) wander into the compound. Entry fee each time you enter park.
$ Shanti Kutir Rest House, near the boat jetty. 5 clean rooms in an old hunting lodge, mostly used by guests of the park director.

Outside the park
$$$$ The Bagh, Agra Rd, 4 km from town, T05644-228 333, www.thebagh.com. Set in a beautiful orchard, space is everything here. There are 14 elegant, well decorated, centrally a/c rooms with outstanding bathrooms. Attractive dining room, lovely pool, beautiful 200-year-old gardens, some may find facilities rather spread out. Recommended.
$$$-$$ Sunbird, near the park gate, T05644-225701, www.hotelsunbird.com. Attractive red-brick building with clean rooms with hot shower, better on the 1st floor. Now also 4 deluxe cottages, pleasant restaurant, friendly staff, bike hire, good value, well maintained. Highly recommended.
$$-$ New Spoonbill, near Saras, T05644-223 571, www.hotelspoonbill.com. 4 good-size rooms, nice decor and a family friendly vibe. There is also the original **Spoonbill** down the road with cheaper rooms but still

a good standard with shared bathroom, run by a charming ex-army officer, courteous and friendly service, good food, bike hire.
$ Crane Crib, Fatehpur Sikri Rd, 3 km from the park, T05644-222224. Attractive sandstone building, 25 rooms of wide-ranging standards and tariffs, all reasonable value. Small cinema where wildlife films are shown nightly, bonfires on the lawn during winter and welcoming staff. Run by the honorary warden of the park. Recommended.
$ Falcon Guest House, near Saras, T05644-223815. 10 clean, well-kept rooms, some a/c with bath, owned by a naturalist, good information, bike hire, quiet, very helpful, warm welcome, off-season discount.
$ Kiran Vila Palace, Saras Circle, 300 m from the park gate, T(0)7597-694894, www.hotelkiranvila.com. Nicely decorated rooms set back from the road, so a little quieter.

⊛ Festivals

Bhandarej to Bharatpur *p172*
Feb/Mar In Karauli, Sivaratri.
Mar/Apr Kaila Devi (28 Mar 2014, 17 Mar 2015). Held in Karauli.

Bharatpur *p172*
2-4 Feb Brij Festival, honours lord Krishna with folk dances and drama relating the love story of Radha-Krishna.

⊖ Transport

Bhandarej to Bharatpur *p172*
Train Nearly all trains on the main Delhi–Mumbai line stop at Gangapur City, 30 km from Karauli.

Bharatpur *p172*
Air The nearest airport is at Jaipur (175 km).
Bus Buses to Bharatpur tend to get very crowded but give an insight into Indian rural life. The main stand is at Anah Gate just off NH11 (east of town). To **Agra** (55 km, 1½ hrs), **Deeg**; **Delhi**, 185 km, 6 hrs; and **Jaipur** 175 km, 5 hrs.
Train From: **Delhi (ND)**: *Golden Temple Mail 12904*, 0740, 3 hrs; This train also leaves Bharatpur at 1030 for **Sawai Madhopur** (2½ hrs) and **Kota**. To **Delhi** *Golden Temple Mail 12903*, 1504, 3½ hrs.
An auto-rickshaw from train station (6 km) to park Rs 80; from bus stand (4 km), Rs 50.

Keoladeo Ghana National Park *p172*
Cycle There are bikes for hire near Saras or ask at your hotel; Rs 40 per day; hire on previous evening for an early start next day.

⊙ Directory

Bharatpur *p172*
Banks SBBJ, near Binarayan Gate, may ask for proof of purchase, or refuse to change TCs.

Ranthambhore National Park

The park is one of the finest tiger reserves in the country, although even here their numbers have dwindled due to poachers. Most visitors spending a couple of nights here are likely to spot one of these wonderful animals, although many leave disappointed. Set in dry deciduous forest, some trees trailing matted vines, the park's rocky hills and open valleys are dotted with small pools and fruit trees. The reserve covers 410 sq km between the Aravalli and Vindhya hills. Scrubby hillsides surrounding Ranthambhore village are pleasantly peaceful, their miniature temples and shrines glowing pink in the evening sun before they become silhouetted nodules against the night sky. Once the private tiger reserve of the Maharajah of Jaipur, in 1972 the sanctuary came under the Project Tiger scheme following the government Wildlife Protection Act. By 1979, 12 villages inside the park had been 'resettled' into the surrounding area, leaving only a scattering of people still living within the park's boundaries. Should the tigers evade you, you may well spot leopard, hyena, jackal, marsh crocodile, wild boar, langur monkey, bear, and many species of deer and birdlife. The park's 10th-century fort, proudly flanked by two impressive gateways, makes a good afternoon excursion after a morning drive.

Arriving in Ranthambhore National Park
Getting there and around The national park is 10 km east of Sawai Madhopur, with the approach along a narrow valley; the main gate is 4 km from the boundary. The park has good roads and tracks. Entry is by park jeep (gypsy) or open bus (canter) on four-hour tours; 16 jeeps and 20 canters are allowed in at any one time to minimize disturbance. You can book online. Some lodges can organize trips for you or there are a couple of jeeps and canters reserved for same-day bookings, which involves a queue and elbows and you may get gazumped by hotels paying over the odds for a private jeep. Jeeps are better but must be booked in advance so request one at the time of booking your lodge (passport number and personal details required) or try online. Visitors are picked up from their hotels.

The park is open 1 October-30 June for two sessions a day: winter 0630-1030, 1400-1800; summer 0600-1000, 1430-1830, but check as times change. Jeep hire: Rs 800-1200 per person for up to five passengers; jeep entry Rs 125; guide Rs 150. A seat in a canter, Rs 500-550, can often be arranged on arrival, bookings start at 0600 and 1330 for same-day tours;

advance bookings from 1000-1330. Individual entry fees are extra: foreigners Rs 200, Indians Rs 25, camera free, video Rs 200. The powers-that-be do keep changing regulations on all park entry in India, so double check with your hotel beforehand.

Tourist information Rajasthan Tourism ① *Hotel Vinayak, T07462-220808*. **Conservator of Forests/Field Director** ① *T07462-220223*. **Forest Officer** ① *T07462-221142*. A very informative background with photography tips is available on www.ranthambhore.com.

Climate Best from November to April, though the vegetation dies down in April. Maximum temperatures are 28-49°C. It can be very cold at dawn in winter.

Background

Much of the credit for Ranthambhore's present position as one of the world's leading wildlife resorts goes to India's most famous 'tiger man', Mr Fateh Singh Rathore. His enthusiasm for all things wild has been passed on to his son, Dr Goverdhan Singh Rathore, who set up the Prakratik Society in 1994. This charitable foundation was formed in response to the increasing human encroachment on the tiger's natural forest habitat; in 1973 there were 70,000 people living around Ranthambhore Park, a figure which has now increased to 200,000.

The human population's rapidly increasing firewood requirements were leading to ever-more damaging deforestation, and the founders of the Prakratik Society soon realized that something needed to be done. Their solution was as brilliant as it was simple; enter the 'biogas digester'. This intriguingly named device, of which 225 have so far been installed, uses cow dung as a raw material, and produces both gas for cooking, negating the need for firewood, and organic fertilizer, which has seen crop yields increase by 25%. The over-whelming success of this venture was recognized in June 2004, when the Prakratik Society was presented with the prestigious Ashden Award for Sustainable Energy in London.

Wildlife

Tiger sightings are recorded almost daily, usually in the early morning, especially from November to April. Travellers report the tigers seem "totally unconcerned, ambling past only 10 m away". Sadly, poaching is prevalent: between 2003 and 2005, 22 tigers were taken out of the park by poachers operating from surrounding villages – a wildlife scandal that spotlighted official negligence in Ranthambhore. Since then the population has recovered somewhat, with about six cubs being born each year. Across the country, the Tiger Census of 2010 revealed that tiger numbers are up by 295 making a total of 1706 tigers. The current estimate is that there are 31 adult tigers in the park. As well as Save the Tiger campaigns from Aircel, there is a Travel Operators for Tigers group which many of the hotels in Ranthambhore are a part of.

The lakeside woods and grassland provide an ideal habitat for herds of chital and sambar deer and sounders of wild boar. Nilgai antelope and chinkara gazelles prefer the drier areas of the park. Langur monkeys, mongoose and hare are prolific. There are also sloth bear, a few leopards, and the occasional rare caracal. Crocodiles bask by the lakes, and some rocky ponds have freshwater turtles. Extensive birdlife includes spurfowl, jungle fowl, partridges, quails, crested serpent eagle, woodpeckers, flycatchers, etc. There are also water birds like storks, ducks and geese at the lakes and waterholes. Padam Talao by the Jogi Mahal is a favourite water source; there are also water holes at Raj Bagh and Milak.

Ranthambhore Fort

ⓘ *The entrance to the fort is before the gate to the park. Open from dawn to dusk, though the Park Interpretation Centre near the small car park may not be open. Free entry.*

There is believed to have been a settlement here in the eighth century. The earliest historic record is of it being wrested by the Chauhans in the 10th century. In the 11th century, after Ajmer was lost to Ghori, the Chauhans made it their capital. Hamir Chauhan, the ruler of Ranthambhore in the 14th century, gave shelter to enemies of the Delhi sultanate, resulting in a massive siege and the Afghan conquest of the fort. The fort was later surrendered to Emperor Akbar in the 16th century when Ranthambhore's commander saw resistance was useless, finally passing to the rulers of Jaipur. The forests of Ranthambhore historically guarded the fort from invasions but with peace under the Raj they became a hunting preserve of the Jaipur royal family. The fort wall runs round the summit and has a number of semi-circular bastions, some with sheer drops of over 65 m and stunning views. Inside the fort you can see a Siva temple – where Rana Hamir beheaded himself rather than face being humiliated by the conquering Delhi army – ruined palaces, pavilions and tanks. Mineral water, tea and soft drinks are sold at the foot of the climb to the fort and next to the Ganesh temple near the tanks.

Ranthambhore National Park listings

For hotel and restaurant price codes and other relevant information, see pages 13-16.

● Where to stay

Ranthambhore National Park *p176*

$$$$ Khem Villas, Sherpur-Khiljipur, T07462-252347, www.khemvilas.com. Super-stylish accommodation beautifully adorned with handblock prints due to Villas being part-owned by the founders of Anokhi. There are beautiful rooms, tents and cottages; the latter have stunning open-air bathrooms. The family here were pioneering in tiger conservation and also with creating an eco-friendly camp.

$$$$ Sherbagh Tented Camp, Sherpur-Khiljipur, T07462-252120, www.sujanluxury. com. Open 1 Oct-30 Mar. Award-winning eco-camp with luxury tents and hot showers, bar, dinner around fire, lake trips for birders, stunning grounds and seated areas for quiet contemplation, jungle ambience, well organized. All meals included. Beautiful shop on site. Owner Jaisal Singh has put together a new book *Ranthambhore – The Tiger's Realm*. Highly recommended.

$$$$ Vanyavilas (Oberoi), T07462-223999, www.oberoihotels.com. Very upmarket 8-ha garden resort set around a recreated *haveli* with fantastic frescoes. 25 unbelievably luxurious a/c tents (wooden floors, marble baths), billiards, elephant rides, wildlife lectures, dance shows in open-air auditorium, "fabulous spa", friendly and professional. Elephants greet you at the door.

$$$ Jhoomar Baori (RTDC), Ranthambore Rd, T07462-220495. Set high on a hillside, this former hunting lodge is an interesting building and offers fantastic views of the area. 12 quirky rooms, varying in size, plus a small bar, reasonable restaurant and beautifully decorated communal lounges on each floor.

$$$-$$ Ranthambore Bagh, Ranthambhore Rd, T(0)8239-166777, www.ranthambhore.com. 12 luxury tents and 12 simple but attractive rooms in this pleasantly laid-back property owned by a professional photographer and his lovely family. Pride has been taken in every detail; the public areas and dining hall are particularly well done. Fantastic food including traditional Rajasthani and atmospheric suppers around the campfire. Highly recommended.

$$ Tiger Safari, Ranthambore Rd, T07462-221137, www.tiger safariresort.com. 14 cosy rooms, 4 attractive a/c cottages, very clean, hot shower, quiet, jeep/bus to the park, very helpful, good value, ordinary food but few other options. Recommended.

$$ Tiger Vilas, Ranthambore Rd, T07462-221121, www.tigervilla.in. 10 clean, modern rooms in a convenient location for the park, beautiful decor, reasonably priced veggie food.

$ City Heart, Ranthambhore Rd, 100 m from Ranthambhore Bagh, T07462-202500. Good, clean rooms, some with TV.

$ Continental, set back from Ranthambhore Rd, next to Ranthambhore Bagh, T(0)9414-727157. Beautiful gardens with 4 simple but big rooms and 2 rooftop tents. Pretty, good home-cooked food; great reports from guests. Recommended.

$ Dev Palace, Ranthambhore Rd, near City Heart, T(0)9413-023628, ranthambhoresafari@rediffmail.com. Only 4 rooms, but one of the cheapest options; simple but sweet. Friendly.

◘ Shopping

Ranthambhore National Park *p176*
Dastkar, www.dastkar.org, the original women's collective shop is near Sherbagh, with another branch on Ranthambhore Rd near Ranthambhore Regency. Many locals have jumped on the 'Women's Collective

Crafts' bandwagon but **Dastkar** is the only genuine one. The collective empowers women by making them self sufficient. They started with just 6 women, but now employ 360 women to do quilting, patchwork, block printing and sequin embroidery based on traditional local skills that were dying out. Beautiful fabrics, clothes, toys and collectibles are sold at extremely fair prices. Highly recommended.

◓ Transport

Ranthambhore National Park *p176*
Bus Stand is 500 m from Sawai Madhopur Railway Station. Buses go to **Kota** and **Jaipur**, but trains are quicker and more pleasant.
Train The railway station at Sawai Madhopur, T07462-220222, is on the main Delhi–Mumbai line. To **Jaipur**: *Ranthambore Exp 12465*, 1435, 2¼ hrs. **Mumbai**: *Ag Kranti Rjdhn 12954*, 2038, 13½ hrs. **Jodhpur**: *Ranthambore Exp 12465*, 1435. **Mumbai**: *Ag Kranti Rjdhn 12954*, 2038, 13½ hrs. **New Delhi** (via Bharatpur and Mathura) *Golden Temple Mail 12903*, 1230, 6 hrs; *Kota Jan Shtbdi 12059*, 0705, 5½ hrs.

◑ Directory

Ranthambhore National Park *p176*
Useful contacts Police, T07462-220456. Tiger Watch, T07462-220811.

Ajmer and Pushkar

Although geographically close, these towns could hardly be more different. Situated in a basin at the foot of Taragarh Hill (870 m), Ajmer is surrounded by a stone wall with five gateways. Renowned throughout the Muslim world as the burial place of Mu'inuddin Chishti, who claimed descent from the son-in-law of Mohammad, seven pilgrimages to Ajmer are believed to equal one to Mecca. Every year, especially during the annual Islamic festivals of Id and Muharram, thousands of pilgrims converge on this ancient town on the banks of Ana Sagar Lake. Many visitors are discouraged by the frantic hustle of Ajmer on first arrival, but it's worth taking time to explore this underrated city.

Separated from Ajmer by Nag Pahar (Snake Mountain), Pushkar lies in a narrow valley over-shadowed by rocky hills, which offer spectacular views of the desert at sunset. The lake at its heart (now healthy and thriving after a two-year cleaning project) is one of India's most sacred, and is almost magically beautiful at dawn and dusk. The village is transformed during the celebrated camel fair into a colourful week of heightened activity, but a visit outside this annual extravaganza is also worthwhile.

The village has been markedly changed in recent years by the year-round presence of large numbers of foreigners, originally drawn by the Pushkar Fair, and there is a high hassle factor from cash-seeking Brahmin 'priests' requesting a donation for the 'Pushkar Passport' (a red string tied around the wrist as part of a *puja*/blessing). However, there are still plenty of chances for an unhurried stroll around the lake, or to take the short trek up to the Savitri Temple where you can swap village activity for open swathes of valley and fringes of desert beyond. From on high, the houses crowd the lake's edges as if it's a plug-hole down which all of Pushkar is slowly being drawn.

Arriving in Ajmer and Pushkar

Getting there Pushkar has relatively few direct buses, but Ajmer is well connected by bus and train to the main towns and cities. The station is in the centre, while the main bus stand is 2 km east. Buses to Pushkar leave from the State Bus Stand, and also from a general area 1 km northwest of the station, near the Jain temple. In Pushkar, most buses arrive at the Central (Marwar) Bus Stand, to the usual gauntlet of touts; others pull in at a separate stand 10 minutes' walk east of the lake.

Getting around The main sights and congested bazars of Ajmer, which can be seen in a day at a pinch, are within 15 to 20 minutes' walk of the railway station but you'll need a rickshaw to get to Ana Sagar. Pushkar is small enough to explore on foot. Hire a bike to venture further. ▸▸ *See Transport, page 190.*

Tourist information In Ajmer, there are offices at the railway station and next to **Khadim Hotel** ① *T0145-262 7426, tourismajmer@rediffmail.com, Mon-Sat 0800-1800, closed 2nd Sat of the month.* Both are very helpful. In Pushkar, ask at the **Sarovar Hotel** ① *T0145-277 2040.*

Jaipur to Ajmer → *For listings, see pages 185-190.*

Sambhar Lake
The salt lake, one of the largest of its kind in India, until recently attracted thousands of flamingos and an abundance of cranes, pelicans, ducks and other waterfowl; some 120 species of bird have been recorded. However, the poor monsoons of recent years have caused the lake to dry up leaving only a few marshy patches. Check the situation before visiting. Nilgai, fox and hare are spotted around the lake. The saline marshes are used for the production of salt. **Sakambari Temple**, nearby, dedicated to the ancestral deity of the Chauhans, is believed to date from the sixth century.

Kuchaman
Kuchaman is a large village with temples and relics. Many visitors stop here for tea and snacks between Shekhawati and Ajmer. If you do stop, make time for a visit to the fort; it is a unique experience. Before the eighth century, Kuchaman lay on the highly profitable Central Asian caravan route. Here Gurjar Pratiharas built the massive **cliff-top fort** with 10 gates leading up from the Meena bazar in the village to the royal living quarters. The Chauhans drove the Pratiharas out of the area and for some time it was ruled by the Gaurs. From 1400, it has been in the hands of the Rathores who embellished it with mirrors, mural and gold work in superb palaces and pavilions such as the golden Sunheri Burj and the mirrored Sheesh Mahal, both in sharp contrast to the fort's exterior austerity. The Sariska Palace Group have restored and renovated the fort at enormous cost. You can also visit the **Krishna temple** with a 2000-year-old image, and the **Kalimata ka Mandir** which has an eighth-century black stone deity and you can shop in the **Meena Bazar** or watch local village crafts people.

Kishangarh
Enormous blocks of marble in raw, polished and sculpted forms line the road into Kishangarh, the former capital of a small princely state founded by Kishan Singh in 1603, with a fort facing Lake Gundalao. Local artists – known for their depiction of the Krishna legend and other Hindu themes – were given refuge here by the royal family during the reign of the Mughal emperor, Aurangzeb, who, turning his back on the liberal views of

earlier emperors, pursued an increasingly zealous Islamic purity. Under their patronage the artists reached a high standard of excellence and they continue the tradition of painting Kishangarh miniatures which are noted for sharp facial features and elongated almond-shaped eyes. Most of those available are cheap copies on old paper using water colours instead of the mineral pigments of the originals. The town has a bustling charm, and is an interesting place to wander around.

The fort palace stands on the shores of Lake Gundalao. Its **Hathi Pol** (Elephant Gate) has walls decorated with fine murals and, though partly in ruins, you can see battlements, courtyards with gardens, shady balconies, brass doors and windows with coloured panes of glass. The temple has a fine collection of miniatures.

Roopangarh

About 20 km from Kishangarh, Roopangarh was an important fort of the Kishangarh rulers founded in AD 1649 on the old caravan route along the Sambhar Lake. The fort stands above the village which is a centre for craft industries – leather embroidery, block printing, pottery and handloom weaving can all be seen. The Sunday market features at least 100 cobblers making and repairing *mojdi* footwear.

Ajmer → *For listings, see pages 185-190.*

The **Dargah of Khwaja Mu'inuddin Chishti** (1143-1235) is the tomb of the Sufi saint (also called 'The Sun of the Realm') which was begun by Iltutmish and completed by Humayun. Set in the heart of the old town, the main gate is reached on foot or by *tonga* or auto-rickshaw through the bazar. The Emperor Akbar first made a pilgrimage to the shrine to give thanks for conquering Chittor in 1567, and the second for the birth of his son Prince Salim. From 1570 to 1580 Akbar made almost annual pilgrimages to Ajmer on foot from Agra, and the *kos minars* (brick marking pillars at about two-mile intervals) along the road from Agra are witness of the popularity of the pilgrimage route. It is considered the second holiest site after Mecca. On their first visit, rich Muslims pay for a feast of rice, ghee, sugar, almonds, raisins and spices to be cooked in one of the huge pots in the courtyard inside the high gateway. These are still in regular use. On the right is the Akbar Masjid (circa 1570); to the left, an assembly hall for the poor. In the inner courtyard is the white marble Shah Jahan Masjid (circa 1650), 33 m long with 11 arches and a carved balustrade on three sides. In the inner court is the square *dargah* (tomb), also white marble, with a domed roof and two entrances. The ceiling is gold-embossed velvet, and silver rails and gates enclose the tomb. At festival times the tomb is packed with pilgrims, many coming from abroad, and the crush of people can be overpowering.

The whole complex has a unique atmosphere. The areas around the tomb have a real feeling of community; there is a hospital and a school on the grounds, as well as numerous shops. As you approach the tomb the feeling of religious fervour increases – as does the barrage of demands for 'donations' – often heightened by the music being played outside the tomb's ornate entrance. For many visitors, stepping into the tomb itself is the culmination of a lifetime's ambition, reflected in the ardour of their offerings.

Nearby is the **Mazar** (tomb) of Bibi Hafiz Jamal, daughter of the saint, a small enclosure with marble latticework. Close by is that of Chimni Begum, daughter of Shah Jahan. She never married, refusing to leave her father during the seven years he was held captive by Aurangzeb in Agra Fort. She spent her last days in Ajmer, as did another daughter who probably died of tuberculosis. At the south end of the Dargah is the **Jhalra** (tank).

The **Arhai-din-ka Jhonpra Mosque** ('Hut of Two and a Half Days') lies beyond the Dargah in a narrow valley. Originally a Jain college built in 1153, it was partially destroyed by Muhammad of Ghori in 1192, and in 1210 turned into a mosque by **Qutb-ud-din-Aibak** who built a massive screen of seven arches in front of the pillared halls, allegedly in 2½ days (hence its name). The temple pillars which were incorporated in the building are all different. The mosque measures 79 m by 17 m with 10 domes supported by 124 columns and incorporates Hindu and Jain masonry. Much of it is in ruins though restoration work was undertaken at the turn of the century; only part of the 67-m screen and the prayer hall remain.

Akbar's Palace, built in 1570 and restored in 1905, is in the city centre near the east wall. It is a large rectangular building with a fine gate. Today it houses the **Government Museum** ① *Sat-Thu 1000-1630, Rs 3, no photography*, which has a dimly presented collection of fine sculpture from sixth to 17th centuries, paintings and old Rajput and Mughal armour and coins.

The ornate **Nasiyan Jain Temple** (**Red Temple**) ① *Prithviraj Marg, 0800-1700, Rs 5*, has a remarkable museum alongside the Jain shrine, which itself is open only to Jains. It is well worth visiting. Ajmer has a large Jain population (about 25% of the city's total). The Shri Siddhkut Chaityalaya was founded in 1864 in honour of the first Jain Tirthankar, Rishabdeo, by a Jain diamond merchant, Raj Bahadur Seth Moolchand Nemichand Soni (hence its alternative name, the Soni temple). The opening was celebrated in 1895. Behind a wholly unimposing exterior, on its first floor the Svarna Nagari Hall houses an astonishing reconstruction of the Jain conception of the universe, with gold-plated replicas of every Jain shrine in India. Over 1000 kg of gold is estimated to have been used, and at one end of the gallery diamonds have been placed behind decorative coloured glass to give an appearance of backlighting. It took 20 people 30 years to build. The holy mountain, Sumeru, is at the centre of the continent, and around it are such holy sites as Ayodhya, the birthplace of the Tirthankar, recreated in gold plate, and a remarkable collection of model temples. Suspended from the ceiling are *vimanas* (airships of the gods) and silver balls. On the ground floor, beneath the model, are the various items taken on procession around the town on the Jain festival day of 23 November each year. The trustees of the temple are continuing to maintain and embellish it.

Excursions from Ajmer
Mayo College (1873), only 4 km from the centre, was founded to provide young Indian princes with a liberal education, one of two genuinely Indo-Saracenic buildings designed by De Fabeck in Ajmer, the other being the **Mayo Hospital** (1870). The college was known as the 'Eton of Rajputana' and was run along the lines of an English public school. Access is no longer restricted to Rajput princes.

Ana Sagar, an artificial lake (circa 1150), was further enhanced by emperors Jahangir and Shah Jahan who added the baradari and pavilions. The **Foy Sagar**, 5 km away, another artificial lake, was a famine relief project.

Taragarh (Star Fort), built by Ajaipal Chauhan in 1100 with massive 4.5-m-thick walls, stands on the hilltop overlooking the town. There are great views of the city but the walk up the winding bridle path is tiring. A road accessible by road has reduced the climb on foot and made access easier. Jeeps charge Rs 500 for the trip. Along the way is a graveyard of Muslim 'martyrs' who died storming the fort.

Pushkar → *For listings, see pages 185-190.*

Dozens of hotels, restaurants, cafés and shops cater to Western tastes and many travellers find it hard to drag themselves away from such creature comforts. The village's main bazar, though busy, has banned rickshaws so is relieved of revving engines and touting drivers. There are dozens of temples in Pushkar, most of which are open 0500-1200, 1600-2200.

Places in Pushkar

Pushkar Lake is one of India's most sacred lakes. It is believed to mark the spot where a lotus thrown by Brahma landed. Fa Hien, the Chinese traveller who visited Pushkar in the fifth century AD, commented on the number of pilgrims, and although several of the older temples were subsequently destroyed by Aurangzeb, many remain. Ghats lead down to the water to enable pilgrims to bathe, cows to drink, and the town's young folk to wash

Pushkar

Where to stay
Bharatpur Palace **13** *B1*
Colonel's Camp **10** *A1*
Dia **28** *C3*
Greenhouse Resort **1** *A1*
Inn Seventh Heaven
  & Sixth Sense **4** *B2*
Navratan Palace **3** *C1*
Paramount Palace **5** *B1*
Pushkar Palace **9** *C2*
Sai Baba Haveli **17** *B2*
Sarovar **12** *C2*
Shannu's Ranch &
  Horse Rides **27** *C3*
Shyam Krishna
  Guest House **22** *B2*
Sunset & Sunset Café **8** *C2*
U-turn Guest House **14** *B2*
White House **20** *B2*

Restaurants
Halwai Ki Gali **6** *B2*
Honey & Spice Café **7** *B2*
Karmima **1** *C1*
Little Italy Pizzeria **4** *C3*
Neem Tree Farm **2** *C2*

Ghat ≡

off after the riotous **Holi** celebrations. They also provide a hunting ground for Brahmin 'priests', who press a flower into the hand of any passing foreigner and offer – even demand – to perform *puja* (worship) in return for a sum of money. If this hard-sell version of spirituality appeals, agree your price in advance – Rs 50 should be quite sufficient – and be aware that a proportion of so-called priests are no such thing.

The **Brahma Temple** ① *0600-1330, 1500-2100 (changes seasonally)*, beyond the western end of the lake, is a particularly holy shrine and draws pilgrims throughout the year. Although it isn't the only Brahma temple in India, as people claim, it is the only major pilgrim place for followers of the Hindu God of Creation. It is said that when Brahma needed a marital partner for a ritual, and his consort Saraswati (Savitri) took a long time to come, he married a cow-girl, Gayatri, after giving her the powers of a goddess (Gayatri because she was purified by the mouth of a cow or *gau*). His wife learnt of this and put a curse on him – that he would only be worshipped in Pushkar.

There are 52 ghats around the lake, of which the Brahma Ghat, Gan Ghat and Varah Ghat are the most sacred. The medieval **Varah Temple** is dedicated to the boar incarnation of Vishnu. It is said the idol was broken by Emperor Jahangir as it resembled a pig. The **Mahadev Temple** is said to date from 12th century while the **Julelal Temple** is modern and jazzy. Interestingly enough the two wives of Brahma have hilltop temples on either side of the lake, with the Brahma temple in the valley.

A steep 3-km climb up the hill which leads to the **Savitri Temple** (dedicated to Brahma's first wife), offers excellent views of the town and surrounding desert. It's a magical place in the evening when groups of women promenade the bazars, the clashing colours of their saris all flowing together; while men dry their turbans in the evening sun after washing them in the lake, wafting the metres of flmy fabric in the breeze or draping it on nearby trees.

The **Main** (**Sadar**) **Bazar** is full of shops selling typical tourist, as well as pilgrim knick knacks and is usually very busy. At full moon, noisy religious celebrations last all night so you may need your ear plugs here.

Ajmer and Pushkar listings

For hotel and restaurant price codes and other relevant information, see pages 13-16.

◔ Where to stay

Jaipur to Ajmer *p181*
$$$$ Kuchaman Fort (Heritage Hotel), Kuchaman, T(0)9811-143684, www.heritage hotelsofindia.com. 35 distinctive a/c rooms in a part of the fort, attractively furnished, restaurant, bar, jacuzzi, gym, luxurious pools (including a 200-year-old cavernous one underground), camel/horse riding, royal hospitality, superb views and interesting tour around the largely unrestored fort.
$$$ Phool Mahal Old City, Kishangarh, T01463-247405, www.royalkishangarh.com. Superbly located at the base of Kishangarh Fort and perched on the banks of Gundalao Lake (dries up in summer), this 1870 garden palace has 21 well-maintained a/c rooms, as well as an elegant lounge and dining room, all with period furnishings and marble floors. Beautiful.

$$-$ Sambhar Lake Resorts, Sambhar Lake, www.heritagehotelsofindia.com. 6 cottage rooms by the salt lake, bath with hot showers, friendly staff, camel rides and jeep safaris across the saline marshes and dunes, also short rail journey on diesel locomotive-driven trolleys that carry salt from the pans to the towns. Price includes meals and safaris. Day visit (Rs 500) includes vegetarian lunch, tea and a tour of the salt marshes.

Ajmer *p182*

Prices rise sharply, as much as tenfold, during the week of the **mela**. Many hotels are booked well in advance. The tourist office has a list of Paying Guest accommodation.

$$-$ Haveli Heritage Inn, Kutchery Rd, T0145-262 1607. 12 good-sized, clean, comfortable rooms in a homely 125-year-old building, no hot water in cheaper rooms. Rooms are quite expensive for what you get. Family-run, good home cooking, located on a busy main road but set back with a pleasant courtyard, very charming owner.

$$-$ Hotel Embassy, Jaipur Rd, T0145-262 3859, www.hotelembassyajmer.com. 31 smart a/c rooms in a building newly renovated to 3-star standard. Enthusiastic, professional staff, elegant restaurant.

$ City View Guest House, 133/17 Nalla Bazar, T0145-263 0958. Very basic but charmingly run guesthouse in the warren of the Old City, Indian toilets, atmospheric building, friendly hosts.

$ Hotel Jannat, very close to Durgah, T0145-243 2494, www.ajmerhoteljannat.com. 36 clean, modern rooms in a great location, within the labyrinthine alleys of the Old City, friendly staff, a/c restaurant, all mod cons.

Pushkar *p184, map p184*

The town suffers from early-morning temple bells. During the fair, hotel charges can be 10 times the normal rate. Booking in advance is essential for the better places. Some budget hotels offer views of the lake from communal rooftops; however, local authorities periodically threaten to close down all commercial properties within 100 m of the lake, including hotels and restaurants. To escape the noise of the Main Bazar, choose one in a back street of Bari Basti or near Ajmer Bus Stand.

$$$$-$$$ Greenhouse Resort, Tilora village, 8 km from Pushkar, T0145-230 0079, www.thegreenhouseresort.com. This is a truly unique place with luxurious tents mixed with giant greenhouses growing roses and strawberries and lots of organic vegetables for the kitchen. With a nod to the environment, they are experimenting with water conservation, innovative irrigation and solar panels and the resort is staffed mainly with local people. The beds are stunning and there are all mod cons in the tents. This is a serene place, relaxing and inspiring. Recommended.

$$$$-$$$ Pushkar Palace, on lakeside, T0145-277 2001, www.hotelpushkar palace.com. 52 overpriced rooms including 25 suites overlooking the lake, in a beautifully renovated old palace, with attractive gardens. It looks good but is rather uncomfortable and lakeside rooms have very small windows. Alas, too the terrace restaurant is now closed, so the restaurant is in the courtyard with no lake view.

$$$ Pushkar Bagh Resort, Motisar Link Rd, Village Ghanehera, T(0)9414-030669, www.pushkarbaghresort.com. Out of town this is a heritage-style property with lots of charm. The rooms are decorated with lovely wooden furniture and there are nice communal sitting areas, themed dinners and gala nights.

$$$-$$ Dia, Panch Kund Rd, T0145-510 5455, www.inn-seventh-heaven.com/dia. Fantastic big rooms in a new chic building. Offering just 4 stylish a/c rooms and plenty of open spaces to curl up with a book or look out at Pushkar and the surrounding hills, this is in a quiet part of town away from the bustle. Highly recommended.

$$-$ Inn Seventh Heaven, next to Mali ka Mandir, T0145-510 5455, www.inn-seventh-heaven.com. Beautiful rooms spiral out from the inner courtyard in this fantastically well-restored 100-year-old *haveli*, plus a handful of ascetic but much cheaper rooms in neighbouring building. Lots of seating areas dotted throughout the 3-storey building, including some lovely swinging diwans. Very friendly, informal, excellent rooftop restaurant (baked potatoes from open coal fire in winter), the restaurant goes from strength to strength. Charming owner and a sociable atmosphere. Exceptionally good value. Whole-heartedly recommended.

$$-$ Navratan Palace, near Brahma temple, T0145-277 2145. Comfortable though not particularly attractive. 33 clean rooms, some a/c with hot showers (Rs 300-600), clean pool, small garden with views, well kept.
$$-$ Sarovar (RTDC), on lakeside, T0145-277 2040. 38 clean rooms (the best are in the old part with amazing lake views), some a/c with bath, new rooms good but no atmosphere, cheap 6-bed dorm, set around the courtyard in a former lakeside palace, attractive gardens.
$$-$ U-Turn, Lake Vahara Ghat Choti Basti, T(0)9928-737798, www.hoteluturn.com. A new chic little number right on the lake. The rooms are small due to the age of the building, but with bags of charm. Formerly the **Bhola Guest House**, the 2nd oldest guesthouse in Pushkar. Of the 6 beautifully decorated rooms, you can choose from the 'Princess Villa' or the 'Kama Sutra Villa'. The rooftop café is also a cut above, with nice fabrics and comfy chairs and serves up the usual global fare.
$ Bharatpur Palace, lakeside, T0145-277 2320. Exceptional views of the ghats, 1 very simple room practically hangs over the ghat, 18 unusually decorated rooms, clean bathrooms.
$ Paramount Palace, Bari Basti, T0145-277 2428, hotelparamountpalace@hotmail.com. 16 clean, basic rooms, some with bath, best with balcony, elevated site with splendid views from the rooftop, the highest in Pushkar. Very friendly host.
$ Sai Baba Haveli, near the market post office, T0145-510 5161, lola_singh_modiano@hotmail.com. Nice big rooms around a central courtyard, lots of greenery and hanging plants, lots of potential but needs a lick of paint.
$ Shannu's Ranch, Panch Kund Rd, T0145-277 2043. On the edge of town, with nice quirky, 'rustique' cottages in a garden, owned by a French-Canadian riding instructor, good for a longer stay but could get cold in winter.
$ Shyam Krishna Guest House, Chhoti Basti, T0145-277 2461. Part of a 200-year-old temple complex with 25 rooms around a courtyard, some with *jali* work on the upper floor, run by a friendly Brahmin family.
$ Sunset, on the lake, T0145-277 2382, hotelsunset@hotmail.com. 20 plain, clean rooms, 3 a/c, around a lovely garden, lots of flowers and papaya trees. Well located close to the lake, plus access to the **Sunset Café**.
$ White House, in a narrow alley near Marwar Bus Stand, T0145-277 2147, hotelwhitehouse@hotmail.com. Very clean, impressively white rooms in a well-maintained building overlooking the nursery gardens. Good views from the pleasant rooftop restaurant with excellent food, free and very tasty mango tea. Also nice cheaper rooms available at their sister guesthouse, **Kohinoor**. Recommended.

During the fair
It is best to visit early in the week when toilets are still reasonably clean.
Tourist village Erected by RTDC, this is a remarkable feat, accommodating 100,000 people. Conveniently placed with deluxe/super deluxe tents (Rs 6000-6500 with meals), ordinary/dorm tents (Rs 300 per bed), 30 'cottages', some deluxe (Rs 4000-5000). Beds and blankets, some running water, Indian toilets are standard. Meals are served in a separate tent (or eat cheap, delicious local food at the tribal tented villages near the show ground). Reservation with payment, essential (open 12 months ahead); contact **RTDC** in Jaipur, T0141-220 3531, www.rajasthantourism.gov.in.
Private camps Privately run camps charge about US$150-250 including meals for Regular and 'Swiss' double tent. They might be some distance from the fair ground and may lack security.
Colonel's Camp, Motisar Rd, Ghanera, T0141-220 2034, www.meghniwas.com. 120 deluxe tents with toilet and shower in attractive gardens.
Pushkar Palace (see Where to stay, page 186). Sets up 351 plush 'tent cottages', well equipped with bathroom, furniture, carpet and and heating.

Also check out tent accommodation set up by **Jodhana Heritage**, www.jodhana heritage.com; **Camp Bliss**, www.pushkar camelfair.com and **Royal Safari Camp**, www.royalsafaricamp.com. Many of these camps also set up during the Nagaur fair.

🍴 Restaurants

Ajmer *p182*

Son halwa, a local sweet speciality, is sold near the Dargah and at the market. Delicious street snacks can be found in the back lanes between Delhi and Agra gates.
$ Bhola, Agra Gate. Good vegetarian food, no nonsense service.
$ Jai Hind, in an alley by the clocktower, opposite railway station. Best for Indian vegetarian. Delicious, cheap meals.
$ Mango Masala, Sandar Patel Marg, T0145-242 2100. American diner-styled place with wide-ranging menu including pizzas, sizzlers, Indian and sundaes. The standard is high, portions are large and service is outstanding.

Pushkar *p184, map p184*

No meat, fish or eggs are served in this temple town, and alcohol is banned, as are 'narcotics' – in theory. Take special care during the fair: eat only freshly cooked food and drink bottled water. Long-stay budget travellers have resulted in an increase of Western and Israeli favourites like falafel, granola and apple pie.
$$-$ Little Italy Pizzeria, Panch Kund Rd. High-quality Italian dishes plus Israeli and Indian specialities, pleasant garden setting. They have opened another restaurant **La Pizzeria** near Varah Temple and **Shanti Palace**, Chhoti Basti.
$$-$ Sixth Sense, perched at the top of **Inn at Seventh Heaven** (see Where to stay, page 186). By far the most stylish dining experience in Pushkar. Serving up the usual Indian fare and beyond, with baked potatoes, pastas and fantastic home-baked desserts. Highly recommended.

$ Halwai Ki Gali (alley off Main Bazar). Sweet shops sell *malpura* (syrupy pancake), as well as other Rajasthani/Bengali sweets.
$ Honey and Spice, Laxmi Market. Only open during the day, this little café offers up great coffees like aniseed and cinnamon, renowned banana bread and steaming plates of brown rice and veggies. Daytime only.
$ Karmima, and other small places opposite Ashish-Manish Riding. Home-cooked *thalis* (Rs 15/20) and excellent fresh, orange/sweet lime juice.
$ Neem Tree Farm, outside Pushkar, T(0)7737-777903, www.neemtreefarm. weebly.com. This place specializes in permaculture, natural farming and solar architecture. You can head out during the day for a 'permaculture' picnic or have a dinner in the desert. Great experience.
$ Sunset Café by Pushkar Palace. Particularly atmospheric in the evening when crowds gather to listen to music and watch sunset, lacklustre food. Recommended for ambience.

🎉 Festivals

Ajmer *p182*

Urs Festival, commemorating Khwaja Mu'inuddin Chishti's death in 1235, is celebrated with 6 days of almost continuous music, and devotees from all over India and the Middle East make the pilgrimage. Qawwalis and other Urdu music developed in the courts of rulers can be heard. Roses cover the tomb. The festival starts on sighting the new moon in Rajab, the 7th month of the Islamic year. The peak is reached on the night between the 5th and 6th days when tends of thousands of pilgrims pack the shrine. At 1100 on the last morning, pilgrims and visitors are banned from the dargah, as the khadims, who are responsible through the year for the maintenance of worship at the shrine, dressed in their best clothes, approach the shrine with flowers and sweets. On the final

The pull of the cattle and camels

The huge **Mela** is Pushkar's biggest draw. Over 200,000 visitors and pilgrims and hordes of cattle and camels with their semi-nomadic tribal drivers, crowd into the town. Farmers, breeders and camel traders buy and sell. Sales in leather whips, shoes, embroidered animal covers soar while women bargain over clay pots, bangles, necklaces and printed cloth.

Events begin four to five days before the full moon in November. There are horse and camel races and betting is heavy. In the **Ladhu Umt** race teams of up to 10 men cling to camels, and one another, in a hilarious and often chaotic spectacle. The Tug-of-War between Rajasthanis and foreigners is usually won by the local favourites. There are also sideshows with jugglers, acrobats, magicians and folk dancers.

At nightfall there is music and dancing outside the tents, around friendly fires – an unforgettable experience despite its increasingly touristy nature, even including a laser show. The cattle trading itself actually takes place during the week before the fair; some travellers have reported arriving during the fair and there being no animals left, so come early. If you miss the fun of the Pushkar fair, there are other options, sometimes less touristy around the state. There is the **Chandrabhaga Fair** in Jhalawar, south of Bundi which is a more authentic fair (also in November). Bikaner has a stunning camel fair (December/January) and in Nagaur they have a cattle and camel fair that draws the crowds with camel races, cock fights and folk dancing (January/February).

day, women wash the tomb with their hair, then squeeze the rose water into bottles as medicine for the sick.

Pushkar *p184, map p184*
Oct/Nov Kartik Purnima is marked by a vast cattle and camel fair (30 Oct 6 Nov 2014, 18-25 Nov 2015), see box, above Pilgrims bathe in the lake – the night of the full moon being the most auspicious time – and float 'boats' of marigold and rose petals in the moonlight. Camel traders often arrive a few days early to engage in the serious business of buying and selling and most of the animals disappear before the official starting date. Arrive 3 days ahead if you don't want to miss this part of the fair. The all-night drumming and singing in the Mela Ground can get tiring, but the fair is a unique spectacle. Travellers warn of pickpockets.

O Shopping

Ajmer *p182*
Fine local silver jewellery, tie-dye textiles and camel hide articles are best buys. The shopping areas are Madar Gate, Station Rd, Purani Mandi, Naya Bazar and Kaisarganj. Some alleys in the old town have good shopping.

Pushkar *p184, map p184*
There is plenty to attract the Western eye; check quality and bargain hard. Miniatures on silk and old paper are everywhere. Cheap clothes, baba pants and bags are ubiquitous: **Manu Maloo Antiques and Collectibles**, Badi Basti (sweet street) take the street opposite Gau Ghat past the array of bubbling sweet stalls and you will discover a little hole-in-the-wall shop with a great range of framed pictures and all manner of wooden and bronze objets. Bargain hard, they are interesting but not hugely valuable.

Essar, shop 6, Sadar Bazar, opposite Narad Kunj. Excellent tailoring (jacket Rs 250-300 including fabric).

Galaxy, main bazaar near Varah Ghat – their card says they deal in books, fireworks and ice which is a strange combination. Certainly they have a great selection of books, from my trashy novels to all things yogic.

⊕ What to do

Pushkar *p184, map p184*
Horse and camel safaris
Hiring a horse costs Rs 1500 per day, camels around Rs 400 per day, at most hotels and near the Brahma temple. Ashish-Manish, opposite Brahma Temple, T0145-277 2584, or **Shannu's Riding School**, owned by a French Canadian, Panch Kund Rd, T0145-277 2043. For lessons, Rs 150 per hr (minimum 10 hrs over 5 days).

Body and Soul
Pushkar Yoga Garden, Vamdev Rd, near Gurudwara, www.pushkaryoga.org. Regular hatha classes with Yogesh Yogi and also longer courses.
Shakti School of Dance, Old Rangi Temple Complex, near Honey and Spice, www. colleenashakti.com. You can learn traditional Odissi style dance, tribal fusion belly dance and local Khalbelia Rajasthani gypsy dance.

Swimming
Sarovar Oasis, Navratan hotels, non-residents pay Rs 40-50.

Tour operators
Ekta Travels, opposite Marwar Bus Stand, T0145-277 2131, www.ekta travelspushkar.com. Tours, excellent service, good buses, reliable.

⊖ Transport

Jaipur to Ajmer *p181*
Train and jeep For **Sambhar Lake** take the train to **Phulera**, 7 km from Sambhar

village, 9 km from the lake. Jeeps charge Rs 50 for the transfer.

Kishangarh is an important railway junction between Jaipur and Ajmer, with regular trains from both places.

Ajmer *p182*
Bus The State Bus Stand is 2 km east of centre, enquiries T0145-242 9398. Buses to **Agra**, 9 hrs; **Delhi**, 9 hrs; **Jaipur**, 2½ hrs; **Jodhpur**, 5 hrs; **Bikaner**, 7 hrs; **Chittaurgarh**, 5 hrs; **Udaipur**, 7 hrs via Chittaurgarh; **Kota** via Bundi; **Pushkar**, 45 mins, frequent. Private buses for **Pushkar** leave from near the Jain Temple.
Train Ajmer Station is seemingly overrun with rats and is not a great place to wait for a night train. Taxis outside the station charge Rs 200-250 to **Pushkar**. Reservations, T0145-243 2535, 0830-1330, 1400-1630, enquiries, T131/132. **Delhi** via **Jaipur**: *Shatabdi Exp 12016*, 1545, 7 hrs.

Pushkar *p184, map p184*
Bicycle/car/motorbike hire Rs 10 entry 'tax' per vehicle. **Michael Cycle SL Cycles**, Ajmer Bus Stand Rd, very helpful, Rs 30 per day; also from the market. **Hotel Oasis** has Vespa scooters, Rs 300 per day. **Enfield Ashram**, near Hotel Oasis, Rs 400 per day for an Enfield.
Bus Frequent service to/from **Ajmer**, Rs 10. Long-distance buses are more frequent from Ajmer, and tickets bought in Pushkar may involve a change. Direct buses to **Jaipur**, **Jodhpur** via Merta (8 hrs), **Bikaner**, and **Haridwar**. Sleeper bus to **Delhi**, Rs 250, 1930 (11 hrs); **Agra**, Rs 250, 1930 (11 hrs); **Jaisalmer**, Rs 450, 2200 (11 hrs); **Udaipur**, Rs 250, 2200 (8 hrs) and 2300 (8 hrs). Many agents in Pushkar have times displayed. Pushkar Travels, T0145-277 2437, reliable for bookings.

⊕ Directory

Pushkar *p184, map p184*
Medical services Shyama Hospital, Heloj Rd, T0145-277 2029. **Post** GPO with helpful postmaster.

Bikaner and around

Bikaner is something of a dusty oasis town among the scrub and sand dunes of northwest Rajasthan. Its rocky outcrops in a barren landscape provide a dramatic setting for the Junagarh Fort, one of the finest in western Rajasthan. The old walled city retains a medieval air, and is home to over 300 *havelis*, while outside the walls some stunning palaces survive. Well off the usual tourist trail, Bikaner is en route to Jaisalmer from Jaipur or Shekhawati, and is well worth a visit.

Arriving in Bikaner

Getting there Bikaner is a full day's drive from Jaipur so it may be worth stopping a night in Samode or the Shekhawati region (see pages 101 and 198). The railway station is central and has services from Delhi (Sarai Rohilla), Jaipur and Jodhpur. The New Bus Stand is 3 km to the north, so if arriving from the south you can ask to be dropped in town. There are regular bus services to Desnok, but to get to Gajner, Kakoo or Tal Chappar you'll need to hire private transport. ▸▸ *See Transport, page 197.*

Getting around The fort and the Old City are within easy walking distance from the station. Auto- and cycle-rickshaws transfer passengers between the station and the New Bus Stand. Taxis can be difficult to get from the Lalgarh Palace area at night.

Tourist information Dhola-Maru Tourist Bungalow ⓘ *Poonam Singh Circle, T0151-252 9621, Oct-Mar 0800-1800.* As well as information, car hire is available.

Bikaner → *For listings, see pages 195-197.*

Junagarh Fort

ⓘ *1000-1630 (last entry), Rs 100 foreigners, Rs 10 Indians; camera Rs 30, video Rs 100 (limited permission), guided tours in Hindi and English, private guides near the gate offer better 'in-depth' tours; Rs 100 for 4 people, 2 hrs.*

This is one of the finest examples in Rajasthan of the paradox between medieval military architecture and beautiful interior decoration. Started in 1588 by Raja Rai Singh (1571-1611), a strong ally of the Mughal Empire, who led Akbar's army in numerous battles, it had palaces added for the next three centuries.

You enter the superbly preserved fort by the yellow sandstone **Suraj Prole** (Sun Gate, 1593) to the east. The pale red sandstone perimeter wall is surrounded by a moat (the lake no longer exists) while the chowks have beautifully designed palaces with balconies, kiosks and fine *jali* screens. The interiors are beautifully decorated with shell-work, lime plaster, mirror-and-glass inlays, gold leaf, carving, carpets and lacquer work. The ramparts offer good views of the elephant and horse stables and temples, the old city with the desert beyond, and the relatively more recent city areas around the medieval walls. The walls of the **Lal Niwas**, which are the oldest, are elaborately decorated in red and gold. Karan Singh commemorated a victory over Aurangzeb by building the **Karan Mahal** (1631-1639) across the chowk.

Successive rulers added the **Gaj Mandir** (1745-1787) with its mirrored Shish Mahal, and the **Chattra Niwas** (1872-1887) with its pitched roof and English 'field sport' plates decorating the walls. The magnificent **Coronation Hall**, adorned with plaster work, lacquer, mirror and glass, is in Maharaja Surat Singh's **Anup Mahal** (1788-1828). The decorative façades around the Anup Mahal Chowk, though painted white, are in fact of stone. The fort also includes the **Chetar Mahal** and **Chini Burj** of Dungar Singh (1872-1887) and **Ganga Niwas** of Ganga Singh (1898-1943), who did much to modernize his state and also built the Lalgarh Palace to the north. Mirror work, carving and marble decorate the ornate **Chandra Mahal** (Moon Palace) and the **Phul Mahal** (Flower Palace), built by Maharaja Gaj Singh. These last two, the best rooms, are shown to foreigners at the end as a 'special tour' when the guide expects an extra tip. The royal chamber in the Chandra Mahal has strategically placed mirrors so that any intruder entering could be seen by the maharaja from his bed. The fort **museum** has Sanskrit and Persian manuscripts, miniature paintings, jewels, enamelware, silver,

Bikaner

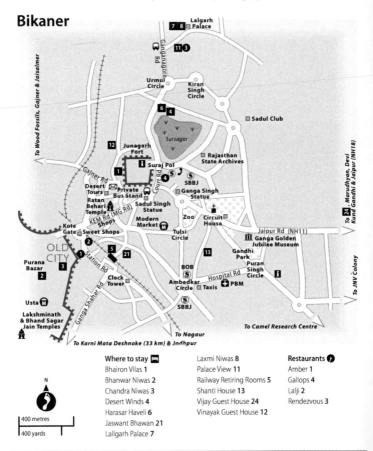

Where to stay 🛏		Restaurants 🍴
Bhairon Vilas **1**	Laxmi Niwas **8**	Amber **1**
Bhanwar Niwas **2**	Palace View **11**	Gallops **4**
Chandra Niwas **3**	Railway Retiring Rooms **5**	Lalji **2**
Desert Winds **4**	Shanti House **13**	Rendezvous **3**
Harasar Haveli **6**	Vijay Guest House **24**	
Jaswant Bhawan **21**	Vinayak Guest House **12**	
Lallgarh Palace **7**		

weapons, palanquins, howdahs and war drums. **Har Mandir**, the royal temple where birth and wedding ceremonies were celebrated, is still used for Gangaur and other festivities. The well nearby is reputedly over 130 m deep. **Prachina Museum** ① *1000-1700, foreigners Rs 50 (guided tour), Indians Rs10, camera Rs 20, small clean café outside is open-air but shady*, in the grounds, exhibits beautifully crafted costumes, carpets and ornamental objects.

Lalgarh Palace
① *Palace Thu-Tue, museum Mon-Sat 1000-1700, Rs 40 (museum extra Rs 20).*
The red sandstone palace stands in huge grounds to the north of the city, surrounded by rocks and sand dunes. Designed by Sir Swinton Jacob in 1902, the palace complex, with extensions over the next few decades, has attractive courtyards overlooked by intricate *zenana* screen windows and *jarokha* balconies, columned corridors and period furnishings. The banquet hall is full of hunting trophies and photographs. His Highness Doctor Karni Singh of Bikaner was well known for his shooting expertise – both with a camera and with a gun. The bougainvillea, parakeets and peacocks add to the attraction of the gardens in which the Bikaner State Railway Carriage is preserved. The Lalgarh complex has several hotels (see Where to stay, page 195).

Rampuria Street and the Purana Bazar
There are some exquisite *havelis* in Bikaner belonging to the Rampuria, Kothari, Vaid and Daga merchant families. The sandstone carvings combine traditional Rajasthani *haveli* architecture with colonial influence. Around Rampuria Street and the Purana Bazar you can wander through lanes lined with fine façades. Among them is **Bhanwar Niwas** which has been converted into a heritage hotel.

Ganga Golden Jubilee Museum
① *Public Park, 1000-1630, Rs 3.*
This museum has a fine small collection of pottery, massive paintings, stuffed tigers, carpets, costumes and weapons. There are also some excellent examples of Bikaner miniature paintings which are specially prized because of their very fine quality.

Around Bikaner → *For listings, see pages 195-197.*

Bhand Sagar
① *Free but caretakers may charge Rs 10 for cameras.*
Some 5 km southwest of Bikaner, Bhand Sagar has a group of Hindu and Jain temples which are believed to be the oldest extant structures of Bikaner, dating from the days when it was just a desert trading outpost of Jodhpur. The white-painted sandstone **Bandeshwar Temple** with a towering *shikhara* roof and painted sculptures, murals and mirrorwork inside, is the most interesting. The **Sandeshwar Temple**, dedicated to Neminath, has gold-leaf painting, *meenakari* work and marble sculptures. They are hard to find and difficult to approach by car but rickshaw wallahs know the way. There are numerous steps but wonderful views.

Camel Research Centre
① *10 km from Bikaner in Jorbeer, 1500-1730, foreigners Rs 50, Indians Rs 5, camera Rs 20.*
This 800-ha facility is dedicated to scientific research into various aspects of the camel, with the aim of producing disease-resistant animals that can walk further and carry more while consuming less water. As well as genetically increasing the camel's tolerances, researchers

are investigating the nutritional benefits of drinking camel milk; camel ice cream is for sale if you want to test for yourself, and coming soon are camel milk moisturizers. It's particularly worth being here between 1530 and 1600, when the camels return to the centre for the evening: the spectacle of 100 or more camels ambling out of the desert towards you is quite unforgettable.

Gajner National Park

Now part of a palace hotel, this park, 30 km west of Bikaner, used to be a private preserve which provided the royal family of Bikaner with game. It is a birder's paradise surrounded by 13,000 ha of scrub forest which also harbours large colonies of nilgai, chinkara, blackbuck, wild boar and desert reptiles. Throughout the day, a train of antelope, gazelle and pigs can be seen arriving to drink at the lake. Winter migratory birds include the Imperial black-bellied sand grouse, cranes and migratory ducks. Some visitors have spotted great Indian bustard at the water's edge. It is worth stopping for an hour's mini-safari if you are in the vicinity.

Kolayat

Some 50 km southwest via Gajner Road, Kolayat is regarded as one of the 58 most important Hindu pilgrimage centres. It is situated around a sacred lake with 52 ghats and a group of five temples built by Ganga Singhji (none of which is architecturally significant). The oasis village comes alive at the November full moon when a three-day festival draws thousands of pilgrims who take part in ritual bathing.

Karni Mata Mandir

① Closed 1200-1600, free, camera Rs 40.

This 17th-century temple, 33 km south of Bikaner at Deshnoke, has massive silver gates and beautiful white marble carvings on the façade. These were added by Ganga Singh (1898-1943) who dedicated the temple to a 15th-century female mystic Karniji, worshipped as an incarnation of Durga. A gallery describes her life. Mice and rats, revered and fed with sweets and milk in the belief that they are reincarnated saints, swarm over the temple around your feet; spotting the white rat is supposed to bring good luck. Take socks as the floor is dirty, but note that the rats are far less widespread than they are made out to be. Sensationalized accounts give the impression of a sea of rats through which the visitor is obliged to walk barefoot, whereas in reality, while there are a good number of rats, they generally scurry around the outskirts of the temple courtyard – you're very unlikely to tread on one. The temple itself is beautiful, and would be well worth visiting even without the novelty of the rats.

Kakoo

This picturesque village, 75 km south of Bikaner, with attractive huts and surrounded by sand dunes, is the starting point for desert camel safaris costing Rs 1500 per day with tented facilities. Staying here makes a fantastic introduction to the practicalities of life in the desert; this is probably the most authentic desert settlement in this area that can be easily reached by road. Good trips to Kakoo are organized by Mr Bhagwan Singh T(0)9829-218237, www.kakusafari.com. You can travel to Kakoo by bus changing at Nokhamandi (62 km) from Bikaner.

Kalibangan and Harappan sites

One of North India's most important early settlement regions stretches from the Shimla hills down past the important Harappan sites of **Hanumangarh** and **Kalibangan**, north of Bikaner. Late Harappan sites have been explored by archaeologists, notably A Ghosh, since 1962. They were identified in the upper part of the valley, the easternmost region of the Indus Valley civilization. Across the border in Pakistan are the premier sites of Harappa (200 km) and Moenjo Daro (450 km). Here, the most impressive of the sites today is that of Kalibangan (west off the NH15 at Suratgarh). On the south bank of the Ghaggar River it was a heavily fortified citadel mound, rising about 10 m above the level of the plain. There were several pre-Harappan phases. Allchin and Allchin record that the bricks of the early phase were already standardized, though not to the same size as later Harappan bricks. The ramparts were made of mud brick and a range of pottery and ornaments have been found. The early pottery is especially interesting, predominantly red or pink with black painting.

Bikaner and around listings

For hotel and restaurant price codes and other relevant information, see pages 13-16.

⬤ Sleeping

Bikaner *p191, map p192*
Budget hotel rooms usually have a shared bath and often serve Indian vegetarian food only. The tourist office has a list of Paying Guest hotels.

$$$$ Laxmi Niwas, Lalgarh Palace Complex, T0151-2252 1188, www.laxmi niwaspalace.com. 60 large rooms and suites which once formed Maharaja Ganga Singh's personal residence, with fabulous carvings and beautifully painted ceilings, all arranged around the stunningly ornate courtyard. Superb bar, restaurant and lounge, discreet but attentive service, absolutely one-off. Recommended. You can also pay Rs 100 to have a tour if you are not staying here.

$$$$-$$$ Bhanwar Niwas, Rampuria St, Old City (500 m from Kote Gate), ask for Rampuria Haveli, T0151-252 9323, www. bhanwarniwas.com. 26 beautifully decorated rooms (all different) around a fantastic courtyard in an exquisite early 20th-century *haveli*. Original decor has been painstakingly restored to stunning effect, takes you back to another era, great service. Recommended.

$$$$-$$$ Lallgarh Palace, 3 km from the railway, T0151-254 0201, www.lallgarh palace.com. Large a/c rooms in beautiful and authentic surroundings, after some much needed renovation the indoor pool is beautiful, there's an atmospheric dining

hall, but mixed reports on food and service unfortunately. Run by the royal family.

$$ Bhairon Vilas, near fort, T0151-254 4751, www.hotelbhaironvilas.com. Restored 1800s aristocratic *haveli*, great atmosphere, 18 eclectic rooms decorated with flair – you can spend hours simply exploring the antiquities in your own room, huge amount of character, lovely indoor restaurant, and great great views across the city and fort from top rooms and rooftop. There's also an atmospheric bar and funky boutique shop. This place sums up the whole Rajasthan experience. Kitsch chic, whole-heartedly recommended.

$$-$ Desert Winds, opposite Karni Stadium, next to Harasar Haveli, T0151-254 2202. www. hoteldesertwinds.in. 22 clean, comfortable rooms with TV, newly renovated, good food, pleasant balcony and garden, friendly family. Run by knowledgable ex-tourist officer.

$$-$ Harasar Haveli, opposite Karni Singh Stadium, T0151-220 9891, www. harasar.com. Notorious for paying hefty commissions to rickshaw drivers; often full when others are empty. Otherwise it's a friendly place, ornate building with nicely decorated rooms, some with verandas and good views, TVs, dining room with period memorabilia, plus great atmospheric rooftop restaurant – you might end up dancing.

$$-$ Palace View, near Lalgarh Palace, T(0)9352-075007. 15 clean, comfortable rooms (all a/c), good views of the palace and gardens, food to order, small garden, courteous, hospitable family.

$ Chander Niwas, near Collector Residence, Kothi No 36, Civil Lines, T0151-220 0796, chandraniwas@yahoo.in. Small place with nice decoration, some rooms with a/c, big roof space, home-cooked food and Wi-Fi.

$ Jaswant Bhawan, Alakh Sagar Rd, near railway station, T0151-2548848, www.hoteljaswantbhawan.com.15 rooms in a charming old building, quiet location, excellent homecooking, lawn, good value. Very popular. Recommended.

$ Shanti House, New Well (City Kotwali), behind Jain Paathshala, T0151-254 3306, inoldcity@yahoo.com. One of the few places you can stay in the old city. It's a new building though, basic and clean with 4 rooms (5 with a/c) and a dorm. They offer tours of the old city and free cookery lessons. Great value and great location.

$ Vijay Guest House, opposite Sophia School, Jaipur Rd, T0151-223 1244, www.camelman.com. 6 clean rooms with attached bathrooms, plus 2 with shared bath. Slightly distant location compensated for by free use of bicycles or scooter, free pick-ups from bus/train, Rs 5 in shared rickshaw to town. Delicious home-cooked meals, pleasant garden, quiet, very hospitable (free tea and rum plus evening parties on the lawn), knowledgeable host, great value. Good camel safaris. Recommended.

$ Vinayak Guest House, near Junagarh Fort, Hanuman Temple, Old Ginani, T0151-220 2634, www.vinayakdesertsafari.com. Friendly homestay run by the manager of URMUL shop and his wildlife expert son who cannot do enough for you, excellent home cooking and cooking lessons, also runs camel safaris, photography classes, village and wildlife tours. Highly recommended.

Around Bikaner p193

$$$ Gajner Palace, Gajner National Park, T01534-275061, www.hrhindia.com. 44 a/c rooms in the elegant palace and its wings, set by a beautiful lake. Rooms in the main building are full of character (Edwardian Raj nostalgia), those in the

wings are well maintained but very middle England. Sumptuous lounge bar and restaurant overlooking the lake, magnificent gardens, boating, good walking, pleasantly unfrequented and atmospheric, friendly manager and staff, no pool. Visitors are welcome 0800-1730, Rs 100.

$ Dr Karni Singh's Rest House, adjoining the home of his forefathers, Kakoo, T01532-253006. Resthouse with 6 simple rooms and 4 rustic huts with attached baths, hot water in buckets, a great experience. Good camel safaris arranged, with the advantage of getting straight in to the desert rather than having to get out of town first as in Jaisalmer/Bikaner.

❶ Restaurants

Bikaner *p191, map p192*
You can dine in style at several of the hotels. Try the local specialities of *Bikaneri bhujia/sev/namkeen* – savoury snacks made from dough. Purana Bazar sells ice-cold *lassis* by day, hot milk, sugar and cream at night.

$$ Amber, Station Rd. Indian, some Western dishes. Popular, vegetarian *thali* is exceptional but some reports of falling standards.

$$ Bhanwar Niwas (see Where to stay, page 195). Amazingly ornate dining hall, good way of having a look around.

$$ Gallops, Court Rd. Excellent views of the fort, but overpriced and disappointing food but good for a rest after exploring the fort.

$$ Rendezvous, close to Palace View Lalgarh Palace Complex. With traditional artwork and Rajasthani decor, this is an atmospheric place serving up a good range of Rajasthani dishes as well as a few other tastes from around the globe. Recommended.

$ Lalji, Station Rd near Evergreen. Popular local joint serving good dosas and sweets.

❂ Festivals

Bikaner *p191, map p192*
Both the following are especially spectacular in Junagarh Fort in the Old City near Kote Gate and some smaller palaces.

Oct/Nov Diwali.
Dec/Jan Camel Fair (15-16 Jan 2014, 4-5 Jan 2015).

Around Bikaner *p193*
Oct/Nov In Kolayat, the Cattle and Camel Fair (6 Nov 2014, 25 Nov 2015 – Kartik Purnima) is very colourful and authentic but it can get quite riotous after dark. Since facilities are minimal, it is best to arrive before the festival to find a local family with space to spare, or ask a travel agent in Bikaner.

☉ What to do

Bikaner *p191, map p192*
Camel safaris must be arranged through private operators. Budget tours (Rs 500-600 per day) for groups of 4 or more; bring water.
Aravalli Tours, opposite Municipal Council Hall, Junagarh Rd, T0151-220 1124. Rs 1800 per person (toilet tent shared between 10 people) for an upmarket experience. Other tours too.
Camel Man, Vijay Guest House, Jaipur Rd, T0151-223 1244, www.camelman.com. Good value, reliable, friendly and professional safaris, jeep tours, cycling. Lightweight 'igloo' tents, clean mattresses, sheets, good food and guidance. Safaris to see antelopes, colourful villages and potters at work, from 1- to 2-hr rides to 5-day trips; Rs 800-1000 per person per day. Deservedly popular.
Vinayak Desert Safari, T(0)9414-430948, www.vinayakdesertsafari.com. Eco-friendly camel trekking with Jitu Solanki who has a Masters degree in wildlife and specializes in the study of reptiles. Camel, jeep and wildlife safaris and village homestays on offer. Highly informed and friendly guide.

⊖ Transport

Bikaner *p191, map p192*
Bus The New Bus Stand is 3 km north of town. Private buses leave from south of the

fort. Rajasthan Roadways, enquiries, T0151-252 3800; daily deluxe buses to **Ajmer**, **Jodhpur**, **Jaisalmer** (8 hrs), **Udaipur**. 2 daily to **Delhi** via Hissar (12 hrs).
Rickshaw/taxi Autos between station and bus stand or Lalgarh Palace, Rs 25. Taxis are unmetered. Shared *tempos* run on set routes, Rs 5.
Train Enquiries, T0151-220 0131, reservations, Mon-Sat 0800-1400, 1415-2000, Sun 0800-1400. For tourist quota (when trains are full) apply to Manager's Office by Radio Tower near Jaswant Bhawan Hotel. **Delhi**: *Dee Intercity 22471*, 0915, 8 hrs arrives DSR; *Bkn Dee S F Exp 12458*, 2220, 8 hrs. **Jaisalmer**: *Bkn Jsm Express 14702*, 2235, 6 hrs.

Around Bikaner *p193*
Bus For **Karni Mata Mandir**, buses leave from Bikaner New Bus Stand, or on Ganga Shahar Rd and at Ambedkar Circle. Taxis charge around Rs 300 return. For **Kalibangan** catch a bus to **Suratgarh** then change; this junction town also has connections to Hanumangarh, Sirsa (Haryana) or Mandi Dabwali (Punjab).
Train The broad-gauge train line from Suratgarh to **Anupgarh**, about 15 km from the Pakistan border, calls at Raghunathgarh, the closest station to Kalibangan; travel from there to Kalibangan is difficult (check at Suratgarh). Trains from Suratgarh:
Anupgarh: *Passenger 10755*, 2¼ hrs.
Bikaner (Lalgarh Junction): *Chandigarh Exp 14887*, 0835, 3¼ hrs. **Bhatinda**: *Chandigarh Exp 14888*, 1955, 3¼ hrs.

❶ Directory

Bikaner *p191, map p192*
Medical services PBM Hospital, Hospital Rd, T0151-252 5312. **Post** GPO: behind Junagarh Fort. **Useful contacts** Police: T100/T0151-252 2225.

Shekhawati

Covering an area of about 300 sq km on the often arid and rock-studded plains to the northwest of the Aravalli mountain range, Shekhawati is the homeland of the Marwari community. The area is particularly rich in painted *havelis*; Sikar district in the southwest and Jhunjhunun in the northeast form an 'open-air art gallery' of paintings dating from the mid-19th century. Although a day trip gives you an idea of its treasures, it is better to spend two or three nights in Shekhawati to see the temples, frescoed forts, *chhatris* and step wells at leisure. Other attractions include horse or camel safaris and treks into the hills. Shekhawati sees far fewer visitors than the better-known areas of Rajasthan, and as such retains something of a 'one pen/rupee' attitude to tourists. This is generally quite innocent and should not be a deterrent to potential visitors.

Ramgarh has the highest concentration of painted *havelis*, though they are not as well maintained as those of Nawalgarh which has the second largest selection. It is easier to visit *havelis* in towns that have hotels, such as Nawalgarh, Mandawa, Dundlod, Mukundgarh, Mahansar, Fatehpur, Baggar and Jhunjunun, and where the caretakers are used to visitors, though towns like Bissau, Alsisar, Malsisar and Churu have attractive *havelis* as well.

Arriving in Shekhawati
Getting there You can get to the principal Shekhawati towns by train but road access is easier. A car comes in handy, though there are crowded buses from Delhi, Jaipur and Bikaner to some towns. Buses leave every 30 minutes from 0500-2000 from Jaipur's Main Bus Station and take three hours. ▶ *See Transport, page 204.*

Getting around You can get from one Shekhawati town to another by local bus, which run every 15 to 20 minutes. Within each town it is best to enlist the help of a local person (possibly from the hotels listed below) to direct you to the best *havelis*, as it can be very difficult to find your way around.

The *havelis* are often occupied by the family or retainers who will happily show you around, either for free or for a fee of about Rs 20. Many *havelis* are in a poor state of repair with fading paintings which may appear monotonously alike to some.

Tourist information RTDC ⓘ *Mandawa Circle, Jhunjhunun, T01592-232909.* Recommended reading includes *The painted towns of Shekhawati,* by Ilay Cooper, a great Shekhawati enthusiast, with photos and maps.

Background

The 'Garden of Shekha' was named after Rao Shekhaji of Amarsar (1433-1488) who challenged the Kachhawahas, refusing to pay tribute to the rulers at Amber. These Rajput barons made inroads into Muslim territory even during Mughal rule, and declared Shekhawati independent from the Jaipur suzerainty until 1738. During this period the merchants lavishly decorated their houses with paintings on religious, folk and historical themes. As Mughal power collapsed Shekhawati became a region of lawless banditry. In the early 19th century the British East India Company brought it under their control, bringing peace but also imposing taxes and tolls on trade which the Marwaris resented. Many of the merchants migrated to other parts of the country to seek their fortune and those who flourished returned their wealth to their homeland and took over as patrons of the arts.

Sikar District → *For listings, see pages 202-204.*

Sikar

The late 17th-century fort was built when Sikar was an important trading centre and the wealthiest *thikana* (feudatory) under Jaipur. It now has a population of 148,000. You can visit the old quarter and see the Wedgwood blue 'Biyani' (1920) and 'Mahal' (1845), Murarka and Somani *havelis* and murals and carvings in Gopinath, Raghunath and Madan Mohan temples. From Jaipur take the NH11 to Ringas (63 km) and Sikar (48 km).

Pachar

This is a little town west of Jaipur in the middle of the sand dunes with a golden sandstone castle scenically situated on a lakeshore. A road north from Bagru on the NH8 also gives access.

Ramgarh

Ramgarh was settled by the Poddars in the late 18th century. In addition to their many *havelis* and that of the Ruias, visit the *chhatris* with painted entrances near the bus stand, as well as the temples to Shani (with mirror decoration) and to Ganga. Ramgarh has the highest concentration of painted *havelis*, though they are not as well maintained as those of Nawalgarh which has the second largest assemblage. The town has a pleasantly laid-back feel. Look for handicrafts here.

Fatehpur

Fatehpur has a whole array of *havelis*, many are rather dishevelled. Fatehpur is worth a visit simply for the **Nadine Le Prince Haveli Cultural Centre** ⓘ *near Chauhan Well, T0157-123 1479, www.cultural-centre.com.* Following a visit to the area, Nadine Le Prince took it upon herself to safeguard the cultural heritage of Fatehpur and the restoration of this *haveli* is exceptional. The frescoes here are exquisite and have served as an inspiration to Nadine's own artwork. As well as the restored *haveli*, there is a fine art gallery, sculpture garden and tribal art gallery and she hopes to create an artistic exchange between local and international artists. Although there are a couple of lacklustre accommodation options in Fatehpur, it would be better to visit from Mandawa.

Jhunjhunun

A stronghold of the Kayamkhani Nawabs, Jhunjhunun was defeated by the Hindu Sardul Singh in 1730. The Mohanlal **Iswardas Modi** (1896), **Tibriwala** (1883) and the Muslim **Nuruddin Farooqi Haveli** (which is devoid of figures) and the *maqbara* are all worth seeing. The Chhe Haveli complex, Khetri Mahal (1760) and the Biharilal temple (1776), which has attractive frescoes (closed during lunch time), are also interesting. The **Rani Sati** temple commemorates Narayana Devi who is believed to have become a *sati*; her stone is venerated by many of the wealthy *bania* community and an annual Marwari fair is held (protesting women's groups feel it glorifies the practice of *sati*). Since 1947, 29 cases of *sati* have been recorded in Jhunjhunun and its two neighbouring districts. Jhunjhunun is the most bustling town in Shekhawati and serves as the district's headquarters – it is preferable to stay in Nawalgarh or Mandawa.

Nawalgarh

Some 25 km southeast of Mandawa, Nawalgarh was founded in 1737 by Thakur Nawal Singh. There are numerous fine *havelis* worth visiting here. The town has a colourful bazar – though lone tourists have been harassed here – and two forts (circa 1730). **Nawalgarh Fort** has fine examples of maps and plans of Shekhawati and Jaipur. The **Bala Kila**, which has a kiosk with beautiful ceiling paintings, is approached via the fruit market in the town centre and entered through the **Hotel Radha**. It also has the **Roop Niwas Palace** (now a hotel) and some 18th-century temples with 19th- and early 20th-century paintings. There are other interesting temples in town including Ganga Mai near Nansa Gate.

The **Anandilal Poddar Haveli**, now converted to the **Poddar Haveli Museum** ⓘ *foreigners Rs 100, includes camera and guide*, is perhaps the best restored *haveli* of Shekhawati. The 1920s *haveli* has around 700 frescoes including a Gangaur procession, scenes from the Mahabharata, trains, cars, the avatars of Vishnu, bathing scenes and British characters. Exceptionally well restored throughout, some of the best paintings frame the doors leading from the courtyard to the rooms. The upper storey of the *haveli* is now a school but the ground floor has been opened as a museum. The photo gallery records the life of congressman and freedom fighter Anandilal Poddar, and the merchant-turned-industrialist Poddar family. There is a diorama of costumes of various Rajasthani tribes and communities, special bridal attires and a gallery of musical instruments.

Other remarkable Murarka *havelis* include the 19th-century **Kesardev Murarka**, which has a finely painted façade, and the early 20th-century **Radheshyam Murarka**. The latter portrays processions, scenes from folk tales and various Hindu and Christian religious themes, sometimes interspersed with mirror-work. Other fine *havelis* are those of the Bhagat, Chokhani, Goenka, Patodia, Kedwal, Sangerneria, Saraogi, Jhunjhunwala, Saha and Chhauchuria families. The paintings here depict anything from European women having a bath to Hindu religious themes and Jesus Christ. Some of the *havelis* are complexes of several buildings which include a temple, dharamshala, cenotaph and a well. Most charge Rs 15-20 for a viewing.

Mandawa

Similar to Nawalgarh, Mandawa has a high density of *havelis* in its pleasant streets and is one of the preferred places to stay in the area with plenty of characterful accommodation. Even the State Bank of Bikaner and Jaipur is an old *haveli*.

Parasarampura

About 12 km southeast of Nawalgarh, Parasarampura has a decorated *chhatri* to Sardul Singh (1750) and the adjacent **Gopinath Temple** (1742); these are the earliest examples of Shekhawati frescoes painted with natural pigments (the caretaker has the keys, and will point things out with a peacock feather).

Baggar

The grand *haveli* of the **Makharias**, 10 km north east of Jhunjhunun, has rooms along open corridors around grassy courtyards; worth seeing if only for the wall paintings of gods and angels being transported in motor cars.

Churu

Set in semi-desert countryside, Churu, northwest of Baggar, was believed to have been a Jat stronghold in the 16th century. In the 18th century it was an important town of Bikaner state and its fort dates from this period. The town thrived during the days of overland desert trade. The town has some interesting 1870s Oswal Jain *havelis* like those of the Kotharis and the Suranas. Also worth a look are the **Banthia** (early 20th century), **Bagla** (1880), **Khemka** (1800s), **Poddar** and **Bajranglal Mantri** *havelis*. The main attraction, however, is the extraordinary '**Malji-ka-Kamra**', which has been lovingly restored in recent years. It's a stunning colonnaded *haveli* which houses some amazing interior scenes and is now a heritage hotel (www.maljikakamra.com).

Tal Chappar

A possible day excursion from one of the castle hotels is a visit to **Tal Chappar Wildlife Sanctuary** near Sujjangarh covering 71 sq km of desert scrubland with ponds and salt flats. It has some of the largest herds of Blackbuck antelope in India (easily seen at the watering point near the park gate itself during the dry season), besides chinkara gazelle, desert cat, desert fox and other dryland wildlife. Huge flocks of demoiselle and common cranes can be seen at nearby lakes and wetlands during the winter months (September to March) where they feed on tubers and ground vegetation. Some 175 different species of bird visit the park over the course of a year, including sandgrouse, quails, bar-headed geese and cream-coloured desert courser.

Arriving in Tal Chappar The best time to visit is just after the rainy season, generally August and September. The enthusiastic and charming forest guard, Brij Dansamor, is a good guide to the area. A local NGO, **Krishna Mirg**, is active in tree plantation and in fundraising for the eco-development of Tal Chappar, providing support fodder during dry months to blackbuck and cranes. **Forest Department Rest House** has five basic but adequate rooms at Rs 300 per double. To book ahead call the head office in Churu on T01562-250938. Try **Hanuman** tea stall for delicious *chai* and the local sweet, *malai laddoo*. The drive to Tal Chappar can be long and tiring but if you are travelling between Bikaner and Shekhawati in a jeep, it is worth making a detour.

Shekhawati listings

For hotel and restaurant price codes and other relevant information, see pages 13-16.

⊜ Where to stay

Sikar District *p199*

$$$-$$ Castle Pachar, Pachar, T0141-222 6920 (Jaipur office), www.castlepachar. com. 16 well-decorated rooms in a fascinating old property with portraits, paintings and weaponry, delicious if very rich food, charming hosts, swimming pool under construction. Recommended.

$ Hotel Haveli (RTDC), Sikar Rd, 500 m south of bus stand, Fatehpur, T01571-230293. Typical RTDC fare with clean rooms, some a/c with bath, pleasant building, dull restaurant. However, if you want to visit Fatehpur, it's better to do it as a day trip from Mandawa.

Jhunjhunun District *p200*

$$$$-$$$ Castle Mandawa, Mandawa, T0141-237 4112 (Jaipur office), www. mandawahotels.com. Huge castle with lots of character, 68 a/c rooms, some in the tower, complete with swing, most with 4-posters and period trappings but rooms vary and beds can be hard so select with care, excellent views, atmospheric, lovely swimming pool, interesting miniature shop with on-site artist, mixed reports, some disappointed with meals (Rs 450-500).

$$$$-$$$ Desert Resort, 1 km south of Mandawa, T0141-237 4112, www. mandawahotels.com. Palatial mud-huts with serene swimming pool and inspiring views. This unique resort puts a new spin on traditional mud huts with interiors ornamented with mirrorwork and glass beads and all the mod cons. Very beautiful, highly recommended.

$$$$-$$$ Grand Haveli, Bawari Gate, Nawalgahr, T01594-225301, www.grand haveli.com. Stunningly restored *haveli* with 19 deluxe rooms and several suites

and duplexes. This impressive building is ornately decorated with frescoes and each room has its own *jhakora* with diwan and stained glass windows. Beautiful restaurant and cocktail bar.

$$$-$$ Jamuna Resort, Baggar Rd, Jhunjhunun, T01592-232871, www.shiv shekawati.com. 14 a/c cottage rooms with attractive mirror work and murals, the 'Golden Room' has a painted ceiling "like a jewel box", frescos, open-air Rajasthani vegetarian/non-vegetarian restaurant serving delicious food, gardens, pool (open to hotel/restaurant guests only), local guided tours. Recommended.

$$$-$$ Roop Niwas Kothi, 1 km north of Nawalgarh, T01594-222008, www.roop niwaskothi.com. 25 rooms in sunny colonial-style buildings. Beautiful grounds with peacocks, pool, horse safaris are highly recommended, qualified guides, good food but service is disappointing.

$$ Mandawa Haveli, near Sonthaliya Gate, Mandawa, T01592-223088, http:// hotelmandawa.free.fr. 18 stunning rooms with modernized baths in a 3-storeyed, characterful *haveli* with original 19th-century frescoes in the courtyard, every aspect is beautiful inside and out, great Rajasthani meals, museum and library. Friendly staff, authentic feel. A real gem. Recommended.

$$ Piramal Haveli, Baggar, T0159-221220, www.neemranahotels.com. Stunning 100-year-old home, restored sensitively with a few roaming peacocks, excellent vegetarian meals and attentive service, quirky original frescoes.

$$-$ Narayan Niwas Castle, near bus stand, Mehansar, T01595-264322, www. mehansarcastle.com. Rooms in the fort, converted by Thakur Tejpal Singh. Only 16 rooms are open (out of a total of 500); Nos 1 and 5 are really exceptional. Attractive wall paintings, pleasingly unspoilt. This is a well-loved place. Delicious meals (cooked by

Mrs Singh), home-made liqueurs, charming owners, a *Fawlty Towers* experience.

$ Apani Dhani, Jhunjhunu Rd, 1 km from railway station, 500 m north of bus stand, Nawalgarh, T01594-222239, www.apanidhani.com. 8 environmentally friendly huts and 3 beautiful tents on an ecological farm run by the charming and knowledgeable Ramesh Jangid. Attractive, comfortable, solar-lit thatched cottages traditionally built using mud and straw, modern bathrooms (some with 'footprint' toilets), home-grown vegetarian, immaculately presented, relaxing atmosphere. Accommodation and education in one enticing package. Cooking lessons also possible. Very special place. No alcohol permitted and modest respectful dress requested. Recommended.

$ Shekawati Guest House, near Roop Niwas, Nawalgarh, T01594-224 658, www.shekawatiguesthouse.com. 6 clean, well-presented rooms and also now a circle of simple, yet beautiful thatched cottages, as well as an attractive thatched restaurant run by the friendly qualified cook Kalpana Singh. The food is exceptional and cooking classes can be arranged, as can local tours. Check out their organic garden. Recommended.

$ Thikana, T01594-222152, www.heritagethikana.com. Comfortable rooms in attractive building. Family-run and welcoming, good locally grown food.

$ Tourist Pension, behind Maur Hospital, Nawalgarh, T01594-224060, www.apanidhani.com. 8 rooms, some family-sized, in a modern house run by Rajesh, the son of the owner of **Apani Dhani** (see above), and his wife Sarla, an excellent cook. Some nice big rooms, beautiful old furniture made by Rajesh's grandfather, very welcoming. Another guesthouse has opened up calling itself **Tourist Pension** near Roop Niwas; make sure you come to the right one.

① Restaurants

Sikar District *p199*
$ Natraj Restaurant, Main Rd, Sikar.
Good meals and snacks, clean, reasonable.

Jhunjhunun District *p200*
$$ Roop Niwas Kothi, Nawalgarh. For heritage experience (and unreliable service).
$ Shekawati Guest House, Nawalgarh.
For delicious, hygienically prepared fare.

④ What to do

Shekhawati *p198*
Camel safaris
A typical 5-day safari might include Nawalgarh–Mukundgarh–Mandawa–Mahansar–Churu (crossing some of the finest sand dunes in Shekhawati); 3-day safaris might include Nawalgarh–Fatehpur. Also 1-week country safaris to Tal Chappar Wildlife Sanctuary. The cost depends on the number in the group and the facilities provided ranging from Rs 800-1500 per day. 1-day safaris arranged by the heritage hotels cost about Rs 800 with packed lunch and mineral water. **Mandawa** (see Where to stay, page 202) offers trips.

Horse safaris
Roop Niwas at Nawalgarh (see Where to stay, above) offers 1-week safaris staying overnight in royal tents (occasionally in castles or heritage hotels) to cover the attractions of the region. The most popular take in the Pushkar or Tilwara fairs. You can expect folk music concerts, campfires, guest speakers, masseurs, and sometimes even a barber, all with jeep support. You ride 3 hrs in the morning and 2 hrs in the afternoon, and spend time visiting eco-farms, rural communities and *havelis* en route.

Trekking
There are some interesting treks in the Aravalli hills near Nawalgarh starting from Lohargal (34 km), a temple with sacred pools.

Local people claim that this is the place recorded in the *Mahabharata* where Bhim's mace is said to have been crafted. A 4- to 5-day trek would take in the Bankhandi Peak (1052 m), Krishna temple in Kirori Valley, Kot Reservoir, Shakambari mata temple, Nag Kund (a natural spring) and Raghunathgarh Fort. The cost depends on the size of the group and the facilities. **Apani Dhani**, see Where to stay, page 203, arranges highly recommended treks with stays at the temple guesthouses and villages for US$50 per person per day (minimum 2 people).

⊖ Transport

Shekhawati *p198*
Bicycle Apani Dhani, Nawalgarh. Arranges cycle tours in Shekhawati.
Bus All major towns in the region including Sikar, Nawalgarh and Jhunjhunun are linked by bus with **Jaipur** (3-6 hrs) and **Bikaner**, and some have a daily service to **Delhi** (7-10 hrs); it's best to book a day ahead for these as buses fill up.
Jeep For hire in Nawalgarh, Mandawa and Dundlod, about Rs 1500 per day.
Taxi From **Jaipur**, a diesel Ambassador costs around Rs 3000 for a day tour of parts of Shekhawati; with detours (eg Samode) and a/c cars coming in around Rs 5000.

Local hire is possible in Mandawa, Mukundgarh and Nawalgarh. Also see Car hire in Delhi, page 63, as Shekhawati lies on a sensible if slightly elongated route between there and Jaipur.
Train Most trains through Shekhawati are slow passenger services, which tend to run to their own schedule. Most begin their journeys at **Rewari** (see Bikaner, page 191), and connect with **Bikaner** and **Jaipur**. Check locally for current schedules.

Contents

Footnotes

Index

Titles available in the Footprint *Focus* range

Latin America	UK RRP	US RRP
Bahia & Salvador	£7.99	$11.95
Brazilian Amazon	£7.99	$11.95
Brazilian Pantanal	£6.99	$9.95
Buenos Aires & Pampas	£7.99	$11.95
Cartagena & Caribbean Coast	£7.99	$11.95
Costa Rica	£8.99	$12.95
Cuzco, La Paz & Lake Titicaca	£8.99	$12.95
El Salvador	£5.99	$8.95
Guadalajara & Pacific Coast	£6.99	$9.95
Guatemala	£8.99	$12.95
Guyana, Guyane & Suriname	£5.99	$8.95
Havana	£6.99	$9.95
Honduras	£7.99	$11.95
Nicaragua	£7.99	$11.95
Northeast Argentina & Uruguay	£8.99	$12.95
Paraguay	£5.99	$8.95
Quito & Galápagos Islands	£7.99	$11.95
Recife & Northeast Brazil	£7.99	$11.95
Rio de Janeiro	£8.99	$12.95
São Paulo	£5.99	$8.95
Uruguay	£6.99	$9.95
Venezuela	£8.99	$12.95
Yucatán Peninsula	£6.99	$9.95

Asia	UK RRP	US RRP
Angkor Wat	£5.99	$8.95
Bali & Lombok	£8.99	$12.95
Chennai & Tamil Nadu	£8.99	$12.95
Chiang Mai & Northern Thailand	£7.99	$11.95
Goa	£6.99	$9.95
Gulf of Thailand	£8.99	$12.95
Hanoi & Northern Vietnam	£8.99	$12.95
Ho Chi Minh City & Mekong Delta	£7.99	$11.95
Java	£7.99	$11.95
Kerala	£7.99	$11.95
Kolkata & West Bengal	£5.99	$8.95
Mumbai & Gujarat	£8.99	$12.95

Africa & Middle East	UK RRP	US RRP
Beirut	£6.99	$9.95
Cairo & Nile Delta	£8.99	$12.95
Damascus	£5.99	$8.95
Durban & KwaZulu Natal	£8.99	$12.95
Fès & Northern Morocco	£8.99	$12.95
Jerusalem	£8.99	$12.95
Johannesburg & Kruger National Park	£7.99	$11.95
Kenya's Beaches	£8.99	$12.95
Kilimanjaro & Northern Tanzania	£8.99	$12.95
Luxor to Aswan	£8.99	$12.95
Nairobi & Rift Valley	£7.99	$11.95
Red Sea & Sinai	£7.99	$11.95
Zanzibar & Pemba	£7.99	$11.95

Europe	UK RRP	US RRP
Bilbao & Basque Region	£6.99	$9.95
Brittany West Coast	£7.99	$11.95
Cádiz & Costa de la Luz	£6.99	$9.95
Granada & Sierra Nevada	£6.99	$9.95
Languedoc: Carcassonne to Montpellier	£7.99	$11.95
Málaga	£5.99	$8.95
Marseille & Western Provence	£7.99	$11.95
Orkney & Shetland Islands	£5.99	$8.95
Santander & Picos de Europa	£7.99	$11.95
Sardinia: Alghero & the North	£7.99	$11.95
Sardinia: Cagliari & the South	£7.99	$11.95
Seville	£5.99	$8.95
Sicily: Palermo & the Northwest	£7.99	$11.95
Sicily: Catania & the Southeast	£7.99	$11.95
Siena & Southern Tuscany	£7.99	$11.95
Sorrento, Capri & Amalfi Coast	£6.99	$9.95
Skye & Outer Hebrides	£6.99	$9.95
Verona & Lake Garda	£7.99	$11.95

North America	UK RRP	US RRP
Vancouver & Rockies	£8.99	$12.95

Australasia	UK RRP	US RRP
Brisbane & Queensland	£8.99	$12.95
Perth	£7.99	$11.95

For the latest books, e-books and a wealth of travel information, visit us at:
www.footprinttravelguides.com.

footprinttravelguides.com

Join us on facebook for the latest travel news, product releases, offers and amazing competitions:
www.facebook.com/footprintbooks.